WOUNDED
TITANS

ALSO BY MAX LERNER

It Is Later Than You Think
Ideas Are Weapons
Ideas for the Ice Age
The Mind and Faith of Justice Holmes
Public Journal
The Portable Veblen
Actions and Passions
America as a Civilization
The Unfinished Country
The Age of Overkill
Education and Radical Humanism
Tocqueville and American Civilization
Values in Education
Ted and the Kennedy Legend
Wrestling with the Angel
Magisterial Imagination
Nine Scorpions in a Bottle
Thomas Jefferson: America's Philosopher-King

WOUNDED TITANS

AMERICAN PRESIDENTS AND THE PERILS OF POWER

MAX LERNER

EDITED AND WITH AN INTRODUCTION BY
ROBERT SCHMUHL

ARCADE PUBLISHING ★ NEW YORK

FIRST EDITION

Library of Congress Cataloging-in-Publication Data

Lerner, Max, 1902–1992
    Wounded titans: American presidents and the perils of power / by Max Lerner ; edited and with an introduction by Robert Schmuhl. —1st ed.
      p.   cm.
    ISBN 1-55970-339-3
    1. Presidents—United States—History. 2. Presidents—United States—Biography. 3. Presidents—United States—Election—History—20th century. 4. United States—Politics and government—20th century. 5. Power (Social sciences)—United States—History. I. Schmuhl, Robert. II. Title.
E176.1.L37 1996
353.03'13—dc20   96–25031

Published in the United States by Arcade Publishing, Inc., New York
Distributed by Little, Brown and Company

10 9 8 7 6 5 4 3 2 1

BP

Designed by API

PRINTED IN THE U.S.A.

CONTENTS

PART III

ELECTING A PRESIDENT

ACKNOWLEDGMENTS

W HEN RICHARD SEAVER, President of Arcade Publishing, was first approached about his possible interest in a collection of Max Lerner's writings on the presidency and presidents, he immediately recognized the merit of such a volume. He previously had worked with Lerner on several books—including the thirtieth anniversary edition of *America as a Civilization* and *Nine Scorpions in a Bottle*—and they had been long-time friends. I am most grateful to him and to Timothy Bent, senior editor at Arcade, for their valuable counsel and assistance. Sean McDonald, Assistant Editor at Arcade, sensitively gave shape and coherence to a sprawling manuscript.

The Lerner family deserves special words of gratitude. Since 1992, we have worked together on five different book projects, and Edna Albers Lerner as well as sons Michael and Stephen helped however and whenever they could.

Evelyn Irsay, who served as Max's assistant for many years, personifies efficiency and loyalty. When asked to locate an array of columns from the library of the *New York Post*, she responded both cheerfully and quickly. Max was lucky; so am I.

At the University of Notre Dame, where Max occupied the W. Harold and Martha Welch Visiting Professorship of American Studies from 1982 to 1984, the Institute for Scholarship in the Liberal Arts provided a travel grant to consult Lerner's papers. Dean of the College of Arts and Letters Harold W. Attridge and Associate Dean Jennifer Warlick, the Institute's Director, help create an environment that fosters work leading to books.

Professor Donald P. Costello, former Chairman of the Department of American Studies, was responsible for bringing Max to Notre Dame, and he worked with Peter Lombardo, Director of Continuing Education, in planning the public lectures on "The Wounded Titans" that were delivered in 1984. The audiotapes of these lectures proved useful, and I am grateful to both of them for their friendship and kindnesses over the years.

Professor Thomas J. Stritch, editor emeritus of *The Review of Politics*, offered valuable comments on a draft of the introduction, as he has done with so many other efforts at composition. He continues to teach in more ways than he knows.

Nancy Kegler, who functions as much more than a secretary in the Department of American Studies, was responsible for preparing the manuscript of this book. Her wizardry with the computer made the work of the editor much easier—and is, as always, greatly appreciated.

Finally, Judith Roberts Schmuhl and Michael Robert Schmuhl remained at a safe distance from a certain room in the house as another book took shape. They tolerate, even encourage, literary and political obsessions. Saying thank you never seems enough.

—R. S.

EDITOR'S
INTRODUCTION

M~AX~ L~ERNER~ ~SURVEYED~ the White House from several vantage points: columnist, historian, biographer, sociologist, psychologist, philosopher. Whether describing the presidency's institutional and symbolic role or taking the measure of the people who fought to occupy the nation's highest office, Lerner produced essays designed to explain—steadily and whole—the possibilities and perils confronting anyone driven to scale the summit of American political power.

A polymath and public intellectual never confined by the fences of academic boundaries, Lerner increasingly trained his attention on presidential subjects during his last four decades as a journalist, scholar, and teacher. For him the White House assumed a significance similar to Herman Melville's white whale, a compelling object of fascination and ambiguity, worthy of the long hunt. The pursuit entailed a succession of literary encounters.

After completing his monumental thousand-page opus, *America as a Civilization* (1958), Lerner analyzed the changing dynamics of world politics, including the centrality of the U.S. presidency, in *The Age of Overkill* (1962). Then, retreating from the present to the past, he spent several years working on a biography of Thomas Jefferson, whom he considered America's "philosopher-king."

Later, during the 1980 presidential primary season and with Senator Edward Kennedy as a candidate, *Ted and the Kennedy Legend* appeared. This book provided Lerner's psycho-critical commentary on the White House quests by the brothers Kennedy: John and Robert as well as Edward. Moreover, throughout these years and until his death in 1992, he composed hundreds of his syndicated newspaper columns and several lengthy essays about the knotty realities of White House governance at a time of tumultuous transformation both at home and abroad and demanding American leadership.

Writing and lecturing about the presidency, presidents, and wishful seekers of the Oval Office were nothing new to Lerner. He had served as political editor of *The Nation* between 1936 and 1938, and had contributed frequently to *The New Republic* and other publications during five years as a professor of political science at Williams College (1938–1943).

In 1943, with democracy at stake during the Second World War, he shifted back to full-time writing. He was appointed editorial director of *PM*, the experimental, liberal-leaning New York newspaper that tried to avoid outside pressure by publishing without advertising. Starting at *PM* and continuing for nearly five decades, Lerner wrote a regular and popular column—as often as four times a week—with the *New York Post* his home newspaper the last forty-three years.

The presidency and national politics were frequent topics. Ultimately, his readership became much larger, with the Los Angeles Times Syndicate distributing Lerner's columns to papers in the U.S. and abroad. Besides writing his books and articles, he returned to college teaching in 1949 and faculty appointments at several universities occupied the next forty years. In his quarter-century career as a professor of American Civilization at Brandeis University, he consistently offered classes focusing on White House actions and world affairs, a continuing trend in subsequent academic posts.

However, beginning in the 1970s, his fascination with the American presidency—its unrivaled powers and dangers—developed into an abiding concern. He outlined and started three different books about contemporary presidents he had studied closely and known. By focusing on these figures, Lerner intended to draw conclusions about the office and its consequences on the nation as a "civilization" as well as on its standing internationally.

Initially, he began a volume called "A Gallery of Presidents," which carried the subtitle "The Mind, Faith, Psyche, and Impact of Six American Presidents from Franklin Roosevelt to Richard Nixon (1933–1974)." Lerner saw these six presidents—Roosevelt, Harry Truman, Dwight Eisenhower, John Kennedy, Lyndon Johnson, and Nixon—as what he termed "the Titans of the Twilight." He compared them to America's first six presidents, "the Titans of the Dawn": George Washington, John Adams, Thomas Jefferson, James Madison, James Monroe, and John Quincy Adams. The first two paragraphs of the opening chapter establish the frame and theme of Lerner's approach:

> In some notes for a draft of Franklin Roosevelt's First Inaugural, jotted down in a session of talk with the President-Elect, Raymond Moley scribbled, "sick world—forged into unity by rings of fire." The words didn't appear in the final version. Yet if the phrases were in fact his, Roosevelt showed a premonitory insight not only into the trials of his first term but into the whole history of the presidency since. The years from 1933 to 1974—from the bank holiday of the Great Depression to Richard Nixon's resignation—proved to be the years of the firestorm.
>
> The presidents who were the latter-day Titans, seeking at once to appease the gods of history and to steal fire from them, were Roosevelt, Truman, Eisenhower, Kennedy, Johnson, Nixon. They had their mettle tested in the storm of fire that scarcely let up from that first Roosevelt day to the last Nixon day. But something more was tested in those tumultuous years—the American presidency itself, whose power these men wielded and whose burdens they carried.

By rendering these figures and their impact, Lerner sought "to see these six presidents as whole human beings, within a presidency that is many things and therefore must be seen as a whole. It is to see the presidency within the total culture and society and civilization. For the presidency is at once part of the American power system, its authority and legitimacy system, its consensus system, its economic system, its class system, its status system, its leadership and elite system, its incentive and reward system, its access system, its identity and awareness system, its mythical and magical and symbolic system, its cohesiveness system, its values and beliefs system."

As with other subjects he explored, Lerner knew a comprehensive treatment could only come from tracing the intersecting connections that create a pattern for meaning and understanding. The circles for schematic diagrams he often drew on blackboards always overlapped. In lecture notes for "How to Study a president," seven clusters of inquiry link together to form Lerner's analytical method: "psyche/character," "life-cycle," "power/leadership," "polis/polity," "epos/time," "ethos," and "eros."

From his early work on "A Gallery of Presidents," Lerner developed the image of presidents as titans who, though powerful by virtue of their office, found ruling in the American republic a succession of trials and testings. As he wrote in one of the countless notes he made for the volume, "The presidency is a rack of pain as well as a dream of glory." He subsequently changed the title of the book project to "The Wounded Titans: A Revisionist View of Nine Presidents in an Imperial Era—From Franklin Roosevelt to Ronald Reagan," and in the draft of a first chapter made his figurative language of the metaphor sharper: "Like Prometheus who stole fire from Heaven, these latter-day Titans sought to confront the gods of history and to steal fire from them. Prometheus was punished by being chained to a rock, while a vulture pecked at his liver. It is not a bad fable for the wounds the presidents suffered."

Captured by the vivid phrase "wounded titans" and all that it symbolized, Lerner offered a series of public lectures at the University of Notre Dame called "The Wounded Titans: American Presidents—Character and Decisions, 1933–1983" during the spring of 1984. Afterward, he wrote an extended essay about the presidents since Franklin Roosevelt. One paragraph he excised for reasons of space amplifies his larger meaning:

> Presidents are constantly tempted, by the drama and magic associated with their office, into thinking of themselves as something other than men. Yet they govern at the sufferance of forces they scarcely understand—of Fortune, of Necessity, of Power, of History. They woo these gods, covet their mastery, rail at them, try to strike a pact with them. There is a limbo to which they have been democratically sentenced, between the earthbound all-too-human world to which they must revert, and an unbounded freedom of action, like that of gods, which they can never reach. Hence their periodic rebellions like the Titans against Olympus with a hubris which rarely goes unpunished.

Shortly after publishing his magazine article with the bold headline "Wounded Titans," Lerner composed chapter-length studies of Roosevelt and Truman for his proposed book. He envisaged it as being similar to Richard Hofstadter's *The American Political Tradition* (1948)—individual studies of significant political figures with broader historical and cultural implications throughout. However, a series of serious illnesses interrupted completion of full-scale assessments of the other presidents. He wanted to do justice to these figures, and needed full powers of concentration for such work. So he set the manuscript aside, shifting his attention to more manageable book projects: a personal narrative, *Wrestling with the Angel: A Memoir of My Triumph over Illness*, published in 1990, and to a collection of his constitutional and legal essays, which appeared in 1994, *Nine Scorpions in a Bottle: Great Judges and Cases of the Supreme Court*. Despite two bouts with cancer, a major heart attack, and other maladies, he also worked on prefatory or postscript chapters to new editions of five previously published books—*America as a Civilization*, *It Is Later Than You Think*, *Ideas Are Weapons*, *Ideas for the Ice Age*, and *The Mind and Faith of Justice Holmes*—while also continuing what he wryly referred to as his "strange necessity," the syndicated newspaper column.

Three years before his death at the age of eighty-nine and amid other commitments, Lerner made one last attempt at writing a presidential volume. Although most of his energy then was devoted to a book challenging the thesis advanced by Paul Kennedy (in *The Rise and Fall of the Great Powers* [1987]) and others that the United States was experiencing national decline—working titles included "America Ascendant" and "The American Trajectory"—he also began a study of three presidents. Called "The Emperor Presidents," the flowing subtitle reveals a dramatic shift in outlook from the concept of "wounded titans": "How Franklin Roosevelt, Harry Truman and Dwight Eisenhower Reached the White House, Met Dangers, and Built an Empire for Freedom in the West."

Nowhere in the prologue, which is triumphant in tone, is there a suggestion of crippling problems—either institutional or personal—limiting a president's exercise of power and leadership. In Lerner's view, Roosevelt, Truman, and Eisenhower were "the Founding Fathers of the America of our time," with the nation under them responsible for making a disordered world a more ordered one. Explaining the phrase "emperor presidents," he says:

> Thomas Jefferson, no friend of interventionism, spoke of his vision of America as "an empire for liberty." The phrase captures my meaning magically. It has little to do with the territorial imperialism of William McKinley and Theodore Roosevelt's America. My three Presidents didn't hunger for an expanded terrain on which to run up the American flag. They responded to expansionist dangers that came not from "empires for liberty" but empires for enslavement.

The presidents had to become the shapers of coalitions of nations which came to be called the "Free World" and "the West."

The process began with Franklin Roosevelt's coalition war against Nazi Germany and the Japan of the war-lords. It ended when Dwight Eisenhower turned over the burden to a younger generation. What he handed on was America's recognized leadership of a *democratic imperium*—a political, economic, and military entity, but more essentially (with all its discordances) a moral community that aimed at world order.

What prompted Lerner to shift from thinking in terms of "wounded titans" to "emperor presidents"? In part, it was a response to the historic moment—the collapse of Communism in Eastern Europe, the end of the Cold War, and the breakup of the Soviet Union. The United States and American ideals had prevailed in a forty-five-year, twilight struggle between global superpowers that had always engaged Lerner, who himself immigrated from Russia as a boy in 1907. Freedom and democracy, cornerstones of America as a civilization, were now embraced in countries formerly closed and totalitarian. In part, too, a book about three presidents was more compassable and somewhat less demanding for a writer bedeviled by illness and bent on completing several more books. (When he died, Lerner had on his desk a list of more than thirty titles for original works or new editions he intended to finish.)

Another factor explaining the change in outlook is that Lerner kept an open mind and criticized any form of rigidity standing in the way of responsible inquiry or action. Writing in 1985, he remarked: "In leadership, as in life, rigidity is the enemy." Interestingly, the three presidents he proposed to examine had been assessed by him in quite different terms earlier.

As a newspaper columnist providing running, day-by-day commentary, Lerner had been in the main an admiring supporter of Roosevelt, a frequent challenger of Truman, and a constant critic of Eisenhower. Years later—and functioning with the longer perspective of the historian and biographer—Lerner described FDR in much less approving terms than before, while both Truman and Eisenhower rose dramatically in his estimation. The revised thinking occurred primarily because the passage of time made it possible to evaluate the consequences of presidential decisions and actions. Emerging scholarship, based on new historical sources and varying angles of vision, resulted in a continuing process of reinterpretation.

Despite his initial enthusiasm to work on the book about the modern-day influence of America and "The Emperor Presidents" simultaneously, Lerner was unable to finish either manuscript. Entitling the first chapter of his presidential volume "The Flawed Paradigm: Franklin D. Roosevelt," he traced the rise of FDR to the presidency but quit writing, in mid-sentence, at the inauguration of 1933. What does exist is remarkably similar to the treatment in the earlier effort, with some passages appropriated verbatim from the essay in "Wounded Titans." Whether Lerner would have cushioned his criticism of FDR's last decisions, especially how he dealt with the Russians at the Yalta Conference in 1945, is anyone's guess. However, the image of a "flawed paradigm" suggests that this presidential portrait would have included its share of warts.

As could be expected of someone who called an unfinished memoir "Delight of Battle," Max Lerner did not, in the Dylan Thomas phrase, "go gentle into that good night." Indeed, Lerner struggled to meet deadlines and to complete book projects until his last days. Appropriately, since it was the presidential primary period when he suffered his final illness, most of his journalistic writing then examined the emerging campaign. Yet for what turned out to be his last column (written on April 23, 1992, just six weeks before his death on June 5) he offered a history lesson and farewell to a favorite subject. He surveyed the presidents who, from his perspective, meant the most to the twentieth century. As he had written with conviction several times since the 1970s, Truman stood out above all others for the endurance of decisive actions.

Throughout his writings about the presidency and individual presidents, Lerner stressed that the nation's future would to a considerable extent be determined by what occupants of the White House did—or did not do. Wounding of some kind would always occur; that is in the nature of being human and of hardball democratic politics. Yet while forming policy and exercising power, a modern-day titan is uniquely capable of mastering the possibilities to lead—in a commanding way—America and the world.

—Robert Schmuhl

AUTHOR'S PROLOGUE

THOSE OF US WHO SEE ourselves as political observers have the illusion of centrality. Yet in fact politics, however important in the collective life, is only one of a number of angles of vision, all radiating out of a deeper intellectual and moral center. Each of us, in our life journey, experiences an odyssey in which that center is a moving one. Change and continuity, transition points and crises and resolutions—these are the true life story.

In my case there were five general phases. The first was my radical political phase, from the early 1920s well into the 1940s. While my basic orientation was toward Marx and Veblen and their economic determinism, I never questioned the primacy of a radical politics that flowed from it. Yet Franklin Roosevelt was the turning point in this phase, and his New Deal convinced me that while capitalism was crucial as an institution, our real fate would be determined by what happened to political democracy. True, I was still writing—as late as 1937—that "the New Deal is the naked fist of the capitalist state." But my constitutional and Supreme Court articles all through this period (specifically "The Supreme Court and American Capitalism" and "Constitution and Court as Symbols") were more sophisticated than that statement suggests.

As with my contemporaries, antifascism confirmed my basic radical phase. Yet the staff debates and my writings, during my years as political editor of *The Nation*, raised some doubts about Communism, especially about the Soviet purge trials and the Spanish Civil War. The result was a section on "The Six Errors of Marxism" in my *It Is Later*

This unpublished essay, written in the late 1980s, describes different phases in Max Lerner's political thinking and introduces his perspectives on the presidency and presidents.

Than You Think (1938). The book itself heavily emphasized a "democratic collectivism" domestically, and a "collective security" in foreign policy, which formed my basic popular front position. My experience on *PM* and its successor the *New York Star* (1943–1949) was also largely based on my popular front philosophy.

Several things happened in my second phase, in the middle and later 1940s, to change and deepen my perspective. One was the war and the atom bomb. The potentials of the bomb combined with a second event—my efforts along with the right-wing Zionist "Bergson Boys" to pressure FDR on the Holocaust, and my visit to the cremation camps—to shape a political philosophy that I called "tragic humanism" (in an article in *The American Scholar*). A third was my closeness to the Alger Hiss case and other treason trials, and my observation of Communist tactics in the trade unions, which raised doubts about the popular front. Finally there was my reading of Machiavelli, Freud, and Justice Holmes, and my writing about all three, which gave me the beginnings of a framework that would make my early economic determinism seem archaic.

I see my third phase, from 1949 (when I joined the *New York Post*) to 1957, as a movement from *political camps* to *civilizations*. During that period I traveled widely, lecturing around the U.S. and visiting most of Europe and much of Asia as a foreign correspondent. One thing my travels did was to convince me that nowhere did any form of socialism work. (This was later strengthened by my year of teaching in India, 1959–60.) I was also affected by Harry Truman's rebuilding of what had been lost in Western Europe and Douglas MacArthur's rebuilding of Japan. I found an intellectual forum for this change in my civilization readings—in Nietzsche, Spengler, and Toynbee, but especially in Tocqueville. (In the early 1960s I wrote a short book titled *Tocqueville and American Civilization*.)

These developments culminated in my writing *America as a Civilization*, the idea for which had come to me in the closing phase of the war when I was a war correspondent in Germany. I worked at the book for twelve years, discarding a first draft that was too close to the model of America in the liberal books. I finally trusted the evidence of my own travel and thinking, and finished the book toward the end of 1957. Its importance for me, in rereading it, was that I found I had broken with my liberal-Marxist political gang sufficiently to affirm the primacy and creativity of America as a civilization.

My position increasingly became one of emphasis on the political reality principle, using William James' distinction between the "tough-minded" and "tender-minded." This was best expressed in my only book on world politics, *The Age of Overkill* (1962), which I began during my year in India and finished in Rome in 1962. It represents my first approximation of a new perspective—a willingness to face the reality of the nature of Communist expansionism, an affirmation of democracy as a way of life, worldwide, and a confrontation of the potential within humanity for both radical evil and creative good.

My fourth phase came in the acceleration of change in the 1960s. I tried to stay on top of the too rapidly changing culture and society, but it was a traumatic as well as exciting period for me. I was part of the cultural revolution, especially in the encounter-group movement and the erotic revolution based on the Kinsey and Masters work. Yet I saw the cultural costs of the "anything goes" dynamism. Politically I supported both JFK and LBJ, but without much enthusiasm. My support of the Vietnam War was largely a reaction to my memories of the dangers of appeasement, and I turned against it well before the war was over.

If there was a symbolic turning point that was decisive for me, it came in foreign policy at the start of the 1960s. I had sent copies of a draft of *The Age of Overkill* for criticism to several colleagues who had been generous about my *America* book. Their responses expressed shock to the point of trauma. But the episode I recall most sharply occurred during the Cuban missile crisis, when Herbert Marcuse, at a meeting on the Brandeis University campus while I was away, proclaimed "Castro Si, Kennedy No!" When I met him the next day and offered to debate with him, his answer was that there could be no dialogue with a fascist. We had each moved beyond the point of no return.

My fifth phase began in the early 1970s and was mainly connected to graduate teaching (after my retirement from Brandeis) at several universities, eventually in California and for two years at Notre Dame. This stretch enabled me to make a more fundamental effort than earlier to develop my own conceptual base and my own method of getting at my inquiries. It was no longer a question of whether and how much I believed in Marx and Veblen or Machiavelli or Freud or Weber or de Tocqueville, but how I could construct my own frame of perspective and discourse.

I came to understand the importance of the dominant political culture and the role of the liberal-Marxist intellectual elite in it. In

1982 I formulated a critique of that culture in my inaugural address as the Visiting Welch Professor of American Studies at Notre Dame and have followed it up since. I began to make the concept of the life journey a central one, applying it with a psychohistorical bent in my book on the Kennedys, in 1980, and in an extended essay on Thomas Jefferson. And I started a long-range venture on the life history of recent presidents, titled *The Wounded Titans*.

Two crucial perspectives have been what I call the *organismic* (both in the person and in the civilization) and the *integrative*, pulling my various approaches together into a paradigm of my own. I find the concept of organismic health, in both the individual and society, to be crucial to my thinking, and along with health a polar approach to life that sees *Eros* and *Thanatos* not as dichotomies but as containing each other.

I can't say that I have moved away from my early political positions to a more conservative one for the simple reason that I no longer find those concepts meaningful. If I had to describe myself today it would be as a tough-minded centrist, concerned with helping to create a new political culture to counter and replace the dying liberal-radical one.

PART I

ASPECTS OF
THE PRESIDENCY
AND SOME
ASSESSMENTS

FOREWORD

THE VIRGINIA QUARTERLY REVIEW, in its Summer 1952 issue, published Max Lerner's essay "The Style and Genius of American Politics." This article—which he later revised and expanded into two chapters of *America as a Civilization*—marks the beginning of Lerner's more comprehensive probing of the presidency.

Although some of his previous writing had focused directly on individual presidents and on contemporary political affairs, he devoted much of his earlier attention to constitutional, cultural, or philosophical concerns. During the 1940s, among other publishing projects, he edited and introduced volumes of the works of Aristotle, Machiavelli, Thorstein Veblen, and Oliver Wendell Holmes, Jr.

Especially from the 1970s on, Lerner became preoccupied with the interplay between presidential power politics and the personalities occupying or craving the office. Despite an effort to be as encompassing as possible, he returned to particular themes—such as the relevance of a president's past experience and private life—in drawing broader conclusions about what he often called "the magnificent burden" of the presidency.

—R. S.

THE STYLE AND GENIUS
OF AMERICAN POLITICS

EVERY CIVILIZATION HAS A GOVERNMENT of some sort, but each differs from the others in the way it organizes and conducts its political life—its mode and style of "politics." Jakob Burckhardt, writing on the *Italian Renaissance*, noted that the men of the Renaissance made even the state a "work of art." The Americans make their state, as they make their armies and corporations, a vast organizational achievement: they speak of "the business of government." The most telling complaint the sound middle-class American can make against any administration is that it has been wasteful of the "taxpayer's money." On the local level, politics is often regarded as a "racket"—that is, a cushioned berth in which you can make a quick and easy dollar. And viewed in terms of spectator sports in a competitive society, politics is also seen as a vast competitive contest played for the big stakes of office and power, but nonetheless a game: "the great game of politics."

But the observer will be misled if he concludes from this that Americans view government solely through the economic eyes. Here is another instance of the polarity of the American character. With his ruling passion for freedom, the American is contemptuous of any government; he says, with Emerson, that "all states are corrupt." Yet since the days when Jackson clashed with the big banking groups, the "strong" presidents and administrations which used the power of government effectively, whatever their party or program, have received popular accolades as well as the verdict of history. The attitude of Americans toward political power is curiously dual. They hem in their

"The Style and Genius of American Politics" originally appeared in *America as a Civilization* (New York: Simon and Schuster, 1957).

state governors, for example, with a jungle of restrictions; they seek to balance the power of every official with another official; they maintain bicameral legislatures that are clearly archaic; they multiply agencies and offices, from the federal to the local, instead of adding new powers to those of the old agencies. No people has ever had less reason to fear the arbitrary abuse of governmental power, yet Americans have been traditionally reluctant to yield power, and they still tend to deflate it. In time of crisis, however, they have viewed power in a practical and undogmatic way. In every great emergency of the national existence they have yielded their government and leadership the necessary power for meeting it, whether the crisis be civil war, economic collapse, or world war.

Yet while managing the problems of political power with tolerable success, they have also found it necessary to be antistate and antipolitician. Traditional American antistatism (or, better, "antigovernment," since Americans use "state" not as a political but as a geographic expression) has stopped just short of anarchism, although Henry Thoreau and Benjamin Tucker show that a part of the American tradition crossed that line. The American anarchist strain is not, like the Italian or Spanish, mixed with syndicalism or with a peasant hostility toward the tax gatherers; nor is it, like the Russian, mixed with a revolutionary aim. It flows, rather, from the tradition of individual self-reliance. The American, especially in rural America, felt he could get along by himself, and that the power of the mastodon government threatened the conduct of his life. In urban America antistatism has been somewhat diluted by the mingling of ethnic strains, the necessity of government involvement, and the turmoil of collective life. Yet even in places where antistatism remains strongest, the attitude toward government has been split—positive when its help is needed, resentful when it seems to interfere.

Compared with the genuine if ambivalent antistatism of the individual, the laissez-faire element in American thinking—the antistatism of the corporation—seems spurious. American business has not refused to accept state authority when it has taken the form of subventions, tariffs, or subsidies. Laissez-faire has been therefore an opportunist antistatism. It has found an echo in the American mind largely because the formative years of American political thinking were the years of revolt against British power, themselves reminiscent of the period of British revolt against their own absolute monarchies. Corporate spokesmen had a convenient chance to clothe their cause in the garments of the struggle against Tudor and Stuart absolutism. Thus the anarchist and the rebel latent in every American joined with corporate power to proclaim that "that government is best which governs least." Or, as someone put it: "In God we trust; in government we mistrust."

Therefore, the most characteristic trait of the American political style became the impulse to belittle politics and the professional politician. The American is prone to be suspicious of every government he elects. Nose-thumbing has become his traditional gesture, not only to show contempt for the politician but even more, to exercise the freedom to express contempt for those whom they have presumably chosen to govern them. The darling of the newspaper caricaturists has for decades been the bloated, gorilla-faced, cigar-in-mouth fellow with the watch chain across his paunch. In the political zoology of the American mind he combines the qualities of swine and fox, feeding greedily at the public trough, plotting cunningly to win and retain power. In recent years his primacy in the caricatures has only been challenged by the bureaucrat—the only word in English, as Harold Ickes put it, that can be hissed although there is not a sibilant in it.

The politician and bureaucrat are fair game, sacrificial kings to whom the Americans grant power but whom they reserve the right to stone to death. The poorest, meanest, most misery-ridden fellow—the town drunk perhaps, the farm ne'er-do-well, or the city derelict—can say anything, no matter how scurvy, about someone in public office. Not only does he have the legal right, but doing so performs a therapeutic function: it shows who is boss, whose is the ultimate power, thus giving him an outlet for his frustrations and consoling him for the disparity in power and income between himself and his target.

The belittlement of politics is partly responsible for the rise of the professional politician. What you despise and attack you do not involve yourself with. This has meant a break with the Jacksonian doctrine of rotation in office, based on the belief that there are no mysteries to governing. All that is required is common sense, integrity, and devotion to the public good. Any able citizen can therefore do it. This was itself a way of rationalizing the spoils system, and for wresting politics away from the elite. In the big city, with its strata of new immigrants who were largely illiterate and grateful for aid and guidance, the professional politician found his home.

A vicious circle came into being: contempt for politics as predation made Americans shrink from the task of government; but the more contempt they felt the larger the vacuum into which the professional politician moved, and the more violently they recoiled from the result. Most able young people turned their talents to business and professions where greater rewards lay, greater glamour and prestige. The arts of government, which the Greeks had deemed the noblest arts within human competence, came to be seen as defiling. In recent years a growing awareness of this gap between politics and creative talent spread among the colleges and has served to counteract the tendency. This awareness was especially evident after World War II among the young veterans who came back to complete their studies under the G.I. subsidies and brought new blood into politics.

Professionals operate not in public office itself but behind it. The officeholders—the mayors and governors, the state legislators, the whole array of county and state administrative officials, even the congressmen themselves—are men of varying ability and integrity who may hold office for a few years and then return to private life. The threads of continuity in the skein of power are woven not by them but by the party managers, the men who make a lifetime career of manipulation and alliances and who have become masters of the "deal" and the "fix." They swing the whole vast structure of patronage, political profit, and power, using apathy as their medium and the party machinery as their leverage. There is no career tradition in officeholding itself, as in England, and this gives the professional political managers their chances. As Lincoln Steffens discovered after years of interviewing them, and many other newspapermen have confirmed, they are likely to be men who combine an ancient cunning with a massive will and the freshest energies of a new country.

I have spoken of the political apathy of a large portion of the American people. But this is part of a pattern that includes also streaks of "good government" reformism and considerable emotional and political invective. The history of American political campaigns is studded with outbursts of political passion, rough-and-tumble tactics of political combat, hyperbolic professions of patriotism, and the assignment of diabolical traits and motives to one's opponents. The deflationary gap between this verbal extremism and the actual continuities of power in the hands of professionals is likely to produce the kind of despair that leads to apathy, so that American politics offers to observers the aspect of violent alternations between activity and quiescence, and between moralism and cynicism. This is true of foreign policy as well, with its alternations between isolationism and a crusading fervor.

However, what emerges in the foreground of the pattern is a deep pragmatic strain in American political behavior: not moral doctrine and dogma, for which there is considerable scorn in the anti-intellectualism of a "practical" people, but a grappling with whatever needs to be done—and doing it. There is little doctrinal commitment in American politics. The party combats do not involve ideological terms but, rather, an assessment of personalities and what they are likely to do. The rise in independent nonparty votes is a sign that this is increasingly rather than decreasingly the case. Unlike the Europeans, the Americans have had no "grand" political theory; they rarely talk of the "state" or even of "government," but, rather, of "*the* government" and "the administration." It is almost as if there were a fear of principles because they might lead to commitments from which it would be difficult for one to extricate oneself. This does not, of course, prevent the waves of fanatical feeling and the suppression of unpopular ideas that have swept the nation, especially after wars. Yet America has never endowed fanaticism with national power. It has thus far managed to avoid enthroning an authoritarian national leader or subscribing to any party-line "truth."

One of the great political documents, which is worth studying for the light it sheds on the American political style, is the series of commentaries on the Constitution that have come down to us as *The Federalist Papers*. The three collaborators—Hamilton, Jay, and Madison—were of different political leanings and were later to play very different roles, yet their political preferences were submerged in their common assumptions about the art of government. They had read widely and deeply, had studied the new political science of their day, and were skillful in conscripting the beliefs and experience of antiquity to the purposes of the new venture in government. They were not closet students but men who focused on action. They had a sense of the fragility of the social fabric and at the same time of the tenacity of social habits, yet even as conservatives (which all of them were in varying degree) they had a capacity for bold political innovation. They were realists who, long before Marx, saw the implications of what we have come to call class structure and class conflict in relation to politics, yet they never lost their overriding sense of the national interest. They knew about the elements of the irrational in men, elements which they called "political passions," and sought to set limits to the power of government to prevent the tyrannies that might arise in the name of the majority. Yet though they elaborated on the checks and

balances in a "mixed government" of separated powers, they were trying to create an affirmative state with more centralized power than any
republic had ever possessed, to perform the jobs of taxation, defense,
and control over the vital processes of the nation. What they sought
was a government "energetic" enough, in the terms of their own day,
"to preserve the Union."

By combining practical daring with conservative techniques for
controlling the underlying radicalism of the whole experiment, these
men—like the whole group that framed the Constitution—expressed
the American political genius not only of their own day but of later
centuries as well. Americans have had to govern a vast territorial expanse, hold together diverse ethnic and sectional and economic
groups, and organize a rapidly mounting mass of wealth and power.
How well they have done it will long be argued, but that they have
done it at all—and still maintained a tolerably free society—is no mean
achievement.

The American governmental system, in practice rather than in theory,
has made some notable contributions to the arts of government. The
outstanding ones are *federalism* as a working equilibrium; cleaving to
the rule of law, especially through the technique of *judicial review* by
both state and federal courts; the *constitutional convention*, a way of for-
mulating and revising the fundamental law; the *two-party system*, a
method for insuring the freedom of political opposition and for organizing power and its transfer; *presidential government* as opposed to par-
liamentarianism, and presidential leadership and responsibility as
against the unstable shiftings of cabinet government; and the creation
of *semi-independent administrative agencies*, to carry out the burdens of
democratic control of industry under conditions of technological
progress.

I put these in terms of political techniques and institutions largely
because Americans themselves think of them in those terms. One
could argue that the rule of law (although not judicial review) and the
party system were both derived from British experience, and that to a
lesser extent this holds true of the administrative agencies as well. Yet
the question is one not only of originality but of application. Americans have not been nearly as innovative in the realm of government as
they have in the realm of industrial technology. While they continue to
imitate the Founding Fathers, the Founding Fathers themselves imitated no one. The political genius of America has not been for formu-

lating doctrine but for finding a practical political contrivances and management, and for adapting old forms to new conditions. Rarely has a nation, in the course of almost two centuries of constitutional history, been able to maintain its ability to balance the conflicting drives of property and democracy, of majority power and individual freedom in the face of the changes and chances of growth and power.

It is here that the American political genius best shows itself: in persisting to believe in *a majority rule and the democratic idea*, along with a commitment to *civil liberties and the image of a free society*, combining them with a pragmatic approach to power and the *arts of equilibrium*, and the belief in presidential leadership to achieve *effective government*.

The basic elements of the American government were shaped in an agrarian era, for the needs of a small-scale agrarian society. But it would be unwise to conclude that they are hopelessly out-dated in a large-scale industrial society, and that the old machinery should be scrapped—perhaps along with some of the old ideas as well, like democracy and civil liberties. There has been a tendency in American social thought to consider "social lag" as a crime against progress and humanity; and many may wonder whether a bundle of institutions and practices set in a constitutional code long ago, and changing only when change is forced upon them, can have greatness.

On reflection, there is nothing wrong with the old institutions and ideas, provided they had a valid meaning to start with. In government, unlike industry, basic ideas and techniques may be as old as Aristotle and still embody a permanent truth. Although the American Constitution is committed to paper, it has left room for the changes compelled by growth and time. While the Constitution is procedurally conservative, it does not operate in a substantive way to enshrine any particular economic, political, or social beliefs. It may prove as effective in protecting a liberal policy from reactionary assaults as protecting the laissez-faire dogmas of economic conservatism. Americans have shown something of the British knack for making day-to-day changes in practice but letting the customary practices become the acknowledged "usages" of government. That is why Americans have never taken seriously the various projects for a thorough "modernizing" of their government, to make it more logical or orderly. They have let well enough alone. Lord Bryce is reported to have said that "Providence has under its special care children, idiots, and the United States of America." Which may be another way of saying that given America's industrial development and power, even a clumsy and unwieldy political system can be a success. America has had the Midas touch; everything that a rich nation touches turns to gold.

With this Midas touch there has also been a brashness that has irritated foreign observers, a lack of self-restraint that has shown itself in periodic witch hunts, a Congress whose utterances have sometimes made elected figures seem more stupid than they are, and a press whose outbursts have at times reached manic levels. This has led many observers, especially Europeans, to conclude that the American political style lacks balance and maturity, maturity especially. There is some truth to this and it may be set down to the zest of a still-growing society (although in periods of anti-Communist hysteria one is tempted to call it, rather, the paranoia of a declining one). But I would argue that the imbalance is largely in the outward aspects. As with much else in their life, Americans like their politics pugnacious. They believe in what Samuel Lubell calls "democracy as arena." Despite the outward violence and even childishness of word and manner, a balancing mechanism is often at work.

PRESIDENCY
AND DEMOS

ONE OF THE MIRACLES of American government is how it has managed, with its creaking machinery and its capacity for deadlock, to respond to emergencies. Part of the answer may lie in a dynamism, which at the moment of crisis gathers its deceptively hidden reserves of strength and comes crashing through. The most crucial governmental agency that shows this elasticity for change and a gift for mastery is the American presidency. But only the stronger and more skillful presidents have been able successfully to break through the net of obstructions blocking any attempt to organize the national will. This is one way of defining the task of presidential leadership.

Americans have learned the truth of the remark that modern democratic government is "just one damn crisis after another." That is why the center of gravity of American political life has shifted from the other two branches over to the executive power. The system which in the early phase of the republic was called "congressional government," and, in the laissez-faire decades of the late nineteenth century, "government by judiciary," must now be called "presidential government."

For a man of deep convictions, getting nominated for the presidency is itself a major feat, for to appear "available" in the eyes of the political managers he must be judged moderate, however militant outwardly. The life of every preconvention candidate thus becomes a heroic wrestling match between conscience and canniness. Andrew Jackson was nominated on the wave of a mass revolt within his party, Lincoln and Franklin Roosevelt both seemed relatively mild men be-

"Presidency and Demos" originally appeared in *America as a Civilization* (New York: Simon and Schuster, 1957).

fore their elections and only showed their strength after, Theodore Roosevelt became president when McKinley was assassinated, and Wilson received the Democratic nomination only after the bitterest of fights in the convention and then only with William Jennings Bryan's help. Wendell Willkie was nominated in 1940 when the Republicans wanted someone who was not an isolationist who could run against Roosevelt; in 1944 he was passed over partly because he had been beaten but also because in the intervening years he had too clearly shown his deep liberalism and a set of internationalist convictions. Very often, a candidate whom the convention delegates support strongly, like John Bricker in 1940 and Robert Taft in 1952, fails to get the nomination because the managers read the public-opinion polls (especially from the urban "key" states) and conclude that he could not be elected. The conditions for reaching the presidency are so haphazard and arbitrary that the nomination too often falls to a genial, mediocre candidate who means well, commands a popular following, and doesn't seem too intractable.

But while the tradition has been against nominating candidates of committed views and creative powers, the mantle of the American presidency has the potential to shrink or expand to the stature of whoever wears it. It is roomy enough for a big man to fill it out; a small man can make it shrink enough to fit him. It has been worn alike by a Buchanan and a Lincoln, a Harding and a Roosevelt.

Apart from the textbook discussions of the president's constitutional powers, there is little question that the actual powers of the office have grown. Of course, presidential power has ebbed and flowed depending on the incumbent. But the trend—despite the massive powers that Jefferson and Lincoln exercised—has been unmistakable. There are some melancholy commentators who feel (wrongly, I think) that the growth of presidential power has largely been at the expense of states' rights and the separation of powers. Others ask where in the Constitution one can find specific language granting some of the many powers recent presidents have assumed. The usual answer to the latter is that the presidency operates on the comprehensive executive power, which includes any residual powers required for an effective government and not specifically denied by the letter and spirit of the Constitution. Another answer is to quote Theodore Roosevelt's famous "stewardship" theory, which holds that the president wields these residual powers in stewardship for the people.

The tendency has been to take a functional rather than legalistic view of the presidency. There are things that none of the other branches of government have explicit power to do, and that the states cannot do adequately, but that must nevertheless get done. There are conflicts that can be resolved only by the power and prestige of the presidency, crises that require someone who can muster the drive to meet them, and who can answer for how well or badly they are met, and policies that require an individual to take the responsibility.

Even this functional, elastic view of the office takes in the possibility that presidential power lends itself to abuse. Roosevelt's threat to "pack" the Supreme Court to push through his reforms was widely denounced at the time as a dictatorial move. The "destroyers-for-bases" deal he made with Great Britain before America entered the war rested on a notably elastic interpretation of its constitutionality offered by his attorney general. President Truman, who was considered less "strong" a president than Roosevelt, had three major encounters with the limits of presidential power: once when he threatened to break a national railroad strike by conscripting the railroad workers in the army, again when he committed a large military force to Europe (and later to Korea, in the U.N. "police action") without declaring a state of war, and finally when he sought to resolve a steel-industry lockout and strike by declaring a national emergency and taking over the steel mills. He was checked on the first, was successful on the second (which illustrates that the real elasticity of presidential power lies in foreign policy), and on the third he was sharply rebuked by a historic Supreme Court decision that raised questions about the scope of implied powers.

The whole question of presidential power is enmeshed in a faulty idea of how the presidency is related to the sources of its power. The Constitution, under the Supreme Court's interpretation, provides the channel through which the president's powers flow; but those powers themselves derive from the president's relations to the events around him and to the minds and purposes of the people whom these events affect. These are the true sources of presidential power. It is sometimes said there are two Constitutions: the written document and the unwritten one. The second Constitution, which is more meaningful, is to be found not in the applications but in the outlines of economic power, religious convictions, ethnic loyalties, rural and urban divisions, and attitudes toward war and peace, with all of which the president must reckon as exactingly as he reckons with the written Constitution.

It might be better to say that the *authority* of a president is even more important than his *power*, because the authority shapes and decides what the power shall be. I use "authority" in the sense of the president's habitual command of popular consent. The sources of the president's authority are subjective—flowing from his personality, his political style, his conduct of the office, his impact on people—rather than being objective and forever imbedded in a constitutional document. If he has a commanding grasp, contagious appeal, political artistry, and a mastery of his purposes and methods, then he will carry authority no matter what powers he claims or forsakes, and his authority will work magic to bolster the claims he stakes out. If, on the other hand, like John Adams or Herbert Hoover, he fails to carry authority, then even a limited view of the presidential power will get him into trouble, and even a clear grant of power will prove ineffectual.

The president has not only massive powers and authority; he has also massive burdens that weigh him down. The presidency eats men. The demands on the incumbent are at once imperative and paradoxical.

Once elected, a president must manage to unify the nation that has been temporarily split by the election ("We are all federalists, we are all republicans," Jefferson said in his first inaugural), yet not abandon the program he has been elected to carry out. He must be national leader without ceasing to be party leader, and party leader without alienating the factions into which every party splits. He must frame a legislative program without seeming to deprive Congress of its exclusive control over legislation and get it through Congress without seeming to drive it. He must head up a vast and sprawling administrative system of whose workings he can know only the tiniest fraction, yet whenever anything goes wrong he must stand accountable to the people for every detail. He must select, recruit, and hold administrative talent on the basis of merit, while "playing ball" within the patronage structure. He must coordinate the workings of the thousands of interlocking cogs of the governmental machine, yet somehow find a space for creative concentration on great issues. He is by the Constitution the sole organ of foreign policy in a peacetime Great Power, and in time of war or "cold war" he is commander in chief of a powerful military machine and head of a vast war economy. He must express and carry through the people's wishes, yet he must function as educator in chief, helping them to formulate their wishes and organize their opinion. He must be a symbol of the world's greatest democracy—its vigor, its effectiveness, its potentials—and, as a symbol, remote; yet he must also have the human immediacy that gives the ordinary American the sense that he is not lost and that he has someone to speak and act for him. He must be all things to all men, yet also a bold leader hewing out a path in a single direction. In short, he must be Pooh-Bah and St. George at once.

Obviously only a comic-strip Superman could combine all these qualities. Actually the presidential function is filled at any one time not by one man but by a number of men. Except at the top level, even most of the major decisions are made from day to day by a group of men each of whom serves as his alter ego in some area of policy. When a new president is elected, the commentators are as likely to turn their klieg lights on the "men around the president" as on the president himself.

No president can avoid the formation of juntas around him—insiders who are bound to have a vague conspiratorial air to the outsiders. Sometimes such a junta is actually sinister, as with the "Daugherty gang" who ran the White House under Harding; others only seem so to opposing groups within the president's own party and to the opposition party. Thus Roosevelt had his "Brains Trust," Truman his "cronies," Eisenhower his "Regency" group. Actually there are circles within circles of influence and power radiating out of the White House. To take the Eisenhower administration as an example: there was a formal Cabinet to which the president delegated his powers over each decision-making and administrative area; there was the National Security Council, which possessed immense power and included the secretary of state and several of the president's crucial advisers; there was an inner Cabinet group, in which the secretaries of the treasury, of state, and the attorney general played the principal roles; there was an inner White House Staff group, led by Chief of Staff Sherman Adams and Press Secretary James Hagerty; there was an inner congressional group, consisting of several trusted leaders of both Houses along with the staff liaison people who served as links with Congress; and there was an inner group of the president's close friends—the "Regency" group—including leading political and business figures, who advised him from the start on crucial matters and kept a supervision over affairs on the two occasions of his serious illness.

I must add that since the president is chief executive, the question of what kind of executive he is is an important one. Given his military experience, Eisenhower operated in the White House also with a line-and-staff organization, leaving most matters for decision to the men in charge of the respective areas, and leaning heavily upon his chief of staff. His tendency was to lay down the general line of policy and then stay out of things, even relatively important things, until real trouble arose, when he came back into the picture with his power and authority to clear up the trouble. Truman, at the other extreme, arose early every day, worked intensively, had his finger on all important matters, was chary of too-inclusive delegations of power, swept his desk clean, and was ready the next morning to begin again briskly. Compared with both of them, Roosevelt was a sloppy administrator who might delegate overlapping areas of power to several of his lieutenants and could not keep his own hand and mind out of any of the areas: as he was his own secretary of state, so he was his own secretary of the treasury and his own military-strategy staff.

There is room for a number of types of the executive mind in the presidency. But what is crucial in every case is that the president should avoid at one extreme the danger of so much delegation that he loses contact with the processes and temper of his administration, and at the other extreme the danger of becoming so preoccupied with details that he loses sight of his grand goals and strategies, and has no time or energy left for reflection on them.

In the end the presidency is thus a one-man job, and that one man cannot escape either the burden of or the accounting for it. The inventory of the tasks of the presidential office is a reminder at once of how capacious and exacting it is. Even more, it defines where the center of gravity of the office is—in the special relation of the president to the American demos.

That is why the people's instinct, in reviewing the history of the presidency, has been not so much to ask whether presidents have been "liberal" or "conservative," men of thought or men of action, but whether they have been "strong" or "weak" presidents. The strength or weakness with which they have exercised their functions has been partly a matter of their own character structure and inner drive, partly of the philosophy with which they have approached their office, but to a great extent the result of the tensions they have had to face. A man of seemingly ordinary capacities, like Harry S. Truman, showed how the presidency stretches a man as well as eats men, and how great is its capacity to educate the man who holds it.

Even the strongest of presidents learns that the presidential office is the veriest Gehenna unless the people make it tolerable; that whatever powers any particular president seeks to assume, it is the ultimate power of the people that grants or checks them; and that a president is helpless except insofar as he can win the people's confidence. This relation between leader and demos is at the heart of the organization of the American political will.

Arthur M. Schlesinger, Sr., polling a number of American commentators, found that the six "great presidents" were Lincoln, Washington, Franklin Roosevelt, Wilson, Jefferson, and Jackson, in that order. I should agree with Clinton Rossiter in adding Theodore Roosevelt to the list. Yet the notable theories of political leadership, especially the theory of "charismatic" leadership and of leadership as vocation, as developed by Max Weber, apply much more to European leadership politics than to American presidential politics. When the American thinks of his government, he thinks first of the president as its symbol. But while the president is often cursed extravagantly, he is rarely praised extravagantly. This is what Kenneth Burke has called the "debunking of the chosen symbol." Except in a rare instance like that of Eisenhower, the symbol is there to do a job under pitilessly critical examination, not to be followed blindly and adoringly. However sacred Americans may consider the Constitution itself and its judicial guardians, the bent is toward the deflation of authority in individuals.

Partly this derives from the American skepticism of all political power; partly too from the structure of authority in the American family and school system, where the emphasis is not on paternal power but on the development of individual self-reliance; partly too from a market system of caveat emptor in which the individual keeps himself continually on guard against being made a "sucker" from a too-unwary eagerness. Whatever the psychic sources, however, the fact is that Americans as a nation have rarely shown a sustained capacity for clinging to a political father. The only important exceptions were Washington ("the father of his country"), Lincoln (seen as "Father Abraham," although mainly in retrospect), and Franklin Roosevelt, who was a father symbol in a time of depression and world war, and then mainly for the minority groups and the underprivileged and excluded. To these must be added the figure of the soldier-as-man-of peace, in the person of Dwight Eisenhower, whose father image was at once authoritative, kindly, and carefully kept above the party battle (although he was a shrewd politician) and who rounded out his image, as American fathers so often do, by incurring a heart attack and having an intestinal operation. But the records of the presidential office show torrents of popular and partisan abuse of men like Adams, Jefferson, Madison, Jackson, Lincoln, Johnson, Cleveland, Theodore Roosevelt, Wilson, Franklin Roosevelt, and Truman—usually on the score that they were tyrants and dictators. A nation that has never recognized political masters needs to reassure itself continually that it is not falling under one.

The leadership qualities of Franklin Roosevelt and Dwight Eisenhower deserve special scrutiny because their common and contrasting qualities illumine the nature of "charismatic" leadership in the presidency. James M. Burns, by calling his study of Roosevelt *The Lion and the Fox*, placed him in the tradition of Machiavellian strategy, and there is little question that Roosevelt used imaginative daring and pugnacity along with the cunning of maneuver. Both qualities led him deep into party politics, where he fought the unfaithful within (he was one of the few presidents who tried to purge congressional leaders of his own party) and smote the heathen without.

Eisenhower had less both of the lion and the fox: he was not savage in attack, but usually soft-spoken; and he affected the style of staying outside political involvement and keeping above the party battles. His total political style was thus an unusual one among American presidents. He was not an intellectual, like Wilson or Jefferson; nor a lusty exponent of the strenuous life, like Theodore Roosevelt; nor a dour Puritan, like Coolidge; nor an introvert, like Lincoln, with a flair for jokes and an undercurrent of tragedy. He was the soldier-statesman combining the two qualities more strikingly than anyone before him since Washington. If he had some of the fuzzy outlines of another soldier-president, Ulysses Grant, who never quite learned what had happened to him when he fell among the businessmen and politicians, he was far less of an amateur in politics than he liked to seem. He knew the political uses of the genial, warming smile, of folksiness and of the earnest moralizing little sermons with which he sprinkled his press conferences. He understood the deep American impulse toward the belittling of politics, and by seeming to avoid partisanship he could win more converts to his cause than the most partisan leader. He came at a time when Americans wanted peace desperately, after a war and a cold war, and his political style as a soldier who knew war and could therefore bring peace exactly fitted the felt psychological needs of his time. He was widely supported during his first term both within his own party and among the Democrats on issues of war and peace, particularly when he met the Russian leaders at Geneva. The genial conflict-avoiding bent of Eisenhower and his reliance on the decision-making of the men around him weakened his second term, and were of some danger to the presidential position: increasingly Eisenhower himself became an image—and a very popular one—while the burdens of the office were more dispersed than they had been before. While the Democrats used the slogan of a "part-time presidency" in the campaign, this dispersal of the duties and powers of the office was not wholly due to the president's illness but was integral to his personality and his political style.

Yet this is unlikely to recur often in the future. The greater probability is that the burdens of the office will increase, and that the American president will, as in the past, have to win everything the hard way. He will have to meet the problems and opposition of Congress, his Party, the judiciary, the press, the power of Big Labor and the Big Corporation, the rivalry and jealousy of sections and classes. Presidential government thus becomes an obstacle race, and the Great President the Great Hurdler.

In this context the fear that a president will abuse his powers, while real enough, is only one phase of the danger. The other phase is that all but the stoutest of heart, the firmest of will, and the most passionate of conviction will give up the struggle long before they have achieved their objective. It is only widespread popular support that will enable any president to clear his hurdles. Unless the people are with him all the way he cannot carry through his program. His last chance of having the people with him is at a time of grave social crisis and in a national emergency, and then only if he is a consummate tactician. The presidential office is like a field headquarters, which operates best in the heat of critical battle. But the fact that it has come through well in every period of crisis is proof that in an age of disintegration, democratic government is not too fossilized and inflexible to survive.

The president combines within himself the double function of reigning and ruling. Using Walter Bagehot's idea that every government must have a "dignified" element in it, this element in America is divided between the presidency and the Supreme Court. Of the two, the president is more subject to vituperative attack but by that token more constantly present in the minds of the people. He occupies the center of the national stage. He is a "republican king." As with the British monarch, his daily life and acts are constantly under scrutiny, and his personality style (along with that of his wife) sets a pattern that is more or less consciously imitated by millions of Americans. The fact that Woodrow Wilson read detective stories, that Franklin Roosevelt collected stamps, that Eleanor Roosevelt worked hard at welfare problems and international affairs, that Dwight Eisenhower was an ardent golf amateur, and that Mamie Eisenhower wore bangs and had a gracious manner left an impact upon the reading, stamp-collecting, and golf-playing habits of American men and on the life style of American women. A president's smile or frown or look of anxiety, when reproduced in the press, may influence the stock market and the action of foreign governments, but even more the habitual demeanor of Americans whose image is formed in the presidential mirror.

There is also another kind of presidential image—the composite picture that the people keep in their minds of the traits a president ought to have. For example, he ought to come from a small town rather than a big city, since the tradition of a superior virtue and strength in such origins has survived the decline of the small town itself. He is likely to be of West European family origin—English, Scottish, Dutch, Swiss, German, or some mixture of them. No American president has yet derived from Scandinavian, Latin, East European, Slavic, or African origins. He is likely to come from one of the big states with a heavy electoral vote which can help swing him into the presidency. He is most likely to be a lawyer by profession and a politician by passion. If the presidential aspirant is either a businessman or a labor leader, the chances are heavy against him. He must have managed to preserve an integrity of family life and (except in a few instances) avoided any public disclosure of violation of the sexual mores of his culture.

Like the corporation, the presidency has been caught up in the managerial transformation of American life. In one sense it can be said that the president is himself a "manager"—in foreign relations, in war and peace, in economic affairs, in the daily functioning of the government. But it would be truer to say that the president has become a kind of chairman of the board, while the real managers operate the day-to-day affairs of the government and even make substantial policy decisions. When President Eisenhower had a heart attack in 1955 the national government went on functioning much as it had done before: there was an "inner group" operating under Sherman Adams, who was in effect the president of the corporate managerial nucleus, and who never burdened the chairman of the board with anything except crisis problems and top policy-making decisions. The effect of this is to bring the president into the decision-making picture only when and where something goes badly wrong, and only when broad new policy needs to be formed. The president thus becomes basically a conciliator between opposing factions within his administration, a resolver of crises, a god from the machine stepping out of the sky to restore order from chaos. This may help explain why the dignity and distance of the presidential office are maintained even in the most constant struggle and bitterness of the daily political arena. Eisenhower, for example, was rarely branded with the stigma of what his underlings did. Under other presidents as well, notably Franklin Roosevelt, the underlings who were unlucky enough to threaten the image which the administration wished to preserve in the popular mind have often had to be sacrificed.

Given this position, the president must rely on the people he picks to carry on the daily work of the government. He operates under the written Constitution as defined by the courts; but, even more, he operates under an unwritten constitution, composed of a body of executive orders which are drawn up by the presidential assistants and are based often only on the fact that some previous president had done something of the sort. The process of constitution-making thus resides in the presidency far more than in Congress and rivals the similar process in the Supreme Court. As a distributor of power, the president not only bestows his blessings on a large number of lucky individuals who come in for the political prizes and flock to Washington when their man has won: he also blesses a particular class or segment of the population. Under Roosevelt's New Deal the intellectuals got a chance at power; under both Roosevelt and Truman the labor groups were similarly cut in; under Eisenhower a large number of corporate executives, major and minor, eagerly found their place in the Washington power hierarchy.

But even with the maximum degree of delegation of presidential duties to staff and advisers, the presidency remains a tense and crushing office, and is likely to take its toll in the future as in the past. This has made the problem of presidential succession, in the event of death or disabling illness, more crucial. The likelihood is that Americans will be more aware of the importance of the vice president in the presidential succession, and that the Throttlebottom type of vice president is on his way out.

PRESIDENTIAL
LEADERSHIP IN
THE NEW AMERICA

THE TESTING OF AMERICA took many forms, but mainly it was a testing of presidents and the presidency itself in the frame of a turbulent world of adversaries and allies. The centrality of the office, for good or ill, was clear in the late 1950s under Dwight Eisenhower, and even clearer in the new presidential generation that stretched from John Kennedy and Lyndon Johnson through Ronald Reagan's 1980s.

After Eisenhower there was scarcely a president under whom the prime question did not arise: whether this complex political organism called America was in truth governable. The answer had to be reaffirmed under each, in testings that reached deep into the fiber of both the president and the people.

Whoever held the office became the world's most closely watched man. No monarch was ever followed more closely—his health and illness, his fluctuations of mood, policy, and advisers, his successes and blunders, his poll standing, his stormy and peaceful times, his crises and resolutions.

He was a prince who had strayed into a democracy. He had countless Machiavellis to instruct him in the principles of *virtù*—today's leadership principle. His face appeared upon a hundred million screens and his name was pronounced endlessly, in praise or imprecation, from African savannas to Russian steppes to German universities to teeming Chinese cities to some marketplace in Central America.

"Presidential Leadership in the New America" is a section of the postscript chapter to the thirtieth anniversary edition of *America as a Civilization* (New York: Henry Holt and Company, 1987).

His own countrymen, in their efforts to define him, end by defining themselves. A recurring positive image on the screen, as the British monarchy knows, can be an antidote against fragmentation, giving the viewers a sense that they are not a congeries of discordant atoms but a society with a center. Whether the center holds is a more troublesome question I shall return to.

What about the man behind the image? After Eisenhower, who closed the Roosevelt-Truman presidential generation, the men of the new generation that came in with Kennedy, Johnson, and Nixon were still seen as Titans, having to carry the burden of the nation and the imperium. But they were wounded Titans, bearing the scars their lives had left on their character and temperament. A subdiscipline called "psychohistory," with roots in Freudianism and developmental psychology, emerged in the 1960s and 1970s and had some influence. Mostly it took the presidents as its theme, reading their character into their presidential decisions, and their early life enactments into their character.

It shed some light on its subjects, after the fact, but its predictive power was slight, and there was always something unfinished about it. The psychic linkage of health or hurt with character, and that in turn with event, was too fragile to bear the implacable weight of context and history. From Franklin Roosevelt through Ronald Reagan, each president offered a succession of revisionist presidential historians a different puzzle, of mingled irony and paradox, for the changing consequences of presidential decisions played havoc not only with their answers but sometimes with the premises underpinning their questions.

Yet the presidents were special variants of a genus—the American as political man. The heart of their training, early or late, was in the electoral process as a prelude to the governing process. Together these formed "politics." Despite my earlier lament at its "belittling," Americans in time came to accept politics with a mixed skepticism and affection, and a number of them crowded into the arena, eager to take the stir and stench of battle because the prize in the end was their Grail.

The chief agents of change in the electoral system—computer and TV—transformed American politics by operating on political man. The key to the change was imagery. Where the verbal image suggested by the printed page and the disembodied voice of radio had been completed by reader and listener, TV offered its viewers the embodied image and voice. In a democracy of images everyone shared them—sound, symbols, message, emotions, fantasies, and all. By mediating the reality for their viewers the medium *became* a species of reality. Hence the kernel of truth in Marshall McLuhan's "The medium is the message."

What took place on the screen was a representation of life but—especially for the young, who had it built into them early—it also became life itself. The viewer thrust his skills, dreams, hungers, purposes, all his selfhood, into the image, and together the viewer in the image and the image in the viewer fused to form the reality.

Two things have happened to the electoral process in consequence of this pervasive technology. For one, the new electoral elite embraced a corporate model, with specialized skills applied to issue demographics, strategy brainstorming, and carefully tested TV advertising of the candidate. His role was less than heroic: he was at once the product being marketed and the ornament and beneficiary.

The second event is the breakthrough of media-oriented primaries as the force field in which the choice of the party's presidential candidate is all but determined. This is linked with the weakening of party authority and loyalty, the crumbling of the brokerage function of party leaders at nominating conventions, the obligatory planning over years for the primaries sweepstakes.

The metaphor of an election horse race still clings to the popular imagination, but with the new media it needs some recasting. The voters who watch it on TV are not just spectators. They are themselves at the heart of the action, identifying with a candidate as a possible winner, but also swept up in the momentum which a surprise win in early primaries gives him. The electoral process is thus opened to the acceleration effect which turns political man into a highly volatile one.

The idea of a distinct American political culture goes back to the New Deal, but the presidential crises and the mounting media role after the early 1960s gave it sharper shape. There was substance aplenty for fervent congressional investigation and talk-show commentators to feed on, over the quarter-century stretch from Kennedy's Bay of Pigs through Nixon's Watergate, Carter's hostage crisis and Reagan's Iran arms deal.

In terms of drama two things stand out to define the mood of the political culture. One is its relation to a succession of tempestuous presidencies in a fever-chart alternation of loves and hates, magnified by a structural media hype. The second is the bloodhound intensity of tracking down the scent of presidential malfeasance by Congress and the media.

Beyond this theater the central feature of the political culture is the dominant academic and intellectual elite that serves at once as the source of its ideas and passion, the critic of its achievements, and the validating agent of its legitimacy. There was no administration that did not feel its sting at some point, no president who was not eager for its good will. It embraced Theodore Roosevelt, Woodrow Wilson, Franklin Roosevelt, and John F. Kennedy. It was condescending to Dwight Eisenhower, hostile to Lyndon Johnson, implacable to Richard Nixon, contemptuous of Jimmy Carter and of Ronald Reagan.

The political culture may be seen as a triangle, with the public at the base, the political elite at the tip, and the intellectual and media elites forming the two sides. Together they shape the temper and climate of the political culture within which governing takes place. The first imperative of a president, as the most visible member of the political elite, is to swim in the sea of the people. But on how well or badly he performs his governing function he is assessed for his place in history by an often adversarial intellectual establishment which has its own politics and ideology, and is often far removed from the minds and lives at the base of the larger culture.

Shelley called the poet the true "legislator of mankind." The role now devolved upon philosophers, critics, commentators, political and social theorists. During the half century that started with the presidency of Franklin Roosevelt, the political culture became a tenaciously liberal establishment, drawing on the state-oriented energies in both parties. Roosevelt's political culture survived his disastrous policy toward Stalin and the Soviet Union.

Whether a lasting counterestablishment can emerge to challenge it is still being tested. Eisenhower and Reagan, both popular conservative presidents, could win two presidential terms and a segment of media approval. But they failed in their efforts to recruit a policy elite from the knowledge class, especially in foreign policy, and an enduring support system that could translate their popularity into viable policies.

Richard Nixon was strongly moved by an antiestablishment animus that—along with his character—was a key to Watergate. But even if he had avoided resigning he could not function as president because he had no political culture to reestablish and legitimize his authority. Ronald Reagan was able to recruit the initial makings of a political counterculture and governed for six years. But he too discovered, with the Iranian arms deal, that his vast popularity could not provide a frame for effective governing as long as mounting questions remained unanswered. It was proof again that while a president is at the core of government he cannot truly govern without a political and media culture that become the custodians of his authority.

Thus a president functions not only by his constitutional and prerogative *powers* but also by the *authority* that enables him to employ them. The powers come from the Constitution, written and unwritten. The authority comes largely from the political culture. In every instance of an imperiled presidency in the 1960s, 1970s, and 1980s it was credibility that was at stake. Without it, authority cannot be exerted, and without authority the full range of power cannot be invoked. Thus credibility and authority go with the perception of the person and character, and power goes with the office. But power cannot be released effectively without an empowerment by the people's belief in both the office and its incumbent.

It is clear now that the legitimacy of a presidency rests in the people and the political culture. But it must constantly be retested in the fires of extreme crisis, when the authority of a president is imperiled.

Aristotle's "man as a political animal" had to be radically revised in the new America to include political woman. Her entrance into the political culture as into the economic—fought for a quarter century—was finally accepted. She also made her way into the intellectual elite, which legitimized both. Women proved formidable as activists because they were driven by an intellectual as well as a political passion. That passion found expression in a cluster of "women's studies" in universities and a spate of revisionist theories in every discipline, from history and politics and psychoanalysis to theology.

Once aroused in rebellion the quest for freedom and equality (the rhetoric seemed always to come from politics) took on a demonic liberating force of its own. It released talents in women they had considered for centuries to be a monopoly of men, including business and political skills. A woman had reached the Supreme Court and another had been nominated for vice president. Why not a woman as president?

It would be seen as the final validation of the women's revolution. But it would take longer for women in the new America to move beyond the economic and political to the realm of relationships and resolve some of the contradictions of their liberation.

★

There were contradictions as well in the perception of the role of government. Just as the political corollary of a welfare economy in FDR's day was a strong and positive government, so the political corollary of a self-sufficient entrepreneurial economy in Ronald Reagan's day had to be a nonburdensome, nonintrusive, noninterventionist "weak" government. Yet like his predecessors, Reagan found that for the foreign-policy sector a high-defense interventionist "strong" government was an imperative. It was an exercise in the schizoid that is likely to haunt governments to come.

In the calculable future America will be confronting two major models in its foreign policy. In one (as in the People's Republic of China) Communist governments have almost total control and the people little. In the other (as in Iran) theocratic elites have taken over the government or (as in Lebanon) have dissolved it into a terrorist anarchy. Without either ideology or theology to inspirit the people the new America must operate in a world environment that—except for the Western imperium—is obsessed with one or the other model. Yet with all their war technologies America and its imperium must in the crunch fall back on consent, consensus, and the "national interest."

Whatever its attractive force, America faces the harsh reality of a world governed by the triple passions of nationalism, race, and religion. It is a world of a few great powers and of adversary imperial blocs but also of a multitude of ministates seeking their place in the United Nations sun, a world to which law has not yet come, one without a moral community that can run beyond the writ of each nation's power elite. In the vacuum of law and community the common currency tends to be the one furnished by arms dealers, and the characteristic lingua franca, that of terrorism.

The paradox of power in the 1970s and 1980s was the impotence of the strong, with the overkill weapons they did not dare use, facing the resource-fullness with which the weak used their weaponry of terror—kidnappings, hijackings, the detonated car- or truck-bomb. The vulnerability of air transport, the easy access of terrorists to a global TV audience, and the sanctity that the individual human life claimed in the West combined—if only for a time—to fashion an age of terror. Looking back we see the 1960s, with all its violence, as largely a decade of principle. But we are likely to see the terror 1970s and 1980s, in the phrase W. H. Auden used about the appeasement 1930s, as "the low, dishonest decades."

Confronting the near anarchy of such a world, the American governing elite had constantly to balance the strategic imperatives and the geopolitical realities with the long and deep tradition of idealist principles. The years of bipartisan support for global policy initiatives, under Truman and Eisenhower, would be hard to restore. After the Vietnam experience and the War Powers Act, interventions of any sort had a stiff gauntlet to run. If short-range war risks were thereby diminished, the price exacted might be inaction by a soft democracy and increased war risks further down the road.

Whether strategic interest can prove a strong enough dynamic for effective action in the global arena was a question not yet decisively answered in the 1960s, 1970s, and 1980s. Could it survive the principle of checks and balances, the failures of bipartisanship, the feuding of liberals and conservatives and of Congress and the executive? Could it, with these obstacles, sustain an enduring foreign policy? The Vietnam experience left in its wake a widespread fear, much like the isolationism of the 1930s, that strong foreign-policy actions would lead to war.

It made covert action difficult because of a deep skepticism as to whether this really served "reasons of state." Justice Holmes spoke much earlier of "the dirty business" of wiretapping. Unlike the older European and Asian societies, Americans were uneasy with whatever seemed dark and dirty, which violated both their open society and their national character. They wanted to bring everything into the light, to see whether rules had been defied and laws broken.

While a few covert actions succeeded, the major ones, under Eisenhower, Kennedy, Carter, and Reagan, ended badly, hurting the presidents and the nation. They raised doubts about the maturity of the covert segment of the political culture and shed light on what happens when American innocence and openness collide with the imperatives of secrecy.

The chances of shaping a reality-grounded foreign policy in a world of stratagems and fanaticisms are still incalculable. America is a young civilization, with only two centuries of existence, in a world of old civilizations steeped in history, less devoted than Americans are to the sacredness of the individual life, more adept at cunning and political survival.

WOUNDED TITANS

Every president of the United States has had in him a little of Job and a lot of Jehovah. Each has complained of the woes that go with his burdens, and each has acted like a god in issuing demands and wielding power.

The modern presidency began in 1933 with Franklin Delano Roosevelt, and he became the paradigm American leader of the twentieth century. He sired a presidential line, established a style, and cast the longest shadow. Roosevelt was a titan, and he made the presidency so large that each of his successors has been a titan by virtue of office. But he was, like each of them, a wounded titan.

Why "titan"? I use the term not to confer on these modern presidents some unqualified grandeur (most were all too human), but to suggest that they came to be seen—and to see themselves—as more than mere men. Why "wounded"? Like all men, each was wounded by his life history, but presidents have their special wounds. With few exceptions, the passion that drove them toward their dream of high office left them scarred when they finally reached their lonely pinnacle. Once there, they often were savaged in the vise of their office by a culture which briefly celebrates "stars" but rarely honors heroes. A president's wounds come not just from his psyche but from the democracy he is called to lead.

But so, fortunately, do his strengths. American presidents are not mere victims, buffeted by the circumstances of their histories and experiences; they are active agents in the midst of life, coping and resilient. I see them not as segmented characters but as whole men,

"Wounded Titans" was published in *Notre Dame Magazine* (Autumn 1984). An expanded version of the essay, "Of Presidents and their Splendors & Miseries," appeared in the British journal *Encounter* (June 1985), and is reprinted here with the original title.

capable of growth: and to understand a whole man, an analyst must find in each man's character the clue which suggests a resolution of his personality's splits and contradictions, which lights up their relation to the whole. To seek the clue is to encounter, in Yeats's line, "the fascination of what's difficult." I want to seek that clue to the lives of each of the modern presidents who have left the stage of history, Franklin Roosevelt to Jimmy Carter, and in Ronald Reagan too.

The man who would become the paradigm president was a coddled only son, with a patrician lineage at Hyde Park and a posh education at Groton and Harvard, which were scarcely the stuff of the "log-cabin" myth. But he came to the White House in 1933 after surviving three crucial tests of his ability and character. For FDR, these were his service as secretary of the navy under Woodrow Wilson, his tenure as governor of New York, and his personal struggle to overcome infantile paralysis.

It was the illness that prepared him best. Roosevelt had taken command of it and had learned how to take command of a people in panic. He taught them that strength (like "fear itself") can become a self-fulfilling prophecy. Crippled himself, he taught a nation crippled by fear how to walk. He demonstrated in ample measure what Machiavelli called *virtù*—courage, instinct, wiles, vision—the capacity for leadership.

He had preternatural antennae. A leftward wind was blowing across the world in his time and he rode it. He was permeable, soaking up impressions from everyone around him, translating them into slogans and actions. To counter his contemporaries Mussolini and Hitler, he fashioned for himself a necessary image of strength. He sensed that history would overlook his critics' accusations that he was building a dictatorship, but that it would never forgive him weakness or passivity. He had much of the shaman in him; he governed by his magical knack for using the people's hunger for symbols and yearning for leadership.

The lapse of time, however, has opened chinks in the burnished armor of Roosevelt's reputation. The initial impact of his New Deal was mostly psychological; the economy never recovered from the Depression, but, rather, limped with the nation toward war. His domestic initiatives—the antibusiness stance, the creation of the welfare state—started a costly fifty-year romance with the social engineering of a new statism.

Roosevelt's reputation as war leader and peace organizer has suffered radical attrition. We now can see that he was slow to understand the nature of the menace of Hitler; and when he finally did, the aspect he grasped was less Hitler's evil than his propaganda skills. "I will meet the propaganda of the word with the propaganda of the deed," he told me in an interview at Hyde Park. When he finally did enter World War II, it was not via Europe but via Pearl Harbor—an episode that he and his war leaders either botched badly or handled deviously. In any event, by December 7, 1941, a largely unassisted Europe had gone dangerously far toward disintegration.

He held the alliance together by playing the "coalition" theme earnestly and grandly, but he made costly mistakes in the war's execution. He turned a stony face to pleas to bomb the Nazi extermination camps because he feared that Hitler would use his propaganda machine to accuse him of waging a "Jewish War." By demanding unconditional surrender, he hemmed in Hitler's foes in Germany and probably prolonged the conflict. He did not understand his ally Stalin or the nature of Soviet Communism. Toward the war's end, Roosevelt decided to check the eastern sweep of American armor, a move that had grievous political consequences. By Yalta, his stamina was exhausted and his judgment faulty.

How did this happen? Roosevelt operated within a frame of three major propositions. One was that Britain had to be aided and saved, but that the British Empire was an antiquated and dying system, to be replaced by Wilsonian self-determination. The second was that, to keep Stalin from suspecting a "deal," there could be no surrender terms for Germany that might have shortened the war and kept the Soviet armies from their final occupying drive through Eastern Europe. The third was that a friendly and satisfied Stalin was the indispensable element for a postwar United Nations world.

None of these propositions worked for him. Worst of all, he neglected the reality principle of military-political decisions. When his military aide, Admiral William D. Leahy, chided him about his Yalta concessions, he replied that Stalin's armies occupied the ground in Poland. Yet he allowed—even urged—them to drive to Berlin, thereby violating the first principle of geopolitics—possession of the turf.

His problem, in the end, was that he did too much too completely. In the process of managing the polity and waging the war, he created a political culture in his own image—a culture that lacked figures of stature to challenge him. No one was around to correct the faults in his world view. The intellectual and political culture which surrounded him (of which I must ruefully admit I was a part) shared his view of most things, including Communism. FDR was a brilliant political practitioner, but neither his intellect nor his instincts enabled him to transcend the narrow culture he had created. And in his feeble final years he overstayed his time of effective leadership.

Franklin Roosevelt is still remembered as a titanic figure. But we now can see how flawed a giant he was.

Roosevelt's successor forced Americans to reassess their thinking about the kind of preparation that makes a good president. Harry S. Truman never went to college, stayed close to his father's farm until he was thirty, and failed as a haberdasher before finally turning to politics. It is often said that he was an ordinary man who made a good president—but that isn't true. Truman had a modest background, but he was an extraordinary man, a member of Thomas Jefferson's "natural aristocracy of virtue and talent."

Hewn out of a single bloc of Missouri turf, he got his strength from strong family ties. He came to office with a profound knowledge of history. He had been a nearsighted boy who ransacked his high-school library, taking to heart the fiery precepts of Plutarch's heroes and dreaming of becoming one. Still, his early life was a protracted moratorium as he waited for a destiny that never seemed to come. He had had one crucial experience as a leader—as captain of a National Guard artillery unit in France, where he found that by word and example he could bend unruly men to his will—but his postwar years were feckless, and his early political career was lackluster. Finally, in 1934, after an overlong tenure as a county overseer, he was handed a Senate seat as a reward by "Boss" Pendergast of Kansas City, and the moratorium was over.

In his second term, Truman chaired a difficult Senate committee on war-industry contracts, and in the process became fully his own man. The assignment gave him the prominence that propelled him onto the 1944 Democratic ticket as FDR's running mate. Eighty-two days after taking office as vice president, Truman found himself thrust into a chair that nearly everyone thought was too big for him.

He changed that view by compiling a record that can challenge that of any president of our time. He dropped the bomb, ended the war, kept American troops in Europe, undertook the Berlin airlift, established the Marshall Plan and NATO, recognized Israel, formed the Atomic Energy Commission, used the United Nations to halt an invasion of South Korea, and affirmed civilian control of the military by dismissing the recalcitrant General Douglas MacArthur. These actions were not without cost, but they undid FDR's faulty decisions where possible and laid the groundwork for an essential free-world coalition in the postwar era.

Truman governed against the odds, within a sheath of liberal contempt and McCarthyite savagery. He blundered. He never fully overcame the limitations and bruises of his early life, remaining stubbornly anti-intellectual, and often reducing complex decisions to black-and-white choices. He boasted that he had "never lost a night's sleep" over his decision to bomb Hiroshima; he should have. He was impatient with reflective thought.

Nevertheless, for the most part, Harry Truman managed the government well in his crucial era. His historical sense and his hard-earned mettle helped make him the most successful of the recent presidents, and the least wounded.

In 1952, the Republican Party turned to a war hero to lead it back to the White House after twenty years. The experience of Dwight David Eisenhower as president suggests that Americans might do well to look more often beyond the pool of politicians when seeking a candidate. "Ike" became America's foremost father-figure after George Washington. But his sunny, grinning, All-American image belied an underlying, studied artfulness. He was, in fact, among the wiliest of men.

Eisenhower's family had been left bankrupt by an unscrupulous business partner of his father's, and the experience left its mark. He grew up in an environment that stressed the importance of maintaining prestige and credibility, and the dangers of being deceived. As an army officer, Eisenhower was promoted only slowly. He was best known for his staff work, which combined meticulous planning and personal diplomacy. But he showed great promise, at least to Chief of Staff George Marshall, who assigned him over several superiors to a position in War Plans, and eventually charged him with the military leadership of the pivotal European theater.

That of course was his great testing, and it came late in life and transformed him into a national hero. On D-Day, the White House became Ike's destiny.

He was a leader of useful contradictions. He seemed unambitious, yet he twice captured the presidency. He seemed above politics, yet his adversaries knew him as a subtle maneuverer and a master of indirection. Preoccupied with prestige and credibility, he hoarded his popularity, declining to spend it even for a just cause. The result was what one historian has called a "hidden-hand presidency." Behind a protective screen, Eisenhower called the plays, laid out the strategy, and enjoyed the gap between his seeming and actual roles in human events.

Eisenhower knew that on sticky matters a president can get more done by stealth than by show. He allowed Secretary of State John Foster Dulles to talk about "brinkmanship," but for eight years he avoided entangling the United States in a war. He used American weapons as covered cards in a poker game, cut defense costs for the sake of the economy without diminishing the country's international role, and achieved zero inflation. He was Odysseus, not Achilles, and he left behind a prosperous, secure nation.

Intellectuals, who had incessantly made fun of his fractured syntax, finally have come to appreciate him. As early as 1967, Murray Kempton saw him as "a great tortoise carrying the world on his back."

John Fitzgerald Kennedy is the only American president who must be discussed within the context of his family. The influence began, of course, with the founding father, Joseph P. Kennedy, who had a remarkably ambitious design for his sons. He also had a profound impact on them; his example as a pirate in business, an appeaser in diplomacy, and a womanizer in a very public private life was a difficult one to ignore. He presided over a tightly controlled and controlling clan, programmed to produce at least one president.

The family's ambitions were in one sense a prison for Jack, but in another sense they released in a sickly, confused boy his own incipient identity as a public man. He acted the role with flair. In the 1960 campaign, his brilliant personal style—shown to great advantage in the televised debates with Richard Nixon—helped Kennedy to overcome his youth, his inexperience, his Catholicism. His presidency, too, had grace and class. He approached the office as a task to be studied and mastered; given time, he might have done both.

The substance of his presidency was no match for the style. In his inaugural address, Kennedy swore to "pay any price, bear any burden" for freedom. But he recoiled from confronting the Russians in Berlin, which was what they had counted on when they built their wall there. He botched the invasion of Cuba at the Bay of Pigs. In Laos and Vietnam, he sought the appearance of action without the reality. His underlying thinking, centered on the idea of dynamism, caused a lot of trouble, because dynamism in a society whips up the accelerations of change and removes useful limits, making it difficult to achieve an equilibrium. It was no accident that the traumatic accelerations of the 1960s began in Kennedy's time, and soon included his own violent death.

Death and danger always fascinated Kennedy. He took risks, walked a tightrope over the abyss. He indulged in a macho duel with Castro. He also indulged in a licentiousness that was a by-product of his long competition with his father. His sexual exploits were strikingly stripped of emotions and even of eroticism; he seemed to bring to them the same zest for danger that he brought to some of his international exploits, the same urge to overfly into the realm of the forbidden.

Kennedy succeeded admirably in one great and grave episode of decision-making: the Cuban missile crisis. By basing Russian missiles in Cuba, Nikita Khrushchev sought to present Kennedy with a provocative fait accompli, as he had done with the Berlin Wall. Kennedy responded by warning that the United States would not shrink from using nuclear force to protect its interests, but he also created a middle course, throwing a blockade around the island and offering concessions to allow Khrushchev to save face.

In the Cuban missile crisis, Kennedy found the right mixture of toughness and caution. He had finally reached his full political adulthood. But he had little time to work in his full maturity. The bullets in Dallas put an end to his explorations, and seemed to threaten more than these.

For most of his political life, John Kennedy's priority was his image; and it is his image that has lasted. He had countless affairs, but his greatest romance was with history. JFK was a Byronic president: he sought to make an adventure out of his presidency and his life. His assassination was shattering to the nation's self-perception. We mourned not just for a murdered president but for a lost, romanticized vision of ourselves.

When Lyndon Baines Johnson took the oath of office aboard "Air Force One" at Dallas's Love Field, he was the man best prepared to assume the presidency since James Madison. He probably knew more about the inner workings of the government than anyone before or since. Charles de Gaulle described him as *un homme politique*, the incarnation of Aristotle's political man. He was brilliant, persuasive, ruthless, and effective—yet in the presidency, none of this could prevent his self-destruction.

An understanding of the rich contradictions of this truly imperial figure must begin in the Texas hill country of his boyhood. Lyndon Johnson was the son of a hard-driving, authoritarian father—a failed Texas politician—and a beautiful, cultured, possessive mother. His family suffered financial reversals that subjected them to the humiliation of a decline in status. As a youngster of developing talent, Johnson was caught in these crosscurrents, and he seemed to spend the rest of his life seeking to redress old wounds by the ruthless acquisition and exercise of power.

Strong evidence supports this view. But some who have adopted it have gone too far, reducing Johnson to an evil caricature of greed, rapacity, betrayal, and deceit. They strip him of his humanity and ignore essential facts: that he won the love of some extraordinary women and the loyalty of some wise men who worked for him, and that he used his power to institute social programs of a scope unequaled since the New Deal.

My own belief is that the key to an understanding of Johnson's conflicting ends and means lies in his need for control. Doris Kearns, a historian who knew him well, says Johnson was constantly plagued by dreams of being bound to a chair, powerless to release himself. Clearly, the future president's early years were a chaos of volatilities that left him forlorn in a world he didn't create and couldn't control. He appears to have set himself at an early age to rebuild his world and to make it manageable. That meant choosing his father's profession. Politics brought Lyndon close to men of power, enabling him in part to control events and to manage his own life in what he saw as a harsh Darwinian jungle where only the crafty and strong survived. In time, he proved himself a brilliant technician, able to manage what others had botched. As Senate majority leader, he unleashed a cascade of legislation like a modern Hammurabi.

Unfortunately, Johnson had no philosophy to guide the technics. His world view was limited to "the lessons of Munich," his social outlook to the hand-me-down theories of Roosevelt. He had a need to "get things done," to "outdo" his idol, FDR, to achieve what the tyro Kennedy had failed at and become "the *can-do* president." But he had only a limited sense of what it was that he had to do.

There really were two Lyndon Johnsons, not "good" and "bad" but controlling and controlled. In the end, with the Vietnam War, they became one and the same. The more Johnson felt controlled by forces beyond his reach, the more rigid he became in seeking to control them, detail by detail, helicopter by helicopter. He tried desperately to run the war from the White House, examining bombing reports each night in his bedroom. He had an Alamo conception of making a stand against the enemy to the bitter end. But he lacked the will either to win the war or to abandon it and call it a victory.

Both the Southeast Asian war and the "Great Society" fell victim to Johnson's excess and bravado. He sought to further simultaneously his war abroad and his reforms at home. Both ventures stoked the fiery furnace of social unrest, and unleashed forces beyond his control or understanding. As they slipped away from his grasp, he fell into a frozen inner panic of paranoia and despair.

LBJ had dreamed of becoming the architect of a golden American era, but he came to preside over this century's most traumatic and nearly suicidal decade. In the end, he came to know his nightmare of being strapped and unable to move. He gave up his election plans and died of heartbreak.

Richard Nixon calls to mind Massinger's Sir Giles Overreach. Throughout his life, he pushed himself beyond the set limits. His wounds, like Lyndon Johnson's, were inflicted within a family that bred insecurity, under a father who was harsh and ineffectual and a mother who, Nixon felt, favored his invalid brothers over him. The political vocation, although not his early dream, became his acquired destiny. He studied it faithfully, and found the art of the adversary suited to the salving of his wounds.

What is striking about Nixon is his series of crises, transgressions, and self-examinations, and his inexhaustible resilience. Even more than Kennedy, he explored the limits. He repeatedly found himself stretched to the breaking point—in the Hiss case, the Nixon fund flap, the Caracas melee, Ike's health crisis, his own defeat for the California governorship, his bombing of Cambodia, and finally Watergate, where he went well beyond the limits.

He was always eager for testings, able to define himself only in action, often destructive and self-destructive. He saw life in the purest life-and-death terms of Social Darwinism. He acted as an agent in the free-market moral jungle, and on the occasion of his California defeat, he told reporters, "You fellows are killers, but I believe in your right to kill." More often, his rhetoric was touched by idealism, but his actions usually alternated between the ferocious and the masochistic.

Nixon knew geopolitics better than Johnson, and he probably would not have originally escalated the Vietnam War, which he took so long to wind down. He had undeniable talents, and he formed a first-rate odd-couple partnership with Henry Kissinger. It is true that he dangerously expanded executive power, moving toward what Arthur Schlesinger called an "imperial presidency," but he ran the imperium with a keen sense of the power principle. Nixon based his political strength on the nonintellectual classes. A man of many resentments, he complemented the resentment of a workingman's "silent majority" with outrage at the excesses of a radical-liberal academic and media elite.

Unfortunately, his own resentments projected Nixon into acts so blatantly illegal that they cut him away from his natural support system. He never trusted the course of events and always felt compelled to give history an extra push. He maneuvered, at Watergate, to steal an election he was almost certain to win anyway; in the process, he stole the presidency from himself. The night before he resigned, he knelt in prayer with Kissinger. It is not clear to what God the two men prayed, but they had in common the god of history, and Nixon could be expected not to lose his chance to put in his bid.

As it turned out, those who thought he was finished that night had forgotten his Lazarus-like power of resilience. The last decade has witnessed, in and out of the academies, a largely unpredicted Nixon revisionism. Some of it is a kind of revanchism by liberals against his three successors, a way of making them look bad by making Nixon look good. But most of it is based on a recognition of his strengths as a leader and of his successes as an architect of foreign policy. It is almost as if his resignation from the post he loved above all else had plunged Nixon into a hell so fiery that it made all his previous wounds seem minor, and burned them all away.

Nixon and I have talked relatively frequently and personally since he became author, commentator, presidential adviser, perhaps the first president to preside over his own revisionist rehabilitation in history. His case suggests that wounds incurred during the life journey and presidential tenure are not beyond all healing.

His successor was a minor figure. In October 1973, when Vice President Spiro Agnew resigned in disgrace, an already weakened President Nixon was forced to choose the inoffensive House minority leader, Gerald R. Ford, as the new vice president—one most likely to succeed. The nominee modestly quipped that he was "a Ford, not a Lincoln," and he was right.

When he finally succeeded Nixon ten months later, Ford was convincing at first in his role as national "healer." But he stumbled one month into his term when he pardoned his predecessor. Ford explained that a Nixon criminal trial and probable jail term would further divide the society; and his reasoning was sound. But he should have known that trust was as important as compassion in his effort to heal the nation. In many minds, the pardon broke the trust which Ford had begun to build and raised the question of his own presidential bona fides.

Ford also had to pay for two events that he had little role in bringing about: the final liquidation of the American role in Vietnam and the quadrupling of oil prices by OPEC. He contributed to his own growing image as a bumbler by stumbling physically in incidents reported mercilessly by the media, and by stumbling verbally on the issue of Polish freedom in his 1976 debate with Jimmy Carter.

As president, Ford lacked gravitas, a certain weightiness. He remains in memory what he was: an interim figure. Early in his life, he had been separated from his natural father; he had lost a figure of authority, and he seemed less than fully able to project authority in later life. During a long spell as a congressional leader, he essentially got along with his peers and did nothing to excess. Because of a remarkable sequence of events, this experience carried him to the presidency—but not to an important use of it.

"Good man, wrong job." That was Speaker Sam Rayburn's summation of Eisenhower. It really did not fit Ike, but it sums up Jimmy Carter.

Carter was a man of obvious intelligence, ability, and religious belief who accurately gauged the post-Vietnam and post-Watergate climate in America, and won his nomination and election as an independent and virtuous political outsider. For all his strengths, however, it should be remembered that he defeated the hapless Gerald Ford in 1976 only narrowly—and against the skillful Ronald Reagan in 1980, he was overwhelmed. He came in by a whisker and went out by a landslide.

Carter failed as president because, like Ford, he never figured out how to exercise authority. He seemed more interested in examining his conscience, in ensuring his own worthiness before God, and in attaining a pristine kind of excellence ("Why not the best?") than in exercising power.

This surely was a legacy of his early life in a family oriented toward good works (a sister became a faith healer), and he learned early on to be dutiful. When his father died, he abandoned his career as a naval engineer to return to Plains and take over the family business.

But he stayed ambitious. When he lost a race for governor of Georgia in 1966, he experienced something very like a breakdown; it was resolved with his "rebirth" as a true Christian. He was also obsessed with being a "positive activist" president. During an evening at the White House, as he talked of his Georgia boyhood days with the black boy who played a "brother" role, I sensed that he had an eye on psychohistory.

Carter was infatuated with facts. As president, he stayed up nights with his briefing books; he marshaled details, absorbed them, ate them, expected them to sway the Congress and the people.

He had no coherent foreign policy. His top aides in that realm were at loggerheads with each other, and he lacked the commanding instinct to whip them into line. His favorite theme, human rights, fell prey to the Soviet contempt for them. His prim and proper State Department undercut allied regimes in Iran and Nicaragua. In the end, his vacillation left America naked to its enemies. His innocence was shocked by the Soviets' contemptuous move into Afghanistan, and his reelection was doomed by the Ayatollah's protracted and humiliating abuse of the U.S. hostages.

Carter was at his best at Camp David, sweating out details and acting as mediator between Israeli prime minister Menachem Begin and Egyptian president Anwar Sadat. Those activities were his fortes. Otherwise, he moved too fast, too early, with too little direction and too many projects tumbling into one another. Overall, he lacked a strong philosophy of government, and he surrendered his authority to his crises of conscience. He had a passion for excellence, but his "best" was not good enough because it was largely irrelevant to the demands of governing.

In January 1981, when Jimmy Carter and his Georgians left the White House in desolation, Ronald Reagan and his Californians entered it in triumph, bruiting a "revolution" by one of the unlikeliest revolutionaries in history.

Ronald Reagan's small-town Illinois boyhood was Arcadian in a Mark Twain way but it had its rough edges. Only with Truman has there been such a disproportion between a president's earlier life and his mature performance in office. His inner security survived an alcoholic father, straitened family resources, and the hazards of a somewhat less than starring film career.

The testing experience came in the 1940s when Reagan, then head of the Screen Actors Guild, met a Stalinist attempt to take over the union and learned that it could be resisted. It turned him from an FDR liberal loyalist into a hard-bitten foe of Communism, whose opposition struck close to the bone. His odyssey as a General Electric speechmaker on the rubber-chicken circuit refreshed his insight into blue-collar lives and values. It also prepared him for his spirited and acclaimed TV speech in the 1964 Goldwater campaign and—spurred on by a junta of wealthy California conservatives—for a try at the governorship.

The response of his Hollywood friends was characteristic. "Not Ronald Reagan for Governor," said Jack Warner, the acrid studio head. "Jimmy Stewart for Governor, and Ronald Reagan for Best Friend." It bespoke the shadowy line between make-believe and reality which ran through Reagan's career and gave it a lightness of being to balance his political tough-mindedness. While using consummately all the arts of communication, Reagan has succeeded by always returning to the reality principle.

He was a pragmatic success as two-term governor of California. His start as a national candidate came late, yet even his failed bids for the presidential nomination in 1968 and 1976 carried excitement. When he finally made it in 1980, he had been through a long testing-period that tried his grit and soul, and one just had to take him seriously as a strong leader.

He is the first president since Franklin Roosevelt to have "revolution" authentically attached to his name, for he marks a watershed for the deep currents of American tendency. Historians are bound to see him as a Jungian mirror image of Roosevelt. He has set himself to undoing a half century of state supports and entitlements, and to opening America—and through it the world—to an expansive free-market economy. He will not be spared by history for leaving American troops exposed to massacre in Lebanon, nor for piling up an unparalleled deficit while preaching a balanced budget. Yet a restored economy and an enhanced American world position created the climate of national confidence which won him a second term by a Himalayan electoral majority.

His optimism, his capacity to relate and communicate, his sensory organic feel for the popular mind—these have been Rooseveltian means that Reagan has turned to anti-Rooseveltian ends. But the same imaginative flair is there for carrying off contradictory messages, as in Reagan's heavy Keynesian deficit-spending within a frame of anti-Keynesian "supply-side" economics, and in high-tech "Star Wars" weaponry research joined to a promise to use it for reducing, in the end abolishing, offensive weapons systems.

This is a more complex personality and mind than Reagan is generally credited with. He fits in with a high-tech information revolution but has baffled the nation's political high culture. America's most effective president since Truman and Eisenhower has never been taken seriously by an intellectual and media elite which regards him as indolent, insensitive, slow-witted, and a Doonesbury cartoon figure of fun and grotesquerie.

Reagan may, of course, somewhere in his second term, tumble off the high wire of presidential politics and have a great fall. Despite his remarkable survival capacity I don't rule it out. But if it happens it will be because—while shaping a climate of popular confidence—he has thus far (unlike Roosevelt) failed to build a protective intellectual counterculture that will reach the media and the academics.

Yet I must stop short of an assessment of Reagan because history is not yet through with him. This actor is still on the stage; his actions are too close to yield the luxury of perspective. The moment, for him, is too filled with alarums and excursions and the noise of continuing battle in which presidents are tested.

The same, in a sense, is true of his predecessors: Does history ever let go of them? I doubt it. With every new event of any magnitude, their decisions are seen through a new prism, their minds and characters are put to a new scrutiny. That is what is meant by "revisionist history," and I confess myself a revisionist. I relish both the excitement and the difficulty of watching these presidential portraits emerge and reemerge from the collective study of scholars. I am even willing to incur the pain this process often brings.

I have felt this pain because, having known each of these men and on occasion having been part of the battles surrounding them, I have also known pleasure in seeing some of their individual reputations repaired or heightened, but pain as well at having to eat some of the words of praise or contumely I sent their way in the past.

How, then, can I be sure that my new estimates of these men are better? I can't. But I do have the comfort of additional perspective. More time has passed, some of the archives have been opened; we know more about these presidents and the results of their work. Also, I am older, and more rueful in experience.

I don't care much for the usual typologies by which historians rank presidents as great or near-great, strong or weak, active or passive. I prefer to ask an operational question: To what extent has a given president truly used his power to make America governable, to allow the organic forces of the nation to flourish, and to make life better, or at least more tolerable, for its people?

In the end, Franklin Roosevelt is the paradigm president simply because he did all that amply and grandly—although, in his later years, at great cost to his ultimate legacy. Truman and Eisenhower did all that, too, and their years (1945 until 1961) are remembered nostalgically as a halcyon period when society seemed in equilibrium, its parts in relative balance. That is why newer evaluations of Truman and Eisenhower, including my own, are upbeat. In their time America was governable, and they governed.

Kennedy and Johnson were men of talent; but their policies, especially in Vietnam, let loose forces and accelerations and dynamisms of change that made it hard for them and their successors to govern. Nixon tried hard to set limits on this unwieldy society but ended up breaking the limits himself. Ford and Carter floundered out of their depth. Reagan, after he lays down his burden, will be judged in the long perspective by how effectively he has slowed the thrust of unbridled change—and whether he leaves the country more governable than those who preceded him.

Anyone who has done his duty as a president-watcher in this time of storms and tempests has his own long and short lists of the leadership qualities that are crucial. It is clear from the experiences of the varied cast of characters who have presided over the past half century that the modern presidency requires a remarkable range of abilities and potentials. An effective modern president must be able to learn from experience and change with it. He must be at home with his innermost self, must be able to come to terms with his own wounds and scars and limits—and not wreak them on the nation. He must be able to make decisions with reflection but also with resolution, and to convey, at all times, a quality of quiet command. He must be able to interact with the moods of the common people, and to transmit to them a coherent philosophy of change, continuity, and direction. He must earn and keep their trust about his character and good faith. He must be aware of but unpanicked by the dangers in a world of ultimate weaponry. Above all else, he must recognize the wounds we Americans have inflicted on our civilization, and he must work to help release our best creative energies.

That is quite an order, but I remain a possiblist: about the presidency, and about America.

THE SHAPING OF
AMERICAN PRESIDENTS

Especially during the months before a general election, an echoing question haunts us: What shapes a good president, as opposed to a middling or disastrous one? If there are any signs and omens to tell us, we want to know what they are. Deafened by the cacophony of conflicting claims, charges, and promises by the candidates, hungry to reject the fake and embrace the authentic, the voters wonder how they can tell one from the other.

A scrutiny of past presidents may help to light up some of the dark places by noting the relation between their early and later lives, the logic of their life-histories in terms of input and outcome, the ways in which they faced crises in themselves and the nation, how they met their testings and how they were transformed by them—or not.

I have picked a sequence of six presidents—Franklin Roosevelt, Harry Truman, Dwight Eisenhower, John Kennedy, Lyndon Johnson, Richard Nixon. They come from no Golden Age, no Age of Innocence. They were part of a stormy time—a forty-year stretch from 1933 to 1974, which the historians will someday call America's Iron Age.

They offer a richly varied array of mind, personality, and character, of origins and upbringing and life experience. But they had one thing in common. They were all beset by the wrenching crises arising from America's institutions and freedoms, from its internal tensions and its world position. Sometimes they seemed doomed to govern—under impossible conditions—an ungovernable people who set no bounds on the demands they make on their leaders, who are by turns

---

"The Shaping of American Presidents," which has not been published previously, focuses on "the life journey" of several presidents and how voters can assess a president.

generous and supremely selfish, who love and hate uncritically, and who no sooner enshrine a hero than they turn and savage him as part of the number one American blood sport—president hunting.

I start with some flash point in the life of each of the six—a turning point of crisis and decision from which we can go backward to his beginnings and forward to what lay ahead.

In Franklin Roosevelt's case there are two flash points—one as he faced the agony of a nation in panic fear over the continuing Depression, the second when he faced the certainty of America's entrance into World War II after Pearl Harbor. In his experience and qualities FDR was the paradigm president for all who have followed. He had to fight a major Depression and a major war, and used the qualities of the lion and the fox in both.

The era began with the patrician of Hyde Park, strapped in his steel brace to deliver his first inaugural address, a paralyzed man speaking out against the paralyzing sense of panic in the nation, saying that "the only thing we have to fear is fear itself," promising "action and action now." He had been the pampered only child of an elderly ailing father and an imperious young mother who had a touch of the tyrant. As a child of the rich, he should never have reached the White House in a nation that worships the log cabin as the mythical representation of the virgin soil of the pioneers. He was showered with all the gifts of the gods. He went to Groton and Harvard, toured Europe's cities and watering places, grew up tall, handsome, athletic, and charming, dabbled at law, took his famous "Cousin Teddy" as a model, made a splash as a Tammany-slaying independent in the Albany legislature, got his chance for the national stage in World War I as assistant navy secretary, where he learned the Washington arts—when and how to thrust with strength, when to contrive, connive, and seduce, when to be abrasive, when devious. He learned there how to be something more than a handsome charmer and aristocratic golden boy. He was even, at thirty-seven, the Democratic candidate for vice president, running with the hapless James Cox, with Woodrow Wilson's League of Nations plaguing both.

Yet something else was needed, to keep the shaping early years from being only a slow preparatory dance for something that might come off—or might not. The tempered steel needed for greatness was still to come, and it came with the blight that struck the wondrously formed body. It was the polio experience that brought it off, transforming suffering into self-command and tragedy into a life force.

The early doctors botched it, as he came bitterly to know. It cured him permanently of any belief in the conventional wisdom, whether in medicine, politics, economics, warfare, or diplomacy. When he took command of his own illness and its therapies, he took the first step toward his later command of the nation. The mastery of his disease became self-mastery, and inevitably transformed the working of his brain and will in the years ahead. He became the essential leader who was galvanized by crisis, treating the economy and polity as ailing organisms whose ills could be overcome by intelligence, experiment, and sheer guts. Through his own illness he acquired an understanding of the biofeedback process that makes health, sickness and recovery largely subjective. It gave him also—despite Hyde Park and his Edith Wharton mother—the empathy with others that became a genius for sensing and distilling the common experience.

It is not extreme to say that—far from handicapping him for the presidency—his sickness and the way he overcame it clinched it for him. Despite his patrician origins, his suffering became common ground with the suffering of so many others. It was his substitute for the log cabin.

It was also the heart of the New Deal myth—the recurring hope, throughout American history, for a fresh start toward a more equitable sharing not only of the nation's goods and income but also of life chances. Truman's "Fair Deal," Kennedy's "New Frontier," Johnson's "Great Society" were all paler variants of it. Kennedy alone added grace to hope—Camelot to the New Deal—but it was his death, not his deeds, that reinforced the myth, making it usable for his brothers.

Roosevelt served as paradigm for later presidents in another sense, through a direct relation with the people, evoking from them by an organic dialogue the overcoming of fear and the resoluteness he had discovered within himself. In that sense the words he spoke on that March morning at his inauguration, started to take shape in him during that Gehenna when everything lay in ashes about him and the steely resolve began to form.

He was never a thinker, getting his ideas always from those around him, his "Brains Trust," usually a hodgepodge of the wrong and right people, brought together almost haphazardly because of the "feel" he had for them and not because of any congruity in their ideas. In hard economic terms the nation was little better off at the end than at the start of the New Deal. But what counted was less the economic reality than the way the people perceived it, which kept their energies going until the war economy caught up with the slack of employment.

He did it by a great dialogue in which he was at once educator, in-spirer, and commander, and the people gave his actions the legitimacy that only they can give. His brand of leadership was, in the language of James MacGregor Burns, "transformative" rather than merely "trans-actional," exactly because he had been through a transformation him-self.

A second vignette of FDR must inevitably be the one caught by the cameras at Yalta—the haggard, furrowed face of a sick man, en-folded in a cape, sitting between Churchill and Stalin in what was to be their last meeting, like figures caught forever on a Russian urn. It was not age that had wasted him but the battering the presidency had given his body and mind together for twelve unrelenting years. But even that was not what was finally wrong with him, which made those last years as war commander tragic ones despite their military triumph. Roo-sevelt's problem was political, not military. He made Himalayan mis-calculations in the name of the war coalition and the peace settlement, which led to the virtual ceding of the whole of Eastern Europe to the Soviet imperium—in stopping General Patton's eastward swing that would have carried him to Prague, in yielding to Stalin's Polish for-mula, in appeasing Stalin when he had never appeased Hitler.

He might have made the same blunders ten years earlier. They came from his having attitudes rather than insight in global politics. His ruling idea was that outworn dogmas were of no use to pragmatic leaders. He considered nationalism and empire outworn, but he saw the Soviet Union as part of the future, not the past, and was blinded to Stalin's nationalism and his empire, where he had seen Churchill's and de Gaulle's. In fighting the war he could resort—as he had done dur-ing the New Deal days—to releasing and inspiring the energies of the people. But in the decisions that shaped a postwar world he was at sea, with no experience of his own except the memory of Woodrow Wil-son's failures, and no advisers of stature in foreign policy who could match Truman's Acheson, Eisenhower's Dulles, or Nixon's Kissinger. No president can rise above the level of the prevailing thought of his time. The climate of liberal-populist thought that seeped through to Roosevelt in the first decades of the century was a good enough base for the welfare state which Roosevelt was the first to shape, but on for-eign policy there was only a vacuum. The semi-Marxist liberal ideal-ism that moved into it was not enough to save the later Roosevelt from disaster, nor America from the long postwar Cold War that became its only recourse.

★

Harry Truman was poles apart from the man he succeeded. He was a Missouri farmer and small-town politician, deeply rooted in the soil and in a cohesive family, square in his life style, committed to all the traditional values, a dapper little man who looked like the haberdasher he once was, with no charisma, and with only his Plutarchian heroes and his copybook maxims to guide him.

The world first took notice of him when he was sixty-one, and FDR had died of a stroke, and Harry Truman called the press together and said, ". . . last night the house, the stars and all the planets fell on me." Everyone was aghast that this ordinary man, the embodiment of Mr. Average American, should be holding the world's most powerful office. But looking back over his life, we can now see that in terms of character, psyche, and judgment he was better prepared for the job than any president since Theodore Roosevelt and Wilson, with the exception of FDR.

The striking thing about Harry Truman was that the ordinary, almost banal, life he led until he was fifty veiled from the world the qualities of an extraordinary man. His life unrolled slowly, in a kind of protracted moratorium. Only the start of World War I broke it. In fact, three lucky things happened to Harry: He had good parents—a scrappy, unsuccessful father whom he admired, and a strong nurturing mother; he didn't go to college, and therefore didn't have his values system undercut or learn a lot of things he would have to unlearn; and he did go to war.

The year in France with his artillery battalion, at thirty-four, was Truman's testing time. In getting mastery over the bunch of "Irish roughnecks" who had harassed their earlier captain into resigning, he found he could use angry, earthy language to move men to do his bidding—and to like it. All his reading and experience came together to give him a self-reliant, no-nonsense crispness of command. After some desultory business ventures that failed, the war-service bond led him into local politics and county elective jobs. He didn't reject the links with the Kansas City machine. In his hierarchy of virtues a two-way loyalty counted for more than an abstract purity. "Who is worth more in the sight of the Lord," he asked, "Boss Pendergast or the snivelers?"

But his second testing lay ahead. Close to fifty he looked down the gun barrel of the future and saw no dynamic beyond "minor county office." Then came the great stroke of luck—a U.S. Senate seat fell vacant, Truman campaigned the whole state hard, got it, and wrote in his diary, "I have come close to the place where all men strive to be at my age," and later, "I was now where I really belonged." But after a first undistinguished Senate term the charges of being a "Pendergast tool" multiplied, and the prize that brought him his happiest years was slipping from his grasp. The scrappy Harry emerged, the bantam fighter routed two strong opponents and came from behind to win the nomination again. This time he came through not by friendships or loyalties but by fighting for what was rightly his.

It was a transformed Truman, combative and determined, who came back to his Senate seat. The rest is history—his sustained work in the limelight as head of a committee probing corruption in defense contracts, his happy choice (with no help from him) to replace Henry Wallace as FDR's 1944 running mate, his isolation as vice president in a White House group that ignored him as an outsider, the dread news from Warm Springs, his succession to the summit office whose great atomic secret had been kept from him. After three years Truman found himself faced with a reprise of his Senate experience, in danger of losing the prize of the presidency, unsought but cherished. Again he became the scrapper ("Give 'em hell, Harry"), and won the prize on his own in an upset victory that no one but himself expected him to win. It reinforced the transforming experience of his second Senate race.

Action made Truman, whether in war or office or in the two great campaigns in which his life force asserted itself. Surprisingly, for a president who bore a constant raking fire in office, he became a folk hero when he left it. He lacked FDR's stature, and the nimbus of magic that encircled him. But he was the most *effective* president of the group of six. He bore the burden of decision-making cheerfully. History has a way of giving or withholding its validations, despite our too quick and puny judgments, and history largely confirmed Truman's decisions. With serious doubts about Hiroshima I list the others: the decision to resist the Soviet "iron curtain," going through with the H-bomb, the firing of Henry Wallace and the confrontation with Douglas MacArthur, the quick recognition of Israel, the Marshall Plan, the NATO structure, "Point Four" aid, the Council of Economic Advisors, the enforcement of civil rights in Washington and the armed services ("but Harry *means* it," said a stunned Strom Thurmond).

Harry meant whatever he did, and some of it was petty, but (as Dean Acheson noted) he had "no enfeebling regrets" later. His experiences were the common experiences, his pleasures the common pleasures, his failings and foibles the common ones—as were his strengths. He was neither an ordinary nor average man, but an elemental one—

which may be why he is both Jimmy Carter's and Barry Goldwater's favorite president. I see him as a rooted, earthy figure, cut from a single block of America.

When Dwight Eisenhower came back from the wars in 1945, Harry Truman told him there was nothing within his own reach or that of the people that wouldn't be his. Which meant the presidency. As he drove through the frenzied acclaim of the New York celebration, could he help thinking of how far he had come from Abilene and the failed father and the little band of six brothers?

James David Barber counts Eisenhower as the most "puzzling" of the presidents he has tried to assess. Actually he is less difficult than Kennedy, Johnson, Nixon, or Carter, who offer more treacherous crosscurrents in their mind and psyche. Ike was the All-American Boy, humble beginnings, stardom, winning grin, and everything. The searing fact running through his boyhood was his father's bankruptcy in a small business venture and his bedeviled sense the rest of his life that he had to make good for it to his family and community. Ike's relation to his father must have been the deepest in his life. He always admired business success (his Cabinet was described as "eight millionaires and a plumber"), and he and his brothers all gave themselves to some form of public service in business, as if they were repaying their father's debt.

In his own life, he never lost a contest and won all the prizes. Which may be why he seems less power-driven than other presidents. He didn't need to be driven; winning came with the territory, and was as natural—and necessary—as breathing. He was a one-dimensioned man. His path to the White House followed a straight line that ran through his military career.

He started as an aide to General MacArthur in the Philippines and in the pathos of the "Bonus March." His boss later called him his "best clerk," while Ike countered that he had "studied dramatics" under the temperamental general. But his true testing came with Army Chief of Staff George Marshall, who was looking for a bright young officer and found a future president. "In the campaign of history," Justice Holmes said about Chief Justice John Marshall, "the important fact was that he was *there*." Ike was there when George Marshall needed someone to develop fast into a military leader. It was a meeting of moment and man. The occasion was the first peacetime war games, in Louisiana, and Ike's Third Army came off with a brilliant victory, highly visible in the media.

To widen his horizons Marshall called him to Washington, set him to planning the European war operations, and then put him in charge of carrying it out. FDR jumped the young colonel over a whole array of general officers, and sent him to Europe, where the confidence he had gained in Louisiana and Washington was reinforced on D-Day and its sequels. Lacking Patton's tactical dash and brilliance and MacArthur's imperious sense of history, he had prudence, steadiness, the knack of seeing through the stuffiness of the military bureaucracy, and a feel for military diplomacy.

He became the unique personal symbol of the war. But, while he won the presidency twice and kept his vitality through the tempests of events, he never really accepted politics as a vocation. His love remained the army. His political decisions were not distinguished. Caught up in the turmoil of the McCarthy struggle, Little Rock, the U-2 disaster, the failed Paris summit, the canceled Japan trip, he was always a step behind the event. What he did well was to keep America at peace. He knew how to do it because, as a soldier, he knew the consequences of war. But as president he seemed to be running the country as a father who had to be home but whose mind and heart were far away, in an earlier time and a sterner but simpler vocation.

Of how many presidents can it be said that they owed their office to a father's dream and his will to bring it to reality? Certainly of John Kennedy. He stood, in the glory of Inauguration Day, in the glint of a heavy snow that had fallen on Washington, and said, "Let the word go forth" that his was a new generation come to power, ready "to bear any burden" to preserve freedom. He was a political Golden Boy, with flair and grace, and the élan which his vibrant tone brought to the vocation of politics in the eyes of the young was extraordinary. Yet in fact he was acting out his father's dream.

Joseph Kennedy, who as an Irish Catholic felt rejected by the dominant Boston elite, concluded that the wealth he had made in business would have to be translated into political power before it could bring social acceptance. He knew the ways of both money and power. A son in the presidency would be at once revenge for the exclusion and a way of founding a dynasty of power and position.

The family's first and natural "chosen vessel," into which it poured its energy and resources, was the eldest of the brothers, Joseph, Jr., who had all the gifts of body and mind resplendently. The second brother, Jack, whose work at Harvard was good but undistinguished, seemed content to play a secondary role and looked toward a career as a journalist and writer.

With Joe, Jr.'s death on a dangerous combat mission in a plane that he must have known to be a death trap—the first of the Kennedy tragedies—Jack was anointed the new chosen vessel, and all the family energies were redirected to him. It was the start of a growth process, the first crucial step on the path to becoming the John Kennedy that became a legend—single-minded, driving, using his formidable armory of talents to build a victory for the family in defiance of death, to live out his father's dream and his brother's destiny.

But it was a growth process that did not move as fast as his political career, whose pace was breathtaking. His highly publicized PT boat ordeal in the war, which showed a reckless courage but hardly a sensible action for a commander, was used politically to the hilt. He moved swiftly into the opening of a congressional seat, then into a Senate seat. He narrowly—and luckily—missed getting the vice presidential spot in 1956, on a doomed ticket with Adlai Stevenson. Four years later he reached the White House.

It was too swift. True, he had a model in his living father and his dead brother, and he had a family to spur him, and a sense of political vocation; and he had developed an inner drive of his own. But he had not developed a knowledge of either the economy or of the web of global relations, or the intricate hazards involved in executive decision-making. He used both his House and Senate positions as stages for advancement, not experience or growth. He was neither a true legislator nor a true executive. He had skipped the first and had to learn the second. There had been no time for tempering the sharp sword of Kennedy's mind and welding it into both an inner security and a capacity for command.

These are the dangers of any too swift storming of the presidency. It was true of Eisenhower, and of Kennedy—and later of Jimmy Carter; Truman had been tempered by his long moratorium, even if he had to deal with unfamiliar career and perception crises when FDR died. Kennedy's growth toward maturity, once started, had to take place in a little more than a decade, and while it moved fast it did not move as fast as his career did. He spent more time and energy on getting to the presidency than he did on preparing himself for it. People were misled by his burgeoning myth. He was a "comer;" wherever he went—as congressman, senator, presidential candidate—he carried with him the sweet smell of success. He overcame the issue of his Catholicism with skill, and the issue of his youth and inexperience by invoking the American cult of youth. But though he talked of William Pitt, he lacked Pitt's early flowering genius. The focus of his energies was on tactic, image, and style. On that level he succeeded. People felt that his future was touched with fire, and wanted to be part of it. He even came to believe his own myth, and to value the quality of "toughness" in him, which brought him his narrow victory over Nixon, as equivalent to leadership. Joe Kennedy's grand design for his son was fulfilled, but a more obscure design—incalculable, shaped by unknown hands—was in the making.

Kennedy's testing came soon after he assumed power. He learned from each crisis. From the Bay of Pigs disaster he learned not to put a naive trust in military and intelligence experts, but to get total input before making his own decision. At the summit meeting in Vienna, Khrushchev took his measure of the young president as inept, inexperienced, ripe for bullying. He did not reckon with Kennedy's growth under pressure, which was becoming more important than his proven grace under pressure. The Berlin Wall crisis, where the Russians presented him with a fait accompli, may have been the final fillip to his new knowledge of himself and others.

The John Kennedy who met the Cuban missile crisis had pondered the lessons of these experiences and had matured in his judgment. Everything about his handling of the missile crisis was cool, steady, balanced—from the first announcement of the Russian missile presence to the final choice of the option that would enable the Soviet leaders to save face while yielding. Looking back after the assassination, one gets the sense not only of an unfinished life but also of an unfinished man, for whom political power and sensual pleasure came too readily, who did not have to work hard for the unpaid graces of life. His father's grand plan, his family's help, his own easy charm—all of these brought him the great prize before he had prepared himself to wield it. He had no real authority in dealing with Congress. He set in motion no important initiatives, as compared to Harry Truman, say, in either domestic or foreign policy. His decisions, except in the case of the missile crisis, have on the whole not been validated by history. Yet he ruled men's minds and imaginations by the magic of his image, if not the substance of his decisions. No one in this century—not even Franklin Roosevelt—had so much impact on the young. People came to call his reign "Camelot," and the term became fixed in the popular mind. But blunders or not, Camelot or not, Kennedy grew in office, and both intellectually and emotionally he was moving toward a new wholeness when he was cut down, just at the point of his flowering.

★

There were two flash points in the life of Lyndon Johnson. One was when John Kennedy died, and after all the mountains of energy and tumult of striving he had expended, Johnson found himself suddenly, unexpectedly, in the Eden he had hungered for and had felt shut out of. He had put the blame on people like the Kennedys—the Easterners, aristocrats, intellectuals, snobs, who were darlings of the college students and the media. They were poseurs, he was the doer. He came from the rude Texas frontier, and they scorned the likes of him, but John Kennedy needed him to help him get elected. Johnson went along, both president and vice president totally aware that he was using and being used.

His choice of political vocation came earlier than in the case of any of the six, when he was a teacher in Southwest Texas, barely out of college himself. At twenty-three he went to Washington as an administrative aide to a Texas congressman. He tells how he haunted the hotel shower room, showering four or five times a night to make political "contacts." The power hunger for the presidency formed early in him, with a ferocity to be matched only by Nixon's. He always sought out the men who controlled the power levers behind the scenes, who knew and used power from the inside. He courted their support, but he also learned from them—men like Richard Russell of Georgia and Sam Rayburn of Texas.

No one who got to the White House in this century came better prepared for the presidency—if knowing every twist of the political ropes is preparation. What depressed him was the conviction that, as a Southerner, held at a distance by the Eastern Establishment, he could never make it to the White House, and that lesser men than himself would wield the summit power while—as legislative leader in the Senate—he smoothed their path. This bitter conviction almost came true—and he reached his goal only by an accident that was part of the inherent logic of presidential politics. Although he disliked Johnson, Kennedy needed a power broker like him. Without Johnson's strength in the South and among conservatives, Kennedy could not have made it, and without Kennedy's halfhearted offer—adroitly accepted—Johnson could not have come a heartbeat from the presidency.

Once in the vice presidency, Johnson had reason to rue his decision. He felt wretched, isolated, unused. Kennedy had got what he wanted out of him, and the whole entourage ignored him. The media took the cue, and when the press noticed him at all it was with derision. He tried to give some substance to the office, maneuvering with Senator Mike Mansfield to make the vice president head of the Senate Co-ordinating Committee, but the move failed. He finally had to accept the fact that he had exchanged his former power for the trappings of an office in which he felt humiliated, and which seemed to lead nowhere since he could not count on Kennedy to support him as his successor.

The Dallas bullets changed it all. The death of Kennedy must have carried shock with it but also—dare we say it?—release and even exhilaration. Life builds on death, even when there is love and admira-tion, and between Johnson and the Kennedys there was neither. There followed an exhilarative burst of energy unparalleled even in the "Hundred Days" of his idol, FDR. Johnson showed himself not only as a Senate power broker but—in civil rights and welfare legislation—as one of the great lawmakers of American history.

There followed the 1964 nomination, the Republican blunder in running Barry Goldwater against him, the easy and overwhelming tri-umph in the election. For the first time this hulking, love-hungry man felt himself truly loved. Yet 1968 found him "abdicating" the throne, retreating from a bid for another four years of the power he adored, without which life for him would be a cruel mockery. It was his second flash point, from which he could look back and ask what had happened in his life to change his state and fate so drastically. What had swung him from felicity to failure, from feeling loved to feeling hated and be-sieged?

The key lay in his innermost self, which contained his striving for achievement and greatness but contained also the insecurities that un-dercut and defeated it. Everything about Lyndon Johnson was out-rage—his hulking frame, his ambitions and emotions, his driven quality, his eagerness for reassurance, his peerless storytelling, his con-niving, his hunger for power matched only by his hunger to be loved. He was overbrimming with hyperbole, rambunctiousness, grandiosity, exhibitionism, paranoia—and just plain orneriness. He overdid every-thing. He was in every way the most excessive president in American history, his only rival being Theodore Roosevelt.

Johnson has provided a field day for the psychobiographers intent on explaining his Vietnam disaster in terms of his childhood insecurity and his unsatisfied need for love. Yet this goes at once too far and not far enough. True, he was caught in the crossfire between a too loving and principled mother and a too feisty and obstreperous father, and—striving to contain their conflicts and please both—was never able wholly to live up to either. By this reasoning Johnson's problem was that he had never worked through his early stages of psychosexual development, and never developed basic trust—in others and himself.

But Johnson's tragedy lay elsewhere. With all his talent and his generous striving he was betrayed within, by his unquenchable thirst for principle and greatness, caught within a frame of assumptions and events that made it destructive. It was Johnson's myth that he ruled by persuasion, but what was truer was his uncanny capacity to seek out whatever was vulnerable in a man—his fears, hopes, weaknesses—and touch it as the spring of his conduct; he was thus better at bargaining and trading than at fighting, better at counting heads in a legislature than at moving the hearts of the many. But what he wanted desperately was to prove himself as a leader for his contemporaries and history.

It was his bad luck to preside at the height of America's most turbulent decade, in a time of global ideology and power beyond anything that his legislative competence had prepared him for. The forces engendered by it ripped him apart as they ripped the nation apart. They required a cool head, flexible tactics, a combination of strength and restraint. Johnson could not muster it. As a frontier Texan he remembered the Alamo, as a patriot he resented the Soviet tactics of slicing away at America's allies in the struggle for the world.

His obsession with the Kennedys—which was the ruling passion of his White House years—intensified his contempt for the Vietnam doves. He vowed he would triumph where Kennedy had wavered. He had a faulty assumption: men are divided between thinkers and doers. The truth is that a leader must act as a man of thought and think as a man of action. He, however, wanted to know "what was the right thing to do," and he would find a way to do it.

He was angered that the people did not follow him, and saw them as ingrates misled by the liberals and the media. The worse the situation got, the more he dug in. He mistrusted everyone, isolated himself from the realities, surrounded himself with men who supported his illusion. A more secure man would have been more flexible. A man less ridden by a principle he identified with his own integrity would have rethought the consequences of his course. He was caught in his own rigidity—unable to give up the war, but unwilling to wage it ruthlessly, as Richard Nixon did later.

Johnson is the only president whose dreams—thanks to Doris Kearns—we know about. He had a major recurring dream of being paralyzed, unable to act when action was needed. Somewhere in the obscurity of his childhood experiences he had developed this fear of paralysis. His whole life seems to have been an effort at action, in whatever form, to overcome it. By the irony of his career this fear of being unable to act was what made him rigid. He wanted to fly, but the wings he fashioned—Daedalus-like—melted in the heat of the turbulent 1960s, and he fell to his doom. He wanted above everything to go down in history as the "can-do president," and he ended by finding that he could not.

If ever the U.S. had a tumultuous crisis President, it was Richard Nixon. His first memoir detailed his "Six Crises," but he was never finished with them and never would be. He was a self-made man who also made his own crises. He needed them, fed on them. In his heart he felt unworthy of the love his angry father had denied him and his Quaker mother ("my mother was a saint") had given more unstintingly to his brothers.

More than any other president his life follows a recurring pattern punctuated by triumphs and despairs. It was a pattern of crisis, recovery, victory, overreach, defeat, followed by another sequence of recovery, victory, overreach. Nixon early developed the habit of self-detachment, seeing himself as an actor in history—in fact, as an instrument of history. He had a curiously Puritan feeling about himself, spending his energies (by his own account) not in doing the things he liked but the things he didn't like yet felt he had to do. He saw himself as a Mr. Christian, in John Bunyan's *Pilgrim's Progress*, constantly beset by enemies, trials, and testings, always having to prove himself to men and history.

He was better in defeats than in triumphs. A defeat, such as he suffered in 1960 and 1962, could be reversed by work and planning. Victories were harder because they were heady, made him overconfident, and led him to become an overreacher, scaling Olympus to unseat the hostile divinities but guilty of the hubris of defying the laws of gods and men. Hence Watergate.

In each of his crises there was an adversary to be overcome—Alger Hiss, the Communists, the liberals and fellow travelers, the Establishment Republicans, the media, Daniel Ellsberg of the Pentagon Papers case. Yet one senses that it was not an adversary but Dwight Eisenhower himself—the man who picked him in 1952 as running mate—who put him through some of his most wrenching experiences. The first came with the "Nixon fund" charges and the "Checkers" speech during the first campaign, another when Ike was close to scuttling him for a second term. The general could have been at once mentor and father to him—a kinder father to replace the one whose love had eluded him. But he failed him twice.

When Ike had his heart attack, Nixon experienced a sharp inner crisis amounting to near panic, perhaps retraversing the unresolved love-hate feeling for his own father, and made more intense by the heartbeat chance that he might now become president and the sense of guilt for having wished the outcome.

In 1962, with his defeat for the California governorship, following his defeat for the presidency two years earlier, he reached rock bottom and had to build from there again. Looking back at his life after the hapless press conference in 1962, he must have been in despair at the hairbreadth margin by which destiny had cheated him of the office he had sought so tumultuously. Yet he did rebuild. Then followed six years of his wandering in the wilderness, a lonely but resolute man, until he emerged with his 1968 victory.

When you compare the Nixon of the Hiss case, the Checkers speech, and the post-California outburst, with the Nixon of the Peking trip and the China policy turnabout, there is an undeniable growth. But it was growth on the cognitive, not the emotional, level. Except for Lyndon Johnson, no one came to the presidency so politically experienced, but no one also came to it so psychologically damaged. He was damaged by his family and his early years and by the heartbreak of struggle and the conviction that the game had been played against him with loaded dice.

This, more than anything, serves as a key to Watergate. Nixon saw himself as a fighter against odds, in a hostile city that had been taken over by his adversaries—the reigning climate-makers. Even in 1972, when he won a second term overwhelmingly and stood at the mountain top, overlooking the hills and valleys below, he was not content, and he had to undo. He did not feel that any victory of his was lasting if it left his adversaries in possession of the field on which they would fight the next battle. Hence he had to be smarter, fiercer, more cunning than they. He saw them as the establishment, and himself as a guerrilla fighter.

True, he had captured the citadel, but he still had to harry them constantly in forays from it, using darkness, secrecy, dirty tricks, surveillance, ridicule, persecution, surprise. We now see that there was a point, even after the Watergate break-in, when he could have come clean with it, confessed his initial malfeasance, avoided the fatal cover-up. But such was his character that, even in power, he had to fight with ferocity and guile.

And when finally, after the Supreme Court decision on the "smoking-gun" tapes, he saw everything in ashes around him, he left the White House with a rambling, sentimental speech, full of self-pity, but in his heart doubtless the conviction that history would give him the justice that his time had denied him.

What criteria do I use in my assessments of what shapes a president and of presidential stature? I take them from trying to read presidential biographies and history in our century, including both the triumphs and tragedies of the men from Roosevelt on.

I start with the willingness to face the reality principle in the life of a great power, which means tough-mindedness enough to meet and offer challenges. I move on to the capacity for command—to be in command of crises and to present the image of decisiveness. I add judgment, for without judgment no decisiveness can operate without trauma, for both the nation and the president.

My next triad would start with character, not in the sense of virtue but of the values a man or woman has settled upon in a turbulent life. With it goes credibility—the presentation of a leader's selfhood in a way to win assent and form the consensus necessary for governing. That in turn depends on the capacity for interacting with the people. To call it "communication skills" is to diminish it. The great thing we learned from FDR is that president and demos, in interaction, have a chance to effect and even transform each other.

My last triad starts with perspective—the capacity for thinking in time and seeing both the nation and oneself in history. With it comes a necessary measure of vision and passion, trying to pierce the future. Tying them all together is a sense of selfhood—the president's secure knowledge of who he is, so that he does not have to woo history by a false worship of change for its own sake, but can keep the nation in equilibrium because he can keep himself in equilibrium.

Ripeness is all, as shown in the fruit that grows out of the bud. Looking at each president we must ask: Did he leave America—in its domestic and world equilibrium, its tranquillity and prosperity, its sense of confidence and hope—appreciably better than he found it?

EROS AND POWER

THE AMERICAN PRESIDENCY tells a ferocious story—of the ferocity with which each man has pursued and held on to power. It is a scarring story—of scars given and received by each president. It is an erotic story, not alone in the case of the presidents whose private sexual lives have been made public but even more in the basically erotic relationship that somehow operates between an American president and the people. It is a magical story, because by its nature the presidential function is that of a shaman, and people never cease to hope that the president will cast a spell on the nation's enemies and deliver it from its agonized problems and dilemmas.

This is a chronicle of six presidents in my life—Franklin Roosevelt, Harry Truman, Dwight Eisenhower, John Kennedy, Lyndon Johnson, and Richard Nixon. It has little intimate or "inside" stuff in it and no great revelations. They were men I talked and argued with and wrote about and reflected on. As a columnist, I had to cope with their decisions, castigate them for their sins of omission and commission, weep publicly over their failures, and rejoice just as publicly at their successes.

Each of these presidents left scars on our history, just as his experience left scars on him. Each had a character amalgam of ferocity and guile. And the element of the erotic and shamanistic pervaded the atmosphere around them, even in the case of Harry Truman, whose character and values were square and who had little visible charisma. Whatever other sexual involvements they had, their true sexuality was with the presidency. Their relation to Congress, to their staff, to the people themselves, was one of constant seductiveness. A president is at once seduced by the presidency and is its seducer. He woos, and is

"Eros and Power" appeared in *Playboy* (December 1978) as a "memoir."

wooed by, the admiration of the people. Whatever his enchantments with women, they are bound to be secondary, for every woman in a president's life knows that if his hunger for her competes with his hunger for power, it is power that will win.

Franklin Roosevelt was probably the greatest president of the century, and certainly the greatest magus of them all, in the sheer wizardry of his combination of smiles and wiles with power—Machiavelli's lion and fox together. I got at him through two of his "Brains Trust," Tom Corcoran and Sam Rosenman, whom he affectionately dubbed Tommy the Cork and Sammy the Rose.

Each of the four times he ran, I voted for him, at first with my fingers crossed, the three other times with mounting commitment. I came to believe in the Roosevelt karma and was touched by the fire of enchantment in him, as happens with all erotic seductions. I saw that Roosevelt had unimaginably come at the right time, to show Americans and the world that, whatever ailed capitalist democracy, the remedy and recovery would come from within. It was a hard lesson, but Americans learned it and I think it stayed learned.

I got to know Eleanor Roosevelt before I had any talk with her husband, in that dervish dance of unending committee meetings and that welter of liberal causes and do-gooder letterheads that marked the New Deal faithful. During the Spanish Civil War, we were both passionately committed to the Loyalist cause, and we shared a sense of dismay at Roosevelt's power politics. At a public dinner, just before I gave a speech, I recall her whispering: "Don't pull your punches. We've got to light some fires under Franklin."

It taught me that a president had to be two persons—one to stir people by his fire, the other to stay within the reality principle. At times, Roosevelt played both roles; at others, he needed Eleanor to do the moving and prodding.

When I wrote my first book, in 1938, *It Is Later Than You Think: The Need for a Militant Democracy*, my publisher sent the proofs to Tommy the Cork, who was both FDR's idea man and his hatchet man. Tommy marked them up for the president to read. He warmed my heart and vanity by reporting that the president had been impressed. I was very young, and for weeks I walked about, dazed by my self-image as one of the movers and shakers. The reality, of course, was that FDR's decisions came from a whole mosaic of pressures on him. But I do think that the book confirmed him in his feeling that some of the younger men would support a greater urgency in both domestic and foreign policy.

Part of the book's fallout was a long afternoon talk I had with FDR at Hyde Park. I recall driving up from New York in a battered car. But I felt no malaise about its appearance, because everything around Roosevelt—since he was an aristocrat, not an arriviste—had a simplicity that put you at your ease.

Sitting at his usually cluttered desk, leaning back, his famous cigarette holder between his teeth, he looked as if he had all the time in the world for the young editor turned professor with unruly hair and rumpled clothes. We discussed the Nazi threat, the potential alliance with Europe, the need for collective security, the nature of the presidency, the creative relation between a president and the people. Above all, we talked about power and public opinion in the struggle between a militant democracy and a militant totalitarianism.

When a staff member came in to end the interview, FDR said, "Go away. We're talking philosophy"—which won me forever, even though I knew it was another instance of his political seductiveness. He was not an intellectual, nor did he have much depth. But he did not go beyond his depth. There was an almost perfect fit between his intuitive sense of action and power and his antennae for picking up ideas and phrases that—whatever their source—he made his own.

Rarely has a president shown such skill of maneuver and of confidence—the fox and the lion—in so messy a muddle of events. It made me, along with many others, support Roosevelt in his unparalleled bid for a third and later a fourth term. And when Sammy the Rose, his speechwriter, asked me to do a draft for one of the president's campaign speeches, I did it cheerfully, though my impassioned sentences came out mangled and scarcely recognizable in the final version.

Roosevelt proved a first-rate commander in chief. We all became military strategists in World War II. But toward the end—exhausted, disease-ridden, the sharp edge of his mind dulled—his military decisions had a political fallout that gave the Russians a postwar empire over half of Europe. Eventually, he caught on to the gravity of what he had done, and he spent the tail end of his last term in a postwar effort to hem in Stalin, hoping too late to undo what he had done.

But first he wanted to get the war with Japan over quickly. In the book *My Parents*, James Roosevelt reports that his father planned to use a mysterious new weapon (whose nature he could not reveal even to his son) against Japan. But with all his fierce energy and will and optimism, death did not spare him long enough either to remedy his miscalculations on the Russians or to make the final decision on Japan. Thus, his death ushered in both the Cold War and the Atomic Age.

Looking back at Roosevelt, and given his knowledge of his own physical condition, one of the things that troubled me was why he ran for a fourth term in 1944. He was a battered, spent man. When he was struck by polio, he had forced himself to reenter public life and became governor of New York. With the inspired help of Louis Howe, he fought his way to the presidency, picking the right year—1932—to make his bid. He presided over the tumultuous 1930s, winning a second term more decisively than the first. In 1940, with the war on in Europe, he convinced himself that only his leadership could achieve American unity in a "sick world—forged into unity by rings of fire." But by 1944, thanks largely to Roosevelt's conduct of the alliance, the war's outcome was no longer in doubt.

The point is that Roosevelt wanted to preside over the peace as he had presided over the war. A president who has drunk a deep and long draught of power does not give it up until death or the Constitution forces him to.

When the killer stroke found FDR at Warm Springs, he was with his love of many years back, Lucy Mercer Rutherfurd, who was spirited out of the compound to evade the press. I had learned earlier, from some press friends, about FDR's affair with the glamorous, gentle young woman who had been Eleanor's social secretary when FDR was in Washington during World War I. Eleanor discovered the affair and it ended their sexual relations in marriage.

FDR had other sexual relationships to fill the void and hunger that were within him despite his life of power. Roosevelt's sons Elliott and James bear conflicting witness to a long-enduring affair with his secretary, Missy LeHand. My own guess is that it took place but was an affair of propinquity, not a passionate love. That surely applies to his other affairs as well, including one with my former publisher on the *New York Post*, Dorothy Schiff, which she told me about years ago.

Presidents share with other men of power complex feelings about women. Because the public fanfare is so loud and so unremitting, they need the constant private support that sexual variety provides. A president's life is a massive glory trip. With so much exposure to the public when he must control himself, he seems to need the contrast of the intensely private, when he can let himself go, and if he cannot find it in his marriage bed, he must find it somewhere else. With the world telling him he is a god, he needs constant proof that he is also a man. With the specter of death hovering over him, he welcomes the orgasmic explosion that tells him he is alive and validates his public persona by private triumph. The fact that Roosevelt's legs were withered and crippled made this validation all the more important.

Roosevelt's one and true love was Lucy Mercer, who later (when marriage proved impossible for them) became Mrs. Rutherfurd. But the course of true love was cruelly interrupted by his political ambition, which consumed him more than love did—as it has every president and presidential aspirant.

Of these six presidents, only Harry Truman had a true love in marriage. He was an exception in another respect as well. Alone of the six, he had no ambitions for the presidency until he found himself in it by Roosevelt's death. But then he had his own love affair with it and wanted to stay for a new full term, to show he could get elected on his own and to consolidate his policies.

Things went hard for him. He took on the decision to drop the bomb over Hiroshima, then Nagasaki, and suffered the fallout of criticism. Many historians feel he had a chance, while America had a monopoly on it, to give the bomb to a world agency and make a genuine peace with the Russians. But it would have taken two to make the bargain, and Stalin—sitting on top of the pyramid of his postwar power in Europe—was in no mood to give up his rising arc of power and make a genuine settlement with the despised West.

Early in Truman's tenure, I went to see him at the White House, along with James Wechsler, my editor at the *New York Post*. He sat there in the Oval Office like a bantam cock in a bustling barnyard, newly arrived amidst the din and disarray around him, a bit bewildered but all the more combative for that reason. There was a crackling briskness about him, not of the corporate executive but of the farmer or small-town shopkeeper who wants to get the chores done and the business of the day dispatched with the fewest words and with minimal nonsense. I was young and foolish enough to be less than impressed.

I had a bad dry spell in my feelings about Truman between 1946 and the summer of 1948. I shared it with most of my liberal friends, who felt the gap between Roosevelt as the great dead father figure and this ordinary little man from the Pendergast precincts who appointed generals and cronies to important posts. But Truman, undaunted, won the 1948 nomination despite us, and his acceptance speech at the convention had most of us in the press section on our feet cheering his fighting words. The "ordinary" little man proved to be an extraordinary man, with guts and insight and vision. Although I had declared for Norman Thomas, the Socialist candidate, I found myself—to my own surprise—when confronted by the voting machine in the polling booth, voting for Truman.

His second term brought a series of crises: the Chinese Revolution (the right-wingers blamed him for "losing" China), the Hiss case, the bomb-secrets scare, the McCarthy sinister silliness about subversives, the Korean War, the challenge of General Douglas MacArthur to civilian authority. He surmounted them all. He knew what he wanted, he developed a feel for the power and influence he needed to achieve it, and he had an inner well of confidence in himself that he conveyed to those around him. He was a cocky little man, but for all his bluster, it was a quiet cockiness: "If you can't stand the heat, get out of the kitchen."

Truman did not have the ferocity of personal will that was bottled up in other presidents—Roosevelt and Kennedy, Johnson and Nixon. He was not a driven man. But when there was a contest of wills in a showdown—between himself and MacArthur, for example—it was not Truman's will that faltered. He communicated this to the nation. It knew who was in charge: "The buck stops here." And because they knew, their basic confidence as a people did not falter, and they decided not to get out of history's kitchen. Thus, the Truman years, which were turbulent enough, strike us in retrospect as years of national confidence.

In his squareness, he had none of the magus appeal of Roosevelt. He did not flirt seductively with the people or treat them as a practiced lover treats a woman—with flattery, cajolery, and alternating tenderness and strength. His style was, rather, that of the bantam fighter, and the times when the people responded to him were when they saw their own fighting qualities in him, enlisted on their side: "Give 'em hell, Harry!"

I got to know Eisenhower on his campaign train and plane, in 1952. A *New York Post* investigative reporter had dug up the story of the "Nixon fund"—a kitty put together secretly by a group of California industrialists to help out their man in the Senate. Having won the presidential nomination, Ike had picked Nixon for the second spot because he was young, articulate, and had tracked down Alger Hiss. That was Ike's way of uniting both wings of his party, since Nixon had become a darling of the conservatives. Now Ike was irritated at being burdened with the albatross of a possible corruption scandal. Faced with the question of how he felt about the charges, Ike answered with a heartfelt mixture of homily and bromide, saying he would have to be satisfied that Nixon was "clean as a hound's tooth." As the *Post* representative on the train, at every conference Ike held with us, I pushed hard on the Nixon story—perhaps too hard. At one point, Ike burst out, "Either Lerner gets off the train or I will." I did, because I had a lecture date to fill, but not until I had watched Nixon do his historic "Checkers" speech on TV, insisting that none of the fund's money had gone into his dog's care or his wife's cloth coat or his modest home.

During an interval of friendliness between the candidate and myself on the campaign trip, we had a curious conversation. Ike alighted from the plane at one of the stops, saw me coming down the ramp, and motioned to me to join him. We walked about slowly, talking, when suddenly Ike stopped, faced me, seized my arm and held it for a moment. "You liberal fellows," he said, "don't think much about my mind." I started to blurt out something about his having us wrong. "No," he said, "I know you don't." Then a slight pause as his blue eyes sought me out. "But you know," he said, "there's something more important than the mind." Again, the slightest pause. "And that's the heart."

I can't remember what I said to that. I do recall feeling vaguely uncomfortable, as one feels about having something confided to him more intimate than is warranted by the relationship. After a long pause, Ike went on to talk of how he felt about his war experience with the Germans and the Russians, and about the Nazi camps for Jewish victims.

I was in a fiercely rationalist phase of my life. I was a liberal Democrat and a partisan. In the contest between the head and the heart—for a man who would guide the destinies of an imperium—I felt the emphasis on the heart was weak and mawkish. I was sure that Ike's opponent and my political hero, Adlai Stevenson, would know how to put head and heart in their proper ranking.

Later, telling the story, I always got a laugh at the naive general who preferred the politics of the heart to the politics of the mind. But looking back, I suspect the laugh proved to be on us, not on him. What Ike had meant to say to me—though I was not open to it at the time—was that even in a power game like politics, it was a sense of restraint and decency that counted. His reference to his German experience, including the overrunning of the Nazi cremation camps—in part, spoken to me as a Jew—was also meant to suggest what happened when simple decency was lacking and the politics of hate took over.

What made our conversation the more poignant was that, for all his occasional display of temper, Ike was something of a cold fish in his public life. He never liked Nixon and several times he was at the point of shelving him if he had not mustered public support. He fired his chief of staff for domestic affairs, Sherman Adams, when he got into the "vicuña coat" scandal. He hoarded, rather than spent, his prestige as a war hero and world figure. He watched his popularity curve and kept it high by his above-the-battle stance. He survived two serious illnesses, including a heart attack, and was reelected despite them. MacArthur called him "the best clerk who ever served me," and Ike countered that he had "studied dramatics" under MacArthur.

Eisenhower was no activist president, and the official liberal president raters gave him low scores on energy and effectiveness. But in later years, during the turmoil of the Kennedy and Johnson periods, the president watchers felt nostalgic for the Eisenhower years. Eisenhower had seen enough wars to make him stay out of any more. He went into office with the promise to end the Korean War ("I shall go to Korea" was how speechwriter Emmet Hughes put it for him).

In his sexual life, as well, the traditional moral code faltered and gave way. Ike's affair with Kay Summersby, the Irishwoman who was his London wartime driver, was bound to leak through into the newspaper world. I heard about it very early from two sources—a CBS friend of Harry Butcher's, who was Ike's naval aide and close social companion, and from a tough reporter who made a specialty of knowing where all the political bodies were buried. During the 1952 campaign, there were reports that a book by the lady was being hawked among American publishers with no willing takers. It did not endear her to Ike.

Years later, after Eisenhower's death and before her own death from cancer, Miss Summersby wrote her final account of her affair with the famous general and president. It had an element of heartbreak—the story of a soldier away at the wars and thrust suddenly to the lonely heights of world fame, of a pretty, high-spirited girl whose fiancé had been killed in the fighting, of the enchantment each felt, she with his aura of authority and command, he with her youth and verve, of the gathering tenderness they gave each other, of the ménage they set up, of his plans for divorce and remarriage. The narrative is skimpy where one looks hardest for the details that would give a greater emotional reality to this wartime encounter and wooing. But enough is there for us to guess what it meant, not only for the obscure driver but also for the commander in chief of the European Theater.

There is no good psychohistory of Eisenhower. But the thrust of the conflicting forces in him is clear enough. His was in many ways the classic story of a love affair between a middle-aged, emotionally starved man and his young and admiring secretary-aide. Even the storybook clash is there between the traditional ethic he inherited and the world of possibility opening for him.

At one point in her narrative, Kay relates a conversation in which Ike spoke of his troubled life with his wife and apologized for his sexual impotence. It is hard to guess at Kay's motives—perhaps bitterness at Ike's breaking off the affair, perhaps (as she insists) to keep the historical record straight, perhaps mostly to affirm that she could have made this great man happy. My guess is that the impotence story is overdramatized, probably by the ghostwriter, but that Kay did have subtleties in lovemaking that were new to the general.

As the story is told, via Harry Truman, Ike went so far as to write to General George C. Marshall, chief of staff of the army, to say that he wanted a divorce. Marshall, whose rootedness in the traditional ethic was deeper than Ike's, and who couldn't imagine anyone subordinating his soldierly duty to a personal hedonism, cabled back a peremptory "No"—and is reported to have added, "This is an order." The story is that Truman later pulled the documents out of the file and destroyed them.

In the end, with whatever tumults of rebellion and resignation, Eisenhower broke off the affair. (In a volume of Ike's *Letters to Mamie*, edited by his son, Brigadier General John Eisenhower, Ike kept reassuring Mamie that there was no basis for the gossip. Understandable, but scarcely convincing.) At that moment, too, much was at stake for the whole Western alliance. Later, when he returned to a hero's welcome in New York and the clamor grew for him to run for the presidency, ambition took over.

Quite possibly, by that time the bloom was off the romance, the enchantment gone. There is a pathetic scene in the Summersby narrative, telling how she tried in vain to reach Ike by phone when he was president of Columbia University, and then by chance ran into him on the steps of the administration building. Ike was adamant, scolded her sharply, and told her never to try to reach him again. Clearly, he was determined to close that chapter, whatever it had once meant to him. His career was to move on to the turbulent nomination fight, the election victory, his eight years of summit power, his illnesses, his closing anticlimactic years at Gettysburg, the world plaudits at his death. I can see a scriptwriter someday tackling the Eisenhower life scenario. Whatever he omits, he will include this scene of the general and the driver—once lovers, now strangers, in their desolating encounter on the college steps.

It was the presidency that cast its shadow in advance and that triumphed. The comparison with Roosevelt and Lucy Mercer comes to mind. That was a less clear-cut decision, because Franklin had given his promise to Eleanor to wait a year and think it over, and before the end of the year, the polio attack closed off any choice for either of them.

In Eisenhower's case, there was a chance for a choice, at least outwardly. In fact, no one could resist the lure of presidential power. It wasn't a balked sexual drive that gave Ike his impetus toward power, though it may have helped. No man can resist his hunger for presidential power, whether it be someone with as strong sexual drives as Roosevelt, Kennedy, and Johnson, or as weak a drive as Nixon. Whatever the choice made, it is not even a choice between Eros and power, for presidential power itself already contains the Eros principle to the full.

My first insight into John F. Kennedy's blend of power and Eros was through meeting a beautiful young woman who had been his mistress while he was a congressman from Massachusetts. She helped him in his campaigns and they talked of getting married. Then he saw the chance for his move to the Senate, as a pathway to the presidency—and everything changed. As a senator, and a possible president, he would need a wife appropriate to his ambition—and my friend evidently didn't measure up. She was bitter at being dropped, yet—like almost all of Kennedy's girls—she knew how power-driven he was and was still in love with him.

Unlike Eisenhower, Kennedy was a driven man and a macho president. Everything in his life, including his political exploits and his sexual escapades, was infused with the drive to accent his masculine identity. Part of his inheritance from his father was a competitiveness that extended not only to career but also to sexual conquests.

When I first met him, early in 1958, he was well launched on his presidential drive and was being careful about his public image. We spoke at a book-and-author luncheon in Cleveland, he about his *Profiles in Courage*, I about my *America as a Civilization*. A full house had gathered to take the measure of the ambitious young senator, including a phalanx of Ohio politicians, as well as the usual "literary ladies." He entered amidst a stir of excitement—the kind that surrounds a "comer"—and already there was the mark of the young prince on him. Speaking first, with some generous words about my liberalism, he was careful to distinguish between us, saying that a writer had a degree of freedom in taking militant positions that someone like himself—with the burden of responsibility as a political figure—couldn't do. It struck me as a curious way to present a book on political courage, and I scribbled some notes to that effect on my pad. But I had no chance to use them. When he finished his speech, he left fast, taking no chances, before I could say anything that might involve him in controversy. He was being politically canny.

Was that an augury of the kind of president he would make? Only in part. He turned out to be liberal in his public attitudes, graceful as a phrasemaker, Cold Warish in his foreign policy, competitive throughout, eager to take on opponents who challenged his sense of masculinity, whether the steel companies at home or Khrushchev or Castro abroad.

He was a frustrated man in the presidency. I had a talk with him in the White House during his first year in office. He was the central luminary of a star-studded constellation of liberal celebrities around him. Going to Washington in those days was like going back for Alumni Day at college: You saw everyone you knew. Pierre Salinger was press secretary, Arthur Schlesinger was intellectual in residence, McGeorge Bundy was special assistant to the president for national security, Felix Frankfurter was over in the Supreme Court. Harvard and MIT and the Boston Mafia were everywhere.

Yet the man who greeted me in the Oval Office—half shyly and with some wariness—seemed to lack the gusto of either Theodore or Franklin Roosevelt, his two patrician predecessors. He spent half the time complaining about the way Congress blocked him on measure after measure, with an unholy alliance of Republicans and conservative Democrats against him. He lacked Lyndon Johnson's skill of maneuver and persuasion in his relations with Congress and with party leaders.

At the Vienna summit, Khrushchev had tried to bully the new young president, and Kennedy was still smarting from the hectoring tone the Russian had used toward him. But what stood out in his memory of the meeting—as he described it to me—was his own offer to Khrushchev, "Let us go to the moon together." The eagerness to compete and transcend that brought him to the presidency and made him embrace the confrontations of the Berlin Wall and of Laos and Vietnam led him also to exult in the space race even while he made his offer of a joint venture in space, which Khrushchev either spurned or ignored.

From this angle, his relationship to Fidel Castro takes on a somber new meaning. Castro was, for Kennedy, more than the ruler of a small island ninety miles off the coast of the U.S. He was a young, highly literate revolutionary, obsessed with power. He had many women. He was the very embodiment of the Latin political and sexual machismo. In all these respects, he was Kennedy's archrival, for Kennedy, too, had a feel for power, was highly literate, and was seen by American youth as a fresh symbol of new American energies. And he, too, had many women whom—like Castro—he fitted into the daily and nightly demands of being a ruler.

Could Kennedy's resolve to get rid of the Castro-Cuba problem, however extreme the means, somehow be related to this? From start to end, the Kennedy-Castro duel was a story of mingled intrigue, squalor, high comedy, nuclear dramatics, and, finally, tragedy. It couldn't have been possible except between two such men, who, regardless of the difference in their power base, were so alike in their crucial traits.

It was Kennedy's bad luck to fall heir to the Bay of Pigs adventure, ill-conceived by the CIA under Eisenhower, which he further botched. It was an ominous start. I was in Cuba for a week, in the period between the Bay of Pigs and the missile crisis, and listened to Castro's five-hour speech on the anniversary of the revolution. It was a long defiance of Kennedy and I wrote it up as such. But I didn't know at the time—how could we know?—that the interlacing of the two men would lead to Kennedy's finest hour, the Cuban missile crisis, but also to his fateful involvement with assassination plans and finally, perhaps, to his own death.

Kennedy took the political wars and competitions of the world seriously, as any president has to do if he is not an innocent. Only in that sense was he a "cold warrior." He was no war-loving monster. He was stirred to a competition with Soviet world influence not because he wanted to flex the nation's muscles but because his sense of life as struggle carried over into his foreign policy. He believed that ideas are weapons and that political war is better than actual war.

Like his father, he had an obsession with power and with the erotic relationship as a form of power. He seemed always to tread the edge of danger. He lived a Nietzschean life, dangerously, and, like the Rope-walker in Nietzsche's parable, he died a Nietzschean death.

Since the Warren Report, there has been a ghoulish war of theories about Kennedy's death, with much ingenuity spent on a number of conspiracy theories. It is clearer now that we were wrong in thinking we had to choose between the conspiracy and no-conspiracy versions. It could have been both—that the shooting was Oswald's alone but that he may have had a Cuban control, and perhaps a Russian one as well. If so, it could be Castro's revenge for the CIA and Mafia efforts to assassinate him. This was also President Johnson's guess, as he told it confidentially to several reporters—and he was in a position to guess well. It is one version that makes sense politically, even while it marks a shambles morally.

What was it that trapped a liberal humanist president like Kennedy into permitting a CIA-Mafia partnership, with Castro as target? (The question also poses itself also about Kennedy's use of the CIA to get President Diem of South Vietnam out of the way.)

I think he had a romantic Sturm und Drang take on the presidency and a fascination with danger. His older brother, Joseph, Jr., whom their father had first scheduled for the presidency, died in a secret surveillance flight over Europe, and Kennedy himself came out of the war scarred from his PT-boat adventure. He felt that danger was his destiny. There were many young men like him who had served in the OSS during the war or who joined the CIA right after—young liberals or conservatives from Ivy League colleges, who put their country ahead of everything and who found the covert not squalid but romantic. If Kennedy had not gone into politics, he might have become one of that group. He felt at home with them.

Lyndon Johnson wanted everything, and wanted it right away. He drove others ruthlessly, but he was also driven as few presidents have been, by inner hungers and insecurities that his brusque outward energies couldn't conceal.

While he was still senator and majority leader, I wrote a piece critical of a compromise he had made on a voting formula to end filibustering. He came back at me with a sizzling letter on my misreading of his civil rights record, my distortion of his motives, and, in general, on the idiocy of liberal commentators on any issue affecting the South.

At the 1960 Democratic Convention, there were few of us who

gave him much chance for anything except the quadrennial Southern bid for the nomination that had become more a matter of ritual than of realism. But (as Papa Joe sharply understood) Kennedy as a Catholic and a liberal needed a running mate to help him with the Southern Baptist and conservative vote. Most of my friends at the convention, among the delegates and newspapermen, were outraged by Kennedy's choice of Johnson. I wasn't. It struck me as cold and even cynical politics—but good politics.

When Kennedy was killed, I mourned for him as others did, with the Whitmanesque sense of a captain "fallen cold and dead." But I didn't follow the Kennedy inner circle in their scorn for his graceless successor. True he was a Texas cowboy, not a Camelot hero-prince, but I liked Johnson's Southwestern frontier vigor and even the excesses and the atrocious taste that went along with it.

I opted for Johnson against Barry Goldwater whenever I could during the 1964 campaign. I recall a debate I had with a brilliant conservative, Willmoore Kendall, before a meeting of high-powered public-relations advisers during the campaign. Kendall attacked Johnson on every possible ground, but he reserved the strangest for the end: that it "takes balls" to run the nation's foreign policy in the face of Soviet expansionism, that Goldwater had them and that Johnson simply wasn't masculine enough to possess them. I had earlier heard the same argument from William Yandell Elliott, who had been Kissinger's mentor at Harvard. I cite these minor episodes as footnotes to my proposition that conservatives were even more fascinated than liberals by the links between power and the erotic. Obviously, they differed on who met the challenges of power and with what sexual equipment.

Johnson ran the presidency much as he had run his Texas ranch, and when he retired, he ran his ranch much as he had run the presidency—with a whip-cracking braggadocio, an infinite attention to details, an intrusive assumption that those who worked for him owed him every minute of every day. He labored under the spell of a great myth of control that often goes with an underlying insecurity.

Doris Kearns was a Harvard graduate student to whom Johnson took a shine, and he confided things to her that he had never confided to Richard Goodwin or Eric Goldman or John Roche—each of whom had been his house intellectual for a brief period. She wrote up her psychohistorical theory—that Johnson's insecurity came out of his recoil from a too-dominating father and his attachment to a too-loving mother.

But I suspect it is Texas, as much as Freud, that explains Johnson,

who was no New Frontiersman but an old frontiersman. The individ-
ualists of the Texas frontier wanted freedom from the state, but only in
order to have total control over their baronial domains.

Lyndon Johnson as Senate majority leader was a great controlling
lawmaker. As president, in the hail of civil rights and other Johnson
legislation before the escalating war paralyzed him, he out Hammura-
bied Hammurabi. As he got deeper into the war, he still kept his passion for control. Where he felt superior to Kennedy was in his pride in
being a "can-do president." He clung to the self-image as a double magus, able to keep up the liberal legislation yet control it. But when he
tried to expand the war yet keep it limited—from involving the Chinese or going nuclear—he failed.

If we take the image of the two detectives—the bad cop and the
good cop—who coerce and wheedle a confession from a suspect, Johnson used the tactics of both, artful persuasion and brutal crackdown together. But instead of combining them as FDR combined the fox and
the lion, he commuted between them. On Mondays and Wednesdays
he found himself derided for being a wheeler-dealer; on Tuesdays and
Thursdays for being an unfeeling tyrant; and on weekends, for being a
boor.

He would have done better to make a choice between his selves—
either not to expand the war at the start of his term or to end it as
Nixon ended it, with the carrot of the Paris negotiations and the stick
of the mining and bombing at Haiphong and Hanoi. He could not do
it because, while he willed the ends, he could not will the means.

His whole personality and style led him to the incremental rather
than the total as a method. As Senator Daniel Patrick Moynihan has
put it, he used "little increments of pressure" to achieve his ends. It
worked with Congress. It did not work with the Communists in
Hanoi. Johnson had that "wish to lead others" that William Blake
speaks of. But his ferocity of will had limits. That is why he turned out
to be a loud talker, an energetic actor, an omnivorous devourer of
power, an omnipresent watcher over his domain—but not a destructive man. Nixon was a destructive man. Johnson knew enough to stop
short of destructiveness but did not know how to reach greatness.

Like others of my time and political clan, I found my first take on
Richard Nixon to be hostile. To win his congressional seat, he did a
dirty-tricks job on my Yale classmate Jerry Voorhis, and later, in his
Senate race, he did an even dirtier one on my friend Helen Gahagan

Douglas. While I didn't take the straight liberal line on the Hiss-Chambers affair—I thought Hiss lied lustily and Chambers exaggerated monstrously—the Nixon role in the case stuck in my craw. It was more obvious than a fly in a honey pot that he was feeding on the case, using it to get to the Senate and the vice presidency, and that he was capable of infinite trickery.

It was Alger Hiss, minor bureaucrat, clumsy amateur at unimportant pro-Communist document filching, who made Richard Nixon and thereby made history. I was a devoted attendant at both Hiss trials, and one night in my New York apartment, I listened to Louis Weiss, one of the brains behind the Hiss defense, mapping out the disastrous strategy of the second trial, which tried to turn Chambers into a case history for psychoanalysis. The trials kept Nixon in the headlines, made him an ogre for the liberals but also a folk hero for the many who worried about the betrayal of secrets in a nuclear age. Without Hiss, I am certain that Nixon could not have made it. Eisenhower chose him as running mate because he needed a young conservative who was not McCarthy but who was already a headline name and could bring in the McCarthy vote.

And the liberals? Nixon was our code word for the adversary. We salivated like Pavlov's dog at the mention of his name. During the Nixon fund fracas, we hoped against hope that Eisenhower would drop him, though realistically I was pretty sure he wouldn't. (I still have somewhere a dollar bill with *New York Times* columnist Scotty Reston's name on it, paying off the bet he lost on that to me.) During both of Ike's illnesses in his first term, we all prayed for his recovery, not just out of human kindness but because of the heartbeat that separated Nixon from the presidency. Twenty years before Watergate, we somehow had his number.

On one score we misjudged him—his viability. He may have had his six crises, but he had more than a cat's nine lives. He depicted himself as a Titan who had rebelled against the reigning divinities on the liberal Olympus, a Promethean figure stealing—if not fire, then sulphur—from the gods. For those who believe there is a karma in names (note Truman as True-man), he was, indeed, Nick's-son, with much of Machiavelli in him and not a little of the Old Nick.

While he was politically durable, he was his own worst enemy. He lost the 1960 election mainly because, in his vanity about his debating skills, he gave Kennedy a credibility in the debates that—as a young Catholic outsider—he would not otherwise have had. But after his dolorous defeat in the 1962 California governorship race, he made his "You won't have Richard Nixon to kick around anymore" statement to the reporters, and we all made the mistake of writing him off as a has-been.

We were wrong. His next six years, until 1968, were his wandering-in-the-desert years. I was reminded of Arnold Toynbee's striking phrase "withdrawal and return." Churchill did it after King Edward's abdication, and de Gaulle—who was Nixon's greatest identity figure—did it after he retired from his initial term as president.

During those six desert years of Nixon's wanderings, our little band of liberals saw only what it wanted to see. He struck us as a figure of fun, sheathed in pathos, with shifty eyes and a nervous laugh and scraggly hair and a nose heaven-sent for the cartoonists. We pictured him, beak and claws, as some Neanderthal creature who had become an extinct species swept away by history. When he moved from California to a New York law firm, we missed the cue: We saw him as losing his California power base, when we should have seen him as invading the Eastern Establishment, to rid himself of his old political associations.

The 1964 Republican Convention should have been the giveaway, if we had not been too blind to see it. Nixon craftily let his old enemy, Nelson Rockefeller, fight it out with Barry Goldwater's right-wing delegates. In the campaign, he kept his party solidarity with Goldwater, though he knew it was a hapless and hopeless cause. But in the intervening four years, he wooed and helped Republicans from both camps in Congress and statehouses and gathered collectible political debts. Thus, when I watched him in Miami, at the 1968 convention, he could present himself as a moderate middle-road figure between Nelson Rockefeller and Ronald Reagan and overwhelm both. It was an unforgettable lesson in political strategy by a master politician who made us all schoolboys in dunce caps.

I tell this story with sadness. If there had been more liberals and moderates among the Republicans, then someone more adroit in national politics than Nelson Rockefeller and Barry Goldwater could have emerged between 1960 and 1968, and Nixon's path back to power would have been made much harder. It was largely the fault of the liberal intellectual and media elites, who polarized the two parties and could not brook moderates in either. On this score I was as much at fault as the others.

Nixon's Inauguration Day was a hostile one, with Washington

blanketed by antiwar posters. But at the start, he showed himself less an ideologist than we had thought. He had three main themes in his first term—to phase out the Vietnam War, to end the Cold War with Russia and China, to muffle the social divisiveness of the 1960s. He had hard going on the first, did well on the second, came a cropper on the third.

No one, whether among liberals or conservatives, was prepared for Nixon's foreign–policy gambit. Here we all were, busy taking him apart and explaining what baleful springs of action made him tick, and lo, he comes up with Henry Kissinger—close adviser to Nelson Rockefeller—as the prime architect of his foreign policy. No psychohistory had prepared us for that event. The liberal commentators were still lost in the Nixon of the Hiss case, the Checkers speech, the Caracas riots, and the "kitchen debate" with Khrushchev.

It took some doing to undo my own obsessive view of him and shift my perspective. The fact of the Nixon-Kissinger partnership in shaping the foreign policy helped. I thought of it as an odd-couple diplomacy, in which the two partners were strangely unlike but formed a remarkable working team. Nixon had the power and found in Kissinger the scholar-diplomat who showed him what to do with it. Kissinger had the ideas and found in Nixon the hard-bitten politician who would give him the power base for trying them out. The two were like individual scissors that can't cut until they are joined.

I saw Kissinger a number of times, at some length. In a TV interview with David Frost, Nixon tried later to shrink Kissinger's role. He did the same in his *Memoirs*. Ungenerously, he seemed to be saying, "I did it alone," which runs counter to everything I learned from Kissinger and everything the Kissinger watchers believed. Looking back at the strange partnership, we must wonder at the passion for power that made two such different men work together and stick together.

Nixon was ill at ease with Kissinger's unconcealed sexuality, his worldliness, his declaration that "power is an aphrodisiac." He was also put off by the heavy Germanic accent of the immigrant Jew who had not learned English until late adolescence and had then learned it all too well, with the rolling periods of eighteenth-century English prose. The two men had a grudging admiration for the qualities in the other that each lacked, and they managed to swallow the rest perforce. Kissinger knew—as he several times told me—of Nixon's anti-Semitic streak, as he knew of his mean-spiritedness, but he also knew that, once committed, Nixon would see any venture in power politics through to the end. Nixon, in turn, knew that Kissinger still had an academic's hesitancies and second thoughts. But it delighted him to steal this luminary out of the Milky Way—right out from under the noses of the Harvard group and the foreign-policy establishment.

As for Spiro Agnew, I disliked him from the start. My column about him, when Nixon picked him as running mate in 1968, was one of the sharpest I ever wrote. Nixon used him as a weapon to keep the liberal press in line, but his speech on the "effete intellectuals"—written for him largely by William Safire—boomeranged.

There was a curious episode when I was invited to the White House to a dinner and reception for Prince Philip. President Nixon was in a wooing mood, and more cordial to me than my pieces about him had warranted. Among the speakers was Agnew, and, to my surprise, he attacked someone who had called his speech on the press an example of "the rhetoric of a college sophomore." That someone was myself. Afterward, he sought me out as the culprit. "I don't mind your hitting me when I'm wrong. But when I do something right, why don't you liberal fellows give me some encomiums?"

In time, Agnew was forced out of office because of charges about financial wrongdoing as governor of Maryland. Agnew was caught in an ordinary bribery operation, receiving kickbacks from contractors on state jobs, to which his defense was, in effect, that it was common practice and went with the territory. With Watergate, Nixon was caught in a trap of his own making, conceived in arrogance and carried through with a contemptuous belief that somehow he would prove himself above the law because his exploits in foreign statecraft carried him beyond the law. If he had not resigned, he would have been impeached for "high crimes and misdemeanors" as president. Of the two miscreants, I preferred Nixon.

Curiously, both Agnew and Nixon, particularly Agnew, ended with the feeling that the Jews were part of their downfall. As governor, Agnew had been close to Jewish contractors and their intermediaries. When the squeeze was put on them by the federal attorney and they talked to save their skin, Agnew felt betrayed. He saw them not as the sleazy human characters they were but as Jews. How deeply this had eaten into his consciousness became clear later, when he wrote a spy novel in which pro-Israeli American Jews got a heavy going over. Like many others who read the book, I shuddered when I reflected that this man had for six years been at a cobweb-thin remove from the presidency; if Nixon had resigned a year before he did, we would have had Spiro Agnew in the White House.

During the 1972 Republican Convention at Miami, I made friends with several minor members of the White House staff, when the full shadow of Watergate had not yet fallen on Nixon. He cut a jaunty figure during the 1972 campaign that—partly through the dirty-tricks operation to eliminate tougher opponents such as Edmund Muskie—presented him (in the form of George McGovern) with a candidate easy to trounce.

During the campaign, I asked Bill Safire to come to my Brandeis University seminar on politics and speak for his candidate. Safire carried it off brilliantly, to the dismay of my universally pro-McGovern students and colleagues. Safire told me cheerfully that he knew almost as little about Watergate as I did and that the standing instructions from the palace guard were to play it down, to urge everyone to wait for the court to act and to stress that the president was not involved. Soon after the inauguration, I got a note from Nixon, out of the blue, about a column of mine on foreign policy. It wasn't much as a piece, and the letter clearly made too much of it. I sensed Nixon's worry. He was fence-mending.

Thus, there was a special irony for me when I listened to John Dean reading from the White House "enemies list" and heard my name. I felt relieved. It would have been humiliating if I had not been on the list. Yet I was not an enemy of the republic. Something I wrote must have infuriated someone in the palace guard, or even the president himself. I learned what was at the heart of the Watergate corruption—the incapacity to distinguish between political opponents and enemies of the state.

Nixon was sliding downhill, and from the time of the McCord letter to Judge Sirica, outlining a cover-up and offering to testify to get a shorter sentence, Nixon no longer functioned as president but only as a man trying desperately to save himself.

Nixon is not an easy figure for a psychohistorical study. The commentators and scholars who have tried it thus far have mostly botched the job by using a crude psychoanalytical model that portrays him as a mechanical monster crippled by his experiences in infancy and childhood. A more tractable one, from developmental psychology, would see Nixon as a human being under stress, with a life history that he brought to his presidential tasks with both startling success and failure.

As I read him, he was the product of our age—eaten up with ambition, hungry for power, competitive to every prehensile finger and toe. He was in essence an outsider—a Republican in a Democratic era, a conservative in a liberal one, an introvert in an age of extroverts, a foreign-policy buff in a polity of pressure groups and domestic issues, basically asexual in an age of hedonism. He used everyone and everything. Without being truly religious, he used Billy Graham and the old-time religion; without genuine values of his own, he used the traditional value system as a weapon. He felt beset by enemies, some of whom were truly so, while others were enlarged by his sense of encirclement. He surrounded himself with a palace guard, with whom his common bond was the prevailing sense of the sons of bitches to be overcome. For them, as for him, politics was the science of the enemy, and they fed one another's indignation and hatred of the adversary and exulted in their triumphs over him. That was the White House atmosphere. It accounted for the rigid controls handed over to Chief-of-Staff H. R. Haldeman and domestic affairs assistant John D. Ehrlichman, as to a security guard. It accounted also for the enemies list.

Being basically a reactive personality, Nixon was likely to overreact, especially to highly symbolic figures. Daniel Ellsberg was his bête noire, and as much the cause of his fall as anyone, including his formal political enemies. Ellsberg was, in Nixon's eyes, a turncoat who had learned the war's secrets in the State Department and had turned against it, pirating the Pentagon Papers and playing into the hands of the enemy. He was an intellectual. He used and was used by the media. He was an Easterner. He was a product of the activist movements and counterculture of the 1960s. He was a liberal, perhaps a radical. He was a Jew. In short, he was the convergence point of the whole constellation of forces that Nixon faced with hostility.

Nixon overreacted, first by trying to stop the publication of the Pentagon Papers, then by releasing the "plumbers" on Ellsberg and on other leaks, going so far as to rifle the files of Ellsberg's psychiatrist. It is true that the immediate Watergate incident was part of a secret operation by CREEP—Nixon's reelection committee—to gather intelligence for the campaign. Specifically, it may have been looking for evidence of a linkage between Castro and McGovern.

But while four more years of power formed Nixon's concrete goal, in the depths of his psyche he was lashing out at the whole climate of the sixties and its rip-offs. To him, Ellsberg and the Pentagon Papers represented a giant rip-off, with drastic consequences for the nation as well as himself. He convinced himself that a search-and-destroy operation against infiltrators was justified by reason of state, even if it had to be buttressed by secret operations that on any other occasion would be illegal.

He was a man who prided himself on his self-discipline and self-control. Thus, when he reacted against events, his reactions were not resilient but brittle. Intent on never bending, he broke under the deep strain. As he felt himself increasingly cornered, he searched more frantically for some way out of the maze into which he had locked himself. Especially after the Supreme Court ruled unanimously that he must surrender the telltale tapes of Oval Office conversations about Watergate, there was no way out for him except to choose between a hopeless impeachment fight and resignation.

Yet even in those latter days, when his rope was getting ever shorter, he could still be roused by a great foreign-policy challenge. That was true of the Yom Kippur War, when Israel was caught by the Arab surprise attack and needed weapons with which to fight back. There was lethal intramural fighting between a troubled Kissinger, who wanted to help Israel, and the undersecretary of defense, who had been an oilman and had some pro-Arab leanings. The Israelis were desperate. Their ambassador held a twenty-four-hour-a-day vigil in the corridors of power, at the State Department and the Pentagon. The final holdback was the lack of transport. Nixon cut the knot. "Send the stuff on anything that moves," he ordered. They did. The Israelis counterattacked, surrounded the Egyptian army across the canal and tightened the noose around it. This time, it was the Egyptians who cried for help in the form of a cease-fire. The possibility of another Egyptian defeat was too much for both Nixon and Kissinger. They threatened to crack down on Israel and they rescued the Egyptians.

I lunched with Kissinger after one of his shuttle trips and asked him not only about the war but also about the president. Kissinger was, in effect, carrying the burden of the presidency, seeking to salvage by his prestige whatever shreds of legitimacy the executive still had. He knew how Nixon was coming apart, as a mind and as a man. After several hours of talk, Kissinger answered what must have been a pressing call at the table. I could hear some muttered words about the president and saw his face change color. For a moment, he was silent, and then— as we rose from the table—he said, almost under his breath but quite clearly, "That anti-Semitic bastard!"

Nixon was a vulgar anti-Semite, given to outbursts of anger against Jews (and against other ethnic groups as well), but not a classic anti-Semite, in the fascist sense. A classic anti-Semite could not have ordered his secretaries of state and defense to send arms to Israel in "anything that moves," just as he could not have chosen a Jew as his prime adviser and kept him by his side for almost six years.

The final contradiction in this curious man and mind came in his last twenty-four hours of power, and it came in the historic prayer session. Nixon had decided to resign, had issued his last orders as chief executive, had given his speechwriters instructions about his farewell statement. To whom did he turn on his last evening in office? Not to his family, his partisans, his close friends, but to the immigrant Jew with a heavy Germanic accent who—he later said—had never been a friend, only an associate.

We have to ask why, and the answer may resolve some of the contradictions in Nixon. He was mean, nasty, ruthless, vindictive—yes. He wooed and held on to power with ferocity. He lied, both for reasons of state and to save his own skin. He could be sentimental, and turn away at someone's tears, yet also give orders that meant death for thousands and tens of thousands. But having said this, we would have to add that he was a political man, all the beads of whose blood turned to the mastery of events.

This was why Richard Nixon spent that last evening with Henry Kissinger. Had he failed to do so—had either man failed—he would not have been what he was. The two men had made together the greatest journey in the life of each—that journey to the end of the night that spelled out the power and passion of guiding the world's greatest power mass.

Each knew that the other had been his passport to history. Now, as Nixon was forced to relinquish the power that had meant the breath of life to him, he turned to the one man who knew the ruses, the glories, and the cruelties of history. He couldn't step out of history, and face the full extent of his tragedy, without touching base with the man who had studied both history and tragedy. When Nixon asked Kissinger to pray with him, it was not to the Judaeo-Christian gods, Yahweh or Christ, that they knelt, but to the only gods they had in common as political men—the gods of power and blind chance, and the ironies and tragedies and absurdities of history.

In his own curious way, Nixon was a Nietzschean figure, lonely on the mountain, striving for some Superman role beyond good and evil.

But in the end, like the ill-fated magus of legend, the genie he released from the bottle became a whirlwind that destroyed him.

As I look back at these six presidents, I cannot escape a pervasive sadness about most of them. They lived out the great American dream and reached the pinnacle and—except for Harry Truman—were broken on it. Franklin Roosevelt died in office, less from his crippling illness than from the tensions of the presidency to which he had added his own dimension of gaiety and greatness. Dwight Eisenhower survived his heart attack, but he was an unfulfilled man both in his private and in his public life, and the storms that gathered around him in his second term burst on the nation in the 1960s when he left office. John Kennedy was just starting to explore his promise as president when he was shot down. Lyndon Johnson found that skill and will were not enough to hold his universe together, and himself rang the curtain down on his hopes for another term. Richard Nixon was expelled from the Eden he had hungered for, harder than any of the rest; he was his own Lucifer and created his own hell.

Together these six are the latter-day Titans, presiding for forty-two years over a power cluster now entering its third century. For all their foibles, it would be hard to find in any other nation of our time a succession of heads of state who were as eager to wield their massive power well, and who gave it up as reluctantly.

I wish they had suffered less sorrow, and led more fulfilled lives, and been wiser in the crunch. But then, I wish the rest of us had been wiser, too. For our presidents are pretty much what we make them. We choose them, deify them, make myths of them, revile them, hound them out of office, or harass them to their deaths. We are as obsessed with them as they are obsessed with power.

In fact, our obsession with them becomes an erotic obsession, in the sense in which power and Eros are closely linked. We project our dreams on them, wreak our frustrations on them, take out our discontents on them. We take human beings and make gods of them, and when they turn out to be made of clay—human, all too human—we close our hearts to them and try to expunge the pages of history on which their deeds are written. "Make our people governable," a clergyman prayed at Jimmy Carter's inaugural. If we had been less ungovernable, these six men would have lived longer and done better, and fewer of them would have been broken by the ruthlessness of a democracy.

DESIRE AND POWER
IN THE WHITE HOUSE

THERE IS A SURVIVING BAND OF BROTHERS among my press contemporaries who have (like myself) known every president from Franklin Roosevelt to Jimmy Carter. Although I had talks with each president I was never, except perhaps in FDR's case, a real insider. But what made my own angle of vision somewhat different was that I was not only a power watcher but an Eros watcher.

This may seem to many a contamination of each. We kept and still keep them locked away from each other in university catalogues. But I went to school for power in those years to Machiavelli and Marx, and for Eros to Havelock Ellis and Freud, and since I meditated constantly on the gods of power and love I broke down the barriers between them, and in my mind I watched them embrace. I had been moved by Theodore Dreiser's Cowperwood and his fusion of the two in *The Titan* and *The Financier*, and I wrote a piece on "Jupiter" Morgan's fancy doings on Wall Street and in the bedroom, which H. L. Mencken—believer that he was in Nietzsche's Superman—published in the *American Mercury*.

At some point I must have made the decision to move from business titans to presidents. My *Lehrejahre* had been endured under Harding and Coolidge, and my fledgling years as an encyclopedia editor under Herbert Hoover, none of them proper subjects for Dreiserian studies. But Franklin Roosevelt was something different. It was his life that put my prime question to me: What does power do to desire, and desire to power, either in the White House or moving toward it?

"Desire and Power in the White House" was accepted by *Vanity Fair* in 1984, but never published. It develops the theme of "Eros and Power" with more specific case studies.

I was thirty when FDR came to power in 1933, and it seemed to me I had been waiting forever. I talked, taught, wrote, argued, drank, and ate the New Deal. I even fancied Machiavelli as a subtle New Dealer in the Quattrocento, and like him I wrote my first book—*It Is Later Than You Think*—for the reading of my prince, to hearten him to stay on his leftward course.

I met Eleanor Roosevelt early and I barnstormed the liberal-left rubber-chicken banquet circuit with her. In our speechmaking we both tried, as she put it to me during the Spanish Civil War, to "light some fires under Franklin." I had only a half-knowledge, not a clear one, that the sexual fire between them had been wholly snuffed out.

It had happened during Franklin's assistant navy secretary days in World War I, when he and Lucy Mercer fell passionately, and (as it turned out) hopelessly, in love. We in the press kept the minimal gossip about them to ourselves. There was a conspiracy of deception we practiced, unwilling to see the veil torn from the private lives of our favorite president and first lady. But the break came in the otherwise tight little inner circle of Washington dowagers who were the keepers of the social flame. Each of them knew a part of the story.

The result was a series of partial disclosures by biographer Jonathan Daniels, son of Franklin's navy boss, who was the first to break the conspiracy in his memoir *Washington Quadrille*. I was myself more taken with the jeweled rendering of the story in Kenneth Davis's study of the pre-presidential *FDR—The Beckoning of Destiny*. Joseph Lash's moving account in his *Eleanor and Franklin* is notably sensitive to Eleanor's viewpoint.

It all depended upon what participants you knew and what dowagers. Joseph Alsop seems to be the only one to have known them all, and his *FDR, 1882–1945: A Centenary Remembrance* gave the story a gossipy opulence. But somewhere in this wilderness of recountings what got lost was the core of Eros itself. For here is one of the great romantic love stories of American history. Its true poignancy is belittled when it is split away from its central core of the lovers themselves.

Consider it as sheer love story. Lucy Mercer was patrician-born of an old Maryland Catholic family that had lost its money but retained its gentility. To make a living in Washington she was a mobile part-time social secretary for a number of ladies, including Eleanor Roosevelt. She was tall, stately, gentle, beautiful, emotionally deep. It was wartime in Washington, and the busy and handsome assistant secretary was a spirited frequenter of the Washington parties, a bit footloose when Eleanor was away with the children or doing good works. Franklin and Lucy fell headily in love.

If ever there was a natural pair of lovers, destined to an inevitable bonding, this was it. At first they were discreet, but in time they grew more reckless, going everywhere together in a clearly buoyant happiness, writing each other when they couldn't meet. Soon many in Washington knew, and even Eleanor began to know—although she didn't know how much there was to know.

It was a brief, intense episode of some two years' duration. By the end of 1918 it was over. Returning from a European trip, Franklin was too ill to attend to his accumulated letters, and—rummaging through them—Eleanor came upon a number from Lucy, clearly love missives. There was a ghastly showdown, with Eleanor acting the betrayed wife and Franklin admitting all yet cleaving to his new love.

Here a number of versions differ on what decisively kept Franklin from a divorce and the lovers from marrying. One version sees Eleanor as adamant. Another has Franklin's mother, Sarah Roosevelt, threatening to cast him off and leave him penniless. A third sees Lucy's Catholic scruples as the central factor. Certainly, given the long family tradition of Catholicism, a high-profile divorce and marriage outside the Church may have been more than Lucy's gentle nature could cope with.

But it is idle to assign blame. All three pressures converged on the lovers. We are told that "love conquers all," but in this case there was not only a triangle of desires but a triangle of wills, and looking back it strikes me that of the three it was Eleanor's which was the most resolute and prevailed.

In the end how do we judge a passionate love affair? Not, despite our pragmatism, by its consequences. Judged thus, this one was barren. Franklin didn't divorce Eleanor, Lucy and he didn't marry, they didn't live happily ever after. Eleanor never after shared her bed with Franklin until death did them part. They went on together, in the world's eye, as a vigorous husband-wife partnership, with an overlay of affection despite the deep hurt.

Franklin resumed his political life design, and in 1920 ran a hopeless race as vice presidential candidate in the face of the Harding Republican landslide. Then came the blight of polio, and given today's perspective on the emotional factors in health and disease, his heartbreak over Lucy may well have been part of what brought it on. But he transcended both—the broken love and maimed body—and out of the crucible of both came the strength that transformed a light hearted young charmer into the towering figure of the world crisis leader.

Soon after the break, Lucy married Winthrop Rutherfurd, double her age (fifty-eight to her twenty-nine), a wealthy widower with four children. But this didn't end things for Franklin and Lucy. They had drunk the fatal love potion and neither ever recovered from it.

When her husband died of a stroke, in 1941, Lucy and Franklin resumed seeing each other. Sometimes it was at the White House when Eleanor was away and her daughter, Anna Boettiger, served as hostess for her father. Sometimes, under a heavy wartime press censorship, a presidential railroad car would remain overnight near Lucy's home in New Jersey. Often, under a Secret Service guard, he would meet Lucy at a trysting place beyond Georgetown, on Canal Road, where they could drive about and have a few hours together. Once the president took an extended holiday from his wartime burden as guest of Bernard Baruch at his South Carolina estate, where Lucy—living at Aiken—could visit with him. There was finally the recourse of Franklin's cottage at Warm Springs, Georgia, which Lucy could reach with ease from Aiken.

Nothing like it had ever happened before in the history of the presidency—a married president, in the ebb tide of his life but at the crest of his world power, managing repeated meetings with the first and final great love of his life, under the world's nose. Who could grudge them this delayed last boon? It had been a long moratorium for both. The scruples of religion, the demands of family, the claimant voice of the hope for power—they had all intervened, fatefully, the first time round. Now there was the postman's second knock and this time—quietly but emphatically—they responded.

When FDR and Lucy started meeting again, early in his administration, I was teaching beautiful and brilliant girls at Sarah Lawrence College, and I moonlighted at a second job by running the Consumers Agency in Washington. When FDR was battling with his New Deal opponents I was editing The Nation and writing my New Deal book, whose proof sheets Tom Corcoran red-penciled for his boss's reading. When we were on the eve of the war—while I was teaching at Williams College—we had a long afternoon together at Hyde Park, when he told his staff to leave us alone because we were "talking philosophy."

One theme juts out in my memory. It was his stress on action. I brought up the ways in which the totalitarians were trying to capture the minds of the world's youth. "I know it," he answered. "But, Mr. Lerner, they have the propaganda of the word, but we have the propaganda of the deed."

It was an assertive, challenging note, which rang through his whole presidency. Today I can't help wondering about its sources. We pay little heed to the impact of the emotional content of a leader's private life on his public acts. I like to think now that this was not an emotionally starved man, channeling his unexercised erotic energies into public service, but a man at the height of his power of feeling and will and action, expressing again the sense of triumph that his renewed meetings with Lucy must have nourished.

The tragedy was not diminished by those meetings, but they were part of its transcendence. It had been, in the classic sense, a "star-crossed" story. Writing about romantic passion, within the frame of the Tristan story, in *Love in the Western World*, Denis de Rougemont contends that star-crossed tragedy is built into the idea of romantic love. But in our American civilization we suffer at once from a wishful belief that life and love must offer happy endings, and a reluctance to face the tragic that is at the constitution of the universe.

Rarely, whether in America or elsewhere, have romantic love and summit power been found together. In our witless sense of perfectionism we dream of their somehow miraculously working together. They haven't and don't. The deepest yearnings of the heart are incompatible with the steepest demands of power.

I came to know Eleanor better than I knew Franklin. During the 30s and 40s our lives met constantly at those political dinners and lectures and on those letterheads. In the 50s we met and talked fleetingly, since we were both members of the Brandeis University faculty. I have some precious memories of our walking in the shade of the campus trees and talking of the turbulent world outside. I admired her forthrightness and courage as a liberal activist, yet I was saddened by her sadness.

This is not the place to talk at any length about her relations with Lorene Hickock, which have been pretty well attested. We are only now starting to accept the romantic component of same-sex love. The correspondence between Eleanor and Lorene, in the Hyde Park Library, runs to thousands of letters. Most show a strong, obsessive friendship, some an effort to keep their meetings secret and a delight in tricking the too curious world. A number were burned by Lorene. I am glad that at some point Eleanor was able to slake her thirsty heart in a romantic—and yes, also a star-crossed—love for another woman, as passionate in its way as Franklin's and Lucy's.

It is futile to speculate on what might have been. We can only accept how things turned out. It was tragic for all three—a numbing stab of pain for Lucy, a sense of powerlessness amidst power for Franklin, a wrenching bitterness for Eleanor. All three acted out their private pain and their secret dreams in their own way. In all three the pain was somewhat and somehow dissolved, but only with Franklin and Lucy was the dream renewed.

The last scene, of Franklin and Lucy together at Warm Springs, was the memorable one. I had just returned from a spell as war reporter for *PM* in the last months of the war in Europe—the Europe that had been retrieved and given new life by FDR's will. We were all talking about how new the brave new world would be, and most of us—including FDR—had high hopes for it. Hitler was all but defeated, a victory over Japan looked manageable, Stalin was making trouble but FDR would be able to charm and pressure him into line. We held fast to our dream.

Curiously the only recognition that Lucy gets from many FDR historians is her presence that April day, in 1945, in the cottage at Browdell Knoll. It was an ironic scene. The Ulyssean statesman, back from his wanderings (the last at Yalta in February), making some final changes in a Jefferson Day talk he was to give, still bent on the morrow. His two favorite young women cousins were moving about. Elizabeth Shoumatoff, the friend Lucy had brought with her to do Franklin's portrait, busy at her easel after throwing a red-tipped cloak around him. And Lucy, sitting contentedly, embroidering, with a smile that needed no words. I like to think that their last thoughts, before the commanding stab of pain, were of the tempestuous years together, now serene, and of the blessedness of sitting together on some of the tomorrows left to them, with friends they trusted like these.

The stab when it came was sharp: "I have such a headache," Franklin said to one of the young cousins. His head fell forward. Lucy put her arms around him but he had lost consciousness.

The years of cruel demands on his heart and arteries had finally exacted their cost. A young navy cardiologist, Dr. Howard Bruenn, had come to a dark diagnosis of his riddled system. Quartered nearby, he came in fifteen minutes, noted the massive stroke, but it was too late to hold him to life for more than a few hours.

The sadness of it is that Lucy had to be spirited away, back to her

Aiken home, even before Franklin was dead. Yet I like to think, given their star-crossed love, that it was the cunning of history which had them together in that brief final stretch of sun and serenity before the end came.

It was a long weekend afternoon on Paradise Island, in the Caribbean, somewhere in 1953, and a young woman was telling me about her affair with the newly elected senator from Massachusetts. It was either just before or just after he married Jacqueline Bouvier, and she felt deeply bruised since they had been close for years and she had expected he would marry *her*. But his family opposed it, and she wasn't Catholic, and (as a minor celebrity in the fast set) she had the wrong social ambiance. I recall wondering how many beautiful women might have told the same disconsolate story about the young senator.

Like many others I was caught up in watching John Kennedy's meteoritic political career. I was not one of the young Kennedy groupies, being some fifteen years older than he and having taught at Harvard just before he was a student there. My close friend Harold Laski, the British Marxist intellectual, had told me about Jack's Senior Honors thesis (published as *Why England Slept*), which he had read for Jack's father and found unimpressive and *young*. But Jim Burns, a former student of mine who was Jack's contemporary and was to write his first biography, was one of his earliest admirers and I was caught up in the excitement.

In the 1950s, I was teaching at Brandeis and writing for the *New York Post*, and I was hungry for a not-impossible coming president who wouldn't read Westerns (like Dwight Eisenhower) and who would be literate, liberal, and strong. Kennedy captured my imagination, as Adlai Stevenson did before him, but Adlai's star would be dimming while Jack' s was rising.

At the 1956 convention I cheered for Jack's vice presidential bid and was heartbroken when it failed, not understanding that he had barely escaped the oblivion of a beaten running mate of a twice-beaten presidential candidate. When he tried again next time, it was for the highest stakes.

Some personal reservations about his own "political courage" didn't keep me from supporting him for the presidency. I went out on a limb publicly early in 1960 to predict he would be the nominee. At the convention, I spent much of my time with Norman Mailer, whose fascination with Jack was to become obsessive. Listening to Norman, it struck me how much of Kennedy's appeal, for women and men alike, was erotic. Jack seemed to rouse in Norman a competitive machismo, both for power over women and for the women who came with power. As for women, they followed Jack everywhere, threw themselves at him, wanted to devour him. His campaign aides came to classify them as the *grabbers*, the *groaners*, the *squealers*, the *swooners*. Jack was like a media or rock star before he became an active political hero.

I saw nothing wrong in this fusion of Eros and power, as I fear Garry Wills—more Puritan than I—does in his brilliantly written *The Kennedy Imprisonment*. Before any of us, Freud's essay on *Group Psychology* noted the erotic attraction the mass feels for the leader. Kennedy felt it too, and reveled in it, although at one point—standing in the Berlin square where he delivered his *Ich bin ein Berliner* speech—it scared even him. If he had asked the crowd to storm the Berlin Wall, he felt, they would have ripped it apart, brick by brick. No president in American history has combined Eros and power as Kennedy did.

Jack's womanizing was at once the best-known and best-kept secret of his campaign and presidency. We all knew different bits of the gossip but none of us wrote any of it. On his Inaugural night, in a Washington blanketed with snow, the conversations between the dances were less about the New Frontier than about the new young president and his adventures. Robert Frost, in the Inaugural poem he was too snow-blinded to read, had spoken of the "new Augustan age" of "poetry and power." As it turned out it was a new Regency age of sexuality and power.

Even better, Frost might have spoken of danger and power. When I think of Kennedy I think of Nietzsche's Ropewalker balancing himself across the dangerous courtyard of life. He lived for excitement and danger and the tension of seeing what he could get away with, and he injected his sense of excitement into a time of smugness and cynicism.

I add immediately that he was also a cautious, prudent political professional, tough-minded about political risks before he made his decisions—except, alas, for the Bay of Pigs. Not for him the Savonarola intensity of his brother Bob.

The truth is that Kennedy contained all the polar drives within his complex self—the risk-taking and the prudent, the realist and idealist, the liberal and conservative, the drive to action and the observing ego always watching himself, the energetic and the reserved, the imaginative and the bottom-line practical, the sociable and the intensely private. More than anything he was a centrist, integrating these polar drives as well as anyone after FDR.

It was with the Cuban missile crisis that he displayed his true greatness. It was as if all his life had been a preparation for this event, which he met with a disciplined sureness and strength that suggested he had finally grown up. Every quality of his, honed by the White House pressures to a fine edge, were brought into play for this climactic testing. It was a hairy time, when each of us had to examine the very foundations of his thinking and being. Yet it didn't change his essential nature. Most students of his life have been hard put to reconcile the Kennedy of the missile crisis with the Kennedy who had an affair with Judith Campbell at the same time that she was romantically involved with underworld chieftain Sam Giancana.

One way of doing it is to "refuse the field," as the Zen writers put it, and deny—with Arthur Schlesinger—that the sexual adventures have any relevance to Kennedy as president. I find that hard to accept. We must take Kennedy as a total man, which means taking the sexual drive in him along with the power drive, the imagination, and the judgment, and everything else.

Going by what his biographers have dug up in interviews, it appears that Jack was amorous, reckless, and insatiable. Nothing and no one seem to have been out of bounds for the young president. Despite the Camelot legend, contrived after his death, his living parallel was not with the court of King Arthur, which was pretty chaste, but with Louis XIV's Versailles. Jack became the Sun King of our century, with a retinue and a court, and he turned the White House into another Deer Park. Nothing like John Kennedy has ever happened in the erotic history of the presidency.

With few exceptions it seems that Jack was accustomed to using his women, found it hard to relate to them, and—as some of his friends guess—found he may have been incapable of giving and receiving adult love. Most explanations of this take a Freudian path. They run in terms of a family setting where the macho cult of sex was handed down as a male tribal icon from father to sons, and where each brother competed with the others and with their father in sexual prowess. It is a usable interpretation but it doesn't go very far. The way in which Jack Kennedy used the erotic in his life may well have owed much to his father as libido model. Joe Kennedy, Sr., was good at fixing, organizing, pressuring, at making a fortune and using it for power, and he had a joy of living, which Jack captured and transformed.

But what Jack made of this heritage was his own doing. There was nothing soaring about the father, but the son gave the nation a feeling that anything was possible. He gave, especially to his generation and the next, new eyes to see their nation and world, with new nerve ends to sense the challenges and responses of their time. He had a genius for the symbolic. More than "image-making," it took the everyday and tipped it with the flame of the heroic.

It doesn't do much good to argue how much he actually achieved. Certainly not as much as Harry Truman, in his down-to-earth hard bitten way. We need both types of presidents. But there should be nothing novel in saying that there were not two Kennedys but one, and that they were held together by Eros not only as sexuality but as a life force.

Jack took a long time, even in his brief life, to shed the libido model of his father and mature as a whole man. Part of our problem in viewing him is the lingering taboo that keeps us from seeing that sexuality is inherently part of a great political leader. Max Weber, early in the century in Germany, called it *charisma* and gave it a vague religious penumbra. But converging at its very center are the twin drives of sexuality and power, and Kennedy had both in abundance. He went far in eroticizing power.

His problem was that he was better at power than at sex—more disciplined and professional, more innovative and imaginative. On Eros as sexuality he repeated his father's experience, and probably was never as good at it. But on Eros as the life force, the sexuality spilled over creatively into politics and power.

He had a natural political sense with a sexual base that he cultivated and refined. He was not a natural lover; by all accounts he didn't take the trouble to interact and relate.

It has often been noted that he linked sex with power: to overcome a woman's resistance was like winning a campaign; to triumph in bed was like triumphing over Castro. But while Kennedy carried it far, it is found in other political leaders, and in corporate Titans as well. It comes with the territory of Eros and power.

What is more striking is that Jack linked his sexual conquests with danger and mystery. His great early passion was for Inga Arvad, a former mistress of a Nazi industrialist and an intimate of the Goering circle, who was being watched by the F.B.I.; Jack's father got him out of that one, spiriting him off to the Pacific. The well-known case of Judith Campbell, whom Jack shared with a Mafia chieftain, attests to his drive to explore the limits of danger and the forbidden. Less known was his affair with Mary Pinchot Meyer, who had been married to Cord Meyer, high in the CIA. She was talented, delightful, "with a mysterious hidden quality," as Ralph Martin describes her. After Jack's death, we are told, she was "mysteriously murdered, and her murderer was never found."

I have never been shocked by Jack's erotic adventures. He was as drawn to the dangerous in power terms as in erotic, from the humiliating debacle at the Bay of Pigs to his brilliant success at the Cuban missile crisis, when his stern resolve was disciplined by an awesome sense of the risks for mankind.

I see his feeling for Jackie and their children as playing a part in this maturing process. The marriage seemed to have a storybook rightness about it. Jack was captivated by Jackie, as everyone was, but he saw her also as the exact queen for a prospective American court. Clearly, however, he had no intention of forsaking all others—or any. His father's marriage, as a paradigm, was too built into his bone and brain to be burned out. Jackie in turn had no intention of becoming a patient and pious Rose Kennedy. So the marriage became tumultuous.

It might have broken at several points, and it is a tribute to a basic quality of will and constancy in both that it didn't. I speak not of continuity, which was what Franklin and Eleanor Roosevelt had, but of a filament of desire and admiration and connectedness, which was Jackie's and Jack's form of marital constancy, whatever his infidelities.

It had to be a strong marriage to survive so many hurdles. Jack was enchanted afresh by Jackie when she took all France and Europe by storm at his summit with de Gaulle. While she was apolitical, she couldn't help but admire his political verve and style. Their two children brought them close together, and the death of Patrick brought them even closer. There was a reserve of mystery in each that the other couldn't penetrate—and valued. Before Dallas there was a marital tenderness between them that augured well for the future, until Jackie's blood-spattered pink suit signaled the end of everything.

The ropewalker had tumbled into the abyss but it had been a classy act, and one to remember.

When Jack Kennedy was killed and Lyndon Johnson succeeded him, our little liberal world fell apart. Whatever else Johnson had, he had no "style," no "class," and (we felt) he wouldn't fight for the things we believed in. I heard the news of the assassination at an American Embassy party in Paris. I had been trying to study Charles de Gaulle, but I came back to America soon, to study the kind of man whose mind and character now held our destinies in thrall.

At the 1960 Democratic Convention Jimmy Wechsler and I had managed to sneak into a Johnson dinner without invitations, and we felt we had penetrated enemy territory. The whole Kennedy camp despised the Johnson camp, which in turn hated the Kennedy camp. When word came later that Jack had given the vice presidential spot to Lyndon, we were too stunned to believe it. We didn't understand—as Jack did in his cold decision—how crucial it would prove for his election. Nor did we know how galling Johnson's isolation in the vice presidency was for him. Jack and Lyndon had to work together but between their two worlds there was an uncrossable chasm.

There were two occasions when I could study Johnson face-to-face. One was a harrowing evening at a high-powered publishers dinner in Washington in which I was somehow included. Johnson presided over it—except when he was on the phone to the Dominican Republic, deciding to send troops to quell a revolt. In between the phone-calls he argued the case for the Vietnam War. He overtalked, overexplained, overexhorted. He was excessive in everything.

The mordant memory I have of Johnson is of an afternoon with him in the Oval Office at the time of the Tết offensive. The media tide was running strongly against Johnson, and my Brandeis colleague John Roche, who had become intellectual in residence, must have thought of me as the last—if not best—hope to help turn the tide. Johnson held me for hours, urging his case. He argued that Tết was a defeat not for the U.S. but for the Viet Cong—and recent scholarship has tended to back him. The U.S. defeat was a media defeat. I didn't see it at the time and in several pieces, which dismayed both Johnson and Roche, I wrote it that way.

What stays with me was his telephone obsession. He sat with a bank of phone lights at his side, and as one or another lit up he would pick up the phone, listen, bark a crisp Yes or No, and then turn to continue our conversation. That bank of lights and those cords tied him to his world, by which he could control it, using will and wile. Suddenly I caught a glimpse of his desperate need to control, lest he let his world slip away.

Why was his need so desperate? This elemental man, embodying the life force itself, with a set of political skills unparalleled in our history—why did he have so much self-loathing?

The best students of Johnson's psyche take the story back to his boyhood in the hill country in Southwest Texas, and the ups and downs of his father's land speculations—mostly downs—which represented a ghastly reversal of fortunes for the family. To have a father who had once been a respected and dominant figure in the community, and to see him unable to pay his debts, to watch the respect of the people who counted slipping away from him—that was the trauma young Lyndon had to suffer.

It might account for the passion for power he developed, thus winning the respectability his father had lost, and the passion to uncover whatever was vulnerable in people, to unmask their pretensions to respectability and make them pliable to his persuasion.

Politics for Lyndon turned out to be a country for conquest, a force field in which he was to operate with deceit, self-aggrandizement, and ruthlessness. And in the annals of Johnsonology the conventional wisdom has been that Johnson was as manipulative and unfeeling in his many sexual affairs as in his political life.

That judgment won't stand up anymore. It has been undercut, curiously, in a book that gives us the darkest judgment of Johnson's character thus far—of a power-driven, greedy sycophant and sadist, who cared nothing for the causes he championed and was a grotesque and clownish scoundrel. I have had to wrestle with the first of three volumes by Robert Caro on Johnson—his *Path to Power*—trying to fit it into the Johnson I remember, and I find it hard. But in a volume that is a triumph of investigative reporting, Caro has fortunately decided to include a Johnson love affair we had not known until now—an episode so passionate, secret, and lyrical that only young Franklin Roosevelt's with Lucy Mercer matches it.

Alice Glass was the mistress of Charles Marsh, a Texas tycoon who, among his other properties, owned the only newspapers that covered the whole of Johnson's congressional district. She was also (in another sense) the mistress of "Longlea," Marsh's estate in northern Virginia, which he had built for her under her direction.

She was, by all accounts, a thing of wonder—a blond, taller Lucy Mercer, with long shimmering tresses, talented in architecture, landscaping, the arts, well read, widely traveled, with a bent for the unconventional in the conduct of her life.

She was twenty-six, Johnson a young Congressman at twenty-nine, Marsh fifty, when Johnson began spending days and weekends at Longlea. Within a year or two they were lovers, with Alice madly in love with Lyndon and he completely lost in her.

It was a closely guarded affair, fitting into Johnson's obsession with secrecy but also secret by necessity on both sides. Alice's sister and a close friend knew of it, Marsh didn't, while Lady Bird Johnson (who was usually left behind at home) seems to have suspected and perhaps guessed but did nothing about it.

For Johnson the risk of disclosure was immense, since Marsh was his strongest backer and controlled the press that counted for Johnson. Lyndon was risking his political career which had started so well in Congress and which he aimed ultimately at the presidency. Alice was risking her relationship with Marsh, and the Longlea she loved.

It was the only time in Johnson's life, writes Caro, when he did something which jeopardized his self-interest. But then he treats it as an anomaly which need not affect his portrait of Johnson as devoid of values, greedy for power and money alone.

I view it as a strong evidence of Johnson's complexity, which belied any monolithic picture of him. If he was indeed the total monster he is depicted to be, it is hard to understand the romantic, almost lyrical passion of both the lovers.

Caro wonders what a woman as glamorous as Alice, with style, taste, and class, could have seen in this gangly, awkward young man whose nose and ears were too long, who slopped his food into his open mouth at table, who didn't know poetry until she read it to him, who didn't know how to wear cuffs and cuff links until she taught him, and whose vulgarity was crass and total.

I have long ago given up the search for rationality in the ways of lovers. The fact that they are irrational is exactly the point of the nature of love.

Yet I am not too surprised to find Alice falling desperately in love with Lyndon. She was no idiot, but a sophisticated woman with life experience. She had a chance to study Lyndon for some time before they became lovers. He had an ungainly attractiveness of his own and a confidence in his sexuality. His very innocence of poetry and philosophy and the graces of life made him malleable material to be taught and nurtured.

The real question may run in the opposite direction: How could Lyndon, with all his wariness, secrecy, self-concentration, have flung himself into a dangerous liaison with a woman he couldn't use or dominate as he did Lady Bird and everyone else?

The fact that he did give himself suggests a dimension of passion and risk-taking that we have been reluctant to recognize in him. He had a Himalayan hunger for power, but he also had a hunger to be loved and to count. Alice Glass was like no woman he had ever known.

In her own world she counted, even more than he did in his. To possess such a woman was the ultimate validation of self, and worth all the power he risked for her. There is little evidence, thus far, of how strongly he loved her in turn, but one must infer from the risks he took that he did.

Was this only a little interlude of lyrical passion, which in the end could not prevail over the pull of power, and which shouldn't change our basic perception of Johnson's character? I don't think so. When we get acquainted with the scoundrel-politician as lover, and find that he is less of a scoundrel and more of a lover than we had reason to expect, it should shake the confidence of the "undiluted scoundrel" school. The intense phase of it happened early in his life, but it sheds a strong light on who and what he became. The Johnson I talked with, and even more the Johnson whom Doris Kearns describes in her *Lyndon Johnson and the American Dream*—a prime document in assessing him—was not wholly unrelated to the Johnson of the Alice Glass romance.

Along with his power-hunger, linked with his father Sam Johnson, Lyndon—boy and man—had a culture-hunger, linked with his mother, Rebekah. He was able to sate the first drive but never came close to sating the second. It was never certain that he would attend college, and when he did it was a third-rate college and didn't count for him. He never got over it and never made it with the gentry.

His scorn and envy for the liberal elite—supremely of the Kennedys and their claque—grew into a dominating force in his life. His father was a failed politician and land speculator; the son became a summit politician and a ranch owner. But while the son fulfilled his father's dream, he failed to fulfill his mother's.

He was no ideologist and no "issues" politician. The terms *liberal* and *conservative* meant little to him. Running for Congress, he could be a "100 percent Roosevelt" man, and running for the Senate he could distance himself from FDR and Washington. He was concrete-minded, a resultist, or "can do" man. And while he never lost sight of Lyndon Johnson's self-interest there was a measure of caring in him—for the Mexican-Americans like the students in the Southwest Texas Teachers College, for the blacks he knew in the Texas cities, for the people near the base of the pyramid whom he had passed on his slippery-pole ascent to the pyramid's pinnacle.

He associated power—life's hard element—with getting to the top, he associated "culture"—life's soft element—with doing something for these people, in an area of life in which he didn't himself shine. Which was why he saw himself (and it was not mere rhetoric) as an "education president," and why he carried civil rights and voting rights for blacks far beyond what the Kennedys had been able to do.

This is where his mother, Rebekah Johnson, belonged, where his wife, Lady Bird, belonged, and—supremely—where Alice Glass belonged.

He always aspired to women who gave some "class to his life." As a youth he had wooed the daughter of the richest man in town. Lady Bird was several rungs above him on the social ladder when he wooed and won her, and she worked harder and more effectively at the culture ladder than he did. When she learned of Tolstoy's *War and Peace* she not only read it but read it twice. Although their marriage was rocky, it was a true pairing of life partners, not without elements of constancy even on Lyndon's part.

Alice Glass was the sex dream and culture dream suddenly made real. She was the mistress of a magical world of literature, music, architecture, landscape, art. He couldn't lord over her as he had over other women. Did he feel about her as he had felt about his mother, who lit her own little flame of culture in the wasteland of Southwest Texas? It is more than possible.

Lyndon must have poured out to her his dreams, not only of political power but of social meliorism, and we can only conjecture that she responded. But marriage was another matter. Alice and Lyndon talked of his getting a divorce, and of marriage, but however much Lyndon may have reveled in the excitement of the unaccustomed world Alice offered him, a divorce would wreck his political career, and clearly he was not about to do that.

So the dream didn't come true. Lyndon ran for the Senate in 1940, barely missed it, felt dejected by his defeat, but went off to war and returned for a second try at the Senate. And won. Alice married Charles Marsh, divorced him, and married again. She and Lyndon got together again in a turbulent relationship. It didn't end until Alice, outraged at the Vietnam War, broke it off for good.

The picture isn't complete without Doris Kearns, who in the 1960s was a young Harvard political scientist on a government fellowship in Washington. Johnson took a shine to her, and tried to use her as biographer to ensure his proper place in history. She saw his ploy and refused. But he came to trust and need her. It was no erotic affair, but (as she has recounted in her *Lyndon Johnson and the American Dream*) he would come early mornings to the room she used in the

White House and curl up in her bed like a little boy, while she sat beside it, and pour out his childhood memories, dreams, heartbreaks to her.

This was the Johnson who talked as pleadingly as he did to me at the time of the Têt offensive. The pathos of Doris Kearns's Johnson was of a man who had not only lost his way in the Vietnam slough of despond but had also lost his world—and more than his political world. He was still trying to keep it from unraveling and slipping through his fingers, to manage it by organizing his position in history.

Placing Doris Kearns's account alongside the Alice Glass story, each illumines the other. Doris was another young and fascinating culture carrier for him, as had been the glittering woman whom he had won and finally lost. But if he could control this one, he could control his world and history beyond the grave.

THE ARDORS
AND TRIBULATIONS
OF THE JOURNEY
OF LIBERALISM

I OFFER A POLITICAL AND INTELLECTUAL CONUNDRUM: How did it happen that the creed of liberalism, which sat so high on the wall for two-thirds of the century, through the 1960s, should have suffered so great a fall since then? Will all the royal horses and men that form the support system of liberalism ever put this Humpty Dumpty together again?

I use liberalism in its broadest sense, as an angle of vision from which to view the world, politically, socially, and culturally. It is this vision that made it at once appealing and vulnerable at crunch points in its history.

Yet there is no way to grasp liberalism as pure idea isolated from its embodiment in partisan politics, institutions, leaders, and electoral triumphs and defeats. Retrospectively, while other terms were used at the time, its American linkage goes back to the philosophy and vision of Thomas Jefferson and James Madison, just as the conservative philosophy and vision go back to Madison (again), Alexander Hamilton, and John Adams. Twentieth-century American liberalism has been linked with social reform on a wide front, with the Democrats as a party, and with specific presidents and presidential candidates, starting with Woodrow Wilson and Franklin D. Roosevelt and ending with the failed candidacies of George McGovern, Walter Mondale, and Michael Dukakis.

"The Ardors and Tribulations of the Journey of Liberalism" appeared in *The World & I* (January 1990).

Most recently, many had the sense of a watershed event when, in the 1988 campaign, George Bush escalated his attacks on "the L-word." Even more notable than the attack on liberalism was the fact that few stalwarts in public life rallied to its defense. It was not a glory point in the history of liberalism as a standard to raise and a drumbeat to march to.

If we ask when the liberal idea and vision were at their apex, the answer would have to be the years of FDR's New Deal and the postwar decades that followed. As it happens I had a chance recently to go back to a polemical book on liberalism in the 1930s that I published a half-century ago, and rethink it from today's perspective. Taking a hard second look at this phase of liberalism's history, I felt a shock of recognition.[1]

Playing Aristotle's "political animal," we must all make an intellectual and moral journey and give some account of it. I came of age politically in the middle and late 1920s. All the writers I had read at college and graduate school, from Shelley and Byron through Charles Beard, Vernon Parrington, Louis D. Brandeis, Randolph Bourne, John Reed, and Thorstein Veblen, were liberals and radicals. The winds of doctrine that swept through American politics, history, law, and sociology from the turn of the century were liberal winds, and they swept with the gusto of a second American intellectual renaissance. They infused both major parties with a "progressivism" that turned the politics of Theodore Roosevelt and Woodrow Wilson into variations on a common theme. In domestic policy both presidents were reformers. In foreign policy both saw an America that had to play a leadership role on a stage larger than America itself.

The climate of the twenties was bleak for liberals, who recoiled from the crass nationalism of the Republican boom years, wondering whether they would ever recover the vision of internationalist hope that had foundered with the folly of Versailles and Wilson's last years. It was not until the panic of 1929 and the Great Depression that they saw a prospect of regaining national power, under whatever flag or label.

The collapse of the economy did much to undercut their faith in both capitalism and democracy. In 1932 too many liberal intellectuals, not only in the great Eastern centers but also across the nation, en-

---

[1]Max Lerner, *It Is Later Than You Think: The Need for a Militant Democracy* (Viking Press, 1938).

gaged in a dangerous flirtation with Marxism as a system of interpreting the world and Communist revolution as a mystique.

Commentaries on liberalism run the danger of being short-range and blinkered, of missing the perspective of liberalism's long history in Europe as well as America. When the L-word stories broke in 1988 the media were awash with accusations and recriminations. It was as if liberalism had been newly minted, to be accepted or rejected like any artifact of the market. There were no follow-up inquiries into the intellectual and moral history of the complex of attitudes it embodied.

The fact is that, like many ideas in human history, liberalism was shaped in the travail of centuries of economic and social struggle. It was hammered out in the same fiery smithy from which capitalism, socialism, and democracy emerged.

Liberalism defined broadly emerged in Europe (in the sixteenth through the nineteenth centuries) as a liberating idea of freedom from the restraints of institutions grown rigid and oppressive—feudalism, the church, the monarchy, the mercantilist economy. It expressed the striving of new capitalist and middle classes in every society for the assertion of every phase of the individual's selfhood—of his conscience, his use of his reason and personal experience, his ideas and opinions, his energies and talents, his artistic expression, his property, his efforts to better himself and his position in life, his relations to his family, his fellows, his government, and his God.

Seen thus the liberal vision of life—it was no less—was an electrifying force as it swept through Europe. When the old institutions resisted it broke their bounds, reached across the ocean, and found a more hospitable intellectual and social terrain in America. Thus the liberal unsettlement of Europe was resolved by the liberal settlement of America—but in a new mold, within a new equilibrium.

The American—the "new man"—went back to the ancient world for models of "Republican virtue," carried over the European liberal's idea of freedom from institutional restraints, and fused it with a passion not only for equality but with practical, effective government and cautiously balanced powers.

There was room in that yeasty mix for Jefferson's "the earth belongs to the living," but also for Washington's prudent conservatism, Hamilton's "energetic government," and Madison's "checks and balances." It was a new entity that came to be called "democracy." By the time young Alexis de Tocqueville came to America to study it, during

Andrew Jackson's presidency, he became convinced that the world and its future were fated by Providence to embrace it.

Given this perspective, it is critical to note that *liberalism* as a term played little role in the American consciousness until the second half of the nineteenth century. Yet elements of its vision were embodied in the passionate issues by which America was rent—the divisive ones of slavery and freedom, of secession and union, which were not resolved until the Civil War.

It was only when the survival of the Union was assured that the "liberal tradition in America," as Louis Hartz calls it, reasserted itself.[2] Over the decades its specific names varied. With Carl Schurz and E. L. Godkin's struggles against political corruption, the independent liberals were called "Goo-Goos" (for Good Government) and "Mugwumps." During Tom Watson and William Jennings Bryan's era they were called populists. The politicians and intellectuals from Wisconsin and the West Coast saw themselves as progressives. The journalist Herbert Croly, and after him Theodore Roosevelt, spoke of the "New Nationalism," and Louis D. Brandeis and Woodrow Wilson of the "New Freedom."

It was a variegated group, with only a few shared strains to unite them. There was no national party in America to call itself "Liberal," as in England, and only a few serious political thinkers. It was only in 1914 that a magazine, *The New Republic*, called itself "a journal of liberal opinion." Taken as a whole the reform groups achieved many good concrete things, especially in domestic social legislation.

I have noted their strengths. Their weakness emerged more sharply in the 1920s, with the backlash against Wilsonian internationalism, when their idealistic sense of the larger world around them seemed to end. Many turned pacifist and isolationist. Politics became for them a Heartbreak House.

These "reform" liberals—pre–New Deal and later anti–New Deal—felt righteous in what they condemned, but, in their domestic program, it was hard to discover what they stood for. In their stress on

---

[2]Louis Hartz, *The Liberal Tradition in America* (Harcourt, Brace & World, 1962). For some of my efforts in the intellectual history of liberalism, see "Liberalism's Family Tree," in my *Ideas are Weapons* (Viking Press, 1939, 343–47), a review piece on Harold J. Laski's *The Rise of European Liberalism* (1936). See also my article on liberalism in the Encyclopaedia Britannica, 13th edition. For liberalism in American thought, see my *America as a Civilization* (1957; new ed. Holt, 1987, 720–31), and, more specifically, chapter I, "Lament for the Liberal" in *It Is Later Than You Think*.

purity they lost the capacity to govern. In their stress on ideal means they lost sight of attainable ends. In their fear of governmental power they seemed to embrace powerlessness as a virtue. In making a cult of reform they abandoned the cohesive strength of tradition. In their pre-occupation with the gadgetry of governmental change they lost sight of the deep wisdoms of society as an organism.

In their revolt against past codes they turned to a moral relativism that stripped standards of their meaning in a democracy of values. "The trouble with us reformers," wrote J. Allen Smith, "is that we made reform a crusade against standards. Well, we smashed them all, and now neither we nor anybody else have anything left." It was a cry of liberal disillusionment that was to be uttered even more wrenchingly after the high point of liberal relativism in the 1960s.

The conservatives fared no better in the ethical climate of the 1920s. They suffered not from relativism but from a corruption of values in a boom period of greed that spilled over into political scandals under Warren Harding and his White House "gang." Calvin Coolidge's Puritan constraint and Herbert Hoover's Quaker commitment got a majority validation from the voters, but the negative assessment they got from the liberal thunderers in the academies is the one that has lasted. When the market crash hit Wall Street and the Great Depression hit Main Street—and Herbert Hoover failed to grapple with them head-on—the American people joined the professors in their condemnation.

Yet it was not clear what they were condemning. Was it the Republicans in power, meeting greed and collapse with no weapon other than the doctrine of laissez-faire individualism? Or was it capitalism as a total system? Or perhaps even democracy itself?

This was a critical point for the liberal intellectuals, who had shaped an accepted political culture under TR and Wilson and had shown courage in the fight for civil liberties during the postwar hysteria. They had now to confront their sharpest crisis, one that tested their nerve and coolness under heavy fire from thought systems of the right and left: fascism, which derided democracy; and Communism, which meant to hasten—as well as predict—the death of capitalism and bourgeois democracy.

The sorry fact is that the liberal intellectuals suffered a failure of nerve. Hundreds of teachers, writers, and artists signed a public declaration of support for the Browder-Ford Communist ticket in the 1932 presidential election, turning that document into a kind of Communist manifesto exactly when democracy was in its direst peril. It was a craven abdication of belief in democracy and a witless transfer of loyalty to its direct antithesis.

I was at the time an editor of the *Encyclopedia of the Social Sciences* and had been carrying on a fiery dialogue with several colleagues who were sympathetic to the Communist promise. I knew the pressures they were under, given our fierce antifascism and the siren insistence that only the steely power of the Communist faith could overcome the fascist Yahoos. The reception of Marxist theory in America was at its zenith and its seductions were great. And many liberal intellectuals were not sturdy enough to resist it.

In one sense the importance of Franklin Roosevelt lay as much in what he did in salvaging and turning around the liberal political culture as in what he did in energizing the nation. He sensed intuitively that his best chance of sustaining his structural administrative reforms lay through the liberal media and campus elites—the "Brains Trust," the brilliantly managed press conferences, the carefully calculated "fireside chats."

Yet a segment of the liberal culture—whether Republican "Progressives" or Reform Democrats—resisted his programs strongly. When I became political editor of *The Nation*, a liberal weekly, the man who came to symbolize that segment for me was its former editor and owner, Oswald Garrison Villard. There were some important causes he and his group cared about—Negro rights, woman suffrage, prison reform, "good government." But they remained causes for liberals, as they did for a large segment of the old liberal persuasion.

Their causes never added up to either a philosophy or a program. They resisted the rising power of the trade unions in their efforts to become a political force. They believed in political virtue more than in energetic government. They agonized over the victims of "American imperialism" at the turn of the century but feared any encounter with the "Thousand Year Reich" that Hitler had proclaimed. They shied away from any move toward collective security. They were too isolationist to fling down a challenge to either Nazi expansionism or that of the Japanese warlords, and too pacifist to wage a war if there were no alternatives.

They feared "demagogues" like FDR more than they feared inaction, insisting on a weak state when only a strong state could confront both the Depression and the dictators. They espoused a liberalism not of triumphant but of lost causes, and they gloried in defeats in which they had refused to surrender their "principles." They willed ends without willing the means to achieve them. "A purpose to them," I wrote with youthful disdain, "is like a work of art meticulously carved in butter."[3] Even in those early days they struck me as already old, weighted down with their paleoliberalism. Above all, they had lost the "tough-mindedness" that William James—himself a turn of the century liberal—demanded in an overall world view.

Looking back, it is clear that part of FDR's task of renewal was to replace this passive, pacifist, isolationist liberalism with a feistier brand—a "militant democracy," as I called it. FDR was one of the first presidents to use the term *liberal* outright to describe himself and his programs, although he sometimes called it *liberal progressivism* to reach the traditional progressives he was wooing.

The trouble was that FDR himself was not nearly as militant in his global policies as he was in domestic ones. Beset by isolationists of both the left and right, he sought refuge in the rhetoric of futile efforts at "peace" and the politics of appeasement. It hobbled his effectiveness as a world leader and kept him from the joint action with Western Europe and Russia that was the urgent necessity. Writing in 1937, I ventured that unless such action came about there would be a war within two years. Nothing was done and war came in 1939.[4]

To use a diurnal metaphor for the history of the liberal political culture, its experience under TR, Wilson, and FDR may be reckoned the morning of its young, blossoming energies. FDR gave it a new direction and turned it—at least in his domestic New Deal—toward a political reality principle. It took him longer—too long—to reach a similar tough-mindedness about Hitler, and he never reached it about Stalin.

That may be a commentary on the political culture within which he functioned as well as on him. In retrospect this tragically belated struggle of liberalism with its own deeply isolationist drives may have been necessary to prepare the political culture for the war and the postwar testings that were to come.[5]

---

[3]"Lament for the Liberal," in *It Is Later Than You Think*.

[4]For some reflections on this phase of liberalism's history see my afterword to the new edition of *It Is Later Than You Think* (Transaction, 1989).

[5]The best study of the liberal presidential tradition is Alonzo L. Hamby, *Liberalism and its Challengers: FDR to Reagan* (Oxford University Press, 1984), written from the vantage point of a liberal but with critical sympathy. Hamby studies the latter day "exhaustion" of liberalism and (with Reagan) the emergence of a "neoconservatism."

The period from Roosevelt's death in 1945 through Kennedy's in 1963 was liberalism's bright noonday. It built on FDR's domestic initiatives and consolidated them, yet stopped short of instituting a welfare state. Its major achievement lay in foreign policy. Trying to turn FDR's Yalta blunder around, the liberal policy makers built on the "coalition" principle he had used in the war, transforming it into a set of alliances that became a Western imperium.

Of the three presidents in this phase, Truman and Kennedy were liberal Democrats, while Eisenhower was a moderate Republican. In domestic politics, liberalism's movement toward a welfare state was inexorable, characterizing even Eisenhower's moderate administration. On the plane of foreign policy, Truman, Eisenhower, and Kennedy sustained a remarkable continuity of policy in fashioning the Western imperium. Yet under all three the liberal political culture played a more negative than positive role. It was the presidents themselves who had to assert their vision and move beyond the constraints of that culture.

Although liberals now claim Truman as part of the great liberal tradition, they were his consistent adversaries, preferring Henry Wallace as a running mate for FDR in 1944. During his presidency they condemned his Hiroshima bomb decision, were grudging about his remarkable civil rights record, and were even skeptical about the Marshall Plan and NATO, which they viewed as provocations to the Soviets. They fought his 1948 nomination and split their vote between him and Henry Wallace's Progressive Party candidacy, all but denying Truman his hard-fought victory against Thomas Dewey. They were unhappy with American intervention to save South Korea and were appeased only by Truman's courageous dismissal in 1951 of General Douglas MacArthur, who commanded United Nations forces in Korea.

In short, what happened under Harry Truman in containing Soviet power and rebuilding Western Europe was due more to the hard sense of the rough-hewn president than to his liberalism or to the liberal culture.

The liberal presidential canon today has it that FDR laid the foundation for the liberal tradition and that Harry Truman—standing on the shoulders of the giant—"consolidated" it. But in fact Truman was less a consolidator than a mover and changer in his own right. In foreign policy at least it is truer to say that he picked what was usable in FDR's positions and decisions, undid his blundering ones, and gave the nation a hardier and more creative direction.

To test this one has only to ask what would have happened had Henry Wallace, the candidate who was more in sync with FDR's liberal heritage, been his successor. Truman's election was a turning point in which Machiavelli's *fortuna*—the element of sheer chance in history—played an unmistakable role.

The task Truman faced was how to hold on to Roosevelt's electoral coalition while radically changing America's relations with FDR's wartime coalition of allies and its enemies. Truman barely succeeded in his first objective, managing by verve and sheer grit to nose out a 1948 victory with diminished liberal support. His success in the second was resounding. He established a new foreign-policy realism as an enduring model for liberal moderates and moderate liberals to sustain.

Truman refused to impose a Draconian peace on Germany, avoiding the perils of Versailles—the grisly postwar consequences that had Hitler as an end product. He brought America's two major enemies—Germany and Japan—into the community of lawful nations, made Germany a NATO ally and Japan America's chief Asian ally, and helped set both on the path to more effective democracy and greater economic power. With far-sighted generosity, Truman helped an exhausted and war-torn Western Europe with the Marshall Plan aid it needed to begin its postwar recovery and bind together in a defensive military alliance in NATO. Determined to test the Soviet long-range intent and finding it expansionist, with the whole of Europe as its immediate target, he initiated a policy of political containment and nuclear deterrence. Recognizing Israel at the start of its statehood—against determined State Department opposition—and extending aid to it in a close relationship, Truman made that nation a key ally in the Mideast.

The remarkable thing is not only that this was done under Truman in the key stretch from 1945 to 1953 but also that it endured in its main outlines for more than forty years. Presidents of both parties, starting with Eisenhower and Kennedy, followed its basic structural thrust, until the changes in Soviet internal and foreign policy under Gorbachev crowned the Truman-initiated era with success.

Remarkably this policy was sustained for more than fifteen years under two men as different as Truman and Eisenhower—one a failed businessman and county administrator, the other an army professional. Truman's education beyond high school was minimal, Eisenhower's mostly military. Each endured a seemingly endless period of uncertain activity, with his energies unused, until he could find his true "place in life," as Truman put it. Once arrived there, both showed an impressive capacity for adaptation, growth, and learning; and both were lucky—especially Truman—in the men who gathered around them as advisers, most of them Establishment members.

In a vivid metaphor, Truman's key adviser, Dean Acheson, spoke in his memoir of being "present at the creation" of the postwar order. He was the leader of a close-knit little phalanx in high policy-making posts, a band of brothers who worked in close complicity with Truman to change history.

They are now finally seen as the "wise men" they were, neither liberals nor conservatives but a mixed bag of professionals—a pair of lawyers, a pair of bankers, a pair of career diplomats—who were clear-eyed about Stalin and the Soviet Union and how to deal with the challenge they posed.[6] They worked closely with Republican Senator Arthur Vandenburg to shape a bipartisan foreign policy. Across the Atlantic they found a cluster of equally realistic leaders in Jean Monnet, Robert Schuman, Konrad Adenauer, and Alciade de Gasperi. On both continents they formed a coalition of liberals and conservatives, bound together in the best blending of both traditions.

Breaking the twenty-year stretch of Democratic hegemony in the White House, Eisenhower's moderate conservatism in domestic policy diverged from Truman's domestic liberalism. Certainly his indirect, wily foreign-policy style was sharply different from Truman's straightforward openness. But beyond styles there was a striking continuity between them. Together they were the two great architects of the postwar order, and in that sense its two great statesmen.

In his military roles both during and after the war, Eisenhower had come to know most of the world's leaders, had taken their measure, and did not need to parade a high profile. He left that to John Foster Dulles, his secretary of state, who belonged to the same Eastern Establishment as Truman's "wise men" but cut a more openly belligerent figure.

Yet while the confrontational rhetoric of "brinkmanship" was Dulles's—and it drove the liberal Democrats to a high pitch of hostile frustration—Ike's "hidden hand presidency" always allowed him to re-

---

[6]Walter Isaacson and Evan Thomas, *Wise Men: Six Friends and the World They Made* (Touchstone Books, 1981). I add that Truman, with only a high-school education, was a "closet intellectual" (the phrase is William V. Shannon's) and West Point had given Eisenhower a base in diplomacy as well as strategy.

main in control. He rounded out the alliance with Germany and Japan begun under Truman. He ended Truman's Korean War and never got America into a comparable one. True, he was outshouted by Nikita Khrushchev in public appearances, especially in the failed Paris "summit." Yet he achieved the broad purposes of containment and deterrence, kept American defense expenditures low, and was able in his farewell address to warn against the "military-industrial complex"— and get away with it.

In the long perspective of America's world position, FDR, Truman, and Eisenhower may be seen as a fateful triad of leaders. FDR's stature rests in the end on his denying to Hitler his claim to establish his destructive world order. Truman and Ike together managed to deny to the Communist powers, in Europe and Asia, their claim to build a world order that would rival and displace the West with a totally different ethos and with a new "Communist man" as its carrier. Yet all three had to do it against the resistance of the liberal political culture, which was dragged kicking and screaming through the second third of the twentieth century.

Recent historians have depicted the Truman-Eisenhower decades as an era of American world hegemony, or (in Henry Luce's phrase) as the foundation for an "American century." There is a sense in which the two presidents did build a new Western imperium. I distinguish *imperium* from *empire*, since it involves a number of nations freely joined in a collective goal and good, with one as *primus inter pares—* first among equals. But the more acceptable term than either hegemony or imperium is a *Western community of nations*, which kept the possibilities open for a world community of free peoples.

From another perspective the two presidents, even in the temper of their domestic policies, also shared a common quality: that of social and political equilibrium. "Things fall apart, the center does not hold," wrote Yeats. Neither president had it easy in his brand of domestic moderation and international strength. Truman had General MacArthur to contend with, Eisenhower had Senator Robert Taft, and both had Senator Joseph McCarthy. Both presidents were able to prevail because both were committed to a center that would hold, within America and through America within the Western imperium.

John Kennedy's "New Frontier" built domestically on the liberalism of Truman's "Fair Deal" but did not in substance go much beyond it. His inaugural address made it clear that he would be as hard-nosed in confronting Soviet expansionism as Truman and Eisenhower, and just as committed to containment and deterrence.

Yet in the perception of his liberal supporters Kennedy brought with him a new liberal dimension. For one, he offered them a generational politics like no one before him. He brought the message that a new generation had taken over, and that what was young and new was for that reason better, that it saw the challenge of social change more freshly and would be more resourceful in meeting it.

The result was a celebration of generational politics as a new icon of dynamic liberalism. But this sort of dynamism had unforeseen consequences in the highlighting of the "generation gap" and—before the decade was over—in a "New Left," which came to regard Kennedy's young liberalism as antiquated.

During his too brief tenure the young president—along with his brother Robert and wife, Jacqueline—brought "style" to the White House. Every president has a style, for better or worse, but it became stylish for his liberal admirers to speak of Kennedy's "style" as if he had invented the term. It meant the investment of power with elegance and "class" and an insouciant lightness of mood. The Kennedy style meant the presence of Robert Frost to grace the Inaugural ceremony, linking poetry with power, the aging Virgil with the young Caesar. There was style in the speeches, state papers, and press conferences. If any of them got too high-flown there were always Jack's self-deprecating throwaway lines to keep things deflated and acceptable.

With this came the sharpest perception since FDR of the presidential persona as a complement to his liberalism. On this score too Kennedy set a standard difficult for Lyndon Johnson and Jimmy Carter to follow, and even more difficult for the failed liberal candidates. If Kennedy was the first liberal president after FDR to attract support through his charisma, to move people's hearts and stir their minds, he was also the last.

It was the intellectuals who were most attracted to him. A "new class" was emerging in America, broadly defined by vocations and professions that dealt with symbols. It was natural for those who made their living and careers by symbols, whether in words or on film or TV, whether in classroom, courtroom, salesroom, or even boardroom, to be drawn to the symbol maker with the highest profile. The fact that he was fashioning a new liberalism made liberals of them in turn.

He had himself made use of symbols masterfully in his rapid rise to the presidency—with both grace and ruthlessness. In a sense he reinvented liberalism, not in his policies (which were in substance moderate) but in his words, style, and appeal. He invested it with the incandescent glow of his dynamism, in the service of what the liberals held dear—change, youth, surprise, compassion, boldness, and an egalitarianism that did not exclude his own wealth.

It was an attraction the "new class"—or "knowledge class"—could not resist, and they became the new carriers of liberalism. Since they had been trained in the universities and had fanned out from them, they formed an intellectual culture that became increasingly politicized. This new class went beyond FDR's "Brains Trust" to fashion a political, media, and campus elite that has retained its power since—and grown rigid with that power.

It was the sunny afternoon of American liberalism. In that glow the liberals swallowed some policies and events that—coming from any other president—would have been unpalatable. There was the botched invasion of Cuba, the failed Vienna summit with Khrushchev, the building of the Berlin Wall, which elicited no American response, the training of counterinsurgency forces as a phase of the Cold War, and the start of a hot one in Vietnam, particularly the bloody way in which South Vietnamese president Ngo Dinh Diem and his brother Ngo Dinh Nhu were killed with the knowledge of the president. There was also the blood feud with Castro that shadowed his whole tenure, sparking eerie CIA efforts to assassinate the Cuban dictator. But Kennedy also revealed a deep character flaw, which turned the White House into a Deer Park, an excess of *machismo* and libertinism that would have been unacceptable in any president with less liberal brio. In that sense Kennedy anticipated the more widespread permissiveness of the sexual revolution that ended his decade and began the next.

Through it all he learned and grew. He came to understand the depth of rage in the consciousness of blacks, and he was quick to forge links with the prophetic politics of civil rights that Martin Luther King, Jr. represented. He also learned to stand up to Khrushchev's bullying. He overcame his inexperience by working at a perception of reality that his telescoped political education had skipped. He replaced his passivity about the Berlin Wall with his eloquent identification with the German outpost (*Ich bin ein Berliner*). And he even made up for the Bay of Pigs by his more mature and disciplined handling of the Cuban missile crisis. By the time he was assassinated he had become a true president, a capable leader beyond the style, persona, and generational hubris that his own political culture had shaped.

His administration formed a bridge between two Americas—the equilibrium America of Truman and Eisenhower and the tumultuous alienated pressure-group America of Lyndon Johnson. But his importance in the iconography of American liberalism is greater than his importance in the history of the presidency. It flowed from the kind of man and president he was; but even more it flowed from the needs of the liberal culture and from the way both Kennedys—John and Robert—served those needs both in death and in life.

The fate of both Kennedys had as tragic a dimension as any event in presidential history since Lincoln. As an American version of the fall of the House of Atreus it merited something better than the false romantics of "Camelot." If the post-Kennedy loyalists had grasped this tragic dimension they might have used it for a structure of liberal power as sustaining as the Republican tenure after Lincoln's death, all the way to Wilson. In fact they did not. During Lyndon Johnson's time they put their accent on the ways in which both Kennedys differed from Johnson in terms of persona, style, and generational politics. Since then, through the 1970s and '80s, they have shown an unreadiness to understand the contradictions that both Kennedy's and Johnson's liberalism contained, and an unwillingness to resolve them and build on the insights of growth and maturity that Kennedy showed before his death.

The contradictions are now clear enough. The showy gestures of Kennedy's brand of dynamism triggered an acceleration of individual fanaticism and group passions, which exploded, first in the president's death and five years later in his brother's. After Jack's assassination, in deep grief and embitterment, Bobby went further than his brother would ever have gone—embracing a sharper generational politics of more egalitarian compassion, a politics of the streets.

Out of his hatred for both Kennedys, Lyndon Johnson sought to outdo Jack's record. He went further on civil rights and black voting, further on "education" and "Great Society" subsidies, and further on the Vietnam War. FDR too had set accelerations of liberalism in motion in his first two terms, but the discipline of the war enabled him to control them. Had Jack Kennedy lived, he might also have controlled them. As for Johnson, given both the nature of the Great Society he was championing and the demons of the kind of war he was waging, he could not control either. Each fed on the other and both metastasized.

I was in Paris when Kennedy was murdered in Dallas and I recall the rage that swept through Europe in those first hours, notably in the conviction that it must have been the act of a man of the right, especially in conservative Texas. As it turned out, both Kennedys were killed by mavericks of the left, who were the product of the passions that the Kennedy and Johnson accelerations of liberalism set in motion. The genii were out of the bottle. One doesn't have to resort to a Hegelian dialectic to understand that the very splendors of Kennedy liberalism contained within themselves the seed of their own destruction.

During the 1960s, from Jack Kennedy's death to the street battles of the Chicago Democratic Convention, American liberalism went through its fiery crucible of testing. There have been diverse accounts of the sixties and the impact they had on American life. Their impact on liberalism was devastating, not least because liberalism did not face its testings more sturdily, with greater courage of conviction and commitment to its original vision in Europe and America. The failure of nerve it suffered was even greater than the failure in the early 1930s, before the New Deal.

We cannot roll history back and rerun it. But we can rethink its myth of inevitability. The record is one of the storming of university buildings, the show of guns on the campus, the scorn for trusting "anyone over thirty," the contempt for the rule of law, the flight from the rule of rationality, the scuttling of the liberal philosophy by the New Left and of traditional liberal values by the counterculture, the flaunting of the ethic of "anything goes," the outrages inflicted on the symbols of morality, country, and religion. In the face of that record I have to ask what liberalism's history would have been if its professors, its writers, its artists, and its political and cultural spokesmen had condemned and resisted those who were destroying the liberal heritage, instead of joining them.

It is doubtless an idle speculation. Yet I am not so determinist as to believe that it had to be the way it was. The American version of *la trahison des clercs*—the treason of the intellectuals—had no inevitabilities in it. Week after week, as a commentator and historian, I watched the sixties unfold. At point after point its trajectory could have been deflected, curbed, or redirected, if the vision and courage had been there to rescue a great tradition from enemies masquerading as friends and benefactors. The vision and courage did not emerge.

When resistance finally came it was from ordinary people in the middle classes, who saw the danger to their country more clearly than its self-appointed guardians in universities, churches, and statehouses.

They said, "This far and no farther." They proved to be the warders of
the social contract. Yet the memory stayed with them of how close we
came to the dissolution of the social fabric of America. It was this,
more than anything else, that spelled the passing of liberalism's high
noon and late afternoon and the coming of the shades of evening.

How shall we explain and assess the twilight phase of liberalism's journey, from John Kennedy's death in 1963 to the defeat of Michael
Dukakis a quarter century later? The conventional wisdom of the neo-
conservatives, in history and political sociology, sees liberalism as
having doomed itself by the policies of the liberal society—by
ever-increasing spending and taxing, by redistributing incomes due to
pressure-group politics, by counterproductive affirmative actions, by
the "revolution of rising entitlements," by liberal judicial activism
since the Earl Warren Court, by well-intended public actions that did
not take account of the unintended consequences.

It is indictment by way of assessment, formidably argued, and on
its own level I have few quarrels with it. Yet I miss the weight that an
assessment of liberalism as a public philosophy might have given it. I
doubt whether the central wisdom about liberalism's latter-day trajectory lies in the issue-oriented "policy sciences," as Harold Lasswell
called them. When voters send liberal congressmen and state legislators back to their jobs in election after election, they are voting for liberal policies in terms of their perceived everyday practical affairs. On
that level policy-oriented liberalism is not dead, not even moribund.

It is in presidential politics, where voters take a longer view, that
the liberals have suffered repeated and intolerable defeats for two
decades. It is there that the sustained memories of national traumas
and triumphs are called into play. And it is there that issues and policies give way to attitudes and values.

This is not, I assert, a policy dimension. It is a dimension of the
perception of the past and of the direction into the future, a dimension
of the spirit. It is on that plane that long-range concerns—of justice,
fairness, well-being, family bonds, defense, country, even God—are
filtered through the spectrum of critical experience and get translated
into the values a man or woman can live by.

With values we move into philosophy, and with philosophy into
the liberal paradigm. I mean by that, as Thomas Kuhn does in studying the "structure of scientific revolutions," the liberal assumptions
about the nature of man and history, the individual, the state and soci-

ety, change and revolution, freedom and equality and justice, and power and order and how to exercise some control over both.

It is, I suggest, in its paradigm that liberalism as creed and vision at first succeeded and has since given unmistakable signs of failure. The metaphysic of promise on which it recruited generations of believers and nourished them has gone unfulfilled. Its underlying assumptions no longer seem to work.

I set down a number of these assumptions: That economic forces shape political man, instead of the other way around; that every emergency need in society can be resolved by appropriating adequate government funds for it; that, in economics, the public sector is always legitimate, the private always suspect; that the American conscience has been sullied by the past treatment of minorities, and atonement can have no end; that whatever goes wrong with anyone or anything, society must carry the guilt, and that the Emersonian philosophy of self-reliance and individual responsibility no longer applies; that the moral philosophy of justice rests on redistributive justice; that equality requires not equal access to opportunity but equality of result; that the procedural protection of the rights of criminals is more important than the substantive protection of the victim; that history speaks through social change, and it is the duty of judges to make the Constitution plastic enough to give them room to legislate; that national defense leads to war, hence patriotism is a dirty word; that it is always harder, whether in America or abroad, for the left to do wrong than the right; that a moral equivalence exists between the Communist world and the free world; that all values are relative in a kind of democracy of values, rendering value judgments futile; that in an impersonal universe of secular forces a personal God is dead, and there is no radical evil, but man is perfectible through social engineering; that dangers lurk in every technology but the task of government is to make life risk-free; and that American civilization is in decline and we have reached the end of American history as a Great Power.

While most liberals would reject one or another proposition in this recital of the liberal credo, few would fail to recognize its resonance in the liberal mind and faith. If that is so then these basic unexamined assumptions, taken together, exercised an unchallenged hegemony over the liberal mind in its latest phase.

Given their cult of change, the strange thing is that liberal intellectuals, during the 1970s and '80s, allowed their paradigm to be caught in an unchanging web, perhaps beyond escape. With polemical passion, Allan Bloom's *Closing of the American Mind* charged that the liberal campus intelligentsia had not only "failed democracy" by their rigidity but had "impoverished the souls" of those they taught and trained for citizenship in the American polis.

The indictment may be overstated, yet, despite a barrage of liberal responses, it may continue to dominate the discourse in the nineties. We are entering a decade that could define the debate over what central ideas should go into education and governance, and therefore into the formation of the American national character.

The '70s and '80s, in liberalism's history, may be seen as prelude and preparation for this debate. For Richard Nixon liberalism was the enemy to be fought by every means, overt and covert, but because his own crisis of character became the center of the struggle they distorted its true nature. Gerald Ford reverted to the moderate liberal Republicanism of Eisenhower as his model, with less distinction, while Jimmy Carter attempted a neoliberal revival, although it was left to others to articulate the neoliberal combination of the striving individualist brain with the social commitment of the compassionate heart.[7] It was only in the Reagan eighties that conservatives began in earnest to shape something like a conservative paradigm, to parallel the liberal one with mostly unexamined propositions of their own.[8]

Except for the Carter years it has been a long time since liberalism had a commanding role on the great stage of history. I have tried to trace the spoor that led to the major defeats and humiliations it suffered in its Time of Troubles. I may perhaps add one further clue.

It concerns the struggle at once for the brain and soul of America. In the early phase of liberalism, in the *saeculum mirabile* of seventeenth-century science and eighteenth-century Enlightenment, the middle and business classes in Europe and America embraced the scientific discoveries and technological advances of the time. They saw them as a chance to break the old habits of thought and make a new era for man possible.

In contrast, despite their absorption with "revolution," the liberal intellectual and political leaders failed to grasp the true American rev-

---

[7] I have elaborated on this in a chapter, "The New America 1957–1987" that I added to the new edition of *America as a Civilization* (Holt, 1987).

[8] For the neoliberal credo expressing the Carter Vision retrospectively, see Robert Bellah, *Habits of the Heart* (Harper and Row, 1985).

olutions in the past quarter-century, which changed the landscape of modern life. America's information and communication revolutions joined with its entrepreneurial and free-market revolution to reach to the farthest corners of the world. But these revolutions failed to engage the liberal consciousness. Nor did the religious revolution, with its rejection of secularism and its marked return to a sense of the sacral, stir liberals from the cocoon in which they dreamed of past ardors, heroes, and splendors.

Liberals remained trapped in their ingrained fear of new technology and its psychological and social impact, and in their disbelief that venture enterprise could be a major source of creativity. They paid more heed to the crudities of the religious revival than to its regenerative strength. Faced with a revolution of self-assertion in every area of consciousness and conduct, they saw only a cult of narcissism. Roosevelt and Kennedy in their time had wooed and won the young to liberalism. But its latter-day leaders bungled their chance with the technical, entrepreneurial, and religious young—and lost them.

Does liberalism have a future? The L-word itself has been damaged badly, less by George Bush's campaign attack than by the past excesses of the liberals themselves, which made such an attack credible. Strikingly, those who defended its honor in public, to restore its good name, were more likely to be knights of the press, the pulpit, and the blackboard than knights of the electoral corridors, who would be considered legitimate targets at the next election. It is a sign that much of the earlier élan of liberalism has been lost.

Yet liberalism as a historic creed and vision, over time, will continue as a force under whatever name. Reaching for a new banner, some will call themselves "neoliberal," some "moderate." I suspect there will be a strong return to the "progressivism" that flourished early in the century, before Roosevelt's New Deal gave "liberal" a new legitimacy. But the core vision will remain and perchance flourish again, since it expresses one of the polar currents of thought and feeling in men and women as political animals.

Whether it flourishes, or merely survives in a suspended state, depends on whether it can rebuild itself as an intellectual and moral system that responds to the great waves of revolutionary change.

We trace the deterioration of liberalism back to LBJ's Great Society and the welfare state entitlements, and to the assassinations, the street demonstrations, and the New Left of the sixties. They left liberalism with an intellectual base that needed rethinking and rebuilding—

which it did not get. The result was the loss of the presidency in five out of the past six presidential elections and a new set of Supreme Court and federal judges. Even in the House, they currently hold power not as liberals but as Democrats.

The intellectual rethinking and restructuring, when completed, will come later than we think, more likely in the next century than this. It needs starting, for the sake of conservatives as well, for a nation does not benefit from long-term, one-sided political representation. There are new immigrant groups to integrate and scientific and technological advances to be sustained, a competitive edge to be regained. There is order to be restored on drug-infested, crime-ridden streets and a system of justice enforcement to be rescued from procedural pettifogging and overcrowding. A new philosophy of education must likewise be contrived, out of resources from the information and media revolutions, and a new authority won for teachers. There are also family authority structures to be rebuilt, so that the precious seed corn can thrive, not be mutilated. Great diverging constitutional interests must be calibrated and ethical and moral codes clarified, involving reproduction, gender, and erotic relations. While there is world tension to be subdued, there is, as never before, a chance for the newly free world of open economies and polities to enlarge and strengthen its legal and moral community.

This cannot be done if one of the two great movements of political vision remains cut off from the reality of America and the world. Both must be vigorous rivals if they are to compete healthily for the common good.

PART II

A GALLERY
OF PRESIDENTS

FOREWORD

Although fascinated by figures who cast long shadows on the presidency—notably Thomas Jefferson and Abraham Lincoln—Max Lerner devoted his greatest attention to writing about presidents he watched from the 1930s until his death. In his role as a commentator, he followed contemporary political affairs closely. Yet he understood the limitations of deadline journalism and saw value in more extended, historical assessments. In several essays that follow, Lerner traces the "life history" or "life journey" of a president while also analyzing policies, decisions, character traits, and other aspects of "the whole person."

Concentrated attention on Richard Nixon's tumultuous years in the White House proved largely responsible for Lerner's preoccupation with the presidency during the last decades of his life. He saw Watergate as "a passion of the republic," devoting nearly a hundred columns to the subject and its significance to America. Several of these columns are published here.

In the early 1970s, Lerner occupied a place on the Nixon administration's "enemies list." In the 1980s while seeking rehabilitation in a campaign for history, Nixon made a point of keeping in contact with Lerner through correspondence, calls, and meetings. On one occasion he instructed an assistant to call Lerner about an exchange between himself and President Ronald Reagan. "'Ron, have you read Max Lerner this morning?'" Nixon said he inquired. To which Reagan replied: "'Yes, I've read him, Dick. I always read Max Lerner.'"

—R. S.

THOMAS JEFFERSON

AMERICA'S PHILOSOPHER-KING

ON MARCH 4, 1801, THOMAS JEFFERSON, attended by some friends, walked from Conrad and McMunn's boardinghouse, in the raw village called Washington, to the new Capitol. In a crowded Senate chamber, Chief Justice John Marshall, his old political enemy, swore him in as president. He was a tall, freckled, redheaded planter-scholar-aristocrat, with a loose-jointed figure, casually worn clothes, strong but kindly features, and an air of gentleness that belied the sharpness of purpose and will behind it. His inauguration marked the first peaceful succession of power from one party to another in a modern republic. But the power base itself was being shifted. What had started as an armed revolution against the British monarchy and had then become a constitutional government of the owning groups was now being completed by the peaceful revolution of 1800 against privilege and the dead hand of the past.

No wonder he had worked hard on his inaugural address, putting it through three drafts, polishing every sentence and phrase. His words were conciliatory in tone: "We are all republicans; we are all federalists." In his manuscript he put it in lowercase, meaning the principles of republicanism and federalism, not the parties. Yet the real theme of the address was Jefferson's vision of where the strength (or "energy") of the new American experiment lay—not in the idea of power but in the power of the idea of a self-governing republic, continually remaking itself by the will of the people.

He knew there were fears about him because he wanted to turn power back to the states, cut both government costs and taxes, reduce

Originally published in *Quest* (March/April 1977) and titled "The Real Mr. America," this essay is based on a book-length study, *Thomas Jefferson: America's Philosopher-King* (New Brunswick, NJ: Transaction, 1996), ed. Robert Schmuhl.

the army and navy, and retire the public debt. He had repeatedly said "Peace is my passion," which caused many to wonder whether he would expose the new nation naked to its enemies.

His answer was a ringing affirmation of the democratic potential. "I believe this . . . the strongest government on earth. I believe it to be the only one where every man, at the call of the laws, would fly to the standard of the law. . . . Sometimes it is said that man cannot be trusted with the government of himself. Can he, then, be trusted with the government of others? Or have we found angels in the form of kings to govern him? Let history answer the question."

Every new president starts, in his campaign, as a suppliant at the door of power and ends as a suppliant at the door of history, to learn how it will judge him. And history puts the old and ever new questions about him: how much power he wielded, and how; what he was like in mind, character, appetites, neuroses, psyche, vision; how many lives he blasted in war, how securely he built the peace. They are the old questions Freud took from the Greeks—of Eros and Thanatos.

There is a streak of Golden Age thinking in Americans, a cult of primitivism, which makes them dream of the early days as always the good ones. If anyone should have made a good president, it is the writer, thinker, and statesman who has come down through history as a demigod. Jefferson is the only philosopher-king America has had, unless we include the unschooled Abe Lincoln as a philosopher. He hated kings, yet for a time reigned as an uncrowned one. As revolutionary spokesman and as draftsman of the Declaration of Independence, as ambassador to France, as secretary of state under Washington, as party leader and polemicist, he was brilliantly effective. But put to the test of sustained power at the summit, he proved a great man but an indifferent president, a better philosopher than he was a king.

By his nature and conviction he was—in James David Barber's classification—a passive president rather than an active one, and an inward-looking one rather than an extrovert. His conception of the presidency was not the dynamic one that Roosevelt, Kennedy, and Johnson made familiar to our own time. It reached back—in his theory at least—to his basic philosophy.

His view of government and society was part of his view of the cosmos—that it had been formed all of a piece by a divine Intelligence and operated by the laws of Nature, that in the moral universe as well as the physical there were laws and principles that men must discover and live by. He had few illusions about man's essential goodness: "The lions and tigers are mere lambs compared with man as a destroyer." He saw man as predator and prey alike, but he saw governments—unless their tyranny was checked—as the embodiment of the predator. His remedy was a double one: to set limits on the powers and actions of the government, and to educate the people to resist the predators and escape being prey. This meant direct intervention by the people to narrow the powers of government and set up checks and balances on power.

Although he was a revolutionary, he did not believe that revolutions changed institutions. He thought they were not utopian but purgative: they could not create an ideal society, but they could get rid of obstructions from the past, and prevent old forms from hardening into tyrannical ones. Unlike Burke, he had little feel for tradition and the continuities of the social organism over time. This man, himself so deeply rooted in soil, family, party, state, nation, time, kept rootedness out of his political philosophy except in his aversion to cities. He felt, unlike the French *philosophes*, that the present owed no debts to the past and could make no claims on the future. Rarely has America had a thinker for whom the generational struggle was so crucial. He calculated a generational span as eighteen years and eight months, and felt that every generation had a right to pry away the dead hand of the past, start with a clean slate, and work out its own lines of development.

This left Jefferson open to a pragmatism that has marked liberalism in America ever since. It gave flexibility to one whose firm sense of principle might otherwise have turned him into a rigid doctrinaire.

In doctrine he did not believe in a strong executive power or an activist presidency; in practice he tried to hold sway over his administration—effectively in his first term, disastrously in his second. In doctrine he believed in construing the Constitution strictly; in practice, as the Louisiana Purchase showed, he used the Constitution flexibly enough to accommodate an "empire for liberty." In doctrine he was a champion of legislative supremacy; in practice he kept a tight rein on Congress through his party lieutenants in both houses, with whom he was in constant touch. In doctrine he saw a "happy variety of minds" as part of the scheme of creation; in practice, when the going got hard, he engineered the impeachment of judges in his first term and tried to harass and jail hostile editors in his second.

He played host to all the 138 congressmen at dinner, inviting them in groups of eight or ten from the same party every other day, so that usually (counting the diplomats and others) he had a dozen to eighteen guests. In the village of 3,000 that called itself the nation's capital, where the social life was sparse and bleak, an invitation to dine with the president was unlikely to be refused. The guests arrived around 3:30, when Congress was through for the day, chatted for a half hour, found places at the round table (there was no protocol: everything was done by "the principle of equality, or pele-mele"), and enjoyed a hearty dinner, with good and plentiful wine, and with conversation as the main course throughout.

There were no blessings at the start, no toasts were drunk, and talk of politics was discouraged at any time. The conversation ranged widely because the host, who led it, knew something about everything and everything about some things. The talk was of travel, crops, farming techniques, animals, music, cities, wines, literature, building, medicine, science, history, fossils, wars, revolutions. "You never can be an hour in this man's company," wrote John Quincy Adams in his diary, "without something of the marvelous." Later President Kennedy, during a dinner for Nobel Prize winners, called his guests the most extraordinary collection of talents ever gathered at the White House, "with the possible exception of when Thomas Jefferson dined alone." The tribute was generous and graceful, but scarcely factual, since Jefferson so rarely dined alone.

His dinners were a costly burden to him, but they were also an intellectual delight, an arena for the quiet and effortless display of everything he knew and had done, everyone he had met. Although they were nonpolitical in tone, they were in the deepest sense political—a way of holding his party in Congress together, while undercutting some of the attacks on him that were mounting in the Federalist press.

Although a deeply convinced pacifist, Jefferson came to believe in extending America's "empire for liberty" on its own continent. Dreaming of an American empire of his own, Napoleon had forced a declining Spanish monarchy to cede to him the immense, vaguely outlined Mississippi Valley. This set in motion strong pressures on Jefferson from the frontier settlers, who needed New Orleans as a transshipping port for their products. Jefferson sent James Monroe to Paris to talk about buying New Orleans and west Florida, but before he arrived, Napoleon—his forces decimated in Santo Domingo—had decided to move his imperial ambitions toward the East rather than America, and Talleyrand offered to sell the whole of the Louisiana Territory.

Jefferson was staggered by the new nation's chance, sudden and immense, to extend its domain beyond any dream of the most fervent nationalists. The price—$15 million—seems tiny to us, but it was four or five times the annual cost of running the government, and added to the debt Albert Gallatin had whittled down. But the real problem was constitutional, since the president had no explicit power under the Constitution to buy land. At first Jefferson thought of asking for a constitutional amendment, but speed was essential. So he did what history has admired him for: he closed the deal, and rationalized it by saying the people would have wanted him to decide as he did.

When the treaty of purchase came before the Senate, a number of Federalists denounced it as "Jefferson's Folly." Yet later generations of Americans have preferred to see it as Jefferson's glory—the greatest single geopolitical event of American history since the discovery by Columbus.

The new land doubled America's expanse, gave it a structure of agricultural and manufacturing power, and propelled it decisively into becoming in time a world power. It also upset the balance of power between the two major parties, broadening the base of the Republicans and making them a national party with an impulsion westward. While it did not make Jefferson an "imperialist" in today's sense, it made him part of what was to be called the "manifest destiny" of America. Himself a naturalist and ethnographer, and the son of a surveyor, Jefferson sent out the Lewis and Clark Expedition to map the new domain, report on its resources and people, and dramatize its meaning for the rising American national consciousness. He had not abandoned his dream of an agrarian society: he had only found a larger setting in which the dream could be renewed and pursued.

By a stroke of fortune history had offered Jefferson, at an unsuspected moment, a great navigable steam and a vast land empire almost for the asking. Had he been merely doctrinaire, he would have turned a stony face to Napoleon and Talleyrand and rejected the great historic chance because it ran counter to what he had argued and written about the Constitution. But he did not, and thereby he laid the basis for the place of his first term in history.

In 1804 Jefferson was overwhelmingly reelected, despite a bitter campaign in the Federalist press against his personal life and morals. He took his success as fresh evidence of the people's mandate. But in 1805 his troubles began. In his first term, very little seemed to go wrong for him. In his second, nothing seemed to go right—not the Burr conspiracy and trial, nor the embargo, nor the impeachment of

Supreme Court Justice Samuel Chase, nor his vendetta with the anti-Republican press.

Aaron Burr was brilliant, cynical, persuasive, unscrupulous, with a flaring imagination—in short, a fascinating rascal. After being dropped as vice presidential candidate in 1804, he cooked up a grandiose scheme for carving out of the Louisiana Territory an independent republic over which he could rule. Jefferson could have played it cool, and let the legal authorities deal with his actual conspiracy. Instead he overreacted, made a treason trial out of it, and Chief Justice Marshall—who had outmaneuvered Jefferson in the case of the "midnight judges" in *Marbury* v. *Madison*—was now able, in presiding over the trial, to apply a strict definition of treason as overt acts of war or betrayal against the United States. The crucial evidence for treason in this sense was lacking; Burr was acquitted, and Jefferson was left looking both foolish and vindictive.

He had an even more hapless time with the French and British depredations on American commerce. It was Jefferson's fate to act out his entire presidential career against the background of swirling struggle between the great European powers—a struggle that locked him into dilemmas not of his own making, presented him with options not of his choosing, and finally proved the undoing of much he had hoped to accomplish.

When the British and French both seized American vessels if they touched at the ports of the other, Jefferson decided to test one of his favorite doctrines—that war was both intolerable and unnecessary, and that the best weapon against both powers lay in economic sanctions. He got Congress to pass a series of five Embargo Acts, stringently forbidding U.S. trade with Britain and France not only overseas but even along the Canadian border.

Not surprisingly, the tactic failed. The British and French were unmoved by a measure that did not hurt them decisively. That Jefferson had stripped the armed forces, out of pacifist principle and for economy, made them contemptuous. Within the U.S. there was sporadic resistance, which infuriated Jefferson. It made him turn each new Embargo Act into a Force Act, with searches and seizures by the army and navy. These in turn embittered the resistance, which Jefferson saw as "insurrection."

When an embargo case involving the port of Charleston came before the Supreme Court, and Justice William Johnson held that presidential acts were subject to due process of law, Jefferson insisted on his "coequal" power to interpret the Constitution and therefore to defy the Supreme Court view. When a lumber-laden raft in Vermont was snatched away from an army guard and hauled to Canada, the culprits were arrested and—on Jefferson's insistence—tried for treason, to set an example to others. Justice Henry B. Livingston, himself a Republican, was shocked by the treason charge, and lashed out at Jefferson for seeking to use the doctrine of constructive treason in a domestic legislative case.

One must judge Jefferson's embargo strategy a dismal failure as an instrument of foreign policy, and a dangerous adventure as domestic policy. Jefferson's idea of passive resistance to the European blockades might have worked if he had used intermediate means. He could have armed American merchant ships and equipped them with convoys, or used a policy of nonintercourse with Britain and France, or both measures together. The embargo was too broad and ineffectual, and did more harm to the U.S. by paralyzing commerce and manufactures than it did to the offending European powers.

Jefferson made the embargo his personal project, watching over its day-to-day operation but doing little to educate Congress and the people on why extreme measures were necessary. Like some later American presidents, he made the mistake of attributing his failure not to his policy but to the opposition to it. He isolated himself from the people, calling the congressional vote to remove the embargo (just as he left office) a "sudden unaccountable revolution of opinion." The pathos of it was that in 1787 he had mocked the fears about Shays' Rebellion, and had written that "the tree of liberty must be refreshed from time to time by the blood of patriots and tyrants. It is its natural manure." When people resist and take up arms, he had said, "the remedy is to set them right as to facts, pardon and pacify them." As president he did none of these.

One must remember about Jefferson that he had a strong will, not easily diverted from its purpose, or softened by adversity. While out of power, resisting attacks on freedom of criticism, he had achieved some abiding victories. When he was in power, he still had his old sense of being surrounded by enemies; and his strength of will became an instrument of repression. Jefferson in opposition met constantly with his fellow party leaders, exchanged letters with countless colleagues, and was deflected by them from potential blunders. Jefferson in power lost the habit of subjecting his policies to prior criticism and—especially after his reelection victory in 1804—he was confident that the people were with him, and came to equate his own thinking and intuitions with the will of the people.

Leonard Levy, a Pulitzer Prize–winning constitutional historian at Claremont Graduate School, courageously took Jefferson as libertarian apart in his *Jefferson and Civil Liberties: The Darker Side*, to the dismay of the established Jefferson scholars, who are protective of him. Quite apart from the Jefferson image, the facts are troubling. A number of Republican theorists of press freedom emerged at the turn of the nineteenth century, broke with the English common law of seditious libel, and spoke up for a wholly unfettered press, much as Justice Hugo Black was to do in our own time. This new libertarianism was bold and radical, condemning not only prior restraints against publication but also prosecution after it, and condemning state as well as national trials.

Jefferson was wary of it. He condemned national but not state antisedition action. When, as president, he felt that the Federalist press had reached "licentiousness" and "a degree of prostitution as to deprive it of all credit," he suggested to a Pennsylvania governor "a few prosecutions of the most prominent offenders. . . . Not a general prosecution, for that would look like persecution, but a selected one." There followed the trial of an editor in Philadelphia, one in New York, several in New England. They all failed, and Jefferson looked foolish.

He could veer wildly on the theme of press freedom. He said at one point, "Were it left to me to decide whether we should have a government without newspapers, or newspapers without a government, I should not hesitate a moment to prefer the latter." Yet this did not keep him from harassing editors by prosecution. A few years before his death he found a middle ground in seeing press freedom as "a formidable censor of the public functionaries," and noting that "it produces reform peaceably, which must otherwise be done by revolution."

As president, he was as foolish about politically overzealous judges as about vituperative journalists. The bone that stuck in his throat was the Federalist judges whom the Adams administration had appointed to lifetime jobs in federal courts just as it left office. Many of them were crassly unjudicial. They galled Jefferson because, massively and symbolically, they stood in the way of his transfer of power. He tried to wait them out, or make life difficult for them but complained that "few die and none resign." His effort at a purge came to a crisis in 1804 with the House of Representatives' impeachment of Justice Samuel Chase of the Supreme Court, who had said intemperate things about Jefferson from the bench. The House presented the charge of malfeasance in office, the Senate sat as a court in 1805, but fortunately—both for Jefferson and for judicial independence—Chase was acquitted. No member of the Supreme Court has been impeached since, although there were rumblings of thunder around the heads of Chief Justice Earl Warren and Justice William O. Douglas.

One may guess that part of Jefferson's thin-skinned sensitivity to his critics derived from their attacks on his private life and morals. At one point a gutter journalist, James Callendar—who had been part of the Republican press stable—failed in his effort to blackmail Jefferson, and then published the story of Jefferson's supposed seduction of a close friend and neighbor, Mrs. Betsey Walker. Jefferson later wrote a friend about the episode: "When young and single I offered love to a handsome lady. I acknowledge its incorrectness." But there is no way of telling whether the husband's charge that Jefferson had made repeated efforts to seduce his wife, or the lady's own charge of a ten-year siege by Jefferson, amounted to more than the fantasies of a wife and the wounded vanity of a husband.

Jefferson's relationships with women have become the thorniest problem for his biographers. He had a strong commitment to his wife, Martha, who died when he was still a young man of thirty-nine, and whose death shook him. But the assumption of most who have written about him, that this great and good man must have forsworn sexuality for the rest of his life, does not necessarily follow. The efforts to sanctify him, as if he were a spinsterish clergyman figure, do justice neither to his intense, passionate nature nor to his basic character as a complex, many-sided, total person.

The storm has raged around the question of Jefferson's relationship to two women—Maria Cosway, American wife of a dandified British miniature painter, who lived in London and visited in Paris while Jefferson was minister; and Sally Hemings, a slave girl at Jefferson's Monticello home, who was also an illegitimate half sister to Jefferson's wife. Jefferson and Maria Cosway unquestionably had a romantic love affair, as evidenced by Jefferson's famous long letter, "Dialogue between My Head and My Heart," which he wrote out of his heartbreak when Maria had to leave Paris for London. They exchanged twenty-five more letters, described by Fawn Brodie as "the most remarkable collection of love letters in the history of the American presidency." Mrs. Brodie's detailed and scholarly psychohistory, *Thomas Jefferson: An Intimate History*, argues persuasively that their relationship was sexual as well as romantic, but that neither of the lovers dared make the break into a marriage that both must have thought of.

The scholarly controversy over Sally Hemings has been even stormier, with Jefferson's traditional biographers dismissing as libel the contention that she was Jefferson's mistress from the days of his Paris household and bore him four children, and with Fawn Brodie marshaling her artillery of evidence to assert it was true. The reader who wants to decide for himself must go to Dumas Malone's masterly six volumes on Jefferson's life and to Mrs. Brodie's massive and lively 800-page book. It is interesting that recent black writers, who uniformly attack Jefferson for having continued to own slaves despite his passionate defense of human freedom, are inclined to accept the Sally Hemings story as part of the facts of life about Virginia plantation morals.

My own guess is that they and Fawn Brodie have the better of the controversy. In his relationships with women, Jefferson seems to have been attracted to the difficult and the forbidden. He was trapped in an age, a class, and a society where miscegenation was practiced but severely punished when made public. He could not have escaped a feeling of guilt about this relationship, as suggested by his long history of migraine headaches. This does not negate my view of him as a whole man, although a complex and guilt-ridden one. Yeats put it well: "Nothing can be sole or whole / That has not been rent."

A week after he left the presidency, Jefferson (at sixty-six) set out for Monticello, riding for days on horseback and for eight hours through a snowstorm. "I have more confidence in my *vis vitae* than I had before entertained," he wrote Madison. For seventeen years he was to live out his life at Monticello, in the groves he loved, on his farms, busy with letters and books and guests, and with a brick factory and mill. He was a world-famous figure. Streams of visitors came to Monticello, some only to see him walk across the lawn. He restored his friendship with John Adams, breaking their long feud, and the two former presidents—lonely, solitary on an American landscape stripped of most of its Revolutionary leaders—exchanged some 160 letters whose learning, high spirits, and versatility of theme are unmatched in the history of American letter writing. "You and I," Adams wrote, "ought not to die before We have explained ourselves to each other."

Of the two men's letters, Jefferson's are more urbane and mellow, expressing an unshattered belief in man's power by reason and education to make his society work. Adams was more convinced of the force of the irrational in human events. When Jefferson wrote him about his plans for his beloved new University of Virginia, which occupied the last decade of his life, Adams answered with the hope that the twin elements of superstition and force "may never blow up all your benevolent and phylanthropic lucubrations. But the History of all Ages is against you."

Jefferson was undaunted. Even the fact that his last years were shadowed by sickness and debts (he was a poor plantation manager and had to sell his library to meet his obligations) did not shake his basic optimism. The end came, symbolically, exactly fifty years after the Declaration of Independence he had written. He survived the night of July 3, and toward midnight—after a fitful sleep—asked, "Is it the Fourth?" He was told, stretching it a little, that it was, and he fell into a coma, which passed into death around noon on July 4, 1826.

In Quincy, Massachusetts, John Adams was also dying, equally intent on lasting until Independence Day. Since he did not know that Jefferson had died five hours earlier, his last words were reported as being "Thomas Jefferson still . . ." The legend was that he murmured either "lives" or "survives" to end the sentence and his life. There is something eerie about the fact that both men died on exactly the day when the nation was celebrating the fiftieth anniversary of the independence they had both helped to win. It was more than coincidence: it was a linked act of will on the part of both.

Even in his last years Jefferson lost little of his political shrewdness. "Take care of me when I am dead," he wrote Madison, his old comrade in the political wars. Surely few political figures could have needed less caretaking for the judgment of posterity. The legend that crystallized after his death made him out to have been bigger than life, so complex that his name and writings were invoked for every cause—conservative, liberal, and radical angles of vision as well as weak and strong presidencies. Everyone saw him through the prism of his own political coloration. But of one fact there could be no doubt—the many-sidedness of his devouring mind. As one reads his letters to Adams the breathtaking web of his interests is revealed: in the sciences, linguistics, anthropology, archaeology and fossil remains, the humanities and classics, music, architecture, farming, in the earth and the skies and the meaning of the cosmos, in the dispersion and variety of the races and their inherent equality as well as differences, in religion, government, aristocracies, morals, education.

As he looked back at his long life, what swam through his crowded memories? He was of the little band of young Virginians who, in their hedonic but intellectually tempestuous life, had shaped themselves into a great governing generation. He had become the spokesman of the American Revolution to the world, drawing on the basic ideas of the European Enlightenment whose child he was, but giving them an analytic sweep and verbal elegance all his own. He had celebrated his state in his *Notes on the State of Virginia*, and his nation in his great public papers. His European education, during his days as American minister, was an intellectual overlay on his essential Americanism; yet without those European years he could not have become the assured man of the world and statesman he became.

He misread much about the French Revolution (he was no disciplined social thinker), but his French experience stood him in good stead as he carried through his own "Revolution of 1800." In his struggles with Alexander Hamilton, both were romantics; Hamilton romanticized the nation, Jefferson the people. Yet it was Jefferson's hard organizing capacity that made him the victor. I count Jefferson, for all his intellectualizing and his lofty revolutionary sentiments, the most brilliant party leader in American political history—at least until Franklin Roosevelt. The miracle was that he managed to project a public image of himself as at once a militant popular leader and a serene philosopher.

In an age like our own, of expanding problems, wary specialization, shrinking perspectives, Jefferson remains witness to the truth that to be a generalist need not keep a man from action, and to be a philosopher need not keep him from power and passion.

ABRAHAM LINCOLN

FROM THE PEOPLE, FOR THE PEOPLE

LINCOLN AS WAR LEADER

WITH HIS *ABRAHAM LINCOLN: THE WAR YEARS*, Carl Sandburg completes the life of Lincoln begun in *The Prairie Years*. Taking the total achievement, there is nothing in historical literature that I know quite comparable with it.

I generally distrust the meeting of perfect writer and perfect theme. There is a blueprint seemliness about such conjunctions that rarely issues in a creative product. The surprising thing about Sandburg's writing on Lincoln is that in this case the results are good: The democrat, the poet, the storyteller, the earthy Midwesterner, the singer of the people has managed somehow to write about another democrat who was also something of a poet in his way and a vast storyteller and an earthy Midwesterner and a product of the popular mass. He has sought to depict him on a canvas broader than anything else in American biography: over 2,000 pages of text, hundreds of illustrations, a hundred pages of index. Even the four-volume *Life of John Marshall* by Albert Beveridge, expanded by long discussions of cases and decisions, seems dwarfed. Sandburg has brought to his theme a brooding vigor and compassion, a precision of detail, a lyricism, a gusto for people and experience that would be hard to match among American writers. And the work he has given us is not only a biography of Lincoln and a history of the Civil War. It is itself a battlefield, a sprawling panorama of people and issues and conflicts held together only by Sandburg's absorption with the central figure.

The New Republic published both "Lincoln as War Leader" (December 6, 1939) and "I Thought of Lincoln" (February 10, 1941). Lincoln was also the subject of several newspaper columns by Lerner, which follow.

The historian's art has been narrowed by the academies to the point of making people believe that there is only one right way of setting down a history. Sandburg's way is as characteristically his own as Carlyle's was when he wrote of Cromwell. It is the right way for him because through it he can best express his own basic drives and outlook. He is in these books three things: reporter, poet, lover.

As reporter he sets down what happened with the athletic matter-of-factness that the best journalists put into their craft. But it is a reporter who has a million and a half words at his disposal, and so Sandburg empties his notebooks into his pages. But while nothing is too minute to be put in, there are no superfluous interpretations. The facts are allowed to speak for themselves, yet almost always they are so arranged (with a simplicity that almost conceals the cunning) that they do speak and have something to say. And Sandburg has the reporter's passion for concreteness. We always learn the exact numbers of everything, the exact look of everyone who enters the story. There is something even a bit frightening about the detail. I think I can understand Sandburg's intent: the Lincoln literature has grown so vast that a definitive factual work was needed to gather together everything available and valid. The result has one great flaw: the sense one gets of a curious one-dimensional plane, in which the detail gets the same loving attention as the big event, at a considerable sacrifice of perspective. Sandburg is a little like a painter in the primitive style. He is your true democratic historian. In his universe all facts, once they have been validated, are free and equal. Yet he gives his material thereby an unforced character that should cause the biographers who come after him to bless him. Unless I miss my guess, Sandburg's *Lincoln* will become an inexhaustible storehouse from which will be drawn a myriad of other Lincolns.

There is also Sandburg the poet. A poet turning to biography and history is likely to flaunt his Muse or, by an inversion, to be ashamed of it and suppress it. Not Sandburg. The America of Lincoln, the teeming years of suffering and battle and greatness, lie drenched in the moonlight of his lyricism. The Sandburg here is the Sandburg of the Chicago poems, celebrating America and the obscure ways of life, setting his words down with neither elegance nor precision but with a curious random obliqueness that nevertheless manages almost always to reach its object. "Out of the smoke and the stench, out of the music and violet dreams of the war, Lincoln stood perhaps taller than any other of the many great heroes." Thus Sandburg. What biographer who was not Sandburg's kind of poet would dare say "music and violet dreams" when describing war, or juxtapose "violet dreams" with "the smoke and the stench"? Yet while there are passages verging on the dithyrambic, particularly at the end of chapters, the whole tone of the book has a quietness and restraint that only one who has mastered his subject and is sure of it could afford.

I have mentioned Sandburg the lover. I know of no other word that will describe the twelve years spent in wooing the material, the care lavished on every detail; or the complete identification with the subject that allows him to analyze Lincoln without once raising his voice in shrillness, and with the effortlessness of what might almost be a reverie. Nor do I know of any other word to describe the deep and shrewd tenderness for common people throughout the book, such as one might expect from the author of *The People, Yes*.

Sandburg has evidently taken care not to write the sort of contemporary book that underlines the parallels between yesterday and today. He has given us Lincoln the man, Lincoln the war president, America in the war years. If there are morals to be drawn for today, he has left it to us to draw them.

I am not averse to drawing my own. But one does not need the stimulus of the modern instance to find excitement in the task of human interpretation that every Lincoln biographer has faced. Sandburg's *Lincoln* stands out not for its sharpness of thesis but for its very lack of the monistic view. It has a catholicity and an unforced quality that are rare in biography, without succumbing to mere straddling and the colorless. One gets the external man and the internal tensions. There is no attempt to prettify, to play down crudities and failings; neither is there any hint of exploiting them. All the lumbering awkwardness of the man is there, his gropings and fumblings, the way he entered the reception room at the White House and made people feel he was the man in the room who was least at home. But the simplicity of the man is also there—a simplicity that, in Emerson's phrase about him, was "the perfection of manners."

Throughout the book we find ourselves on the verge of the symbolic. To quote Emerson again on Lincoln, "He exerts the enormous power of this continent in every hour, in every conversation, in every act." Sandburg spells that out in detail, while he never lets us lose the sense of the symbolic relation between Lincoln and the American energies. And he manages also to convey Lincoln's tortured sense that there had been imposed on him a task too great for a human to bear. It is here that one strikes the deepest chord in Lincoln. The fatality of it: that he, with his tenderness for everything living, should become the instrument of death for tens of thousands; that he, who always saw the danger of men's control over men, should have in his hand the destinies of millions; that he, who always shrank from action, should at the peril of his people be galvanized into a train of actions with vast inscrutable consequences. From this viewpoint there are two peaks in the book: the chapter on Lincoln's laughter and religion, and the analysis of how Lincoln had to tell his stories in order to relieve the intolerable tensions within him; and the chapters on the assassination and the country's mourning. To the latter especially Sandburg brings his most complete gifts, telling the story with the subdued reverence of a passion play, and with a fatality as if the actors were moving in a dream. Here one reaches great writing.

It is a bit of luck for us that these volumes should appear just when the question of the conduct of the war by democracies is so much in our minds. One will not find here, as in the Baker volumes on Wilson, much discussion of the now frayed theme of American neutrality. But there is a store of stuff on the question of what happens to a democracy when it goes to war.

Lincoln has gone down in American history as one of the "strong" presidents, who flouted constitutional restrictions and established a dictatorship in order to win the war. The view is not without its truth. Yet never has a government waged so fierce a war as Lincoln had to wage, and departed so little from the democratic spirit. Lincoln the war president, Lincoln the commander in chief of the national armies, Lincoln who suspended habeas corpus when it seemed an indispensable measure and who backed up the arrest and expulsion of "Copperhead" leader C. L. Vallandigham of Ohio by General Ambrose E. Burnside—that Lincoln never ceased to be also Lincoln the humanist and Lincoln the democrat. He was sore pressed as no American president has ever been. He made mistakes, but as one reads the Sandburg volumes they seem to have been mainly on the side of excessive tolerance rather than lust for power. He had to deal with all the plagues that beset a war government—the militarist mind, the messianic mind, the bureaucratic mind; with war passions and hysteria, with patrioteers, with the lynching spirit, with lethargy, with an opposition so bitter it verged continually on sabotage and treason. He had no genius for organization, little capacity for delegation, little administrative ability as it is generally understood. But with all these limitations he never once lost sight of the main chance. He had a way of cleaving to the heart of a problem that baffled subtler and more expert and sophisticated minds. There were men around him with more powerful wills, men with a greater commitment to humanitarian and radical values. But there was no one who saw better than Lincoln the dilemma and task of a democracy at war: how to win the war with the minimum sacrifice of traditional liberties and democratic values.

In a world in which there have been so-called war leaders like the Daladiers and the Chamberlains, we have reason to be proud of Lincoln. We have reason to be proud that with every opportunity for setting up a dictatorship, he did not succumb; with every opportunity for betraying democratic values under the guise of war necessity, he did not succumb. Long before the end of the war he was giving his best thought to the problem of a humane peace and a constructive plan for rebuilding the defeated states. I have no intention of saying that Lincoln was wholly consistent in the strength of his humanism. There were forces in American life that proved too powerful for him, for the cause of the North was tied up with the cause of a predatory capitalism, and the Reconstruction that followed Lincoln's death was almost devoid of either democratic or human values. Yet there was never a time when it was more important for us than now to know the capacity of a democracy to turn up greatness of Lincoln's sort from its humblest sons—a greatness that will survive the grime and savagery of war.

If I read my own Lincoln somewhat into Sandburg's pages, there is room for others as well. He has given the coming generations the material out of which to construct a succession of Lincoln images. All the material is there—from the day that Lincoln boarded the train at Springfield to ride to his inauguration, down to the day when his coffin was placed in a flower-heaped vault in the Springfield he had left. What four years were crowded between those two boundaries! The hordes of people, office-seekers, handshakers; the jokes and stories, deep, illimitable stories, lighting up what was comic and contradictory in life; the grim wild humor of a president-elect conferring with his advisers as to how he might travel through Baltimore on his way to his inauguration without being lynched; the Cabinet officers, with their intrigues and jealousies; the vast decisions and petty details; the generals, and the heartbreaking search for military leadership that would be confident and firm and aggressive; the violent attacks in Congress and the press; the drama of emancipation, and the harrowing uncertainty of its consequences; Father Abraham; the seesawing of war's fortunes; the draft riots, the desertions, the Copperheads; the unending delegations of politicians and ministers and zealots and cranks; Jay Cooke and the financing of the war; the profiteering and poverty, at one extreme costly furs bought with war profits, at the other the starving families of soldiers; the European diplomats and statesmen puzzled by this ungainly fellow who told crude stories; the faith of the masses, growing and deepening every year; the rows of hospital cots, the faces pleading and rebuking; the dream of sudden death and the deep inner conviction that it would come; the unerring course of Booth's bullet; Whitman's threnody; the grief of the people. And then the legend.

✭

I THOUGHT OF LINCOLN

There will be many political dinners this year [1941], as always, to celebrate Lincoln's greatness. Wendell Willkie is scheduled to speak at one, Thomas Dewey will contribute his Lincolnism to another, and Clare Boothe hers to a third. The orators will orate, the well-fed and sleekly dressed thousands will applaud. There is nothing new in this. Yet this year as never before, in a national crisis deeper than any since the Civil War, we must reassert that Lincoln is not the monopoly of a party with whom today he has nothing in common.

He belongs, as leader, to the whole American people. And he is today the most complete and satisfying symbol of leadership we have. Leadership has two facets. At any moment a people needs not only a leader for the present but a leader for the past as well. And the man in the past to whom a people turns is just as important a fact about it as the man to whom it turns in the present. There has been a vast amount of guff written about Lincoln, and he has grown to the proportions of a legend. Yet, legend or not, the fact is that with every year Lincoln has been emerging more clearly as our great historical leader.

There are reasons for that, reasons which reach down to our sense of equality and our will to live. For Lincoln was a democrat, a man out of the people who never tore the roots that bound him to them. And he was a humanist who felt deeply about inequality and inhumanity wherever he saw it. And he was a nationalist in whose mind the survival of the united nation came first. And he was a strong president who, when the time came for decisive action, knew how to act decisively. We tend to forget today that Lincoln's decision to risk a destructive war was a hard decision to make, and by no means as inevitable then as it seems to us now with the hindsight of history. All these qualities are the qualities that make great leadership in a crisis democracy. Whether he knows it or not, Mr. Roosevelt is being measured in our minds to that fit, as every leader will be measured as long as Americans have the task of making out of their democracy a strong state and out of their strength a living democracy.

There were many things wrong about Lincoln and the American democracy of his day. There were draft riots because the burden of service fell on those who could not buy their way out. There was bribery, inefficiency, appeasement. There were breadlines and banquets, profiteering and cowardice and criminal complacency. There were partisans to attack Lincoln from the political left and right, men who called him a baboon, accused him of selling out. But through it all, for all his veerings and indecisions, he clung tenaciously to his single-purposed course.

Given what the Civil War means to us, there are things also in our America of today for which we should apologize to those who died under Lincoln's leadership. I heard from a refugee just arrived from Marseille of the conditions in the prison camps for German and Spanish refugees in France; and then I looked at the obstacles our State Department is placing in the path of their coming to our country, and I thought of Lincoln. I read Leigh White's account of the butchery of innocent Jews in the slaughterhouses of Bucharest, and then I read the speeches of our appeasers, and I thought of Lincoln. I thought of Henry Ford's fight now against his workers, and of the preparations being made by Bethlehem Steel to fight labor, and I thought of Lincoln. I read of the Jim Crowism still practiced in the American army, and of the fifteen Negro sailors dishonorably discharged from the navy because they had protested against discrimination, and I thought of Lincoln. I had a letter from a brilliant Negro professor who wrote that the vast body of his people saw the need for destroying Nazism: "How grimly ironic therefore that we should have to beg for our chance to help"; and I thought of Lincoln.

It is easy to idealize Lincoln and to read into him your own views and beliefs until they become his as well. But it is even easier to deflate than to idealize, to set him down as just a shoddy horse-trading politician. He was not that. If ever there was a man in our history who had the difficult stuff of heroism, this was the man. He was no absolutist and no program-builder. But neither was there any cant in him, as we know when we read his ironic letter to the delegation of ministers protesting as Christians against the war. He did a hard job well, with dignity, firmness, and—in the midst of desperate measures—with compassion. Always he had the distinguishing mark of greatness, the ability in any problem to get at the jugular. He saw when he came to office that the crux of adequate presidential power in an emergency lay in the president's role as commander in chief. And, although a hard-bitten realist, he could know the meaning and the value of a dream.

He was no great leftist. Yet the American progressives have made a mistake not to claim him as one of them. Why have they, with a few exceptions, steered shy of him? Has it been some curious snobbishness—the knowledge that Lincoln is in the very stream of the American tradition, and the feeling that the left needs something more esoteric and marginal before it recognizes the stuff of heroism? If so, they have been cruelly wrong. For whether on a national or a transnational plane, Lincoln, as the American common man raised to a heroic pitch, has in him the power to give meaning to the past and shape to the future.

★

FEBRUARY 9, 1959

The generation that followed Lincoln's death saw him as the Great Emancipator and the Great Martyr. For later generations of Americans he became the crucial folk hero, a legendary figure through whom we were able to express our hunger for a homespun symbol of giant stature—at once tough and tender, rowdy and wry; full of jokes, yet always on the margin of heartbreak; terribly human in his gawky, fumbling ways, yet also the one abiding figure in American history with the authentic stamp of immortality.

Every era fashions its own image of Lincoln, out of the material that the historians furnish, but also out of its own drives and needs. What is our image?

The Lincoln I see, as I have been browsing through a pile of several years of new Lincoln books, is a lonely man, deeply split, who spent most of his life finding out who he was. But once he found out—in the early years of the Civil War—he showed passion and tenacity, and a sure sense of what he wanted and where he was going and how to get there.

We call this kind of search, in the jargon of our own day, the "quest for identity." Lincoln would have rejected the high-flown term, but not the fact. His law partner, William Herndon, said Lincoln had told him his mother was illegitimate. There must have been other racking doubts he had about himself, and sometimes I have felt that the "house divided against itself" was inside Lincoln himself. Yet when the crisis broke all around him, something happened within him to steel his will and make him all of a piece.

Lincoln's lowly origins are part of the homespun–folk-hero figure. But what is not underscored enough is that out of this common stuff came one of the chosen of the earth, perhaps the greatest leader the American nation has had. Our social thinkers have often enough pointed out that there must be a "circulation of the elite" in every society. If a nation cannot draw constantly upon the vigor and passion of the young men who come from humble stock, and raise them to the seats of the mighty, it will die.

We need to remember today, in the midst of our own debates about the schooling of our young people, that we can as readily find the material for leadership somewhere on a lonely farm or in a city slum as among the sons of the cultured. But how the unlikely raw material of Lincoln came to be developed and trained, how it was shaped by time and circumstance and his own inner fires into the Lincoln who played his brief but transcending role on the stage of history—that can never be told with certainty. If we could read this story aright—the story of a great education, almost without the benefit of schools and teachers (he did have a teacher—Mentor Graham) we might know what to do with our young talent today.

The Lincoln I see was an earthy figure, who showed that a leader can be shrewd, hard, and realistic without hardening into one of those "practical men" who always bring their country and cause to disaster. One has only to read about how Lincoln managed to get the presidential nomination in 1860, how he used patronage, how he kept changing generals until he had the men he wanted, how he kept from drowning in the swirl of strong undercurrents of politics during the Civil War, how he got himself reelected, how he resisted pressures from the "radicals" yet adopted many of their ideas—one has only to read about these phases of Lincoln to see that he knew how to get what he wanted.

But I do not see Lincoln as simply one of the regular run of politicians. The political strain in him is remarkable mainly in contrast with the twin strains of tragedy and compassion—strains that are as important for American leadership in a missile age as they were during the Civil War. The only difference is that Lincoln had these qualities and none of our leaders today do.

The Lincoln I am describing left his impact on sensitive and powerful minds, and on the minds of millions of people, right across the face of the earth. We make a good deal today about the need of fighting an "ideological" struggle with the Communists, and the need for finding the right phrases, symbols, and techniques to wage it. Lincoln had an eye for the world impact of his actions, and he had a good way with his words, which he didn't coin as he ran but which he polished in solitude hour after hour. Yet what made him the great world symbol of democracy was his own figure—Lincoln as a person in thought and action.

The Lincoln I see was an intellectual, with a wonderful sense of the complexity of life and thought. Yet the complexities were in his own mind. In what he uttered, after wrestling with the demons, there was a piercing simplicity of approach—to law and labor, to slavery and freedom, to the self-government of people, to the agonies of fratricidal conflict, to life and death.

His capacity to put these insights into words that ordinary men could understand was met almost mystically by a similar response from the people. There are few of our historic leaders about whom we can say to so great an extent that their careers embodied a great dialogue between the people and themselves. At a time when this dialogue is so strangely silent as now, it is good to think back to a man and a time that expressed it.

★

NOVEMBER 15, 1978

Memphis, Tennessee—For a wondrous stretch during an afternoon in Memphis I was Abraham Lincoln and spoke his deathless lines.

I'd been invited to talk to the history and politics students at Memphis State University, and since it overlapped with Aaron Copland's visit as an artist in residence, President Billy Jones was struck by the lightning idea of having me appear with Copland when he conducted his great *Lincoln Portrait*.

It was brash of me to agree. My musical education had been limited to some violin lessons when I was a teenager in New Haven. I once played in an early movie theater there and was fired on my second night. I read music roughly as well as I read Sanskrit.

Yet how could I resist the chance to take second billing to Copland in the performance of the *Portrait,* and thus touch the hem of the well-worn but tough garment of Lincoln's thought and passion?

It was this that enticed me. The Lincoln words in Copland's *Portrait* had long ago reached deep into my unconscious. When Copland, at the piano, did a first run-through with me, the words I was to read came back with a searing strength. "Fellow citizens, we cannot escape history."

The Illinois farm boy had somehow found the voice and words for every call to action in every crisis since the Civil War. "The fiery trial through which we pass will light us down, in honor or dishonor, to the latest generation." And then the clincher: "We . . . hold the power, and bear the responsibility."

It was a phase of Lincoln I had almost forgotten—this man's stern refusal to let any member of Congress, any party opponent, slip out from the burden of responsibility that goes with power.

Then the great words, still not known widely enough, from his 1862 message to Congress: "The dogmas of the quiet past are inadequate to the stormy present. . . . As our case is new, so we must think anew, and act anew. We must disenthrall ourselves, and then we shall save our country."

But how disenthrall ourselves? By finding rock bottom in our faith: "As I would not be a slave, so I would not be a master. Whatever differs from this is no democracy."

Copland wrote his *Portrait* eighty years after Lincoln spoke these words. It was in 1942, after Pearl Harbor, in a difficult year of the war. It has been performed scores of times since the first with William Adams as narrator, with Carl Sandburg, Henry Fonda, Marian Anderson. I was in a good line of descent. There will be doubtless others to come.

On the day of the concert I spent the morning playing a tape of a past performance, watching for the interweaving of musical and verbal phrase, letting the simple, strong beats hammer themselves into my brain. During the dress rehearsal with the orchestra I felt like a novice approaching the mystery I had watched but never taken part in.

And then the thing itself. At a lectern a little to the side of Copland's, I listened to the folk ballads he had woven into his own musical conception. Then unbelievably my cue came, and there I was on my feet, speaking the great words, saying "That is what Abraham Lincoln said."

And as the musical chords mounted I forgot I was there, and once more I was a young immigrant boy in New Haven, reciting to the bare walls of my room the great Gettysburg lines: ". . . that we here highly resolve that these dead shall not have died in vain—that this nation, under God, shall have a new birth of freedom. . . ."

I thought of the ungainly young man who didn't impress his townsfolk much, who—they thought—was too awkward in relating to others, and a little too calculating as a politician. I thought of his deep depressions and the way he wrestled with them, and how he wrestled with the war and its trials and transcended them.

Then suddenly I was back in the hall again, seeing the faces in the audience—young faces and old, black faces and white, furrowed and seamed faces and smooth ones—engrossed faces in an unlikely South that had once fought Lincoln and hated his words but had now inherited them.

Clearly they were caught up in the magic of Lincoln's words as I was. Then I spoke the last line: ". . . and that government of the people, by the people, for the people, shall not perish from the earth." And the worn words took on a newborn freshness, and I felt at peace with my country and its people and myself.

★

FEBRUARY 18, 1985

We celebrate Lincoln's and Washington's birthdays together but we make more to-do about Lincoln. In part it is because he was a martyr, but mostly because he was more complex and interesting as a modern man.

One could build a case for Washington as the larger figure, the true Founding Father.

He had prudence, perspective, command, a sense of limits. Only he could have set the new United States in motion because only he evoked the requisite trust and awe from all.

Lincoln was something else again—lonely, turned inward, yet somehow wielding authority. One thinks of him in paradoxes.

He was the frontier lawyer and storyteller who was also the most reflective of all our presidents.

He was immovable in resisting the secession of the South, and, at any cost, saving the Union. Yet his heart broke as he visited the wounded of the war he had unflinchingly accepted.

His formal education was minimal: one year of schooling, but his self-education was rich.

He knew Shakespeare's tragedies and histories and could recite whole passages. He had read all of Gibbon's *Decline and Fall of the Roman Empire*.

While the young Lincoln didn't have even a tiny fraction of the information with which a child today is battered, he knew how to ponder the meaning of what he knew.

He was reflective without being indecisive. He knew the *Hamlet* soliloquy too well to play Hamlet as president. Joseph Alsop has wondered why Lincoln liked *Macbeth* best of the Shakespeare tragedies. It may have been because of the blood theme in it.

Some recent Lincoln historians have noted how the metaphors of blood and struggle and transcendence run through his speeches and writings. How could they not? The metaphors described his presidency and foretold his death.

Mostly his struggle was against government-as-usual and thinking-as-usual.

"The dogmas of the quiet past," he wrote Congress in 1862, "are inadequate to the stormy present. . . . As our case is new, so must we think anew, and act anew."

When accused of violating the Constitution to pursue the war, he answered that unless he could save the Union, he couldn't save the Constitution.

It was dangerous thinking, as all fresh thinking is. He perished in consequence but the Union did not.

While today we suffer from the fragmenting of society, brought on not by fresh thinking but by unthinking, we do not suffer from the fragmentation of the nation. No minority dares secede from the American nation. People everywhere in the world want to join it.

These are the two political fathers we celebrate—the stern one, with command and authority, and the compassionate but unyielding one, with heartbreak but with strength, who taught all the sons to think freshly.

FRANKLIN D. ROOSEVELT

THE FLAWED PARADIGM

FRANKLIN ROOSEVELT WAS A PRESIDENT on a grand scale—grand in his impact on his time, grand in his achievements—and grand in his blunders. He has to be America's paradigm president. We use him as a criterion for measuring his successors, and Rooseveltology has accordingly become less a discipline of assessment than a liberal canon of presidential greatness.

He is still the icon of the dominant political culture and has sired a whole presidential line. He left a style of governing, a security net of agencies and institutions, a tradition of regulatory activism, and the example of vigorous interventions in global macropolitics. Their influence has been felt for a half century. But he also left a burdensome statism and a sharply divided world to his successors as the dubious harvest of his magisterial decisions.

The challenge he presents is to trace how his life and temperament had prepared him for the conquest and wielding of power, how his decisions arose out of his thinking, and how they now stand revealed in their consequences.

First a personal note. I spent my youth and early manhood under FDR. I was thirty when he became president and forty-two when he died. I supported him on his liberal left, first as a *Nation* editor, later as editorial writer and columnist for the newspaper *PM*. I had a part in his constitutional battles and even backed him on his Supreme Court "packing" plan of 1937. I was in close touch with his "Brains Trust" advisers and worked briefly for him in the early New Deal. I wrote my first book, *It Is Later than You Think* (1938) as a Machiavelli guide for my prince—it earned me an afternoon of talk with him at Hyde Park.

The essays about Franklin Roosevelt and Harry Truman appear here for the first time.

I voted four times for him as the indispensable national leader and was a stalwart in the liberal political culture that owed its energy to him and that he used as a support system. When he died I was desolated and felt he was irreplaceable.

It took me years to disengage myself from his sorcery. With no other president have I struggled as hard to reach an independent assessment. It has meant cutting myself away from my earlier self, so inextricably linked (as it seemed) with the Roosevelt image. But I cannot be less true to my present angle of vision, reached after so painful an inner struggle, than I was to the self that I was then.

A president's life history is a sequence of interacting force fields, within himself and his environment, that propel him (with a logic only partly clear, even to himself) toward a goal that later gives the entire sequence its historic meaning.

In Roosevelt's case the first force field is the unlikely one of patrician birth and lineage, and shining, pampered boyhood years among the Hudson River landed gentry, and a posh education on the Groton-Harvard axis, through political apprentice years in Albany and wartime Washington, to a failed vice presidential bid in the lost-cause campaign of 1920, when he was thirty-eight.

Yet while it went against the grain of the log-cabin myth, it was not as unlikely as it seemed in a democracy oriented to the cult of the upward-mobile "common man." FDR and Theodore Roosevelt ("Cousin Teddy") belonged with the great founding presidents of the Republic—Washington, the Adamses, the Virginia dynasty from Jefferson through Monroe—who were all landholding patricians. It was part of what gave him his security. Out of his sureness of family and historic setting flowed much of young Franklin's sureness of being.

An elderly, ailing father and a beautiful, controlling young mother were a pair straight out of Edith Wharton's turn-of-the-century caste society. Sarah Delano Roosevelt was a possessive and intrusive mother whose efforts to control her only son's life were part of her drive to hold together a world increasingly threatened by changing mores. But his sense of selfhood may have been strengthened in resisting her possessiveness and perhaps in turn he took over some of her imperiousness.

At Groton he found a quasi–father figure in the headmaster, Endicott Peabody, a fisher of young souls who preached noblesse oblige to the rich boys in his stewardship. When James Roosevelt languished and died, Franklin—at Harvard at the time—reached out to the lasting phase of trust in a Father God whose tutelage he was never to doubt, confident that what happened to him was part of a divine watchfulness.

At school and college his presentation of self, in journalism and plays, fused with his sense of life as eventful and as theater. But his prime influence was the image of his cousin and strong career model, TR, who cut a wide swathe in the news and in history just when Franklin was most impressionable. His father's side of the family being Democrats and TR's Republicans, he saw no reason why he should not some day add a Democratic Roosevelt presidency to a Republican one.

He was a young man in a hurry. There has been some debate about his early—and fateful—marriage to his gawky young cousin, Eleanor Roosevelt, but surely the fact that she was a direct niece of the president—and that he came from Washington to give her away—could only have added to the challenge of making a choice not his mother's. The attention their honeymoon European trip drew followed inevitably from the TR connection.

Although Frances Perkins, on meeting him, thought him a lightweight, this was no shallow rich man's son who danced with the girls and charmed his elders but a young man who knew where he wanted to go and did not doubt the vocation for getting there—the conquest of the fabulous mountain of presidential politics. To a group of his fellow law clerks he mapped out his plan for the ascent. It followed strikingly TR's course—state legislator, assistant navy secretary, New York governor, and then (skipping TR's vice presidency) the presidency itself. To his little audience—given his name, connections, flair for people—it did not seem an impossible dream.

In 1910, at twenty-eight, he ran as a Democrat for a heavily Republican seat in the New York State Senate, won it, and led an insurgency against the Tammany choice for U.S. Senator. TR could not have bettered it. His foes proved slippery but the national press adopted him as a spunky young Tammany-buster. He aligned himself early with Woodrow Wilson in 1912 as the winning presidential nominee, and was rewarded with TR's old assistant secretary of the navy post. As second-in-command to a permissive chief, Josephus Daniels, Roosevelt virtually ran the department. He found it a priceless learning-by-doing experience, hammering out the personal style he later used in the governorship and the presidency.

It was a selective, experimental style: to find expertise where he could, to listen, to choose an amalgam of contending policies, to bully, to charm, always to be seen as a reformer, but a practical one, and always to be (or seem to be) in command. He also learned the Washington arts of political infighting: when to thrust with strength and smite an opponent, when and how to contrive, convince, and seduce, when to be abrasive, when devious—in short, the Machiavellian arts of the lion and the fox.

How to fit a passionate love affair into this life context? The liaison between Franklin Roosevelt and his wife's social secretary, Lucy Mercer, has troubled the biographers because it seems a gleaming tragic episode, with a pathos of its own, but somehow unrelated to Roosevelt's larger design. But was it? She was beautiful, sensitive, part of a Maryland Catholic family that had lost its money but retained its gentility. At some point in the midst of the war, she and the handsome, spirited assistant secretary of the navy—whatever his other wanderings at the time—seem to have fallen passionately in love. Recklessly they went everywhere together while Eleanor was at Campobello, and the dowagers who watched over doings in Washington's social circles knew and gossiped about it. When Eleanor inevitably discovered Lucy's telltale missives, what followed was a triangle of wills, and the story is that Eleanor's proved the most resolute. Yet we are talking of a resolute man in his late thirties, accustomed to command, and of the only great love he—or Lucy—was ever to have. *Amor vincit omnia*, we are told. But in this case love did not triumph over its obstacles. For reasons still obscure there was no divorce and no marriage. In the world's eyes Eleanor and Franklin continued in their partnership, but Eleanor never again shared her bed with Franklin. Lucy married a man twice her age, becoming Mrs. Rutherfurd. Franklin resumed his political life design. Clearly it did not include overcoming a mother's shock, a wife's adamant resolve, a sensitive political culture. Knowing something of his design we have to ask whether he had second thoughts about what the entire episode would do to his burgeoning political hopes. That may well be how desire and power resolve their conflict in the lives of presidents-to-be. In FDR's case, an experimental pragmatism seems to have won out. So the episode did have context after all.

For a stretch after the war little in FDR's life seemed to go right. Wilson's collapse after Versailles threw the Democrats into confusion. Their 1920 convention chose FDR, at thirty-eight, to lend grace and fire as vice presidential running mate for a lusterless James Cox. Eager to become the young leader of a new Democratic "progressivism,"

FDR made a thousand speeches and appearances, straining his ener-gies for the doomed ticket and (the only time he followed sentiment, not interest) taking a pro-League of Nations position. For once he misread the popular mood of reaction against the war, the peace, the League, and Wilson.

He was dismayed by the electoral earthquake of Harding's victory, and—jobless—looked about for ways to stay in the public eye. Friends noted a frenzied dimension in him, which triggered a reckless expen-diture of energy and self—getting overheated, immersion in the icy Newfoundland sea—which in turn may have been the occasion for his polio.

Thus 1918 to 1924 were the years of a broken government post, a broken love affair, a broken marriage, a broken body. It strikes us to-day as a "mid-life crisis" in which his career, relationships, indeed his whole life were thrown off balance. In the life history of every hero there is this perverse break in the upward arc that shows his fragility and evokes our empathy. It is the years of wandering in the wilderness. For FDR it was the stretch when his life design, so vauntingly pro-claimed to his fellow law clerks, seemed to be going down the drain.

Thus we need to understand that FDR's testing by polio was not the isolated event we have made it, but was imbedded in a larger context of loss and adversity. But it was also the most immediate and concrete event of all, and—for him and for us—it came to stand for them all.

The experience was not one to teach him the virtues of orthodoxy but, rather, of experimental action. After the early doctors had misdi-agnosed his illness he had to find the right doctors and the right self-help regimen. It took months of patience, practice, will, even to move his little toe. For years he refused to accept the verdict of the doctors that he would never again be able to walk. He endured all the agonies of treatment with indomitable hope and single-mindedness. The blighting polio became his White Whale, to be hunted down. He learned to live with his heartbreak, and the struggle for life itself cen-tered his energies anew on life's essentials.

There is a long-standing dispute about how crucial the polio ex-perience was for FDR. Writing of his father's "personal Gethsemane," James Roosevelt said "it was not polio that forged father's character but . . . father's character that enabled him to rise above his affliction." This dispute can be a mare's nest. There were dark spaces in FDR's psyche along with the splendor of light. There must have been some desolate watches of the night, in that back bedroom on East 65th Street where he fought out his inner battles against the perversity that life had visited upon him. Could a man who had always gloried in his body fail to be dismayed at the prospect of spending the rest of his waking life strapped in a wheelchair?

I see the polio attack and the ordeal of recovery as a pivotal phase not only in the shaping of FDR's psyche but also in the reshaping of his political will in a denser form than ever. Now the presidency was for Roosevelt not only a high prospect but political anodyne and best revenge as well. The command of his illness became a form of self-command, which, in history's own due time, was translated into the command of a nation. It taught FDR that—like "fear itself"—strength could become a self-fulfilling prophecy. It taught him also, I suspect, that the best answer he could make to life was to pursue his power design with the same intensity with which he had pursued survival.

What remained was his political career. At this point in FDR's life the best medicine was the sheerest politics, his best doctor Louis Howe, Roosevelt's eccentric, spirited Pooh-Bah, his accomplice since state Senate days. Howe worshiped Roosevelt as a Carlylean hero and was heaven-sent for the tutelage of the stricken great prince. He knew every behind-the-scene staffer, trusted no one, and had an instinct for the public pulse. Roosevelt needed Howe to lift himself out of his life crisis and to thrust him toward the presidency. Howe needed Roosevelt to give his failed life meaning and mission. It was a marriage of true minds which together responded to what Kenneth Davis has called "the beckoning of Destiny."

Together they dreamed an outlandish dream—that a still pain-ridden man who could not walk, aided by a dwarflike gnome of a provincial newspaperman, could somehow sail into port with the highest prize of all. It was a strange partnership—the high-toned political grandee teamed with the hard-up scribbler who had a clandestine network of those who were rarely overtaken by events because they knew where the bodies were buried. Between them they combined the suasion of sweetness and light with the necessary hardball tactics of pros who had put aside amateur imaginings.

What did FDR make of the desert bleakness of his out-of-power years? There were eleven years between FDR's paralysis and his presidency, and eight of them—up to 1929—were dominated at home by Republican peace and prosperity, a stretch which Paul Johnson has called America's "last Arcadia." It was a wasteland period for FDR and the Democrats. What did it do to his political drive and to his thinking?

Because he was no intellectual, he made the false assumption that he had no context in the history of ideas. This does both the man and his times an injustice.

A leftward wind was blowing through the world in his time and he rode it. After the turn of the century a liberal intellectual Renaissance took place in America, matching that of the 1820s through the 1850s. Behind the Democratic political leaders from Bryan through Wilson were clusters of rebel thinkers. There was a "new history" and "new politics" (Beard, Robinson, Veblen, Patten, Mead, Cooley), a "new philosophy" (James, Dewey), a "new jurisprudence" (Holmes, Brandeis, Cardoza, Pound). Innovation and renewal were in the air; everything was freshly minted, newborn.

The common element was a modernizing liberal revolt against the formal thinking of the status quo, replacing it with a state activism to deal with the pathologies of the new industrialism. To be at once up-to-date, down-to-earth, and humane jibed with young Roosevelt's temperament. While he was never a thinker or much of a reader he was open to this intellectual climate, perhaps the most permeable president ever; ideas seeped into him by osmosis. He soaked up impressions from everyone around him, translating them into slogans and actions.

Yet nothing had quite prepared him for the collapse of the Wilsonian world of idealist internationalism and for the Republican twelve-year takeover of the presidential office and power. With the Republicans riding high nationally, FDR's grand strategy was to wait out the cycle of their dominance, meanwhile presenting himself to the splintered and demoralized Democrats as a leader with a vision beyond faction. While nominating Al Smith in 1924 as the "happy warrior," and again in 1928, FDR stayed out of contention both times as improbable years for a Democrat. He hinted in a widely discussed book review that he might be the Jefferson of his time, yet he possessed nothing like Jefferson's world perspectives or his coherent theory of government. He was groping for a patchwork combination of the "new nationalism" that TR got from Herbert Croly and Alfred Mahan and the "new freedom" that Woodrow Wilson got from Louis D. Brandeis.

It was not as a man of ideas that we must view him in this phase between the polio and the White House, but as a deeply political man in the pit of the political battle. With no other twentieth-century President was there so total and skillful an embrace of the political vocation. He was not power-driven in Lyndon Johnson's and Richard Nixon's sense of a life of power hunger, yet driving and driven he was by reason of being presidency-driven. Everything else—love, family, health, staff, friends, supporters, allies—was subordinate and instrumental to that goal.

With it all he had a conviction of irresistible destiny, which—whatever its base—was subjectively important. One may argue, as Kenneth Davis does, that destiny was behind his critical decision to succumb to a Smith-engineered draft for the New York governorship run. A livid Howe thought it a spineless timetable blunder, four years early, that would set Roosevelt's entire career at risk. I see it as an uncanny case of Roosevelt's political instinct, which told him that it was better to seize the immediate moment of reality when things were going for him, instead of waiting for an incalculable future.

As it turned out, Roosevelt's razor-thin yet stunning victory in the face of a Hoover national landslide over Smith heightened the éclat of his name. It gave him four years as governor to build an image and record for the nation, which would compare with Hoover's battered image and Depression record when the true time came.

Once in Albany the former state legislator and navy administrator had for the first time to govern—and in his own style, not Al Smith's. He governed effectively but not distinctively. He no more foresaw the Depression than Herbert Hoover did, nor was he any clearer than his fellow politicians about its nature and dynamics, or how to deal with it.

But—a political man to the bone—he knew how to stay ahead of the rest with a more glittering public image, and the kind of record to make—farm aid, hydroelectric power, trade union encouragement, social legislation, and especially relief for the unemployed. It touched all the bases and confirmed him as a national figure while also making him few enemies.

FDR used the governorship to the hilt and wooed everyone—business, the unemployed, the reform groups, the internationalists, the isolationists—in what was to become the politics of the "great coalition." But beyond this mélange, as the end of the 1920s exploded into a wasteland of joblessness and despair, he projected the image of a reform-minded political humanist who had the strength to intervene if necessary.

FDR annexed for himself the feeling in the air that something new would have to be done, by someone new, to keep the surging tide of revolution and threat in Europe from engulfing America.

The 1920s were enamored of the "engineering" of social change—Howard Scott's "Technocracy," Thorstein Veblen's "engineers" who would replace the "price system," Herbert Hoover as engineer and technocrat who believed in voluntary self-ordering of the national enterprise with governmental guidance.

With the start of the Depression the prize of a Democratic presidency suddenly shone with brilliance. FDR's rivals in the 1932 primaries and state conventions—Al Smith, Newton Baker, John Garner, Governor Albert Ritchie—presented a varied churned-over array, none of them tuned to the new mood of the nation. Actually FDR was Wilson's unacknowledged but true heir, with an energy and imagination to rival his former leader. For eight crucial years in Washington he had watched, talked, and dreamed Wilson, whose blunders and strengths became his political catechism. He used Wilson and his grand manner as modes of becoming truly presidential.

The oft-quoted 1932 Walter Lippmann comment—that FDR was "no crusader . . . no tribune of the people . . . no enemy of entrenched privilege," but only "a pleasant man who, without any important qualifications for the office, would very much like to be President"—sheds more light on Lippmann as political prophet than on Roosevelt. Lippmann could not know that only when FDR became president would he fill the glorified roles Lippmann listed. So FDR wheeled and compromised, and Louis Howe, Edward Flynn, and James Farley made deals for him (including one with William Randolph Hearst and John Garner) at the 1932 convention before he could become president and make his New Deal.

The recruiting of a campaign "Brains Trust" was critical. Earlier presidents—Jefferson, TR, Wilson—had writers and thinkers as a natural part of their milieu. But FDR took the risk of scaring the conservatives by openly establishing a resource group for ideas, spanning the political spectrum from moderate liberals, such as Raymond Moley and Adolf Berle, through Sam Rosenman, to socialist Rexford Tugwell. It helped recruit an entire new political culture. It brought most of the youth into his coalition, later made the liberal segment of the Washington-based correspondents his willing allies and accomplices, turning his press conferences into triumphs of his personality.

It was early vintage, highly charged Roosevelt, including the breaking of precedent (flying to Chicago for his acceptance speech) and the symbol-conscious phrasemaking ("the forgotten man," "the New Deal"). In rapid succession the constituent elements of a governable crisis America were moving into place. It was a unique campaign. A certain winner was hinting, however craftily, at a still-undefined new order to replace the failed one. And an emerging leader was meeting a people ready and waiting for him.

After FDR's landslide victory there was a drawn-out interregnum until late March, when Hoover could not govern alone and Roosevelt refused his repeated pleas to govern with him. Hoover tried several times to ensnare him into a united stand on the world financial crisis but FDR stayed aloof. The day before the inauguration Hoover again asked, "Will you join in a joint proclamation closing all the banks?" Mrs. Roosevelt, listening at a partly open door, heard FDR say, "The hell I will. If you haven't got the guts to do it yourself I'll wait until I am president to do it."

Come what might, he was determined to make a clean start, for dramatic timing and for history's sake. Thus, when he came on the stage it was not as a savior with a sword or a book or a mapped-out plan, but as a leader with a sense of the dramatic and a will to action. Unfortunately he had only the haziest idea of the intellectual frame that would alone give direction to the action.

The inauguration was pure theater. The bank crisis dominated it, but also the anticipation of what Roosevelt's speech would be, since it was his first action. Moley had done the draft, and they spent an evening polishing it, while FDR wrote every sentence in his own hand, presumably to keep "the little man" (Louis Howe) from feeling he had been bypassed—but it also misled several of FDR's biographers. The ruse, at the very start, was characteristic.

The impact on the nation was instantaneous. The line Howe had inserted—"the only thing we have to fear is fear itself"—came either from Thoreau or from a department store ad in Washington, but it reached its mark. The promised "action, and action now" took the concrete form of round-the-clock working sessions of a Cabinet task force to order the closing of the banks.

Congress was not in session, and in its absence FDR could have governed by decree, as Europe's dictators were doing. He chose not to, calling a special session of Congress and using it to generate a responsive excitement from the people. What surprised him—and Eleanor as well—was the intensity of response in the mountain of White House mail. Too many people were eager to lay down the burdens of freedom and embrace a regime that would release them from their anxieties and fears. Roosevelt was saying that they had to face them, and that it had to be their action as well as his. So he drew them into the circle of his leadership.

The European models, of Lenin, Mussolini, Hitler, were no viable choices for the American Puritan small-town self-image. But the model of the well-run American corporations—U.S. Steel, Ford—was. FDR had an emerging collective mentality to top. There was a growing sense, never clearly articulated in the media, that the government should be run on responsible corporate lines, by someone efficient who would put everyone to work and make the farms and factories prosper again.

So Roosevelt remained faithful to the political process, although he quickened and intensified it. The cyclone of legislative and executive action, which we know as the "Hundred Days," set a pace of innovative change rivaled only by Lyndon Johnson after 1964. And he reinforced it all by his radio "fireside chats," with their superb use of the president's role as educator.

With his lieutenants Roosevelt seemed to invent the world anew, contriving governmental controls and entitlements unparalleled in America. They included farm supports, bank and security exchange controls, government generation of energy, rural electrification, federal relief, make-work (WPA) jobs, youth work camps, collective-bargaining protection, social security—all of it supported by progressive taxation and deficit financing. Within a space of four years FDR and his little band created a centralized welfare state that has lasted more than fifty years, and only began to be turned around in the 1980s. Never in the history of Western democracies have so few built a federal infrastructure so fast that has survived so long.

Some critics have faulted him then and since for failing to use the crisis to nationalize the banking system and the key capitalist institutions. But this is to misconceive Roosevelt. Despite his populist gibes at the "money-changers in the Temple" he was not bent on overthrowing capitalism. He had been all too busy, in his feckless earlier years, with inventive schemes for making quick money as a capitalist himself. What he wanted to save was democracy, at a time when it was being derided and threatened. Marshaling enough governmental power to reform capitalism and make it workable was part of that. He was a career politician, not a zealot with a mission, nor a power-hungry demagogue, nor an ideologue messing with the engineering of human souls.

Roosevelt was thus a master builder, but of a very special sort. What he built was less an economy than a controlled bureaucratic polity, a welfare society of group entitlements, a culture of state-dependent pressure and interest groups—in short, the "positive state." Did he have to do it? At the time, most of us were convinced he did, and we applauded it. Life was lonely, chancy, estranging, and Everyman was glad to have a safety net poised under him and in time came to demand it as something society owed him. Like Topsy, that was how the welfare state grew.

Yet it was no solitary act of creation. It had been gestating ever since Woodrow Wilson's spate of federal reform legislation in his first term, and the agencies of his war bureaucracy in his second. These had formed the prime seedbed of FDR's government experience and ideas.

If the New Deal "worked," it was because FDR displayed, more than any president before him, a *magus* or *shaman* quality, a capacity to communicate to people his sense that anything was possible. A number of leaders have "charisma." But FDR appealed to two crucial elements of the American national character—its experimentation and its resilient optimism.

In sheer economic terms the New Deal failed, but not dramatically, as Hoover had. Hoover's economic sin was his passionless isolation from the wretchedness of the jobless, homeless, hopeless, and the political sin of his symbol blindness. His failure was more immediately devastating than Roosevelt's and left him a figure of pathos and ridicule. Roosevelt's failure was more protracted and concealed. But FDR had a fallback strategy, that of economic statism, which made the state the fountain of succor against contingency. It gave him enough political success to reelect him in 1936 and keep the polity going until the war-readiness economy could finally overcome the inhibitions of investment and management risks and create jobs in a proto-military Keynesism.

If Roosevelt was a Keynesian in practice, he was an unwilling and unconscious one. He was scornful of Keynes and his theories. His gut instinct was not for economics but politics—for power and behavior and how institutions work. True, he had believing Keynesians like Lauchlin Currie and Marriner Eccles as advisers, yet there were few fiscal leverage strategies, and the Keynesian impact came only with the war industries.

The unemployment and production levels tell the story. In Roosevelt's last New Deal year, 1937, unemployment fell to 14.3 percent (Hoover's worst had been, by the crude estimates of the time, 25 percent, with many believing the figure much higher). But by 1938 it was up to 19 percent again. The start of the war in Europe, in 1939, bringing a zooming American war production, set investment going again, and by 1941 production in dollar value was back to 1929 Hoover boom-year levels. Where Hoover suffered four years of steep economic decline, Roosevelt suffered eight years of a lethargic economy, yet his fame rested on his having done what Hoover failed to do.

His long-range problem was to find, underneath the jaunty Roosevelt, his true center of moral and political gravity. Were he more of an ideologist he might have found it in his political philosophy. Yet his own method was to respond to pressure, overcome obstacles, and create agencies and institutions, and out of that process the New Deal "philosophy" emerged.

   His crisis years in finding his gravity were 1936 and 1937. He had run through two New Deals—the emergency legislation of 1933–34, and the more sharply antibusiness motif of 1935 and 1936, aimed at the public utility holding companies and the core power structure of the economy. His indecision about the thrust of his 1936 campaign, and therefore of his second term, was finally resolved by moving to the left. Those of his corporate enemies who had earlier "met their match" in him, he said in his 1937 inaugural, would now find that they had "met the master."

   It was more than rhetoric, and more also than Roosevelt's "auto-intoxication of ideas"—Moley's shrewd phrase about him. The populist in FDR knew that the voters needed an enemy symbol, and that the public utility barons would serve admirably. But FDR himself also needed an enemy. The stricken young god in his wheelchair had covered over his wound with his exuberant life force, but it was still there.

   Part of the art of politics is where you find and place your enemy. FDR placed him on the right, where his vaguely Marxist political culture did. He placed his most dangerous enemy, Huey Long, on his right, as a fascist or proto-fascist, although Long's distributist ideas were on the left. Competing with the Communists for the capturable populist strain and the intellectual youth, FDR refused to allow anyone of importance on his left. But placing the corporate conservatives on the far right resulted in a skewed political geography, making Hitler and the Nazis blood brothers to the American managerial class rather than to Stalin and the Soviet leaders whose totalitarian methods and ethos they shared. This deeply flawed view had consequences for Roosevelt's wartime view of the Russians as difficult partners of democracy, but partners still, and therefore outside the circle of the enemy who had to be "mastered."

In reaching for domestic allies FDR sought them leftward among the intellectuals. They were emerging as a self-conscious elite and have remained one ever since, thus making their alliance with FDR one of the fateful events of our time. It happened within the frame of an ethnic breakthrough in higher education. The unspoken but implacable academic quotas began to collapse. Young Jews emerged for the first time as a prime intellectual force in the political culture. FDR's liberalism validated their liberation from the ghetto of the university quota system, and they came in turn to associate the release of their creative energies with the Roosevelt years.

Political observers have always stressed FDR's "Great Coalition" of interest groups but what held them together was that their leaders— among labor, blacks, Jews, farmers, youth, even the city machines— had links with the intellectuals in the political culture. Thus what may be called the "Roosevelt Enlightenment" became his strongest political resource, largely through the skills in symbolism that are at the political heart of the republic of the mind.

FDR's mammoth 1936 victory over Alf Landon, a moderate Republican who never had a chance against him, was a "realignment" triumph that made the Democrats the majority party and validated the Roosevelt "Great Coalition." It also tested the capacity of FDR's mind and character to ride success as they had ridden adversity.

He flunked this testing. He had shed Ray Moley, and Louis Howe was dead. Howe's last words to Vice President Garner were "Hold Franklin down," and to another friend: "Franklin's all alone now." He was right. Roosevelt had used his Brains Trust effectively because his mind was a marvelous instrument for filtering and resolving conflicting opinions. But he needed challenge—and got little. His uncurbed euphoric impulsiveness was no substitute for governing.

His ill-advised "Court-packing" plan of 1937 was a prime example. The Supreme Court had been striking down a mounting portion of the New Deal laws and agencies which FDR saw as his major claim on history, and he tried to push through a law giving the president the power to appoint up to six new justices in place of those who failed to resign after the age of seventy. A measure of hypocrisy is built into democracies, but FDR's was too patent in his tortured legislation and its dishonest rationale. I say it ruefully, having supported him strongly at the time. In the end, through a chain of events and court tactics that outflanked him, FDR's Court-packing plan folded, although he could claim that he had lost the battle but won the war.

If FDR's critics expected the Court fiasco to chasten him, they failed to fathom the depth of his confidence in his own judgment, whose infallibility there is little evidence he ever doubted. He returned to the attack in an effort to purge two prestigious conservative Democratic senators in 1938, and again he failed. When FDR felt threatened and was unchecked, he often overreached. Unlike Lyndon Johnson and Richard Nixon after him, he did it not out of insecurity, but out of inner security.

He had to pay for these setbacks as well as for the continued failure of the economy to right itself. The Democrats lost a substantial number of seats in the 1938 election, and his 1940 encounter with Wendell Willkie was the first to give him a scare. But he may have needed these close encounters to reassure himself that he was, after all, not a status quo possessor but a rebel. I should amend Richard Hofstadter's much-noted essay head—"The Patrician as Opportunist"—to read, "The Patrician as Rebel."

In perspective FDR's strategic problem at first turned on how to stay out of a war, then later on how to get into the war in Europe, then on how to win the global war, and finally on how to structure a postwar world. In his first phase he used the conservative isolationists as a protective screen against the liberals who were pressuring him to intervene against the aggressions by the Japanese militarists or the totalitarian leaders in Europe. His rhetoric was different from that of the isolationists but his aims were the same.

James MacGregor Burns calls the first-term FDR a "pussyfooting politician" on foreign policy. I should extend his phrase to much of the second term as well. Certainly he was reluctant to provoke the Catholic hierarchy over the arms embargo that crippled the Spanish loyalists. Except for the "quarantine" speech in 1937 FDR's foreign-policy statements, even as late as 1938, read like anti-interventionist tracts.

The moral lights seemed to be going out all over the world. By 1933, when Hitler came to power, to join Mussolini and Stalin and the Japanese warlords, the will to power of ruthless ideological and na-

tionalist leaders had moved into the moral vacuum left by the confusion of values and the lack of collective action for security.

It was a hard time for FDR, who found himself unprepared and
without intellectual and policy bearings in a storm of global power systems, groping for the hard-wire realities. He had little notion of what
to do about it, other than to protect the nation against war entanglements by parroting the term *peace* and embracing the *neutral* embar-
goes, whose passivity was the exact opposite of his New Deal activism.
My generation of interventionists had the feeling of losing time as
FDR moved ever so slowly to grasp the collective-security principle.

FDR's early strategy—to alarm the people to a warlike mood
about the plans of the dictators but to stop short of stirring their fears
of getting caught in a war—was too contradictory to be a policy. Thus
FDR felt himself engaged, as he told William Allen White, in an exercise of "walking on eggs." This had not been true of his domestic New
Deal, when he seemed capable of walking on air and even on water. In
time he got the arms embargo lifted and a "cash-and-carry" policy established for Britain's benefit. But it was part of a long and almost fatal
moratorium, which wasted some good years while FDR spent his popularity on his Supreme Court and party purge adventures. He could
have used some of his postelection prestige to back up his "quarantine"
speech by modernizing the military.

Even Hitler's seizure of the Rhineland (his own generals were certain he could not get away with it) and of the Sudetenland did not
shake the FDR who sent Chamberlain a "Good Man!" message before
he left for Munich. Until his State of the Union messages of 1939 and
1940, Roosevelt saw "peace"—as Wilson had done—as American non-
involvement in war, instead of seeing it as the product of a network of
national wills that make armed expansionist adventures prohibitive.

These are no historical afterthoughts of mine. I argued them in *It
Is Later Than You Think*, which I wrote in 1937 and early 1938 while I
was political editor of the liberal weekly *The Nation*. I linked internal
reforms ("militant democracy") with "collective security" pacts abroad,
including the Soviet Union, and argued that time was of the essence,
and that precious little of it remained for action. Tom Corcoran,
FDR's legislative draftsman, tactician, and lobbyist, showed me a set of
galleys he had marked up for the president. But given FDR's inaction I
had some doubts.

Roosevelt lacked a "Brains Trust" in global policy equivalent to
his domestic one. Of his secretaries of state, Cordell Hull was a shrewd

man but inadequate to the stormy occasion, and Edward Stettinius was a cipher. FDR's pivotal ambassadorial choices—Joseph Kennedy to London and Joseph Davies to Moscow—were impulsive and frivolous. Harry Hopkins, who became increasingly his prime partner as well as emissary on foreign policy, had a quick mind and tongue, but he worked in FDR's shadow and did not know enough and was not strong enough to keep him from blundering.

In large part the American political culture was as unready for the global crisis as its armed forces. There were no defense thinkers and on global problems the intellectuals were at sea. The isolationism of the right was fortified by the bastard economic determinism of Charles Beard and the Nye Committee myth that arms sales and the "merchants of death" were what led to war. The answering interventionist voices were a few writers (Lewis Mumford, Waldo Frank, Archibald MacLeish), a theologian (Reinhold Niebuhr), and a gaggle of foreign correspondents (John Gunther, William L. Shirer, Dorothy Thompson, Edward R. Murrow).

Why did Roosevelt stretch his presidency through a third and fourth election? Only a liberal president in a liberal political culture could have cut so sharply against the grain of the two-term tradition. A conservative Republican would have ended in a storm of criticism for aiming at a dictatorship.

Roosevelt got away with it because enough people felt he was indispensable at a time of global crisis. I was among them. Overcoming my hesitations I voted for him a third and fourth time. I reasoned that in a Hitler-dominated world there would be no two-term tradition and no presidency to worry about.

We did not yet know just at what point FDR decided to run for a third term. My own guess is that it came sometime in 1938, after his ill-fated domestic adventures, when he learned that the war-and-peace problem could not be resolved by being neutral but would take some positive efforts to get into the war and win it. He dallied for a time with James Farley, Robert H. Jackson, Harry Hopkins, and William 0. Douglas as possibilities to replace him, dangling the prize before each, never serious about any, for all along he wanted it for himself.

His wiliness was never better displayed than in floating these trial balloons so that—each being found wanting by comparison with himself—they would all be shot down. In the end, by the spring of 1940, FDR must quite genuinely have convinced himself that he was in fact the indispensable choice to see America through the stormy war period he saw as inevitable.

So FDR lied in the 1940 campaign, when he said "I will not send a single American boy" to fight in a war in Europe. By 1940 FDR as a hardened pro probably knew two things—that the only way to save America was to bring it into the war, and that he might lose the election if he told the truth about it. Given the country's fear both of Hitler and of war, it was a case of a politically necessary lie.

Once reelected, Roosevelt—late as the hour was—turned his resourceful energies to helping England and (later) Russia, to modernizing the unprepared defense services, to building a war-readiness economy. He got enabling legislation (Lend-Lease, conscription) through Congress. He entrusted the administration of the economic build-up to the corporate managerial professionals, no longer the enemy he had targeted in 1936 and 1937.

During the year between his election victory and Pearl Harbor he was at his magnificent best. Wendell Willkie as president might also have pursued an aid-to-Britain-and-Russia policy and a defense build-up, but no one could match Roosevelt's bag of political tricks, his magisterial manner, or his imaginative fire. FDR in 1941 almost made up by his brilliance of maneuver for his foreign-policy confusions of his first two terms. History has strange ruses for reaching its ends.

The thesis that Roosevelt knew of the coming Pearl Harbor attack, and shut his eyes to his knowledge, may not be quite as "vile" as Joseph Alsop has called it, but it will not stand up. The evidence is too spotty to condemn Roosevelt for anything more than a devious wiliness. Given the "Magic" code-breaking operation, the top American brass knew the Japanese were poised to strike somewhere, but probably guessed it was at the British or Dutch possessions, closer to Japan. They could have treated an intercepted message with genial neglect. Since they could not get Hitler to attack, they were probably more than half-praying the Japanese would. Nevertheless they were stunned by the swiftness, daring, and precision of the attack.

In the end, however costly and traumatic, it solved Roosevelt's prime problem of getting into the war. He was right about the "day of infamy," which was documented by the intercepts on Secretary of State Hull's desk when he talked to the Japanese emissaries ("hypocrites and pissants" was how he described them later). The Japanese military elite, running the show totally, was betrayed by a power hunger and a bastard Shintoism into an impossible duel with American technology. The unintended consequence of Pearl Harbor was to galvanize the unity and will to war of the divided American nation.

Thus the "infamy," however repugnant to him, served FDR's larger purpose. The burning ships and slain sailors and officers were cruelly tragic victims. But in the grand perspective of history the major victim that was slain at Pearl Harbor was American isolationism.

Five days after Pearl Harbor, Roosevelt was even luckier, with Hitler's impulsive declaration of war against the U.S. What made it an eerie one was that he had tried at every point to avoid a war with America and its massive industrial power. But now, with his ally Japan at war with America, he would not wait passively for FDR to move first in a war declaration. In his declaration speech at Berlin's Kroll Opera House he noted "the world-wide distance" that "separates Roosevelt's ideas and my ideas." His world vision was apocalyptic. If Roosevelt was bent on a showdown to the death then Hitler would make it a twilight of gods that Roosevelt would rue.

When the war finally came FDR steeped himself totally in it, eating, drinking, sleeping, dreaming it. Everything before it had been only a preparation for this role on which so much of history hung. It offered decision making and action galore. Even when the news from the battle sectors was "all bad" (as he put it in his first war "fireside chat") it was the meat his dauntless spirit fed on. It tapped the deepest springs of a will that had seen him through the hell of polio and helped him govern a people in a Depression wasteland. It differed from Stalin's "patriotic war" and Churchill's stoic "blood, toil, tears, and sweat," but each man knew his own home front.

He had conducted the New Deal as a war and had gloried in the martial language of its battlefields and enemies. He could now act out a real life-and-death war, on a global scale unparalleled in history, in multiple battle sectors, leading a formidable coalition of allies against an enemy alliance. He cherished his secret trips to the summit conferences, "firsts" for an American president. On state occasions he preferred being introduced in his commander-in-chief role. He haunted the War Room, built for him to match Churchill's, and was proud of knowing the geography of his briefings, and impatient with aides who did not reckon with his knowledge gained on his World War I inspection trips. He wanted it understood that as commander in chief he was no amateur but a pro.

His top industrial and military professionals were good at their tasks and—once he had chosen them—he did not meddle with the execution of the larger economic and military strategy he had set.

On the economic side his critics on the left accused him of surrendering his prime chance to establish a war socialism, but they misread his priorities, which called for winning the war, not establishing socialism. On the military side he had a happy choice in his chief of staff, General George Marshall, who exercised an eerie professional authority. Jumping General Dwight Eisenhower over his seniors in service to command the European theater, they both agreed to put coalition military diplomacy ahead of strategic brilliance. But from neither Marshall nor Eisenhower could he count on the kind of challenge to his basic military-political strategy that every war leader needs.

It is a striking fact that while FDR counted on the industrial and military professionals for their expertise he often bypassed State Department officials and ambassadors, and relied on personal sources for information and advice. From Upton Sinclair's "Lanny Budd" series to Herman Wouk's *The Winds of War,* this was the stuff on which admiring writers built a picture image of an authentic commander in chief. But in fact it was Roosevelt's weakness, not his strength, to have appointed ambassadors like Joseph Kennedy, to London, whom he had to bypass, and to have as secretary of state Cordell Hull, who ran his own detached imperium, or an Edward Stettinius whom everyone overlooked.

What was centrally at fault was that the Great Improviser, who had succeeded in improvising the New Deal and became an inspired professional politician, now set to improvising a war command at which he was at best a gifted amateur, and for which he had no group comparable to his earlier Brains Trust to help him. Berle, Moley, Rosenman, Corcoran, and Cohen all had legal, verbal, and intellectual skills superbly fitted for their tasks. Harry Hopkins, whom FDR had drafted to take their place in the war setting, had wit and talent and a considerable adaptive capacity, but as a geopolitical diplomat he was no Metternich or Talleyrand. He suffered from a digestive malady that went long undiagnosed and wasted him. He spent his body and heart in the service of the leader he worshiped, after whose mind he fashioned his own. There are few chronicles in history at once as moving and tragic as this story of two grand invalids on the edge of death, bringing their country through the war but faltering at its last stage because—with all their hardened experience—they lacked the final necessary preparation of judgment and toughness of mind.

"A second-class intellect. But a first-rate temperament." This was Justice Holmes's view of FDR when the new president paid a visit to the old warrior and jurist who had been a president-watcher since Lincoln, had known them all, and was hard to impress. FDR's conduct in the critical triad with Churchill and Stalin for roughly five years and the Grand Strategy he followed both toward his comrades-at-arms and toward Hitler are worth some study in testing this assessment.

Did Roosevelt have an overarching Grand Strategy for the war? It can be summed up in a series of injunctions: Run the war by the joint commands of a coalition and do anything to hold it together. Follow a "Europe First" policy: put your combined pressure on Hitler's Fortress Europe first, while restricting Douglas MacArthur to a holding operation in the Pacific. Insist on unconditional surrender. Share the occupation of Germany among the four coalition partners. Let the nation that holds the territory won in its sphere of influence set up new governments, after promising free elections. Trust the Russians and win their trust in turn. Prevail on them to share in the final defeat and occupation of Japan. The days of empire are over: in the colonial world apply the self-determination principle. Make the wartime coalition a basis for the United Nations and use it to build an orderly, peaceful postwar world.

In working out this Grand Strategy FDR played the conciliator within the coalition—a Prospero bent on casting a spell of peace over the discordances of prosecuting the war. But his contending associates each tried to use him against the others, while he in turn thought he was driving *them* in a wide tandem.

Yet who was driving whom? Of the partners Churchill fared worst despite their vaunted closeness, because he had a diminished power base, and Stalin fared best because he knew how to play on FDR's two great weaknesses—his liberal idealism and his failure of nerve in a coalition power struggle.

The fascinating correspondence between Roosevelt and Churchill reveals that while their personal ties were genial and much of their language sparkled with the raillery of close friendship, their relations were far rockier than the surface showed.

Churchill had wooed FDR and American power ardently when England stood alone, and had invoked the new world to restore the balance of the old—and won his bet as a survivor. After Pearl Harbor he felt exultant and brushed aside an aide's wary reference to America. "Now that she is in the harem," he said, "we talk to her quite differently." In time the superior American power asserted itself, and Churchill as a realist had to defer to it.

Roosevelt knew that he sat on a pyramid of growing power, while Britain's was slipping as it lost its economic edge and its imperial base. Churchill in turn was exasperated with the arrogance of a callow new world power, while Roosevelt had a cavalier disdain for what he saw as Churchill's benighted obsession with a dying empire.

Each was an aristocrat who had chosen the political vocation, each had been savaged by life, had wandered in the wilderness and returned in triumph. FDR had a record of political instinct and domestic achievement, while Churchill had switched camps erratically and was considered "unreliable."

Both were confidence men, not in the meretricious sense but in that of a leader's necessary nimbus of wiles and wizardry. But FDR had an eminently practical mind while Winston Churchill had a history-searching one. FDR, with his stamp collection, his ship models, and his desk cluttered with memorabilia, saw history in terms of its artifacts and residues. Churchill had a literary and conceptual sensibility. He took the prophetic view, watching for the intangibles of history in its broad movements of civilization-linked ideas. For Roosevelt the drama of history was played out in the theater of actions, for Churchill in the theater of will and ideas. But it was Roosevelt and not Churchill who saw himself, and was seen by the world, as the symbolic world leader—and both men knew it.

The Hitler-Roosevelt duel is one of the fateful confrontations of human history, ranking with the polar roles of Lenin and Wilson in the generation before. Roosevelt's career in power coincided almost exactly with Hitler's—from 1933 to 1945. The entire unfolding of Hitler's vision of conquest and vengeance was there for him to read. He came in time to understand Hitler's expansionism but not his psychic makeup nor the full reach of his inhumanity.

Hitler had his ambitious grand strategy—to isolate each nation in a geopolitical and psychological sequence, and to use their cumulative economic and military power to intimidate his successive targets. It was a brilliant strategy but vulnerable at its riskiest links, since it could afford no timetable blunders and no strategic failures. After his string of successes from the Rhineland and Sudetenland through France, Norway, and the Netherlands, he failed in his air war against Britain and took a giant risk with his belated Russian campaign in late June 1941. It was while he was mired down in the Russian mud and snow around Moscow that he made his final blunder of declaring war on America.

Of the prime players in the global drama Churchill and Stalin, who had both surprised him with their tenacity, gave way to Roosevelt as the archenemy in Hitler's mind. He denounced FDR as "the man who is the main culprit in this war." He was the demonic wraith Hitler wrestled with, day and night. Once America threw its full weight of manpower, matériel, and wealth into the coalition whose effective leader and symbol Roosevelt became, Hitler knew the odds had shifted against him.

It was not only American power but also Roosevelt himself that made the crucial difference. FDR added the dimension of his name and fame, his fiery symbolism, his mastery of the arts of public suasion. Hitler—and Goebbels too—knew something of what that meant. It broke Hitler's grand strategy apart.

Up to then he had counted on isolating and conquering each of his target nations in sequence—even Russia, which was proving the hardest. But Roosevelt changed all that. Hitler's invasion of Russia brought a shift in American war resources to Lend-Lease aid for Stalin. America's formal entrance into the war, less than six months later, meant the Hitler would have to face a huddle of enemies to the bitter end. He would have to prevail everywhere, against every enemy from Russia to North Africa, in a coalition animated by Roosevelt's flamboyant energies and cemented by American power and Roosevelt's will. This was not what Hitler had meant at all.

These years, 1941 and 1942, and this role as coalition leader, marked the acme of Roosevelt's greatness. Whatever his earlier falterings and miscalculations, he now used his power and talent to the utmost. He had joined with Churchill to keep Britain afloat in its island fortress, and America's support had been no mean element in the British will to hold on. He had joined with Stalin to keep Russia viable while Russian resistance—less Communist than "patriotic"—bled the German armies half to death. He had thrown in American forces, giving the war against Hitler priority over the war against Japan. So 1942 was the touch-and-go year. By 1943 Hitler knew that while he might postpone his doom he could not escape it.

Hitler's apocalyptic vision, refulgent with light for him, was also his great blindness. He was heir to two entrenched German myths— the Teutonic dream of racial purity and superiority, and the dream of conquest eastward (*Drang nach Osten*) to incorporate the Russian plains into Germany and populate them with pure Teutonic stock. In his mind the two dreams fed and reinforced each other. In the crunch of action they clashed. Had Hitler's invading armies come as liberators from Stalin's tyranny they could have enlisted the anti-Soviet discontents in countryside and cities and weakened the resistance. But they came as scornful conquerors and tyrants, to depopulate and repopulate what they had long coveted. The Russian people saw them as the worse evil and fought them for the Motherland.

By 1943 the tide had turned everywhere—which is when FDR overreached. Like some other great leaders he was better in adversity than in a growing victory. Riding the crest he turned to laying down the conditions of peace. In a press conference at Casablanca he yielded to a spur-of-the-moment impulse that he had not communicated to Churchill, playing it on his own. It was the vow of "unconditional surrender," and was doubtless meant to reassure Stalin and keep divisive German peace feelers from splitting the coalition.

Yet its consequences were dismal. Exactly at the point when the war turned against Hitler he cut himself and the Allies off from a strategy of encouraging the internal forces in Germany that could have shortened the war. The Office of Strategic Services had done psychiatric studies of Hitler, including one that correctly predicted that Hitler would kill himself rather than surrender.

A possible Allied strategy would have aimed at the aristocracy, which was never sympathetic to Hitler, and the army officers who preferred not to go down with him and could have overthrown and killed him—as almost happened anyway. Instead, the unconditional-surrender strategy hardened the German will to fight to the end. A shortening of the war could have saved millions of lives—those of the camp victims and of Allied as well as German soldiers. It might also have kept the Soviet armies from taking over Eastern Europe. It was a decision as momentous as it was shortsighted and impulsive.

The 1944 elections took place in the closing phase of the war in Europe, when Hitler was already beaten but before the outlines of Roosevelt's accommodation with Stalin had emerged.

FDR was clearly dying—clearly enough so that the insiders (especially the big-city bosses) managed luckily to ditch Henry Wallace and substitute Harry Truman as running mate. FDR's condition had been persistently misdiagnosed for years, until a young navy cardiologist—Commander Howard Bruenn—took over. He was in an advanced stage of cardiovascular disease. To campaign again was to court death; to enter on another four years of the most taxing office in the world was to embrace death as a sure thing.

But FDR, ever the great denier, denied this reality too. What else was he to do? To give up the presidency was to give up the war and the peace and life itself. So FDR ran for the fourth time (and for the fourth time I voted for him), and he beat Thomas Dewey, although by the closest popular-vote margin of all four. At Camp Pendleton, near San Diego, and again at the Bremerton naval shipyard, he suffered angina. But in the face of the Republican campaign on the "hidden issue" of his health he persisted in showing himself to the crowds, and toured New York and its boroughs in a driving rain.

It was again vintage Roosevelt. He was on his favorite stamping ground—electoral politics—and he knew how to win against Dewey even if he was to prove helpless against Stalin. His inaugural was a statement of wishful hope instead of a hard-bitten reality principle. Quoting Emerson he said, "We have learned the simple truth, that 'the only way to have a friend is to be one.'" Two days later he left for Yalta.

Would Dewey have been equally hopeful and helpless? There is no way of knowing. But judging from the views we know of his foreign-policy adviser, John Foster Dulles, the diplomatic positions of a Dewey administration—and perhaps its military-political strategy—would have been less high-minded perhaps but certainly more tough-minded than FDR's.

It was in his relationship to Stalin, the pivotal sector of his policy, that Roosevelt lavished his most determined energies, took his biggest gamble and met with his most grievous disasters. He understood Stalin even less than he did Hitler. Just as he underestimated Hitler's evil because evil was not a category in his political thinking, so he underestimated Stalin's cunning and ruthlessness—a more surprising weakness, considering his own finely honed political instincts.

While he dealt with Hitler as the enemy and with Churchill as an ally he could take for granted, he dealt with Stalin as the ally he had constantly to woo and win over. His decision about unconditional surrender probably turned on his fear that Stalin might either become suspicious or make a deal with Germany, and it cut off Roosevelt's chance of sharpening the war and of keeping the Soviet armies from their final occupying drive through Eastern Europe.

His dominant anxieties were to get Stalin's help with an assault on Japan, and to persuade him to work with America in the postwar United Nations. It is uncertain whether he reckoned with the bomb being made at Los Alamos—at his direction—to make the Japanese sue for peace. In any event it did not affect his sense of needing Stalin. By 1943 he was also becoming obsessed with the map of the postwar world and with the need to bring in Russia as a goodwill peace partner, through a spheres-of-influence division of the power spoils, and through decision-sharing and power-sharing within a United Nations run by the five Great Powers.

The two objectives are tied together, as indeed FDR's political-military war decisions and his postwar thinking were intimately tied. He was in this sense all of a piece.

He operated within a frame of three major propositions. One was that Britain, once saved, was needed (like France and China) for the United Nations, but that the British Empire was an antiquated, dying, and mischievous system and had to be replaced by new self-determined nations.

A second was that Stalin and his regime were no different, psychologically and morally, from America's other war allies, and that the sentiment most crippling to a stable and secure peace was anti-Communism. Thus FDR was the first and foremost anti-anti-Communist. Casablanca, Teheran, Yalta were the result.

A third was that a United Nations mechanism that profited from the experience of the League of Nations could avoid its blunders, provided the Great Powers of the war coalition used it for a peacetime coalition.

Roosevelt's failures in his latter-day decisions for the war and the postwar period flowed from these propositions. They were the more surprising because they came from the same level on which his New Deal success had been built—his understanding of power realities. He failed to see that, except for Russia, the war had broken the power structures of Central and Eastern Europe—of Germany, Austria, Poland, Italy, Greece, Turkey, Czechoslovakia, and the whole complex of East European nations—and that its ending would leave a power vacuum at the heart of Europe. The breaking of Nazism as an idea and the danger done to the idea of democracy early in the war would also leave an idea vacuum.

He also failed to understand that someone and something would have to move into both vacuums. The someone would be whoever had troops and tanks on the ground and planes in the air over it, and who had shown the will to use the power. In the end it proved to be Stalin. The something would be the idea with a mystique that would combine with the power. That idea proved to be Communism. But neither result was inevitable if Roosevelt had acted with strength and understanding.

His failure to act was due—applying Holmes's assessment—not to his temperament but to his thinking. In temperament he was still the power broker he had been in his New Deal days. Watching Roosevelt, in his talks with Harry Hopkins, as they made one decision after another about the fate of nations, it struck Churchill that FDR was acting as a "conjurer," dispensing magic all around. Churchill tried to do the same. One of the vivid scenarios of the war was the meeting between Churchill and Stalin in Moscow, where they parceled out parts of Europe and the Middle East between the Russian and Western camps. It was all done (so the legend goes) on a single piece of paper that Churchill had brought with him. But Roosevelt and Stalin had the power for the magician's role and Churchill did not.

Roosevelt's idealist strain made him deny his power-broker role in deciding on spheres of influence even while practicing it. He recalled the criticisms Woodrow Wilson had incurred for playing that role at Versailles. Yet at both occasions it was sensible enough, if done with some discrimination.

The real problem between the Western democratic Allies and Stalin lay not in the areas parceled out but in the remaining ones, which Stalin hoped to possess by force of arms before Roosevelt and Churchill dared to intervene. This was true of Poland, Czechoslovakia, Hungary, Yugoslavia, and as much of Germany itself as he could claim by force. He did not have to recall Versailles. His peace conference rested on his armies. For him diplomacy used the same means as war and was continuous with it.

With all the weight of American power, Roosevelt felt powerless in the crunch. It is hard to judge at what point he lost his capacity to shape history. Certainly at Yalta it was already too late. Yalta marked the formal validation of the power Stalin had already taken in the field. When FDR's military aide at Yalta, Admiral William D. Leahy, urged a tougher stance in the bargaining with Stalin over the composition of the Polish regime, FDR answered ruefully that the power realities were on Stalin's side. After all, it was Stalin—and not Roosevelt or Churchill—who had his troops in Poland. And despite all the talk about Stalin's puppet regime and elements from the democratic exile regimes, it was the naked power reality that counted.

The historic turning point came on the field of the common war against Germany, in military decisions that were in fact political decisions. By making the wrong military decisions Roosevelt and his top commanders in the European theater, including Generals Marshall

and Eisenhower, made the wrong political ones. With a few sharp
exceptions, notably General George Patton, who was counted a right-
wing political weirdo, everyone was under the spell of Dr. Win-the-
War. The idea was to knock Hitler's military power out, by whatever
means. If Stalin was willing to let his armies bear the brunt of savaging
Hitler's armies—and be savaged by them—then all power to him. Roosevelt gave the large direction to the military-political strategy in the
final phase of the war, as in the earlier phases, and his generals went
along. They were not eager to bloody their divisions. Stalin was.

So Roosevelt allowed, even invited, Stalin to drive through Eastern and Central Europe to Berlin, thereby violating the first principle
of war-and-peace geopolitics—possession of the turf. If anyone else
happened to be president—Wendell Willkie, Thomas Dewey, Henry
Wallace—the historians and the political culture would have called it
the idiocy it was. But it was Roosevelt, and it is a measure of the spell
he casts over us that few even now dare condemn his actions and inac-
tions outright. How can we criticize a president when he is the very
model we use for criticism?

What criticism there has been has focused on Yalta, which misses
the point because it was a diplomatic occasion after the military decisions had been taken. General Patton, reading the situation far better
than his superiors, had asked for orders to head for Prague and get
there ahead of the Russians. The gasoline for his tanks and trucks was
denied him, first by General Omar Bradley, then by Eisenhower. They
had support from General Marshall and from Roosevelt himself. What
else could FDR say, having settled on a high policy of letting the Russians get to their objectives and meeting them at Torgau, as the price
for Stalin's good behavior?

Yet the Patton gambit would have been a desperate one, even if
worth the gamble. It would have required a different mind-set for
FDR and a different political-military strategy, reaching back into
1943, as early as the Casablanca and Teheran conferences. It might
have involved Churchill's strategy of an Allied invasion through Southern Europe, moving rapidly into Eastern Europe, rather than the
cross-Channel invasion, which had so much distance to cover before it
could challenge Stalin's drive.

By late November 1943, with the Teheran Conference, when
FDR and Stalin first met, FDR's Grand Strategy was in place. Stalin
had not yet started on his drive to the East European capitals and
Berlin, which was timed to the June 1944 D-Day operation. But Roo-

sevelt had no political-military strategy that could deny Stalin his territorial objectives. So he fell back on concessions and personal relations. The concessions were to legitimize Stalin's 1939 conquest of the Baltic States, and to accept in principle his terms on the Lublin puppet government (although he stayed out of the formal discussions, lest he lose the Polish vote in 1944).

It was at Teheran that he launched his drive to charm Stalin, after a sleepless night of planning how to do it. The "how" was to do it by cracks at Churchill's expense until Stalin smiled and finally "broke out into a deep, hearty guffaw. . . . The ice was broken and we talked like men and brothers." The guffaw and the brotherly talk were to prove expensive for FDR, Europe, and America.

At Yalta similarly FDR refused to meet with Churchill for a brotherly exchange, lest he awaken Stalin's suspicions of an Anglo-American agreement on terms. He found a formula for a Polish government, which Stalin cheerfully accepted because he saw it for the face-saving device it was—and as cheerfully proceeded later to break. FDR also agreed—in return for Stalin's promise to help in the attack on Japan—to give Russia concessions at the expense of Chiang Kai-shek, which enabled the Chinese Communists to start on their road to victory.

Once boxed in, there was little FDR could do in power terms. He might have tried to outrace the Russians to Berlin and the Eastern capitals, which was what the Nazi leaders and generals waited for. Stalin had as much to fear from such a confrontation as Roosevelt. He knew the strength of the American forces and economy. But while FDR had wooed him in their personal encounters, Stalin had played hard to get. He had taken FDR's measure and his own, and knew that at the crunch it would be FDR and not he who would flinch. FDR wanted to be a high-minded global leader. Stalin wanted only Russia's power and his own. Thus he outfoxed, out-thought, and out-maneuvered the man who had organized Hitler's defeat and saved the Western tradition and values.

FDR was very much himself and no one else. He tried hard not to be Woodrow Wilson, seeking to avoid the peace blunders and rigidity that doomed him. He appointed two Republican Cabinet members— Henry L. Stimson and Frank Knox—and he avoided a postwar peace conference like Versailles. Yet his roots in the Wilsonian worldview were deep and, for all his good intentions, he got caught in a fatal rigidity of his own.

The "Atlantic Charter" and the "Four Freedoms," the product of his early meetings with Churchill, were strongly Wilsonian but also good political warfare against Hitler. I was involved—along with Archibald MacLeish, Reinhold Niebuhr, E. B. White, and Malcolm Cowley—in composing a widely distributed pamphlet on the Four Freedoms. We had the sense of working in the shadow of the little group that drew up Wilson's "Fourteen Points."

FDR in turn, to some extent, also worked in Wilson's shadow, but warily. To overcome the weakness of the League of Nations he inserted sanctions into the United Nations making the Security Council— an instrument of the Great Powers—rather than the Assembly its core. Nor did he wait for a big overarching peace conference but turned the need for Allied planning into a portable feast of strategy summits, moving in a mounting progression from conference to conference, to lay the base for an ultimate peace based on a harmonious equilibrium between the victorious powers.

The result was to entangle war decisions and peace objectives, and make the postwar world map dependent on immediate military situations in the worst possible mix. No theory of war-making or peace-making could envisage such a process as a healthy one for either.

As a corollary it necessarily made FDR dependent on the temperament and mood of Stalin since it was for him to decide what kind of government he would or would not command in the territories he controlled. The picture of the leader of the free world truckling to the totalitarian overlord of the Russians is a demeaning one. No one can argue with FDR's acceptance of Stalin as an ally at a time when Russia had to be supported to break Hitler's power. But Churchill's willingness in June 1941 to "make a pact with the Devil himself" was a clearer-headed approach than FDR's eager embrace of Russia, along with the brutal "human engineering" of Stalin, whose cold-blooded death-sentencing for millions of peasants exceeded even Lenin's ruthlessness. It was a phase of Roosevelt's vaunted pragmatism, and his assessment of Stalin's iron resolve was borne out by the final victory of Leningrad and the destruction of Hitler's army there. But it reached beyond pragmatism in Roosevelt, to a personalism which led him to focus on Stalin as a man and a temperament, and write off the whole structure of both Communism and nationalism, which formed the engine that drove the man. This blindness to the reach and inner meaning of ideology was also operative in his miscalculation of how far Hitler would be driven by his murderous grandiosity.

One might argue that this is all hindsight and that FDR could not know as much about Stalin and Communism as we do today. But the Soviet state had been in power for a quarter century and could be known by its fruits. A truer view of Stalin and the Soviet Union was available to FDR—from the first ambassador he had sent, William C. Bullit, who had watched the Russian Revolution and its leaders from Moscow and whose embassy experience had disillusioned him. There was a group of journalists and scholars, including Louis Fischer, James Burnham, and William Henry Chamberlain, who had studied the experience of the Purge Trials, the Spanish Civil War, the Nazi-Soviet Pact, and the iron repressions, and whose counterview to that of Roosevelt, Hopkins, and Ambassador Joseph Davies was available to be drawn upon. Woodrow Wilson had a sterner view of Lenin and had joined in the Allied effort to support the anti-Bolshevik forces and failed ingloriously. FDR did not intend to make the same miscalculations.

To hope, as FDR did, that nations united in war would therefore also be united in peace was too amateurish a verbal trap for a sophisticated leader to fall into. The war united their national interests against a common enemy, but with the enemy defeated their national interests were once more caught up in conflict.

He was also betrayed by the fallacy of the instrument—his belief that an organization could provide peace when there was no peace but only the hope of goodwill. A world statesman must have vision, and here FDR followed Wilson's high lead. But having failed in the territorial decisions his vision was fixed on the United Nations as instrument, and on persuading Stalin to become part of the solution there. As a result he developed a rigidity, as Wilson had done, and paid a heavy price for it—the division of Europe, the enslavement of half of it and the endangering of the other half by the shadow of its power. Instead of becoming part of the solution Stalin and his emerging Soviet empire became a deeper part of the problem.

Just as Wilsonian was FDR's support for the principle of national self-determination. He linked this with an "anti-imperialism" that made the mix, as it proved, destabilizing. Like other "progressive" Western leaders, Roosevelt and Hopkins were under the spell of an economist they may never have read directly—John A. Hobson—who dominated the anti-imperialist climate of their time and who saw imperialism as an evil child of capitalism. A more famous thinker and revolutionary, Lenin, had used Hobson in turn to shape the thesis that imperialism was the "last stage of capitalism," involving wars of increasing intensity and leading to the victory of Communism.

By these combined theses on imperialism Roosevelt was himself their best illustration, as was the war he had brought America into. But that did not keep him from cutting down the positions of Churchill, pressing him to grant independence to India and to follow the self-determination pattern elsewhere. The exasperated Prime Minister declared that he had not "become his Majesty's First Minister to preside over the liquidation of the British Empire"—and ironically had little choice but to do exactly that. By destabilizing the empires, through the self-determination slogans associated with his name and fame, Roosevelt heightened the options for Communist power—once it was strengthened in Russia and Eastern Europe—to move into the power vacuum in Africa, Asia, and the Middle East by coups and insurgencies. Thus FDR's fears of British and Western imperialism gave Soviet imperialism its chance to take off with half of Europe in tow and the Third World to penetrate.

One ends with a profile of a man of winning temperament and overpowering presence, brilliantly effective in a peaceful domestic revolution and in war management, totally confident of his judgment even in areas where his experience—however lengthy and varied—had prepared him in many ways but not in the one way that in the end counted. That was an understanding of the large frame of geopolitics when facing an illusionless master of it like Stalin. In that confrontation Roosevelt proved to be more trusting and high-minded and less tough-minded than a great national leader had any right to be. His thinking simply did not measure up to his temperament.

His illusions did not stop at his estimate of Stalin but included his estimate of himself. He saw himself as a cool pragmatic realist, unflappable, unfoolable, unbeatable, and capable of charming and disarming his allies as well as his antagonists. But he also came to see himself as a lofty leader giving direction to the world, to dismay the demons of darkness and enhance the glory of the angels of light. But his faulty judgment sometimes confused them, and he failed to grasp the ironies of history that bring unintended consequences in the wake of grand intentions.

At no point can an assessment of Roosevelt as man, mind, character, and temperament be separated from the cultural context in which he worked. In the process of managing the polity and waging war he helped create a political culture in his own image—a culture that increasingly lacked figures of status to challenge him. The circle of his advisers narrowed and their range of experience and outlook diminished. Hardly anyone of moment was around to correct the faults in his worldview. The intellectual and political culture that surrounded him (of which I must ruefully admit I was part) shared his view of most issues, including Russia and Communism. If anything, the academic and media elite was more pro-Soviet than he and—as on the Nazi-Soviet Pact, the "phony war," Lend-Lease, and the Second Front—leaned on him when he faltered.

He was a brilliant practitioner of politics, but neither his intellect nor his instincts enabled him to transcend the tyranny of the narrow culture he had helped create, which now in turn held him in its vise. The rebel in him, who had performed so effectively against the enemies on the right, would not turn toward the end against the enemy on the left—or even recognize him as such. So he went down in what was hailed as a glorious victory, and paid a fearsome price for it.

He might have retired in 1944 with the victory all but won, but he did not, and he overstayed his time of effective leadership in his last years, his stamina exhausted and his judgment scarred, in an office in which he saw himself as the indispensable hero. He was a shadow of the man he had been. His young stalwarts had mostly died or left him and only Harry Hopkins lingered like a wraith. Eleanor was often absent and their estrangement became more hopeless. As his difficulties with Stalin grew, so did his own languor. His disease-racked body caught up with him. His work spells grew shorter, his fatigue greater. He had breathing problems and was sensitive to cold. There is a hypothesis now, backed by his son James, that these were symptoms of a post-polio regression which often happens—years later—to its victims.

The trip to Yalta exacted a savage penalty from his organism, which was no match for a Stalin riding the crest of his territorial and diplomatic victories. On his return journey he received three monarchs in succession—Farouk of Egypt, Haile Selassie of Ethiopia, Ibn Saud of Saudi Arabia—but the power and the authority he exerted could not make up for the sorry fact of Yalta.

Gallantly as he tried to recover, he was a president going through the motions, wielding power over millions who did not know he was dying. The one consolation was the return of Lucy Rutherfurd, whom he had been seeing secretly since her husband's lingering illness and death. In some ways the memory of their love was what the intervening years of struggle and triumph had been about. She was at the Warm Springs cottage with him, quietly smiling as she knitted, when the cerebral stroke and hemorrhage hit him that April afternoon in 1945. The Tristram potion of power, replacing love, had begun to wane, but I like to think that in those closing days the potion of love had returned.

He was mourned and is remembered for the titanic figure he had been, and his name still resonates with his exploits, for he remains the paradigm president. But we now see how flawed a paradigm it was, which may enable future presidents to free themselves—as happens in the history of science—for experiments and experience that take account of his failures as well as his triumphs.

HARRY S TRUMAN

THE PLUTARCHIAN PRESIDENT

WHEN HARRY TRUMAN SUCCEEDED Franklin Roosevelt and sat in the familiar chair at Roosevelt's desk, everyone thought it was too big for him. For a time he thought so too, but before long he and they knew differently. However we may rank him, Harry Truman did more than anyone since Lincoln to compel us to rethink what prepares a president for stature in history. He has also made us rethink Lord Acton's overvalued proposition about the unusually corrupting effect of high power, and Chaucer's observation about Prince Hector—that "great power and moral virtue are seldom seen in one person together."

He came of no dynastic stock, never went to college, managed and worked his father's farm until thirty-five, tried various ways of making a living (including a failed haberdashery shop) before turning to politics, and was fifty before he could break away from a lackluster county overseer's life into national politics, to run for the Senate as a choice of the Pendergast machine of Kansas City.

It was an unlikely preparation for functioning as the head of the American imperium during more than seven stormy years after Roosevelt. Yet I question the now encrusted Jacksonian tag for him (first used by Roy Roberts of the *Kansas City Star*) to prove that an "ordinary man" can make a good president. Let it be said, against all the obfuscation, that he was not an ordinary but an extraordinary man, who remained in ordinary circumstances, undiscovered by others and by himself until long after most other men on their way to the presidency had shown their mettle and captured attention. What he illustrated was Jefferson's conviction, in his great correspondence with John Adams, that a democracy requires "a natural aristocracy of virtue and talent"—or (in our current usage) character and ability. Truman, possessing both, was a distinctive man, a natural aristocrat.

Talent crops up in unexpected places and at incalculable times out of the soil of American experience. Truman's roots went deep into the

Missouri ground, and he grew up with strong family ties. He was a nearsighted boy who ransacked the town and school libraries, read biography and history, took to heart the fiery precepts of Plutarch's heroes, and in his secret life myth dreamed of becoming one.

In terms of genes and family ecology Truman's inheritance laid a bedrock base of character for him. Even if the Senate and presidency had never happened to him he would have left the impression on his community of a strong, candid, straight-shooting man, as well as an able one. The families of his four grandparents were all pioneers who had come to the Missouri frontier from Kentucky—sturdy, self-reliant, and salty. They were farmers, traders, speculators, adventurers, part of the ongoing westward migration, moving about on the frontier of the Middle Border, restless for a good piece of land and a home for the family, eager in the American fashion to make some money and improve their situation. The women too were fully engaged in the daily coping with land, climate, family, and the vicissitudes of life. There were no weaklings in the larger family constellation, no sniveling or self-pity. Self-help and self-reliance were the operative life strategies.

This was the continuing Puritan ethic, transplanted from its original New England locus to the Midwest and the Middle Border, stripped of some of its earlier dourness about life's pleasures, more than touched by the spirit of American business enterprise. Truman's father and both his grandfathers dabbled in various moneymaking ventures, as Harry himself did in his early manhood years, but the necessary margin of ruthlessness and wiliness that went with the smart Yankee trader on the frontier seemed to be almost wholly absent in them and him. In this respect his heritage was a conflicted one—to "make something" of oneself, but not at the expense of a strict code of personal values and morals.

It was a heritage of intense individualism, with disdain for rank, ceremony, "side," one that stressed the authentic selfhood of the person, beyond the distortions of success, happiness, fulfillment, power that have attached to individualism in our time. This was neither wholly the Benjamin Franklin ("Poor Richard") acquisitive brand nor the Walt Whitman "leaves of grass," "I sing myself" brand that we usually think of as dividing the field of individualism. It was characteristic of the region, a Mark Twain individualism, scornful of pretense, stubborn, somewhat perverse, fiercely asserting the authenticity of the natural man.

There was one thing finally the Middle Border frontier gave to the later Truman—a political flexibility that he did not have to sweat for because it came with the territory. The rural areas of Missouri, which were Truman's political base, had been Confederate in the Civil War, and Truman carried a tang of the Baptist South with him that gave him a common world with John Nance Garner and Sam Rayburn of Texas. But Kansas City and Sedalia had also become strongholds of Catholic and black migration. Thus Truman's roots in the Pendergast machine made him acceptable to the other big-city machines that controlled the Democratic Party, and to the labor, Catholic, and black leaders who (with FDR) had become increasingly influential in it. Without this mix of appeal Truman could not have won his second Senate race in 1940, or the 1944 vice presidential nomination, nor triumphed in his only presidential run in 1948.

In his immediate family models there was an adventurous horse-trader father who was always ready for land or commodity speculation as well and always failing at it—and a strong, steady mother who was (like many frontier women) the family's culture carrier, and furnished the element of continuity that a child needs to feel secure.

Luck played a large role in Truman's life, but even the bad luck was at times turned to his advantage. Harry's "flat eyes" as a young boy meant he had to wear glasses to function in his immediate environment, which kept him from the rough children's games and kept him around the house and turned him into a chronic reader and a demon letter-writer. But to ward off the consequent cries of "sissy" and his own fears of being one, it also led him to wear a habitual mask of hair-trigger sharpness and no-nonsense tough-mindedness about the world.

These influences may explain in part why this young man of a strong innate gentleness was always clipped and "businesslike" in his style, why he turned to masculine ventures (farming, oil-drilling, a zinc mine, banking, the National Guard, war service), why he became part of a hard-driving political machine, why he assumed a "Give 'em hell" stance of militancy in his campaigns.

Born in 1884 Truman was sixteen at the turn of the century, and should thus have been exposed to the same innovative liberal and radical doctrine that reached FDR at Harvard and Columbia Law School and were part of the great liberal intellectual renaissance in the first decades of the century. But Truman could not get to a college or law school where these academic influences might reach him. He applied to the Naval Academy as the only free higher education he could get, but was turned down because of his eyes. He might have entered a Missouri college but his father broke his leg and Harry had to run the family farm at Grandview until he left for the war. When he worked earlier as bank clerk in Kansas City he talked of night law school but could never afford the time. He once said that farming, banking, and war were the three basic experiences a man should have—and he had all three. Yet he was the first president since Abraham Lincoln and Andrew Johnson without any higher education.

Perhaps this saved him from learning many things that were not so, which is a way of saying that while Truman missed out at digging into the complexity of ideas he also was protected from the confusions and distortions of reality that came with the intense academic liberalism of his time—to which even a pragmatic FDR succumbed in his final years.

He was a late bloomer, but his character and style were set early. He had to adapt to his skimpy schooling, and he did it by knowing what he knew in psychological and moral depth and in sharp common-sense assertiveness. His later boast that he had read all the books in the Independence town library, including the encyclopedias, was of course self-protective. William V. Shannon, in calling him a "closet intellectual," overshot the mark—although in the right direction, not the usual condescending one. Truman had a strong streak of anti-intellectualism, as witness his contemptuous remarks about Harvard graduates and other "overeducated SOBs." This masked his insecurity about his own lack of higher education. But he was a closet psychologist and something of a moral philosopher about the life journey, which absorbed him in his reading of biographies.

In the wake of books, like Thomas Carlyle's *On Heroes, Hero-Worship, and the Heroic in History*, there was an awakening American interest in the lives of great and distinctive men, including generals, statesmen, and "captains of industry" like J. P. Morgan and Andrew Carnegie. It reached far into the reading culture, as far as Independence.

One of the notable events in Harry Truman's boyhood was his mother's gift, on his twelfth birthday, of a four-volume set of biographies, *Great Men and Famous Women*. It was subtitled *A Series of Pen and Pencil Sketches of the Lives of More than 200 of the Most Prominent Personages in History*, and edited by Charles Francis Horne, who couldn't have known how a nearsighted boy in a Missouri town would devour the volumes year after year—lives and sketches and all.

They were Plutarch in Victorian dress, and from them, with the taste they strengthened for classical history, the boy turned to Plutarch's *Parallel Lives* and to the grand theme of Edward Gibbon's *The History of the Decline and Fall of the Roman Empire.* This was self-education in the great tradition. The Plutarchian virtues were added to the Puritan values, and to both of them were added somehow the searing lessons of the Roman Empire, laid down unimaginably as a residue in the mind of a boy who would someday govern the American Empire.

Amidst the prosaic tasks of his young manhood the reading hunger was never slaked. Even in the haberdashery shop (so Eddie Jacobson's wife recalls) the slack hours would find Harry Truman in the back of the store—reading a book. We have never quite recognized that he was one of the *readingest* presidents we have had—not on the intellectual level of Jefferson, the two Adamses, Madison, or Lincoln, but in his own right as someone for whom print was (in Emerson's great phrase) "the daily bread of his eyes."

Having laid a character base his life problem was to lay a skill base, so that he could make a living and—in his own phrase—"make something" of himself. To forgo college in order to run the family farm, at the time of family need, was for Truman an act of simple duty. Yet it was also an act of sacrifice with far-reaching consequences, which he was reticent about ever discussing. It limited his range of skills and experience to the workaday tasks of the farm and to the few business ventures he could undertake. The rest of the wide world of opportunity must have seemed to him a world of doors closed to him—doors he could not even knock at. Hence the note of forced gaiety and of a don't-care wry indifference about the larger world that one detects in his *Letters to Bess* during his long courtship.

Yet the farm days were not without their élan. He had an instinct for managing and for running things that today we call the art of "administration." As a young man he preferred life in Kansas City and his job as a bank clerk; a good banker was probably lost when he had to take seriously to farming Grandview. Yet he approached it methodically, getting into "scientific" farming, fertilizing, and crop rotation. He ran it unsentimentally as a business, but he also spoke truth to the earth, never hurting it for a quick yield. He was to speak truth to each of his projects, ultimately to high power itself while administering it cannily. Not the least of his traits was an innate passion for order, which he applied to every task—small and large.

His first chance to apply these talents to use outside of his immediate gambit came with the war. Until then his life was a protracted moratorium in which he strove and waited for something—he scarcely knew what—that seemed never destined to come off. It was the war experience, as a captain of a National Guard artillery battery in France, that enabled him to break out of Grandview and Independence and his narrow round of daily duties and family obligations, and try himself in the larger world.

It proved the first major testing of his adult life, and its consequences reached beyond anything he could calculate at the time. He volunteered for service soon after America entered the war, helped recruit men for his battery, was chosen as first lieutenant in the 129th Field Artillery, trained at Fort Sill, Oklahoma, ran his battery canteen flawlessly, went with it to France, and became Captain of Battery D—a rowdy, hard-drinking band of 200 who had learned how to break each of its past commanders. Instead, at the first sign of insubordination, he lambasted the whole array of unruly officers and men. The lesson stuck with them.

It stuck with Truman too. He learned that he had what it takes to be a leader of men. In the stress of battle, when the battery came close to panicking under unexpected fire, "Captain Harry" held them in line by sheer will and by a torrent of epithets. It convinced him that he could discipline rough unruly men to his command by word and example.

The war also gave him a little community of his war comrades, which was to serve him better than he knew, as a social context that erased class and religious boundaries. Truman had been an outsider to Bess's "social crowd" in Independence. He had welcomed membership in the Masonic rite, which gave him statewide meetings to attend. But many of his battery mates were Irish and German Catholics from a Jesuit high school in Kansas City. His closest friend was his canteen sergeant, Eddie Jacobson, a Jew. Truman, at heart a joiner and egalitarian, welcomed his war and postwar camaraderie as the great leveler.

The war separation brought his courtship of Bess to a decision point. It enabled Bess to break through her mother's opposition to the match as beneath her daughter's rightful expectations, and it established the enduring equilibrium of the Truman household—Harry, and Bess as "the Boss," and his mother-in-law, who lived with them and held them both in some sense in thrall. Still intent on a business venture as the best way to "make something" of himself, he scraped together some capital and joined Eddie Jacobson in a Kansas City haberdashery shop, which at first prospered and was then caught in a postwar deflation that squeezed out the value of the inventory. For his part Truman refused to seek refuge in bankruptcy and spent years repaying his loans plus interest. But—along with earlier hapless ventures in a zinc mine and an oil field—it ended his dream of business success.

What remained as a second best—politics—proved to be his true career. The haberdashery failure became part of presidential legend. Yet what a stroke of luck it was. Suppose it had succeeded! Looking back at those feckless years of seeking and striving one gets the sense of a young American following the lead of his culture, digging for treasure in the recognized places, when all along the treasure was hidden within himself. Yet not so hidden as to escape the notice of his battery mates, who saw "Captain Harry" as a natural leader. One of them, Jim Pendergast, nephew of the head of the Kansas City Pendergast organization, brought him into the Pendergast clan.

Truman had dabbled in local machine politics as an amateur but now he ran for "judge" (in reality commissioner or supervisor) of the rural Eastern district of Jackson County, and won. He was elected three times and served for ten years—eight of them as supervising judge of the county, comprising a half-million people. He had always hungered to run things and proved a tireless campaigner and good administrator. He established a new system of county roads, as planned by a nonpartisan board, remodeled the Independence courthouse, and built a new skyscraper courthouse in Kansas City.

He had finally found his true vocation. The road to it, however roundabout and wayward, had not been wasted. He had learned skills— on the land, in the bank, in business, and in the army. He had born the burden of debt and the verve of failure. He had learned the reality principle of how life actually is, not always what it should be, but also how to remain true to himself within that reality.

It could not have been easy to make moral ends meet in collaboration with a prime practitioner of big-city machine politics. Truman always insisted that Pendergast never asked him to do anything he couldn't do with conscience, and there is no reason to doubt him. He did it by a render-unto-Caesar separation of realms, giving Pendergast the patronage due to the system, running his own realm by his exacting lights while not looking too inquisitively into Caesar's. It was a nonimperialist ethic, and it served at once as a base for Truman's system of loyalties up and down and for the contempt he developed for the "snivelers" who were not as "worthy in the sight of the Lord" as Pendergast. But the belligerence with which he made this judgment showed that his critics had touched a sensitive nerve.

He had started late at his newfound vocation, in 1922, when he was thirty-eight. He worked at it faithfully for twelve years. Pendergast needed him for support in the rural Protestant area of the county, and for the respectability that Truman's reputation for integrity gave him. In turn he needed Pendergast for the support his machine gave him. It was an honest quid pro quo. Truman was good at his end of it, but it would be foolish to think he was also happy at it. Time seemed to stand still. Or perhaps time moved too fast while he seemed to stand still and nothing new happened. It seemed an unending wait.

In 1934 it ended. Two years earlier Truman had hoped to make a run for Congress, which was the summit he aimed at, but the prize had gone elsewhere. When Pendergast had a tactical need for him in 1934 it turned out to be for a prize more dazzling than Congress—a Senate seat. Pendergast's Kansas City machine was in a power struggle with the rival Democratic St. Louis machine. In the primary both brought out their "ghost" vote—"This is the time," someone quipped, "for all good cemeteries to come to the aid of the Party"—but Pendergast's was better at it, at the height of its power and efficiency. Truman campaigned inexhaustibly, at his own expense, adding to the machine's skullduggery his own reputation as administrator and his influence with the hundreds of county judges who formed the political infrastructure of the rural counties. He won. At long last, at fifty, he had a high political post, and his agonized waiting was over.

That was when he wrote his revealing diary note: "I have come to the place where all men strive to be at my age . . . where I really belong."

Truman's first Senate term was marked by what must be called the "Truman syndrome"—the undervaluing of himself when facing a great office and task, leading others to take him at his word and undervalue him in consequence. The leap from Jackson County administrator to the U.S. Senate was exhilarating, but it was so far beyond his dream as to be almost traumatic.

He lacked FDR's unfailing self-confidence and his sense that power and high place were his destiny and his due. It was Truman's first career venture east, his first chance to test himself against the vaunted names of the national Establishment of both parties.

He announced early that he did not expect to be "one of the great Missouri Senators," and what he may have intended as humility became apologetic and self-demeaning. On his first visit to Washington he described himself to a Kansas City reporter as "only an humble member of the next Senate, green as grass and ignorant as a fool about practically everything worth knowing." Roosevelt and the men around him condescended to the new junior senator from Missouri, when they noticed him at all. For some time (following the bad advice of Vice President John Nance Garner) he made no Senate speeches, as if out of fear of calling attention to himself and making himself vulnerable to those who were bound to view him as a Pendergast "office boy." But this did not save him from being a target, while it exposed him to the risk of seeming a cipher as well.

One gets the sense of an apprehensive outsider coming to Washington for once unaware of his peculiar quality and distinction, seeking to efface himself in that bright galactic firmament of New Deal luminaries, presided over by the greatest luminary of them all. President Roosevelt ignored him, and when he finally received him Truman was almost totally speechless, telling himself later that it was due to his sense of the presidency as an office, not the man.

What made it worse for Truman was the question of how he had come there. In all too literal a sense Tom Pendergast had been the "god from the machine" who had rescued him from oblivion. There were detractors enough, in the Missouri press and in Washington, who came to call him the "Senator from Pendergast," even though anyone who knew him would know that he could be no man's puppet. Truman was helpless to answer, and was in a Washington political environment in which his usual qualities did not work. He was too straightforward to trade votes for administration favors, and too independent to fawn on the existing New Deal power constellation, even while he voted for it consistently out of principle.

Of the men around Roosevelt only Harry Hopkins (as Truman later recalled) was "kind" to him. The rest, including FDR, either took him for granted, since they could almost always count on his vote, or were downright hostile, eager to replace him, figuring that his political fortunes would fall with the collapsing fortunes of his patron, Tom Pendergast, who was in deep trouble with federal law officials during most of Truman's first term.

Characteristically he tried to take his measure of this senatorial office with his usual systematic thoroughness. "I studied up on the lives of each Senator and by the time the session started I knew pretty much the history of every man, and why they acted as they did." Considering some of his fellow senators—Arthur Vandenberg of Michigan, Carl Hayden of Arizona, Alben Barkley of Kentucky, Pat Harrison of Mississippi, J. Hamilton Lewis of Illinois, Burton Wheeler of Montana,

Warren Austin of Vermont, Hugo Black of Alabama, and Huey Long of Louisiana—it was a touching display of faith in acquiring insight into character at second hand, by reading and study. He approached his legislative tasks with the same thoroughness, haunting the Library of Congress and checking out scores of books for office and home study. The new senator from Missouri was still the boy who had ransacked the Independence library.

But that boy was now in a new learning environment, at the hub of world power and at a time of the rethinking of an entire society. He had learned on the farm, at the bank, in the war, in the primitive political give-and-take of Pendergast politics and county-courthouse administration, and had learned well. But he had never taken as broad a learning leap as this one.

Up to this time he had come up against men on a local and statewide scale and had quickly taken the measure of their hardness and talent. But now the scale had suddenly magnified, the more so because the New Deal had brought an inpouring of ambitious and sophisticated men to a Washington dominated by FDR and his in-group.

It was at this point that Truman encountered two men who were to shape his legislative and investigative style. One was Max Lowenthal. I first learned of Truman through him in 1936, when I was editing *The Nation*, and Lowenthal—a Washington original—regaled me from time to time with talk of whom and what to watch on the Washington scene. He had persuaded Senator Burton Wheeler, head of the Interstate Commerce Committee, to investigate railroad finance and reorganization, but Wheeler—who was more interested in fighting FDR's Court-packing plan—left the railroad investigation for Truman to pursue. Thus Truman and Lowenthal, the committee counsel, became a working team.

Lowenthal was fascinated by Truman's zeal to learn and his straight-shooting courage in attacking the vested interests of railroads—including those in his own state. Few other senators, he said, could have withstood the pressures that converged on Truman. Together they dug up evidence on the looting of railroad assets by men who had been enriching themselves even in the severest phases of the Depression. Truman delivered a couple of hair-raising speeches in the Senate on the railroad millionaires and on the "highest of the high-hats in the legal profession" who were guilty of "tricks that would make an ambulance chaser in a coroner's court blush with shame." They got him some media attention briefly, which fell away, but they tell us the temper and strength of the man. These were not the words of a machine boss's "office boy" but of a man learning about the seamy side of high finance and angered and aroused by what he learned.

When Lowenthal, at one point, offered to introduce the senator to Justice Louis D. Brandeis, Truman backed off. "I'm not used to meeting people like that," he said. But in the end he went along, and in time became a frequenter of the justice's afternoons at home, and was entranced by the mind that had captured Woodrow Wilson and shaped his "New Freedom" economic thinking. He had become an almost mythic figure in Washington—half Jeffersonian apostle, half Hebrew prophet.

It was a more eventful encounter for Truman's thinking and skills—and his future—than the research has yet dealt with. The second-term senator who was picked for the vice presidential nomination in 1944 because of his industrious investigations did not spring full-blown into public attention in the early 1940s. He emerged in what seemed his lackluster first term in the mid-1930s as a hard-working, courageous legislative investigator who did not shine on the floor of the Senate but saw himself as "a workhorse, not a show-horse," and who learned by sheer sweat on Senate subcommittees the arts he was to put to such brilliant use in the 1940s.

He became expert on the transport infrastructure of America— the automobile roads he knew so well as county administrator, the railroads he came to master, and the new civil-aviation industry whose regulations he pioneered. He was able to frame legislation in 1938 for a Civil Aeronautics Board, largely because the air industry was newer and had fewer vested interests than the railroads. It took him until 1940 to get a new Transportation Act passed, fighting all the way against the bankers and lawyers who had fattened on railroad financing and reorganizations.

No thinker himself, he needed an intellectual framework to give meaning to this new experience of his, and to sharpen his investigative skills. He found what he needed in Brandeis and his protégé, Lowenthal. From his Brandeis reading and conversations he seized upon his seminal ideas. One was that the corporate and legal barons exercised their control over industrial power and insurance company assets by their use of "other people's money." The second was that the concentration of economic power was inefficient as well as arbitrary—that it was the "curse of bigness." The third was in some ways the most important for Truman—Brandeis's moral belief in politics and economics as the arts of the possible—that a small group of committee men of goodwill, armed with thoroughly researched factual knowledge, can make a difference in taming the monster power aggregates and thus make a difference in the working of democracy and the welfare of the common man.

There is little evidence that these doctrines, as such, carried over in any concrete form into Truman's "Fair Deal" when he became president. But every national leader must at some point find an impulsion that gives shape to his thinking and striving, providing some intellectual and moral form. Truman was not power possessed or power driven. His impulsion came originally from his character and sense of duty. But I have little doubt that his experience with Brandeis gave some form to social thinking that would otherwise be inchoate or else merely borrowed from the New Deal—which Truman all along resisted. By 1940, with both his important legislative bills accepted and passed, Truman had completed his difficult first encounter with the Senate and laid the groundwork for his thinking and method in a second, for the more important investigative experience to come.

I consider the 1940 contest the crucial campaign of Truman's entire career—the prototype of his vaunted climactic 1948 presidential victory, but also the campaign that validated his sense of self after the battering of his first term and made him a prime Senate figure.

Tom Pendergast had stretched the bow of his expanding life style tighter, and grew more negligent about how he financed it. Convicted of tax evasion, he was in jail and his machine in ruins. Transparently honest himself, Truman was an inevitable target-by-association for his political opponents. He had no money for a campaign, his political stock was low, his media support almost nil. Roosevelt, always devious, was dallying with Truman's chief rival in the primaries for the Senate seat, Lloyd Stark, hoping to build a new Missouri power center around him. He sent word to Truman that a reelection bid looked hopeless and, as a consolation prize, offered him life-tenure membership on the Interstate Commerce Commission. Truman angrily refused it, sending back word that he meant to run again, even if his own vote was the only vote he would get.

It was a low point in his political career. From its start he had run with an organization, campaigning hard himself but always counting on its support. Now he was totally on his own if he chose to run again. But characterologically, against all the odds, he had to follow what his whole being demanded—to fight it out, whatever the result.

But as a now seasoned fighter he was not without guile. His readings of the politics of antiquity told him that Stark was an overreacher who could be counted on to destroy himself—with some help. Some of Truman's friends reached Maurice Milligan, the prosecutor who had sent Pendergast to jail, suggested that Stark should not be the sole beneficiary of an easy victory over Truman, and lured him into joining the race—thus splitting the anti-Pendergast "reform" vote. Only then did Truman announce his candidacy. It was a classical ploy, but an honorable one.

The rest was a dogged uphill climb, with Stark ahead most of the way but with Truman edging him out in the closing phase, surprising everyone but himself. He had no money for radio spots as Stark did, had to borrow to pay his skeletal staff, used his skimpy funds for mailings to get small donations, covered most of the counties of the state, often making ten or twelve speeches a day—always unadorned, direct, pungent.

But there was a logic to his campaign strategy. He built it on his honesty and personal credibility, his support of FDR's New Deal and his foreign policies and defense effort, his association with labor (especially the railway unions, which worked hard for him), his speaking out for equal rights for all minorities—including the blacks.

But he was not idle about using traditional politics, salvaging what friends he could of the Kansas City organizations, directing his campaign aides in their trade-offs with the St. Louis organization. A last-minute switch from Stark to Truman by Robert Hannegan, a newly rising figure in St. Louis politics, furnished neatly enough about 10,000 votes, to give Truman his statewide victory margin over Stark of some 8,000 votes.

When he entered the Senate chamber a few days later, his Senate colleagues, to a man, rose to applaud him. They were applauding a politician who had shown himself very much a man, and a man whose integrity did not keep him from being a politician. It was the triumph of a whole man.

It was in his second Senate term that Harry Truman gathered the sweet fruits of his years of striving. He felt exhilarated by his investigative work, and relished the camaraderie as well as the prestige of his new standing in the Senate "Club." If ever he was a happy man it was in the four brief years of 1941–44.

The core of his contentment was his new investigative venture into the burgeoning defense contracts which came with FDR's decision to turn the U.S. into an "arsenal for the democracies." Through his close relations with his constituents Truman was alerted to reports about waste, profiteering, and defective performance in his own state, and made a 30,000-mile "Great Circle" swing on his own, from Florida to Texas to Minnesota, to get an overview of what was there to dig into. In March 1941, under a Senate resolution, he picked his original committee and staff and—with only $15,000 to start with—he began his probe into the pathology of a program of war industries—a probe that reduced the cost of the war by some $20 billion, saved American lives, made him a national figure, and carried him in turn to the presidency.

He was clearly the right man in the right place at the right time. All his vigilance during his years as county administrator and investigative senator had prepared him for this role. So had his studies of the structure of corporations and his conversations with Justice Brandeis.

The first thing he decided was what he would *not* do. He was a Civil War buff, had studied strategies and battles, had visited the battlegrounds at Chancellorsville and Gettysburg, had checked out the only Library of Congress copy of the hearings of the "Committee on the Conduct of the War," which had tried to do too much in too partisan a spirit. The war was for the president to conduct, as commander in chief, and Truman sedulously refused to meddle with it. But the civilian side of it—the supply of matériel, the building of ships and planes, the granting of contracts, the flow of labor—these demanded a watchdog oversight.

It was a staggering task to track down the bottlenecks, the swollen profits, the favoritism shown to big contractors, the neglect of small business enterprise, the overcosting, the shoddy ingredients, the trickster dodges in construction and manufacture that could lead to the loss of thousands of lives. In World War I this had not been done adequately, until the hundreds of postwar investigations—too late. Truman's committee kept pace with the war itself.

The second danger Truman avoided was internal committee squabbling. The committee membership grew from the original five to ten, each senator carefully chosen for his capacity to work, and his compatibility with the others. Truman broke them up into subcommittees, made sure that each of the forty reports was unanimous. He knew the virtues of a Quakerlike consensus, and the corrosive effect of divided counsels on the public. Especially after Pearl Harbor the people were hungry for the operation of the command principle and the show of unity.

His third insight was his insistence on total factualness and the avoidance of publicity overkill. Exactly because he was so deeply moral a man his stress on "getting the facts" took on a moral intensity, since he was operating within a frame of patriotic values. As a result his committee, which actually cut into the sloppy, the sleazy, the inefficient, the corrupt in the defense industries, was not seen as a threat to administrative power or as a publicity-hogging adventure. Truman became known for his straight-shooting and his nonpartisanship in the national interest.

He did not have to seek the press; it sought him. Papers like the *St. Louis Post Dispatch*, which had clobbered him as Pendergast's "office boy," now saw him as a statesman. In a feature story in *Look* on the ten most important Americans in the war effort Truman was the only member of Congress among them. Even FDR, who had ignored Truman when he was not downright hostile, and had been niggardly about the first $15,000 appropriation for the committee, came to regard its work as somehow part of his own achievement.

The story of how Harry Truman became Franklin Roosevelt's running mate in 1944 is one in which neither of them appears at his best—Roosevelt wavering between casual inattention and extreme indirection while Truman showed an obtuse orneriness. It might have all blown up except for the intervention of a strange group casting themselves as "conspirators," who nudged history (no thanks to the two principals) in the direction it finally took.

The bedrock facts were these: From the spring of 1943, FDR was a dying man, and his intimate circle knew it well before the 1944 convention. Henry Wallace—the vice president—had proved himself too credulous and maladroit and too naively left to be trusted in the presidency. Someone had to be found to replace him, in full knowledge that he would probably become president before the term was over, and FDR had to be enlisted not only to embrace him as running mate but also to educate him for the task ahead.

The reality was that there was a dying king and no accepted heir, at a time of danger when a war was not yet settled and a peace not yet framed. It was a time also when FDR's incapacity to envisage his own mortality and to develop alternative talents in the party could prove fatal for the nation.

The situation had a stark clarity about it. Yet what happened was a tangle of confusions and cross-purposes.

There was no lack of claimants for the great prize—Wallace, who refused to be cashiered and fought hard for his passport to the presidency; James F. Byrnes, who was FDR's Pooh-Bah but was anathema to labor and the Catholics; Senator Alben Barkley, Speaker Sam Rayburn, and a host of sectional figures and "favorite sons."

Each had some critical "negative factor," as today's pollsters put it, in being unacceptable to an important voting bloc or (as in Barkley's case) to FDR himself. Within this frame Harry Truman seemed a God-sent solution. He had won national stature with his committee, had no discernible "negatives," and was capable of uniting the liberals and conservatives and the Northern and Southern wings of the party.

A little inner cabal formed, animated by Robert Hannegan, the young St. Louis politico whose 10,000 votes had formed Truman's victory margin in the 1940 Senate election and who was now (with Truman's help) head of the Democratic National Committee. Working with him was Ed Pauley, a Texas oilman with a taste for political maneuver, and several marginal members. Whatever their interests as power brokers they had a deep-structured hostility to Wallace and a heady sense of being kingmakers. Hannegan later said—before his untimely death—that he wanted to be remembered for his feat in making Truman president.

Hannegan's cabal had to persuade two people—FDR and Truman—and of the two Truman was the thornier and more difficult.

The problem with FDR was the trail of false leads he left behind as he wriggled elusively, refusing to be boxed in by anyone—whether Wallace, Byrnes, or Hannegan. He gave Wallace a guarded letter of "personal" support, which he did not mean, since his close political adviser, Ed Flynn, had told him Wallace would be a massive liability. He let Byrnes believe he had a green light, which Byrnes used in a classic maneuver by nailing down Harry Truman to nominate him. Faced by the Wallace and Byrnes moves, Hannegan mounted what became a war of the chits, getting FDR to scribble a note saying "Bob: It's Truman," which later became—in typed-up form—a willingness to run with either Truman or William O. Douglas (by one version, which Hannegan didn't display, it was Douglas or Truman). It seems that Douglas, a strong philosophical liberal on the Supreme Court whose views differed little from Wallace's, played a poker game that impressed FDR. It was as if FDR felt he could pick his successor by the same legerdemain he used in settling clashes between several administrators—making promises to each, rejecting none, confronting none face-to-face, leaving it to chance and struggle to resolve.

FDR had acted very differently in 1940 when he rammed Wallace down the throats of the resisting moderate and conservative convention delegates. But he was constantly fatigued, and there was no one this time he felt strongly about either way. He cared mostly which of the candidates would do least damage to his popularity.

Hannegan had little difficulty in drumming up support for Truman from the groups that counted—the union chiefs, the big-city politicos, the Southern conservatives, the heads of crucial delegations, the convention managers. His headache was with his own candidate, who played the stubborn Missouri mule.

Truman's behavior offers a puzzle for students of his mental processes. He had the world's greatest prize within his grasp if only he reached out for it. He could not help knowing of FDR's condition when Hannegan and the inner circle knew.

Yet instead of quietly going along with the Hannegan group and making himself available, without being hungry for the post, he found an array of reasons for refusing to lift a finger for it. The Senate as an environment—its work and lifestyle—suited him to perfection. He scorned the vice presidency as a sentencing of its occupant to wait for a funeral. He shrank from going through a national campaign where the ashes of his Pendergast years would be scraped over again. He even feared the exposure of his technical peccadillo in having Bess on his payroll—although she earned the pay. Besides, he agreed with Bess that the White House wasn't a fit place to raise a daughter.

Clearly these were rationalizations. Truman had spent his mature life in politics, was no tyro at it, and did not lack ambition. To anyone in his place the prospect of attaining the presidency must have beckoned as a kind of Heaven-sent destiny. Despite all his protests of refusal we must note that at no time did he tell Hannegan to cease and desist.

Why then did he put up such a resistance? In part, I suspect, he scorned to be a supplicant for the post when so many others were, especially with a president who had been too lofty and standoffish about him in the past. But, more important, my reading of him—it must be only a surmise—is that the prospect of the presidency scared him more than a little. A decade earlier, a newcomer to the Senate, he had wondered whether he was up to it. Now the leap to the presidency would be far more formidable than the Senate had been.

So he repressed the reality of the historical moment, and—confronted by a prospect he couldn't face outright—he allowed the tumult of his feelings to turn him into a seemingly serene bundle of passivity, buffeted by the activism of others.

The only thing that could unlock this passivity was to be told by the president himself that it was his duty—even his patriotic duty—to run with him. This was indeed what happened, although—as in a bad suspense story—it was not until the night before the vice presidential nominating speeches were scheduled. The Wallace staff had packed the convention floor and galleries with supporters holding bogus tickets.

Hannegan had gathered a group of politicos, including Truman, in a suite at the Blackstone Hotel in Chicago, and reached the president at San Diego. FDR's voice resounded through the room. Hannegan reported his failure with the "stubborn Missouri mule." In one version FDR replied, "You tell him that if he wants to break up the Democratic Party in the middle of a war, that's his responsibility." Another version has Truman then coming to the phone, listening, then saying, "Well, if that's what you want, that's what I'll do. I've always taken orders from the commander in chief." A possibly apocryphal story has him blurting out later, "Why didn't the SOB say so in the first place?"

Whatever actually was said, it was how history was made. Truman reported his decision to Byrnes, who then dropped out, a forlorn forgotten figure in the big convention hall. To meet the Wallace blitz the group managing the convention adjourned it after the nomination to allow the Truman candidacy to be mounted. Wallace led on the first ballot but was swamped in the second by the man who had only recently emerged to national recognition but who clearly had the support of FDR and the insiders. The Wallace liberals talked of betrayal but with the unions solidly backing Truman they had little credibility.

As for FDR, the campaign was what counted. He had managed to avoid any hostile confrontation but had come close to being saddled again with Wallace, who would have carried heavy political baggage, while Truman had fewer disabilities than any other candidate. But the nation also came close to getting, in Wallace, a presidential successor who would have yielded to Stalin what was still left after Teheran and Yalta.

The campaign was arduous for Truman, who made more than fifty talks and ran into press hostility for his sometimes sulfurous campaign style. It was far worse for FDR, who suffered several anginas on his Pacific "inspection" trip, and—to counter the whispering campaign about his health—endured a cold pelting rain in an open car touring New York City. FDR and Truman lunched on the White House lawn on August 18, and FDR did reveal some secret policy and personal information. He told Truman not to campaign by plane ("I am not a well man. We cannot be sure of my future"), yet did not tell him anything about Teheran or the other summit meetings. The new team won handily, but it is characteristic of FDR that he could not find an hour or two to start educating his probable successor.

The brief months as vice president were a relief from Truman's close to a decade of hard work, as senator, but also an anticlimax. Truman managed a large correspondence and visitors' schedule in his old Senate office and spent some time in the new ceremonial vice president's office, and presided over the Senate when he had to. He performed a chore for FDR in pushing through his payoff nomination of Wallace as secretary of commerce against a resisting and hostile Senate, casting the vote that broke the tie. But otherwise the president, absorbed with his arrivals and departures, with the breaking and re-forming of nations, with a European war drawing toward seeming victory and another waiting to be ended by a dangerous assault on Japan, and with his own rapidly dying body and mind, had no time for talking with a vice president whose existence he and his little ruling group scarcely acknowledged.

Writing some forty years later one cannot fail to be struck by two almost staggering realities about Truman as vice president. One is how utterly he was ignored by the inner FDR circle who must have known that, sooner or later, they would have to be working under a man they had allowed to be preternaturally cut away from them. The second is how isolated Truman was in fact from the great shaping world events that would soon form his universe, how trivial by comparison were the daily routines he concerned himself with, how much in fact the war and peace being shaped were one man's war and peace, which even the most powerful senators over whom the vice president presided had almost nothing to do with, and little real notion of. If ever the image of Plato's cave fitted a group of men, it was Truman and the senators whose working day he opened and closed, who saw not the realities of the world outside but the distorted shadows they cast on the walls of the cave of illusions that enclosed them.

Just as strange, however, is the fact that Truman made little effort to become more familiar with the outlines of the wider world he would probably soon have to deal with. He was the man who had boned up on the life of every colleague when he first came to the Senate, yet the same man was now spending his time on routine mail and visiting firemen when he knew he might at any moment be hurled into a maelstrom.

That he did know it is clear. He recalled FDR's pallor at lunch, how he slurred his words, how his hand shook when he held the cream pitcher. On the night of the election victory, at the Hotel Muehlebach, in Kansas City, he had talked at length about the presidency with a close friend. And walking past the White House with another, he admitted he knew he would probably be living in it.

Why then his passivity, and why his evident surprise when he heard of FDR's death? The fact was that Truman was a present-minded man who avoided probing the future. The day itself was enough; he dispatched it, slept well, and met the next. The man who "hated funerals" didn't relish thinking about this one.

So he probably repressed most of what would have been—in any other man—a tumult of the mind. He wrote a letter to his mother while presiding over the Senate, and he had joined in the ritual libations of the "Board of Education" in Speaker Sam Rayburn's office when he got a message to call Steve Early, FDR's press secretary. Early asked him to come immediately by the front door of the White House. "Jesus Christ and Holy General Jackson," he exclaimed as he started at a run for his car.

The rest has become enshrined in myth and history: how Mrs. Roosevelt placed her arm on his shoulder and said, "Harry, the president is dead," how he asked, "Is there anything I can do for you?," and how Mrs. Roosevelt went gently but unerringly for the jugular—"Is there anything *we* can do for *you*? For you are the one in trouble now."

As he first sat in FDR's chair that so many thought too big for him, he knew of course that he would in the end have to do it for himself. And while he was notoriously ignorant of FDR's largely hidden world of conferences, negotiations, strategies, bargains, and commitments, he was—on the essentials of character, strength, mental processes, problem-solving, and command—better prepared than we have thought.

The trouble is that in Truman's first days, and for decades afterward, the perception of his presidency by historians and other president watchers has been shaped largely by the preconceptions of the post-Roosevelt era. The people as a whole, after the first shock of FDR's death, were pleasantly impressed by the vigor and decisiveness of the new president, as were some of the Cabinet officials and many in Congress. They gave him a political honeymoon for something like a year. But to the New Dealers and their liberal political culture, which FDR had created and had ruled over for thirteen years, Truman seemed an insult to FDR's memory.

The inexcusable thing about him was that he wasn't Roosevelt. He had the bad taste to succeed the martyr president whose name had become, for an entire generation, a synonym for the presidency. Their accepted way to lament FDR's death was to express consternation at the mediocrity, gracelessness, even vulgarity of his successor.

Truman was no Roosevelt-worshiper, and while his positions were pro-New Deal his modes of thinking made him skeptical of New Dealers and their Roosevelt mystique. But he had a sense of awe of the presidency as the most powerful office in the world. His initial sense of inadequacy is reflected in one of his first remarks to the press: "I don't know whether you fellows ever had a load of hay or a tree fall on you. But last night the house, the stars and all the planets fell on me. If you fellows ever pray, pray for me." But everything was moving fast and he got caught up in its imposed rhythm, and his life force and instinct of workmanship came to his rescue.

His mind was not FDR's. But its qualities were considerable. He lacked FDR's imaginativeness and persuasiveness, his capacity to manipulate people, and to solve a problem by devious induction. But Truman had something else. Since his county administrator's job, and especially in his Senate investigations, he had relied on "getting the facts," assessing them in their context, and reaching a decision. Beyond the fact-gathering there was an analytical mind at work. Lifting what was critical from what was less so, digging under the layers of appearance and opinion to get at the operative realities. Linked with this was a taste for analogy, using his boyhood readings about ancient heroes and his memories of machine politics and his army experience as parallels for the problems of grander scale and knottier complexity he had now to resolve. Often it led him into oversimplification and reductionism, but it also gave an unfooled quality to his thinking.

During his first year, he had to resolve how to mend the peace in Europe, both before and after the fighting ceased, how to set up the United Nations, and then how to end the war with Japan. He had to move from a coalition war, which FDR had dominated, using the élan and trust generated by a war, to a peace in which the crumbling of the coalition went along with the corrosion of trust. Roosevelt's decisions— political and military—added up to leadership in a grander style, but Truman's may have been more difficult because he had to work not only in FDR's shadow but also in the context of FDR's illusions.

One of those illusions was that Stalin might be a recalcitrant partner but that he would yield to the right pressures. Just before his death FDR showed some signs of concern about Stalin's continued intransigence on having the governments he wanted in Eastern Europe, but he died still believing Stalin could be managed, that he could be persuaded, bribed, or pressured into behaving well in a continuing postwar coalition world. He died also without having changed the basic military-coalition strategy in Europe, which kept the Anglo-American armies waiting while the Soviet armies kept rolling on into the great capitals of Central and Eastern Europe.

Not only did Harry Truman inherit this: he was largely in its thrall. His attention, during the first weeks, was focused on making his diplomacy toward Stalin firmer and tougher than FDR's had been. The same advisers who had failed to convince FDR toward the end— mostly Ambassador Averell Harriman's group at the Moscow Embassy and in the State Department—now found a sympathetic listener in Truman. He decided to "lay it on the line to Molotov" about the Soviet recognition of a puppet Polish government, and related later Molotov's complaint that he had "never in his life been talked to" that way. But Charles Bohlen's notes as interpreter for the two men do not bear it out. Truman may have intended to speak with an undiplomatic harshness and thus recalled that he did. But he was not ready for a break with Stalin, who didn't scare and didn't yield and who kept complaining that Truman was backtracking on the Yalta commitments and the peaceful understanding he had with Roosevelt.

The fact is that while Truman was determined to be sterner than FDR with Stalin he never meant at this time to break out of the Roosevelt pattern. That came in time with the onset of the "Cold War," but it was no part of Truman's deliberate plan, but of the convergence of events he set in motion. His central paradigm was still that his problem with Stalin was diplomatic and could be settled by a tougher diplomacy. He thought—as many did—that the source of the difficulty lay in the Yalta agreements, which captivated him because they were part of the series of secret conferences from the knowledge of which FDR had excluded him.

So he used them as his focus, and used James F. Byrnes—who had been at Yalta with FDR and had glowed in knowing its secrets—as his close foreign-policy adviser until he could name him formally as his secretary of state. FDR had been his own secretary of state, using Cordell Hull and Edward Stettinius as fronts. But Truman did not trust his own experience in that area, believed in Cabinet government, and admired Byrnes for his sharpness of mind and wiliness of style. Byrnes in turn, who had been a kind of assistant president to FDR on the domestic war front, assumed the role of Truman's assistant president for foreign affairs. Truman gave him a loose rein, trusted his strategy, made him his number two at Potsdam, and let him bask in the headlines in the two meetings of the Council of Foreign Ministers—at London and Moscow—and then forced his resignation.

The fault was largely Byrnes's hubris but in part also Truman's lack of clarity about his own foreign-policy strategy and the limits of his power. There were times when Truman found Stalin's behavior intolerable and noted that the Soviet system was a despotism and its rulers as privileged a class as any in the past. There were other times when he wrote in his diary that peace with Russia was close and would last for "90 years."

It took both Truman and Byrnes some time, amidst their groping and coping, to seize the central fact—that the Russians were in possession of the field. Around the same time, however, they got the news of the success of the Los Alamos test of the bomb. It gave them new hope—and Secretary of War Stimson as well—that they had a diplomatic as well as military weapon that would make Stalin "manageable."

The New Left historians have made much of this "atomic diplomacy," but with the wrong emphasis. What the weapon did was, in time, to make Truman less dependent on Stalin's help in fighting Japan, thus releasing them from one of the strongest holds that Stalin had on both Roosevelt and Truman. But it was not a weapon that could be used against the Russians, and when this became clear any real hope of coercive pressure on the Russians, in taming them in their new empire, vanished. Instead the horror of the shock after Hiroshima made the sharing of control over atomic weapons with the Russians a new center of gravity in diplomacy.

Truman had grown increasingly restive under Byrnes's maneuvers and began to suspect him of intrigue and disloyalty. At one point, by his own account, he sent or read to Byrnes an explosive screed about being "tired of babying the Russians." In any event Byrnes's time had passed and his hold on Truman's trust was over. Truman was moving into a more independent phase and saw Byrnes as yielding too much to Stalin. At that point he was clearer about the Russians in his own mind, and ready for a shift of focus from the helplessness of the Yalta accords and Eastern Europe to what America could do without Stalin's help and Russia's costly "friendship."

But this is to jump ahead of the story. The thing to remember is that too many things were happening too fast, and Truman and his advisers had to sort them out, digest their meaning, and come to decisions. The crux of it was not in diplomacy but in military action and inaction, which is the foundation of diplomacy. Twenty-five days elapsed from April 13, when Truman took his oath of office to V-E day on May 8 when Germany surrendered. They could have been twenty-five days that shook the world. For even before FDR's death Winston Churchill had been beseeching him to allow the Allied armies to counter the swift penetration of Central and Eastern Europe by Soviet armies. The Americans and British were already deep in the Soviet zone of occupation, and had the mobile power to reach Berlin, Prague, and Vienna ahead of the Russians.

Roosevelt of course was adamant against it. So was Eisenhower, who felt honor-bound to observe the demarcation of the Soviet zone and stopped the Allied armies at the Elbe, well south of Berlin, giving Stalin the monopoly of taking Berlin. He also allowed the Russians to take Prague, despite General Patton's urgent offer to lead an armored column to its capture. Marshall went along with Eisenhower in deference to Roosevelt's decision.

But there was now a different commander in chief, who could have changed Roosevelt's decision, substituted his own, joined Churchill in an improvised new plan, and saved Czechoslovakia and much of Eastern Germany. It was around this time Truman was still talking tough and saying of the Russians that "we've got to teach them how to behave."

But he was still in thrall to Roosevelt as war commander and strategist, still convinced that the decisions at Yalta about zones of occupation were right, still in awe of Marshall and Eisenhower. He was also too new in the presidency, with too little self-confidence, to strike out so soon on a course of his own. So the entreaties of Churchill and the British General Staff—which would have had the backing of a majority in the Senate and the nation—went unheeded.

He would only have been following what he should have learned from his experience with Stalin in Poland—that the government whose armies have occupied the terrain is the one whose decisions hold against all diplomatic maneuvering. But there is little evidence that Truman seriously considered making the break with the Russians and with the committed Roosevelt positions. It is irresistible—however fickle—to speculate on what a bolder Truman—like the Truman of the Berlin airlift, of the Truman Doctrine, of NATO, and of the Korean War—might have done. But that Truman had not yet emerged.

With only a few exceptions Truman had to retreat from his position of "toughness" on the Russians. When Stalin accused him of breaking up the alliance, he sent Harry Hopkins to Warsaw to appease him, and Joseph Davies—former ambassador to Moscow and a Stalin sycophant—to explain his retreat to Churchill. The choice of Hopkins and Davies marked a reversion to Truman's dependence on the Roosevelt worldview. On the U.N. the only way Truman managed to get Stalin to yield on the Security Council veto, and accept the position that it should apply only to the Council's actions and not its discussions, was to offer him a trade-off. Add the fact that the Potsdam Conference, which Truman had pushed against his better judgment, turned out to be a disaster. As with Roosevelt at Yalta, it thrust Truman into an ungenerous and unwise belittling of Britain's continuing postwar alliance with America and of Winston Churchill's own role as a decision-maker, if not as a power-wielder. It was an unhappy time for Britain, which was about to lose its empire, and for Churchill who—midway in the conference—lost his bid for reelection at the hands of an ungrateful people. It was also an unhappy time for Truman and Marshall, who, with the ending of the war in Europe, were caught up in the bring-the-boys-back hysteria and had to reduce the American forces.

On the question of Germany, where Stalin was only partially entrenched, Truman found more leeway for making American positions effective. The immediate question was reparations, but it opened up the larger outlines of the German and European future. Truman knew little about Germany, but he had good instincts and gave scope to his best adviser. The political culture was in a crucial transition stage on Germany, moving away from the harshness of the Morgenthau Plan for a "pastoral" Germany, toward the understanding that a starving deindustrialized Germany would sap not only its own but all of Western Europe's economic energies.

As part of the earlier climate, FDR had made the blunder of

agreeing, at Yalta, to the principle of extracting $20 billion from all of Germany, $10 billion of it to go to Russia for rebuilding its economy. Stimson and Harriman, along with Ed Pauley—Truman's choice for the Reparations Commission—all of whom Joseph Davies despairingly saw as conducting an anti-Soviet "palace intrigue" stiffened Truman's resolve on the issue. After weeks of wrangling the upshot was a plan for each of the occupying powers to get its reparations from its own zone—and even this compromise Byrnes had to sweeten for Stalin by recognizing the four Soviet satellite governments.

Yet it was the start of an immensely important breakthrough, for Truman as for his advisers. Despite the enormity of Nazi evil it would not be diminished or punished by adding to the strength of Soviet evil. What was emerging in the White House was the understanding that a strong German economy—without war industries—would have to be the base of an operative German democracy, and that both were linked with the future of a Europe that could resist Communist penetration.

Truman's decisions on the Berlin airlift, the Marshall Plan, and NATO still lay ahead, but they were foreshadowed by the breakaway from FDR on reparations and the German economy. Together they would emerge impressively as a display of the tough-mindedness and vision that, when continued, go to form statesmanship.

More than for any of his decisions Truman is remembered as the president who ordered the dropping of the bomb over Hiroshima. Any assessment of him must grapple with the wrongness or rightness of that decision, within its historical context.

The way I prefer to put it is that Truman was the first president of the Atomic Era. The bomb was not of his doing, but Roosevelt's, who was quite right to have taken up the challenge of the little group of scientists, including Enrico Fermi and Leo Szilard. Robert Oppenheimer and the Los Alamos scientists he recruited were moved by their fear of Hitler as the symbol of destructive inhumanity and of Roosevelt as the symbol of hope. It was this double spur that brought the bomb into being.

But Truman was the one who had to cope with the bomb and its cui bono—toward what good, for what end? No president has been faced with a graver, knottier choice, not even FDR in his initial decision, nor Kennedy in the Cuban missile crisis. Truman was told of the bomb fleetingly by Secretary Stimson, perhaps even earlier by FDR. But his first real briefing came from Brigadier General Leslie R.

Groves, who had directed the Manhattan Project with toughness, verve, and acumen.

Truman was impressed by the Alamogordo tests, as were the jubilant scientists, including Oppenheimer. He sensed the difference that the possession of the weapon could make in American foreign policy, especially toward Russia. But when he told Stalin about it, perhaps too delicately, like Proust's well-mannered maiden aunts, Stalin took it with great coolness. Doubtless he already knew of its making and testing through his spy apparatus. The even greater news, of its stunning destructiveness over Hiroshima, reached Truman on his way home from Potsdam and produced what now seems an undue elation in him.

It was not the bomb's use over Japan's cities that brought the Atomic Age into being, but its manufacture and successful testing. When it became the possession of the scientific community, that was when mankind ate of the fruit of the tree of evil. If Truman had not used the bomb and continued its development it would not have kept the Russians from making and developing it as a monopoly of their own—and perhaps using it with less compunction than the Americans showed during their period of monopoly.

What Truman faced was not a moral decision on the life or non-life of the bomb but a political decision on how best to end the war with Japan, with the fewest casualties, the least sacrifice of American power, and the least danger to Japan's postwar future.

His decision, in retrospect, was the right one. Whatever their rivalries the navy, air force, and army agreed that the final crunch in achieving Japanese surrender would be an agonized one, with heavy American—and Japanese—casualties. There was no way, even with an intense air bombardment and a navy blockade, to avoid an invasion of the main islands. The casualties at Okinawa, on both sides, foreshadowed a drawn-out struggle with estimates of probable American casualties ranging from 40,000 to a quarter million—the estimate Truman cited. American servicemen in both theaters, however patriotic, were tired of the war, and their foreboding about being assigned to the invasion of Japan created a problem.

To end the war quickly, without troop landings and without protracted—and probably fanatical—Japanese resistance, was Truman's prime objective. But there was a linked one that also weighed heavily with him—the question of the Soviet role if an invasion was necessary. Roosevelt had envisaged a Russian declaration of war against Japan as crucial to cutting American casualties, just as the engagement of

Hitler's forces by the Russian armies in Europe had cut American casualties. To get a Russian commitment to enter the war against Japan was part of the logic of Teheran and Yalta. Under Truman too it was part of the logic of Potsdam, where he got Stalin to set a concrete date when Russia would declare war.

But clearly there would have to be a quid pro quo, which would be Soviet power-sharing of the occupation zones in Japan. Truman's experience with Stalin over reparations and the occupation zones in Germany had turned him against further adventures of the same sort in Japan. Why should America store up future grief for itself and take on a troublesome partner in shaping the future of postwar Japan—a partner that seemed all too clearly bent on world expansion?

This was the context within which Alamogordo, with its successful testing of the bomb, gave Truman his chance to end the war and establish a tolerable peace for Japan and America. In saying, as he did later, that he never lost a night's sleep over his bomb decision, he meant to convey his sense of serenity at the time about the moral dimension of his decision. Looking at it with our knowledge of the bomb's progeny—which he didn't have—I feel he should have lost several nights' sleep. When the full extent of its ravaging destructiveness over Hiroshima became known, there is some evidence that he had some compunctions about it.

Yet he was not a president whose politics were governed by a high moralism. He decided according to the reality principle as he saw it. At times he was too swiftly reactive but this was not one.

There had never been any doubt under FDR that the bomb, when completed, would somehow be used. The bomb was political from the start, in the sense that it was conceived, continued, tested, as a weapon against Germany as the enemy and threat and Russia as an ally. When the war in Europe ended and Germany ceased to be a threat and the Russian alliance frayed, the bomb's politics changed, its use against Japan was challenged, and—at least for much of the original band of scientists—its threat to the Russian alliance came to the fore, and consideration of "morality" displaced the politics of the bomb.

Truman was a newcomer, and his first introduction to the bomb came in the midst of his agony of struggle and frustration over Stalin and his anxieties about the casualties still ahead in Japan. This became his politics of the bomb. Stimson and Byrnes, his two prime advisers on the bomb, shared his view. The Interim Committee, which did the initial canvassing of options, spent little time debating the decision to use it. The Science Advisory Committee, including J. Robert Oppenheimer, also recommended it. Leo Szilard and the Franck Committee of scientists which proposed a "demonstration" bomb over an atoll, made their case to Byrnes—without persuading him. The weight of opinion now is that a demonstration bomb would have failed utterly to create the needed "shock" to get the Japanese military leaders to surrender. Even the destruction of Hiroshima was followed by an ominous silence from Japan while its leaders wrangled. This in turn led to the Nagasaki bomb—a blunder by the American generals before civilian control over them emerged. An earlier blunder by the Japanese civilian leaders was to make their overtures to Stalin to act as an intermediary for peace instead of to Washington directly.

The Americans of course, who had read the coded Japanese messages, knew of the peace overtures and Stalin knew that they knew and told them perfunctorily. The fact is that Stalin was even less eager than Truman for the overtures to succeed, since it would mean the end of his hopes to enter this part of the war and share the postwar power.

My own response and that of my circle of friends, as I recall it now, was to welcome the news of both the first atomic explosion, tested at Alamogordo, New Mexico, and of Hiroshima as marking a new era in mankind's history, but urging strongly that we share control of future atomic weapons with some global entity. But we were all fuzzy about what that meant. Truman and his advisers on this issue— Dean Acheson, David Lilienthal, Bernard Baruch—responded to the wave of public feeling by issuing two reports, which caught attention notably through Baruch's use of "The quick and the dead." But they could not enlist Stalin's support, since his sharing of control would hinder his getting the bomb and help him win when he did.

Thus our hopes crumbled, but not because of Truman, who failed at a task where no other president could have succeeded. The bomb, in ways few of us understood, imposed its own technological imperative; once its science and technology became known they took on an autonomous will.

It was a more impressive array of talent than FDR had ever assembled and a more forceful policy than he had ever applied to Stalin. But Stalin was no more inclined to yield to pressure by Truman than he had yielded to FDR's appeals to his goodwill. Stalin's armies were in possession of the area of Eastern Europe and pressure could not dislodge them. And they were moving every day, every hour, toward taking possession of the heartland—Berlin, Vienna, Prague—while the

Anglo-American commanders waited for them at the Elbe or quar-reled among themselves as to what armies should move where, how, and why.

Historians must record that while Roosevelt's diplomatic policies in the last year and more of Europe's war were a disaster, his military policies during the last months of it were a shambles. They must also record that while Truman tried to shift the diplomacy, even though unavailingly, he stood by while his generals carried through the strate-gies associated with the diplomacy and did nothing to change them.

The grand strategy of allowing the Soviet armies to take the three cities had been part of FDR's design for keeping Stalin happy while let-ting the Russians do the fighting in the last months. Stalin was de-lighted. But this made less and less sense as the Anglo-American armies came within reach of the cities and their surrounding fields and industries.

Stimson and Marshall trusted Eisenhower as their man, and Ike in turn was furious at the new British chief-of-staff, Lord Hanbrooke, who wanted to abandon Ike's waiting strategy, and direct the combined forces under Montgomery to head for Berlin and beyond. The armies, which could have outpaced the Russians if fuel had been made avail-able, waited decorously at the Elbe, which was not a strategic line but an arbitrary symbolic one. Thinking he was carrying out high political policy, Ike declared that Berlin was of no strategic importance. It was a curiously narrow definition of "strategic."

The only authority that could have settled the quarreling and bro-ken the impasse was the president. But FDR was too sick or too inat-tentive and stubborn to do it, and Truman after him was too paralyzed by his admiration for Marshall and Ike as military planners, and too ac-customed as Captain Harry to leave such major policy unquestioned. He was also, like the rest, under the spell of the ruling shibboleth of the military hierarchy—that Russia's "help" was so crucial in ending the Japanese war that no price, diplomatic or military, was too high to pay for it.

It was a drama of high, almost intolerable, tragedy. These were men of great ability. They had performed great services and two of them—Eisenhower and Marshall—were to perform greater ones. Yet they were all caught, and Truman too, by a preconceived idea that flowed from its time and climate and had the magic of a name and leader behind it, but outlived its validity. These men of goodwill had high-minded ideas, but without thinking them through or testing them against reality, what happened became a prime example of passivity in decision-making. These decision-makers were betrayed by the idea of comradeship in peace as in war and of wooing an ally who was in reality a predator by sharing power with him.

Curiously Truman, who learned in time to see through the Yalta trap, did not see through the Elbe River trap in time. But we have to report that he did learn, even in the strategic area, and in time he broke through the thrall of the we-can't-end-the-Japanese-war-without-Russian-armies precondition. It was a critical learning experience.

Not long into his administration you often heard the wisecrack, "To err is Truman." There was persistent ridicule of the man in the White House, and I confess I was part of it. When it came to 1948, a presidential election year, an enormous number of people did not want to support him to run on his own for a full term. Two of Roosevelt's sons joined a committee to draft Eisenhower for the Democratic ticket instead of Truman. Nobody thought he could carry the load, and nobody gave him a chance. But the campaign of 1948 for him was a repetition of what the second Senate race in 1940 had been.

I was at the Democratic Convention in Philadelphia that nominated him in 1948, and I remember the correspondents standing and sitting around, feeling so smug. We all felt so smug about this little fellow trying so hard to get reelected. All of the so-called experts said that Thomas Dewey would win, and there wasn't any doubt.

But then, in that hot convention hall in Philadelphia, Truman came out in a white suit looking very dapper, natty, and cool. He had decided that he was going to attack the Republican-dominated Congress and ask for a special session of Congress to come back, daring them to do the things that had to be done. In short, the president was going to run against Congress. The first few sentences were so crisp and incisive, sharp and militant that I got on the table and started waving my arms and cheering, while every other correspondent was doing the same. We were all supposed to be nonpartisan, but Truman's passionate combativeness moved everyone, and he of course showed that all the experts were wrong in picking Dewey over him.

I have already called Harry Truman an extraordinary man—with a sense of clarity, a sense of strength, a sense of direction, but mostly a sense of command. His life was a life of relatedness, and somehow he learned how to judge people. The Truman-Acheson relationship has never been matched for a president and a secretary of state. What a curious pair that was: Dean Acheson—Harvard-trained, aristocrat, dandy—and Harry Truman—self-taught, commoner, man of the Missouri soil. Yet what respect they had for each other. There has not been another team like that. The Nixon-Kissinger team did not have the harmony of the Truman-Acheson team. Nixon and Kissinger worked together, but they hated each other.

Truman picked good men: Acheson, George Marshall, Robert Lovett at defense, General Lucius Clay for postwar Germany. Truman gave these men and others their rope of responsibilities, but he also made it very clear that he was in command. He had the spine a president needs. He had clear purpose in his own mind, and he knew where he wanted to go. He had the capacity to surround himself with people who could tell him what he needed and wanted to know. Then he made up his mind. The buck always stopped at Truman's own desk, for the decision.

The way to judge a president is to ask: What were the president's basic decisions, and what has happened to those decisions in terms of their consequences over time? Domestically, his economic programs were upbeat and expansionist, and he was the first president to care deeply about civil rights for blacks.

His real creativity lay in his foreign-policy decisions, all of them strong, whether we liked them or not, starting with his use of the bomb to end the war and save millions of lives and keep Stalin out of power-sharing in Japan. He kept American troops in Europe, announced the Truman Doctrine for meeting Communist penetration, and worked for foreign aid. He formulated the Marshall Plan, built the NATO alliance, met the Soviet encirclement of Berlin by an ingenious and daring airlift, and recognized Israel as a state. He also used the UN to meet an invasion of South Korea, and reaffirmed civilian control of the military in his dismissal of Gen. Douglas MacArthur.

It's true that some of his foreign policy was inept, especially his handling of the Chinese revolution and the Korean War. Yet he presided over the economic and psychological rebuilding of Western Europe and the new beginnings in Japan, and laid the groundwork for the free-world postwar coalition.

In *Harry S. Truman*, Margaret Truman concludes her evocative memoir with one of her father's typically sharp, direct statements: "Do your duty and history will do you justice." He did and it will.

RICHARD NIXON

THE TORTUROUS DESCENT FROM OLYMPUS

APRIL 20, 1973

NIXON AND WATERGATE

T HE WAY OF A MAN WITH POWER, when he finds himself threatened in its use, is as much a thing of wonder as the way of a man with a maid when a shadow has come over their relationship. Richard Nixon has had the Watergate shadow hanging over him since it emerged during the election campaign. For a time there was a curious apathy about it, perhaps because most people didn't want George McGovern to emerge as president, and so they tried to make the shadow disappear. Hence there was only desultory interest in it, mainly about the men who had been arrested and their possible motives.

The first change came when Federal Judge John Sirica decided to take a hand in ferreting out what lay behind the shadows of the case, and a Senate committee under Senator Sam Ervin began informal questioning. This was helped by the hapless testimony of Patrick Gray during the hearings on his nomination as FBI director, and by the whole controversy over executive privilege for Nixon's White House staff. The second change came with the leaks on the information provided by campaign security coordinator James McCord, himself arrested during the break-in, when the question arose about which of Nixon's staff—if any—had been involved, and how much.

Now comes a new shift, with Nixon's reversal of his earlier position on executive privilege, and his announcement of a new inquiry of his own, with new—and unstated—developments in it. Again the at-

---

Max Lerner chronicled Richard Nixon's fall from the presidency in his syndicated newspaper column.

tention has shifted, this time to Nixon himself—how much, if anything, he knew about the episode from the start, why he has now reversed his stand, whether he has in fact discovered anything new, how he has handled the whole thing, how much candor and truthfulness he has shown the American people.

An observer suspends judgment and awaits further light as the case unravels further—and unravel it will. Judge Sirica, Senator Ervin, James McCord—all of them set the unraveling in motion. I doubt whether anything or anyone can stop it now.

This will be a warm spring and a hot summer. The next few months will be dynamite. Careers and reputations will be blasted. A new chapter is likely to be written in the history of the corruptions of power.

Richard Nixon's problem—whether the "old" or the "new" Nixon's—has always been a quality of deviousness and an itch for manipulation. I don't deny him courage in the decision-making crunch. He has shown it a number of times.

But when he is faced with a crisis of credibility—as was true in the "Nixon fund" case in 1952, and twenty years later in the handling of the Watergate case—his natural tactics are shifty and evasive, until he feels the time is ripe for a change to aggressiveness.

His favorite ploy is the sudden change of mood. After a period of silence and isolation from the people on any issue, there comes the abrupt shift from the defensive to the offensive, from passivity to command. This is again what has happened in Nixon's tactics on Watergate.

But in the present case the inaction lasted so long, the efforts to cover up the unlovely aspects of the case were so obvious, that one wonders whether the change of tactic doesn't come too late to restore the credibility that Nixon has lost.

There are reports of imminent indictments and of resignations of high former and present White House officials. It will be hard for many Americans to believe that all this could have happened without any inkling on President Nixon's part, especially with the McCord evidence of an attempted cover-up. Not since Warren Harding's day, and the Teapot Dome cases, has a scandal of corruption reached so deep into the men around the president.

The past scandals have been concerned with greed and venality. This one goes beyond it, to power corruption. It is hard to guess about the motivations until we know more about the men involved. But clearly it was not greed for money. The Nixon reelection committee had plenty of money. It was crawling out of their ears.

Something far deeper was involved, and more dangerous—the resolve of a small group to keep the president and themselves in power by clandestine means, even if it involved wiretapping, secret surveillance, political espionage. These are not the conventional corruptions of bribery, graft, or influence peddling. They are the core corruption of power.

✶

APRIL 30, 1973

DEAR MR. PRESIDENT

Dear Mr. President: I write this as you wrestle with either gods or demons over Watergate, at Camp David. The walls have come tumbling down around you as well as around your staff. Your universe, so sure five months ago when you were sweepingly reelected, is now a wasteland. But the crisis goes beyond you to the trust of Americans in the presidency, and in fact to the capacity of the government to function.

The prime question for many is whether you have had complicity, not in the action itself but in the attempts to cover it up. Two out of three people in straw polls feel you have been evasive about your knowledge of those attempts. They may do you an injustice. I hope they do. But the mistrust can't easily be pushed aside.

In part it is based on the fact that the events and your statements don't hang together, and in part on your personality. We have known it not as a forthright personality but as a devious one. In your political battles and your foreign-policy duels you have been the Machiavellian prince, getting your effects by force, and a formidable toughness. Most people accepted the combination, as the election showed. But given the mysteries and corruptions of Watergate, guile was the wrong way for you to handle it, and is still the wrong way. Senator John Stennis wants you to "tough it out," but toughness and bluster won't do any longer.

I don't ask you to shed your skin and grow a new one, but if you have any honesty, directness, and humility in you, this is the time to show them. Later may be too late.

You have been asking advice from your friends whom you still trust—like William Rogers and Robert Finch. You can no longer ask John Mitchell. You haven't asked me, but if you did I should give it in three short sentences: Level with America. Clean out the mess completely. Start afresh.

Talk to the people through your "presidential medium"—TV. Speak directly, fully, honestly. They will respond. Don't try to be cute or devious, as you did with the Checkers performance in 1952. Don't try to summon a "silent majority" to redress the balance of the vocal one. Don't be a hound-of-God Savonarola, playing on their passions. Talk as a human being with problems and frailties—a human being who has tried to cut some corners and has been let down by his own blunders as well as by some of his staff and friends.

But also talk as a president whose authority has been undercut by the country's total obsession with Watergate, whose credibility has been badly bruised, and who can't shape either domestic or foreign policy until the mess has been resolved and the authority of the presidential office has been restored.

You can reestablish credibility only if you clean up the mess summarily and completely. This means cleaning up your White House staff. It will be hard to do, since the men involved did what they did, not for money, but because they thought they were protecting your power by keeping the nefarious Democrats from winning. They thought they were your good servants, perhaps even thought they were patriots, which bears out Dr. Johnson's remark about patriotism being the last refuge of a scoundrel.

You will feel you are plucking out your good right arm, but pluck it out you must, for it has gone gangrenous. Dwight Eisenhower depended on Sherman Adams even more than you depend on H. R. Haldeman, and Adams had done far less to deserve dismissal, but the dismissal had to come.

The other part of cleaning up the mess is prosecution. When Prime Minister Harold Macmillan found he had to clean up the Profumo affair, he picked an independent, trusted man to track it all down. When Calvin Coolidge had to clean up the Teapot Dome scandals of the Harding administration, he picked Owen Roberts and Atlee Pomerene as special prosecutors—a Republican and a Democrat.

Henry Peterson and Earl Silbert are fine men, but they have the disadvantage of being part of the Justice Department, which right now bears the political brand of Cain. It won't be easy to find some outsider whom everyone will trust. That kind of detachment seems almost to have vanished. But you must do it.

Having done that you can start afresh. Failing to do it you will be faced by further erosions of authority and there will be calls for your impeachment. What is at stake is not only your career and your place in history, but the capacity of a great democracy to survive a crisis that goes to the very root of its sense of confidence.

✶

MAY 9, 1973

THE VALUES CRISIS

Big Sur, Cal.—With all the talk about Watergate as a constitutional crisis we seem to have missed the deeper crisis of values. True, the presidency as a political institution is in peril, but even more the American belief in basic life values is in peril.

This theme emerged at a seminar here on values and human potentials, at which, inevitably, Watergate came up. Consider what has happened in the domain of values. The administration that made the biggest to-do over traditional values—the work ethic, the Puritan ethic, all the rugged virtues of the ancestral Golden Age—is the administration that has fallen flat on its face over the elementary ethic of honesty and lying.

Where does this leave those—older or younger—who can't resolve their lives without taking the values problem seriously?

I am not speaking primarily of the college young who went through the convulsive changes of the later 1960s. They decided some time ago that the traditional Puritan virtues were for the birds, simply not credible, because their elders who talked about them didn't in fact practice them and didn't believe in them.

I refer here particularly to honesty, steadfastness, commitment. They never trusted Nixon, and are not surprised now. They thought for a time that George McGovern stood for these, then they got disillusioned about him too.

They got out of the traditional values system. They just got off the bus, scrapped it, and built themselves a new contraption, which could be called the challenger values.

Note that they used some of the old bus parts to build it. Honesty, simplicity of life style, directness, commitment: these were taken over from the original Puritan values. But the point was that they took them out of the traditional frame, where they had become tainted with money and power, with success and prestige and security, with the job and career, and they put them in a new frame.

The trouble now is that they don't fit well with a number of far-out uprooted and uprooting values, which are also part of the challenger ethos—but that's another story.

The real indignity that Watergate has done is not to them, who form only a fraction of the population, but to the rest—to the college youth who come from blue-collar, white-collar, and rural backgrounds, and to their parents, mostly in the lower middle class. The young were the ones we saw at Miami, at the Republican Convention, cheering Nixon, chanting "Four More Years."

Their parents were largely of the second- and third-generation white ethnics. Some were Archie Bunkers, yes, but most were earthy people with their measure of goodwill. They really believed President Nixon when he made those campaign speeches about the work ethic, about honesty and self-help, about loyalty and patriotism and the whole freight car full of the traditional virtues. Watergate now inflicts upon them a massive indignity, dirtying what they thought was genuine, and making them feel they were had.

And how about their sons and daughters? The 1970s found them moving away from the leftward, activist movements of the '60s. They became more work- and career-oriented, much as in the late '40s and early '50s. Some became inner-oriented, moving toward religion, whether inside or outside the traditional churches. Many joined the upsurging new fundamentalist creeds, like the "Jesus people," and some (along with the more avant-garde youth) went into new mystical beliefs.

What can we say to them, what do they say to themselves, as the Watergate story unravels? Like the radical youth, who will turn further left on the ground that this shows the corruptions of "imperialism," the blue-collar youth are likely to turn more sharply to fundamental creeds than ever, on the ground that it shows again the corruptions of earthly life without a vivid, immediate, personal God. And some will carom wholly out of the human universe into the transpersonal and supernatural.

I leave the saddest sadness to the end: what Watergate does to the prisoners of war who came back with the feeling that their traditional values of loyalty, courage, steadfastness, and honesty had been vindicated. I wonder what courses through their minds now as they look at the shambles of the value system in Washington?

★

MAY 21, 1973

THE TRIAL OF RICHARD NIXON

Washington—No, not a formal trial, nor yet an impeachment trial, but a trial nonetheless. For what is happening, as the vast TV and radio audience follows the Watergate testimony, is that President Nixon is on trial. He is on trial for whatever knowledge or collusion he may have had involving the whole undercover and cover-up operation, of which Watergate was only the visible iceberg.

In effect the people are sitting in judgment on him, and will continue to sit in judgment as long as the hearings last and the pieces of the jigsaw puzzle continue to come together.

Washington is a poor place to tap the opinion currents. While it is the great fountainhead of new evidence, and streams of reports and counter-reports come gushing from it, Washington is in its own way too isolated from the American crossroads. It is a city of insiders, with a hothouse atmosphere, a city of government people and media people, but not the rest of the people.

But everywhere else in the country the feeling is clear without being bitter or partisan. There is hardly a man on the street who believes the president is telling the whole truth. Most people think he knew of the cover-up but not of the original operation. Many think he knew of both. Very few believe he was an innocent, wrapped in a cocoon of high-level policy decisions, guarded by a protective staff from the facts of life and the undercover operations.

If the evidence at the Senate hearings stands up, it is damning. It suggests strongly that while the president probably didn't know of the specific Watergate operation, he could not have been ignorant of the larger underground campaign, planned and pursued covertly, with secret funds. It more than suggests that he knew about the cover up effort, engineered by his top assistants, including the offer of clemency later for the silence of the convicted.

Hence, as the president's trial proceeds in the court of public opinion, more and more people will conclude that he is lying. If so, what then?

At this point opinion divides sharply. Some feel that if he has lost credibility he should resign, or that if he has been involved in impeachable crimes he should he impeached. Others feel pretty cynically that all administrations get involved in lying—a point that David Wise makes in his new book, *The Politics of Lying*. Still others say quite soberly that there must be a measure of undercover operations and a measure of withholding the truth in every government, that otherwise governments can't function.

Without getting high and mighty and holier-than-thou about it, I can't agree. True, in dealing with foreign governments, historians recognize that kings, presidents, and prime ministers have often lied for what is called "reasons of state." But no reason of state can explain or condone lying to the people who have elected a leader inside a democracy.

This isn't a question of virtue and vice, but of what makes a democratic society work. Very few—if any—of those who are sitting in judgment on the president are angels. If men were angels, as James Madison used to insist, you wouldn't need either government or law. This applies all the way down the line, from the very human senators sitting in that august tribunal of inquiry down to the lowliest sinner on a bar stool, watching the hearings on TV.

There is a working margin of lying in most lives and most governments. But there is a limit to the lies a people in a democracy will tolerate. America is today in the most serious crisis of credibility in the history of the presidency. In such a crisis it becomes crucial to expect that the president will tell the truth. Otherwise he is doomed to conduct at best a limping government and at worst a paralyzed one.

Given what we know of the president's personality, he is likely to stick to his denials as long as he can, and try to "tough it out." But this would be unwise. Democracies usually get along with a saving sense of the frailties of the human animal. But in moments of showdown, when everything depends on a two-way dialogue of candor, a leader's lie of the soul is bound to do irreparable harm to the whole society.

President Nixon had a chance to level with the people right after

Watergate, and he had a second chance right after the elections. He took neither. He has a third and final chance now to say what actually happened, and entrust himself to the people. If he doesn't seize it at the last moment of truth, history and the people are likely to be rough with him.

✴

COUNTEROFFENSIVE

Richard Nixon is fighting for his political life harder than he has ever fought before. But will it avail him?

This is his time of troubles. He has been betrayed by friends. He is beset by enemies, within his own party as well as among the Democrats. He is beleaguered by the media; never has so intense a scrutiny been focused on every operation of an administration, secret or public, as on this one. This, at any rate, is his self-image. And he meets a continued skepticism among the majority of those who have either felt friendly or neutral about him in the past.

In the midst of the Senate inquiry he has made a second major effort to explain what happened. It helps, especially in recognizing the cover-up, and there are passages of contrition in it which must have been hard for Nixon's pride to utter.

But it still doesn't ring wholly true. It is hard to believe that everything he did was done for reasons of national security, in order to keep crucial political intelligence from being revealed. It is also hard to believe that a tough, driving politician like Richard Nixon didn't know about either the input or outgo of his campaign finances.

When Nixon revealed so little in his TV speech, there were desert stretches crying to be irrigated by further information. His second statement adds considerable detail. But now the trouble for Nixon is that every new revelation will be matched against his statement. That means a continuing crisis of credibility.

Is this finally Nixon's last stand, or will there be still another? I feel there is bound to be another, since new contradictions and disbeliefs are bound to pile up, and will need to be dispelled.

The danger is, of course, that this might go on indefinitely, in a chain-reaction sequence, until it finally forces Nixon out of the presidency. Something like it forced Lyndon Johnson out of the political arena, compelling him to take himself out of the running for another term.

Nixon is, of course, as aware of the Lyndon Johnson parallel, as of the Andrew Johnson impeachment parallel. The two historical Johnson cases plague his mind.

To prevent the ghost of Andrew Johnson from haunting him he has first to lay to rest the ghost of Lyndon Johnson. He did it once before, when an antiwar campaign—in the media and on the campuses—was mounted against him.

His answer was a counteroffensive—the historic "silent majority" speech, one of the most effective presidential TV talks in recent history, shrewdly gauged to the audience and the moment. It caught the tide of anti-anti-Nixon sentiment just as it crested, and it changed the climate for Nixon's war and peace efforts.

One might guess that Nixon will do something like this again, not in the context of the war but of Watergate. He may again wait for the right psychological moment, when people start to feel that he is the underdog, and a shabbily treated one. Flag decals are starting to appear on car bumpers, with a simple "President Nixon" next to them. The movement may grow.

Right now the press is riding high, but there is an antiliberal potential in the attitudes toward the press that will crop up if more people decide that the press is crowding the president too hard. There is a gaggle of commentators, of various stripes, hinting darkly of the counteroffensive to come, and saying (with various shades of agreement or derision) that it will be linked to the climate engendered early in the '70s by intense anti-Nixon movements on the left.

On the whole there is far less talk of impeachment than of resignation. To put it differently, the present way of expressing anti-Nixon urgency is to predict that the president will have to resign, or badger him to resign. Part of the merit of the resignation route, for those who care about social peace, is that it would not rip the country apart. Hence the president's repeated assurances that he has no intention to resign, and that he does intend to govern.

It is a way of reassuring foreign governments and the business community here. It also hints that those who want him to resign will have to mount an intense campaign against him, which will in fact split the country.

There is little doubt that a strong impeachment movement, whatever its success or failure, would leave its scars on the country, as the Andrew Johnson impeachment trial left scars on the Reconstruction period. Richard Nixon now confesses to grave misjudgments. One of the problems about punishing him is to find a punishment that will not also make the nation a victim.

✮

JUNE 29, 1973

WHITE HOUSE PARANOIA

The government of Great Britain, speaking through the monarch, announces an annual honors list, eagerly awaited, which makes awards to a deserving elect. Thanks to presidential counsel John Dean's hoarding of White House files, we learn that the Nixon administration followed the British practice, but inverted it into an "enemies list," and kept it secret.

It is a part of the topsy-turviness of our time that when it was made public the enemies list became an authentic honors list. People scanned it avidly to see who had made it, who had not. It was an in-thing to be on it. To be left off the list was like failing to make the big bash that Truman Capote threw for the elite a few years ago. It was to be publicly humiliated.

How different from the McCarthyism days, when being on the infamous radio or TV industry blacklist could spell hardship, ignominy, and even the loss of livelihood. Evidently we have moved forward in our awareness and our sense of paradox, even while the White House group was moving backward in moral fuzziness.

I was busy writing during the afternoon, and it wasn't until I went to a dinner party that I learned I was on the list, and was greeted by the congratulations of my friends, as if I had done something extraordinary.

The fact is that none of us had done anything except his ordinary work by his best lights. I prided myself on making every effort to be fair to the president, but I was severe when he deserved severity. To try to be informed, to strain for perspective, to call your shots as you see them, with no afterthoughts: corny as it sounds, that is what being a commentator is about.

But for men blinded by arrogance and corruption, if you did your job and hit hard when you were moved to, and refused to curry favor, you were bound to be suspect. The distorted angle of vision of the White House staff distorted their image of the commentators as well. You didn't have to be guilty of any act of enmity: it was all in the subjective eye of the beholders, and the quality of vision of the beholders can be judged by the fact that they were up to their eyelashes in Watergate.

It sounds pretty zany, doesn't it? A good psychological term for it is paranoia, when you see enemies, enemies everywhere, and you feel so surrounded by threats that you turn yourself into an engine of threat. A good political term for it is police state.

Each of us has enough of a touch of paranoia to have a personal enemies list tucked away somewhere. Judging from some of my more choleric mail, I am on a goodly number of lists. I have a little list of my own, and who doesn't? When you experience some special, outlandish idiocy, when someone inflicts on you a grievous injustice, you put him down on your mental list. There may be murder or mayhem in your heart. But it eases the pain and frustration to assign the SOB to some Dantean circle of Hell.

For most of us the list ends there, as it does in Gilbert and Sullivan—as people who never will be missed, whom you consign in your imagination to diabolical tortures. I speak of those of us who don't have the resources of the Mafia, or the KGB, or the French Sûreté, or the White House staff. All power, said George Santayana, is delightful, but absolute power is absolutely delightful.

If you have that kind of power, then the temptation is to translate your personal little list, if not into assassination, then at least into wiretaps, tax audits, other tax pressures—efforts to find a private "scandal" to publicize, constant harassment.

My colleague James Wechsler wrote about this dawning understanding of some connection between his being on the enemies list and the fact of having a tax audit made on him for the first time. He hopes it is not paranoia on his part. I doubt whether it is. Several of us have experienced a series of such audits.

But in these Orwellian years a number of commentators on the list are likely to be auditing the behavior of the IRS just as closely as the IRS will be auditing them. Not the least of the disservices the Watergate gang has done the nation is to cast this kind of shadow on due process of tax administration.

✯

THE BUGGED WHITE HOUSE

The news that President Nixon's offices and phones in the White House were bugged from the spring of 1971, and that it was done at his own orders, is the final absurdity of the whole story of an intelligence-oriented, secrecy-absorbed, surveillance-obsessed administration.

The image of a bugged White House is an unpleasant one for Americans who have fancied themselves as living in an open society. If this was also true, wholly or in part, of the Lyndon Johnson administration—as White House counsel J. Fred Buzhardt contends—that doesn't make it less alien to the image Americans had of themselves.

A bugged White House—bugged in a secrecy so deep that it was hidden from all but a few of the president's own White House staff—is the product of a paranoid vision of life. Whether or not it was meant for "historical" purposes (as presidential assistant Alexander Butterfield, head of the taping operation, valiantly insisted in his testimony) or something less virtuous, it was close to an Orwellian vision.

How far American democracy has moved since those days in the Jacksonian Republic when a triumphant horde of the common people, celebrating their victory, swarmed over the White House, which by that act they claimed as their own! They muddied the carpets and carried away fragments of the curtains as emblems of their possession, which made a number of the contemporary and later historians shudder.

But however rude this invasion by the demos, it was an open one, marking an open relationship between president and people. A closed, secretive, bugged White House is the exact opposite. The knowledge of it strips away the last shreds of the innocent self-image of the American Adam.

It raises, for the moment, two major clusters of questions. One is why it was done, and especially in such secrecy. The second is what its impact will be on the present constitutional impasse between the president and the Senate committee over the issue of providing the committee with the White House documents (now including the tapes of conversations) that the committee asks for.

It is idle to argue, as some will do, that a president has the right to order the bugging of the White House conversations he is involved in. The point is that Nixon was not the only one involved in them. Countless others—visitors who came to see him, those who called him and talked with him—were also people with a personality, a self-image, a stake in their privacy, and in the historical record they wanted to leave. It gave the president an immense advantage over them: he knew that he and they were being bugged. They didn't.

It must have crossed the minds of some visitors to the president, in various administrations, that a record of some sort was being kept of their conversations. But usually it was a joking, whimsical surmise, as of something that might be true if it were a stage set in suspense fiction but couldn't be true in actuality, without their being informed about it. Now it turns out to be true, beyond the wild, whimsical surmise.

One can understand its being done to protect a president, who might otherwise be defenseless against distorted versions of what was said, as one can also understand its being part of a record to be deposited in future archives. But in either case both sides to the conversation would need to know about it. The secrecy is what makes it sinister.

If President Nixon argues the case as one of historical archives, it strips him of the moral right to refuse to produce the records for the Senate committee. In the case of the crucial conversations the committee is likely to want—those with H. R. Haldeman, John Erlichman, John Dean, Charles Colson—the president could continue to claim a privilege of secret communication with members of his staff, even if there was an actual record of them and they were thus neither secret nor ephemeral.

He could take his position on the danger of setting precedents for congressional invasion of executive communications in the future, however innocent he might claim these particular conversations to have been. In fact, he might even argue that if they had been sinister, he would have been an idiot to have held them at all, given his knowledge that they were bugged.

It is too early to guess whether the committee will move from request to subpoena, and whether Congress will move beyond subpoena to impeachment. But it is clear that the knowledge of the bugged White House has given the Senate committee a psychological advantage in the constitutional impasse. The Butterfield windfall—the accidental way his evidence came about was nothing less than that—may prove a turning point in the contest between the White House and Senate.

✷

AUGUST 17, 1973

THE DECLINE OF AUTHORITY

President Nixon's TV reply to his critics was less than candid, it said nothing new, and it left the crucial question of the tapes unchanged. But what counts is how the American people settle on an estimate of him in the long months ahead. It will make or break him as president. But it will also depend on a larger estimate of the overall climate in America within which Watergate took place.

In assessing the changes in that climate, I start with a basic distinction between power and authority. Power is what you can do by the office you hold or the function you perform. Authority is how much strength you give to what you do, not by your office or function but by yourself as a person, by what you are. This is true whether you are a teacher, employer, army commander, actor, officeholder, prison warden, psychiatrist, social worker, minister of a church, gang leader, policeman, parent, or President of the United States.

We have witnessed, in the past decade, a fearful decline of authority in America, perhaps in the whole Western world. Not a decline in power, for power is ever-present and inescapable, and if it isn't wielded by some it is wielded by others. But a decline in authority—whatever puts its impress on people and makes them go along willingly and not by coercion. It has happened in government, the economy, the churches, the armed services, the schools, the family itself.

This is what has happened to the American presidency and vice presidency together. In constitutional terms the power is still there. In actual terms it has diminished because the people no longer believe in the integrity of the men filling the offices. It is a question of credibility. If Nixon and Spiro Agnew can achieve a turnabout in their credibility in the coming weeks, it will be among the great performances of history.

There is a good illustration in Theodore White's *The Making of the President, 1972* of how rapidly the authority of the presidency eroded. After describing how Richard Nixon won power again in 1972, White appends a final chapter, "The Temptation of Power," as a kind of epilogue to the narrative.

I am reminded of a memoir that John Bartlow Martin did on events, during LBJ's presidency, in the Dominican Republic, to which he had been President Kennedy's ambassador. He called the memoir, wryly, *Overtaken by Events*. That is what happened to White's fine, dramatic narrative: the Watergate break-in came when he had all but finished his recital, and he found himself overtaken by events. He had to fashion an assessment of Richard Nixon's personality that would tie together his original estimate with the shattering events of Watergate.

In a real sense Richard Nixon was overtaken by events too—but events he had not counted on, events he had himself in one way or another set in motion. Whatever he may have known or not have known about the plots and cover-up, he must have been surprised at the intensity of the national reaction when it came. He has been trying to catch up with the events—and his underestimate of them—ever since.

The greatest moral crisis of the presidency in American history has wretchedly eroded the president's authority. Where once his authority bulged all over the presidential chair, his diminished authority now leaves a vast space all around him.

This has had repercussions—on America's world monetary position, on prices and living costs internally, on the loss of command in the Cambodian situation, on the disenchantment of the Chinese Communists when they found that the head of the world's greatest imperium is not in command of his own national house.

Which raises the question: What will happen to the authority of the presidency, not only of the president? Whether Nixon and Agnew stay in office, or whether only one of them does, or neither, there is bound to be a shift in the balance of authority between the presidency on one side, and Congress and the courts and the media on the other.

I am convinced that one way or another a new equilibrium will have to be struck. It may last a few years or a decade or several generations. That is in the lap of history, and this time we had better not be overtaken by events.

✷

NIXON: A TRAGIC FIGURE?

We still don't know what will happen to him, but under the sting of events the style, personality, and character of Richard Nixon are being projected—in however shadowy a way—on a merciless screen. No president in American history has ever been subjected to so total a scrutiny of what he has done, what he is like, who in fact he is. None has ever been so hard-pressed, none has ever maneuvered so continuously, endlessly, inexplicably.

Each position is occupied, shifted, abandoned, replaced by another in a bewildering succession that leaves the watchers more incredulous and the disclosures more incredible.

The whole business forms a treasure trove for the psychobiographers and psychohistorians who have for years been trying to reach an assessment of Nixon's complex, elusive personality.

Some of the traits they spotted in him have been borne out by recent events: his "loner" quality, his isolation, his soul-searching spells with himself at decisive moments, his proneness to crisis, his secrecy, his deviousness, his passion to win and dominate, his sense of being beset by enemies, his obsession with power, his cult of technique, his distrust of personal or political closeness, his concern about his image, his moodiness, his sense of letdown at his moments of triumph, his willingness to take unusual, risky, and unpopular ways to achieve ambitious goals, his lack of scruple about means when he is convinced of his ends, his love of surprise, his belief that when a leader takes history by storm he will be vindicated by history.

There is a sentence in James David Barber's study of Nixon's political personality, written in 1971, which was shrewdly predictive, and which rings a resonant bell today. "I think that if Nixon is ever threatened simultaneously with public disdain and loss of power," Barber wrote, "he may move into a crisis syndrome." He is today threatened with both. He has shown evidence of the crisis syndrome. But no one can be sure that his resilience won't overcome and survive what might otherwise become a psychological tailspin.

You hear many things about Nixon, whether you listen to the gos-

sip in Washington, New York, Los Angeles, or Cambridge. He will resign, say some. He will commit suicide, say others. He will press the
button and start a nuclear war, say still others. He will engineer a military coup (presumably with Chief of Staff General Alexander Haig's
help), the story goes, and will suspend constitutional government. The
gossip spreads fast, to the world capitals. In every national crisis the all-
too-real dangers are compounded and distorted by hysteria and fanaticism.

Nixon may, of course, be impeached. He might even resign, although I doubt it. I doubt the suicide thesis even more strongly, and I
regard the military coup as sheer absurdity.

But you don't have to go that far to feel a sense of the tragic about
the whole Nixon story. One might object that Nixon doesn't have the
stature for anything like the tragic dimension. I agree that he doesn't
possess the grand mythic quality of the great Greek figures of tragedy.
He seems at this point a harried and doubtless frightened man, moving
more desperately each time to parry each disclosure.

Yet what is truly tragic about Nixon is the expense of talent in a
waste of deviousness, the sense we have of what Nixon could have
achieved, and how he has turned so many potentials into destructiveness and self-destructiveness. Those who are urgently engaged in
chasing and finally killing the king may find such an overall view a luxury, but I think the historians will see it that way.

Kennedy's life was tragic, and not only in his death. He had great
talents, and he committed them to his effort to confront the myth of
Communist power and destiny, and build a countermyth of the young
and valiant democratic hero. In Nixon's case we were misled by his bitter anti-Communism, and he was misled himself, for in spite of all the
garish display it was not his deep drive.

As it turned out, in his presidential years, amidst the passions generated by the war and by the antiwar movement, it was not so much
Communism that Nixon was resisting. It was, as he saw it, the tumults
and violence of democracy. For that crusade, as Watergate has shown,
his ends and means became tragically distorted.

Even with the Greeks, the tragic figure was the man of gifts who
aimed for what seemed to him high purposes and in the process destroyed something more precious than anything he could have
achieved. That is Nixon. We have not finished measuring how much of
the fabric of our institutions has been destroyed. Nor can we tell yet
how much of Nixon has been.

★

THE WALLS CLOSING IN

The odds strike me as better than even that Gerald Ford, translated from the House into the vice presidency, will be translated further into the presidency by the end of 1974. I wish it had been someone other than Ford, who seems an unlikely choice to fill out the presidential term and office.

But it is in the nature of history that in the great crisis of the national life it should offer not a choice between the desirable and undesirable, but between degrees of the undesirable.

Some five weeks ago, after the "firestorm" events in the Justice Department that included the resignation of Attorney General Elliot Richardson and the dismissal of Deputy Attorney General William D. Ruckelhaus for their refusal to fire Special Prosecutor Archibald Cox, I wrote that "Americans are now thinking the unthinkable. Impeachment was for a time only an outside possibility. It has now become almost a probability. It may soon reach the point where it is all but irreversible." The event of the drowned-out tape, with more than eighteen inaudible minutes, has brought the nation even closer to that point.

The question is no longer whether the House Judiciary Committee will vote to impeach: that seems inevitable. The question now is whether the whole House and the Senate will follow its lead.

That is something which will wait on two other events. One is Judge Sirica's "moment of truth," when he decides what to do with the tangled issues of evidence and law over the tapes. The other is what happens when the congressmen and senators go home over the holidays, and sound out the grassroots opinion about presidential impeachment.

President Nixon cannot influence the first event. He can try to influence the second by a renewed, aggressive Operation Candor.

One gets the feeling, very much as in an Edgar Allan Poe story, that the walls are closing in around Richard Nixon. Each time he extricates himself partially his room for maneuver shrinks. His weakness is not crucially in the legal area but in the moral and psychological area.

Thus one may argue and disagree about how the tape to be transcribed by the president's secretary Rose Mary Woods was actually erased, until a finding by Judge Sirica or his grand jury. But it is impossible to explain innocently why Nixon waited for weeks before telling Judge Sirica about it, or even his own lawyers.

Was it secrecy become obsessive, or panic and funk, or a deliberate game plan of the timing of damaging revelations? Whichever you choose is morally indefensible.

What makes Nixon's situation worse is that by now he has all but used up the new White House staff group around him, damaging their credibility as well as his own. This isn't true of Cabinet officials but it is true of the lawyers and the administrative assistants, who don't call the shots themselves, who are often kept in the dark, and who seem unable either to defend him wholeheartedly or to resign.

He has also pretty much used up the protective layers of authority around the presidential office itself. It is a kingly office, and presidents have made use of the awe and pomp surrounding it. But the "divinity that doth hedge a king" is now eroded.

The focus now is on Nixon as a man. Increasingly he is the target of intense study of his personality and character. If he rescues himself it will be by sheer personal cleverness and will, not by the trappings of office.

The resignation route is unlikely now, as long as the case against the president is the web of suspicion that surrounds him, rather than a specific criminal act. If such an act could be proved, either about Nixon's tapes or his finances, it would galvanize the whole moral case against him as well, and make impeachment virtually certain.

In that event the resignation pressure will be resumed, in order to spare the nation the anguish of a divisive impeachment process. In Congress and the press there is talk that the leaders of Nixon's own party would get together to urge him to resign. If so it will be very late for the party leaders to function.

The failure of the party system has been almost as dismal as the failure of the presidency. Where were the party leaders when the palace guard took over increasing powers? Where were they when the Committee to Re-elect the president went off on an irresponsible frolic of its own?

I fear the answer is that they too wanted to win the election and that they were thinking of their own political skins. We often talk a lot of nonsense about "Establishments." What was lacking among the

Republicans was exactly a party Establishment that would bring its weight and judgment to bear on the wild parvenus of CRP and the palace guard, and on the president himself.

✸

SHADOW OF THE ORDEAL

President Nixon is losing, if he has not already lost, the all-important battle of public opinion. I call it that because it is the people who will decide how Congress will vote on his impeachment. The release of the transcripts of the tapes enraged the key Republicans in Congress who felt the president had trapped them into supporting him and then cut the ground away under them, and it outraged a large segment of the people who earlier had stuck to a marginal wait-and-see position.

There are two major currents of fact and feeling operating against the president. One is constitutional and criminal law. The transcripts suggest strong grounds for an indictment of the president for obstructing justice. He and his supporters reach a different conclusion from the same conversations. This will be fought out during the impeachment process, but the evidence of the language itself is pretty strong.

The other major current is morality. Americans are not easily shocked in these freewheeling days, but the transcripts sent a seismic shock across the nation.

In part it was the language. Americans are accustomed to rough talk, even from presidents, as any newspaperman can testify who talked with Harry Truman or Lyndon Johnson. But beyond the (deleted) expletives there was a moral bleakness in the language that one might accept from a skull session of ad men or a pettifogging strategy session of client and lawyers cornered in a legal jam, but not from a president and his close advisers.

One thinks inevitably of George Orwell's essay on how the corruption of language expresses a corruption of politics.

On those ethnic slurs Nixon is reported to have made against Jews and Italians, one is forced back into the contradictions within his personality. Here he was, alone with his closest staff people, off guard, believing himself safe with his secret tapes. It isn't hard, despite Ronald Ziegler, to think of him as slipping into coarse ethnic epithets.

What is hard to reconcile is the split in Nixon. The man who spoke of "Jew boys"—if he did—had appointed one of them secretary of state, and was prouder of their achievements in policy together than of anything in his career. The man who called Judge Sirica a "wop"—if he did—had successfully wooed and won the votes of most middle-class ethnics, including those of Italian descent.

It is as if there were three Nixons—the public one who plans difficult and innovative foreign policies, the one who at another level is capable of what is in the transcripts, and somehow a third Nixon who may reveal himself to himself in those lonely vigils at Camp David but who has not integrated his three selves into one.

The shadow of the ordeal ahead falls on all of us. Raising the specter of a jailed president, *New York Times* columnist and former Nixon speechwriter William Safire has, in effect, asked liberals to call off the dogs and save the nation the anguish of an impeachment process that would not only oust him from office but logically lead to criminal trial, with its consequences.

Nixon could have avoided the whole ordeal for everyone if he had been wholly honest with the nation in those cruel months last spring. There can be little doubt now about the bitterness of what lies ahead.

But history moves inexorably, once it starts moving. It is too late for Nixon to buy immunity from later prosecution by resigning. More important than any other element in the American system is the doctrine of due process of law. That is why the Democratic leaders in the Senate are wise to play down the resignation talk and let impeachment take its course.

The president took huge risks to assure his reelection and what he thought would be his place in history. Now he is fighting for an exit from history with some shreds of self-image. He seems determined to force the House and Senate to vote on him and risk alienating an important segment of their constituencies, however they vote. If they won't lighten his burden (he is saying), he won't lighten theirs.

General Haig's Delphic sentence—that the president would resign only if he felt it was in the national interest—may well be the thread leading out of the monstrous entrapment in which the nation is caught. My hunch is that he will invoke the national interest only when he counts the probable vote in Congress and finds it adverse. In either case—whether the course be resignation or impeachment—it will be the common sense of the people that will call the tune.

★

AUGUST 5, 1974

IT'S TIME HE RESIGNED

It will be downhill all the way now for Richard Nixon on the slippery slope of his declining fortunes. Impeachment by a House majority seems inevitable even before the debate starts, and the debate is bound to seal it.

The one-third of the Senate vote that he needs as his last defense has all but slipped out of his grasp, and by the time the Senate trial starts it will have been reduced to a pathetic Gideon's band of loyalists. Nor is there any chance that at the last moment a group of "recusants" from the enemy camp will cross the battle lines to save him as they saved President Andrew Johnson.

There were two recent trial balloons intended to save him, but neither has worked. The idea of conceding a House impeachment by a formal unanimous vote in order to avoid the damning effects of a House debate was meant to get a quick Senate vote before any further erosion set in for the dwindling Nixon forces. It was too transparent politically and doubtful constitutionally.

The second plan, broached in despair, was to propose an amendment to the House articles that would substitute "censure" for "impeachment." Had the censure idea been seriously pushed a year earlier, before the evidence began to gather avalanche weight, it might conceivably have worked. Today it is too slight and too late.

The more serious question beyond these tactical ones is whether President Nixon will decide to fight it out to the end or resign, now that the handwriting on the wall grows too claimant to be ignored.

Rationally he can cut some of his losses by resigning. He may salvage his pension payments, and—even assuming there will be no plea bargaining as there was in Agnew's case—he may have a better chance to escape later criminal charges than if he fights it out.

By this reckoning the sensible thing would be for him to count the inevitable Senate vote now, rescue the Congress Republicans from their election nightmare, and spare the nation the expense, time, and bitterness of the Senate trial.

My hunch is that Nixon will play it that way. But it isn't a strongly held hunch, because the more irrational elements of Nixon's personality speak against it.

Like many people the president shuts out reality by denying it is there. This is one reason why he has so consistently insulated himself from any unpleasantness, cutting himself off from the people and from the reality principle.

His White House palace guard reinforced his self-isolation and, despite the tough male-bond talk in the transcripts, dealing with techniques, they helped him not to face the essential truth of what had happened.

Like many people the president is also a splitter, putting his broad national purposes and his sense of history in one compartment of his mind and his rough and devious means in another—and never the twain shall meet. This may give him the conviction that he is no guiltier than other presidents have been and make him feel like a fighting martyr to the end.

Many have wondered how President Nixon has managed to survive a drawn-out pitiless ordeal that might have crumbled a frailer self-image and a lesser will. The answer may be that a strong man can survive as long as there is some residual hope to cling to.

But all remaining hope will surely have ebbed away. It would be better all around, for the nation and for the president, if he were to go to the people—on radio and TV—and say that to staunch the blood and bind up the wounds he will resign.

When the pressure for his resignation first came, it came too early to enable him to face himself. Now it should make sense, to him as to us.

★

AUGUST 9, 1974

END OF A GAMBLER

The problem during the last phase of the presidential crisis can be put simply: How do you move the most powerful man in the world out of power when he said consistently that he wouldn't go except by the longest and hardest route?

The question has been resolved at last by President Nixon's resignation yesterday.

What made it harder, during these final tense days of the crisis, was that there were no precedents for what was happening, and where precedents didn't exist we had to create them. On that score we have been, in effect, where the Founding Fathers were at the time of the Constitutional Convention. Every step taken, both by congressional and party leaders, by federal court judges, and also by the president, had to be taken with an eye to the future.

Yet to say, as President Nixon repeatedly said, that he couldn't resign without laying future presidents open to arbitrary political pressures, was a curious way to put it. For it would have meant there could never be any easing of a president out of office—even one who by his own admission had committed great malfeasances—except by the final cumbersome solution of the impeachment process.

If the nation had to drink the cup of impeachment to the last dregs, then somehow we would have done it. But there had to be a better way, with less punishment for both the president and the people.

Looking back at the past few weeks, it is clear that the president was caught in an agonized wrestling between his rational self-interest and his irrational self-image. Once he found that he had lost the people themselves—even his past strong supporters—his self-interest had to lead him to talks with the few congressional leaders he trusted, and a decision to effect an orderly transfer of power.

But there were also signs that his self-image was in conflict with this course. It has been that of a loner, a fighter, one who has been through a succession of crises and has seemed each time to be beaten but has always rebounded and would rebound again. It was the self-image of a man who—like his admired hero-figure, de Gaulle—refused to let history happen to him, but felt he must happen to history.

Yet often in the lives of gamblers there is a last time, when they have gone too far, to the point of no return, and their gamble no longer pays off, and they lose their whole stake. That happened with Richard Nixon. In actuality the game was up, the Congress and most of the people wanted him to go, but the danger was that he would isolate himself in his self-image and not understand what was happening.

Persisting in this self-isolation he would be his own worst enemy. There was even a theory, growing fashionable in some quarters, that Nixon sought out the course that destroyed him, as if he were seeking punishment—that all along he followed a self-destructive impulse that reasserted itself perversely every time he had a resounding success.

As I wrote a number of times, my own guess—despite Nixon's persistent denials—continued to be that he would resign when he counted the Senate votes rather than wait it out to the bitter impeachment end. But I also felt he would try to arrange it so that he would present himself to history as having chosen his own timing, rather than yielding reactively to the pressures around him.

For in the end he had to face the realities about immunity. Resignation would bring with it a vast national wave of relief, and on the swell of that wave a mixture of compassion as well. "There is no desire to hound him into jail," said one congressman, which is doubtless what most Americans feel at this moment.

But would they feel it three months from now, about a Nixon who had insisted on prolonging the confrontation with Congress and embittering and dividing the nation? I think not. And that may turn out to have been the decisive element in the calculation of a man with a crowded tumultuous life who at one point went too far, a gambler whose hole cards had been exposed.

☆

SEPTEMBER 9, 1974

MERCY WITHOUT JUSTICE

It was the wrong action to take—understandable but unwise and wrong.

"I do believe with all my heart," President Ford said in announcing his pardon of Richard Nixon, "that I . . . will receive justice without mercy if I fail to show mercy." It is good to temper justice with mercy, but how about placing mercy in the context of justice? Does President Ford feel that the way to escape suffering justice without mercy, "as a humble servant of God," is to mete out mercy without justice as President of the United States?

I take him at his word that it was a decision of conscience, but does that make it the right and wise one? The question is not only what Ford's conscience dictated, but also how it jibes with the moral sense of the rest of America, and what impact it will have on America's future. That is the crucial test.

No one questions the president's constitutional power of pardon.

But the people will ask how he has used that power, and whether he has abused it.

It took courage to make the decision, since Ford knew how unpopular it would be, and the storm it would arouse. But courage, however desirable a quality, isn't enough. Richard Nixon's Cambodian decision took courage too, but it was nonetheless the wrong decision.

Ford's decision was spurred by compassion, but compassion also isn't enough. There must be a cool, careful calculation of the nation's interest, including the need not only for compassion but also for justice. In the long run history will judge Ford by how wisely he weighed these two factors.

The nation was in a double bind on the question of punishment or pardon for Richard Nixon. If he was to be indicted and tried criminally, there was danger (as President Ford noted) of prolonging the national debate and perhaps starting again the turmoil of polarized opinion that had for a time subsided. But if he was to escape indictment and trial, there was the danger of a widespread disillusionment with the failure to live up to equal justice under the law.

I feel that President Ford overestimated the first danger, that of social divisiveness if Nixon were tried, and underestimated the second danger, that of social disillusionment if he escaped trial. In fact, the upshot of Ford's pardoning decision may be that the nation will be afflicted by divisiveness as well as disillusionment, and will thus have the worst of both worlds.

Inevitably there will be questions raised about what was actually behind the decision. People will ask whether there had ever been an understanding about it between the two men, even one short of commitment. They will ask how it happened that, after having made two public statements saying he would not use his pardoning power before legal proceedings had started against Nixon, he nevertheless reversed himself. They are bound to ask whether there might have been fear of what would emerge in the course of a trial.

I don't say these doubts and fears are true, but only that they are inevitable. Because they are inevitable, the pardon doesn't settle the social agony. It will be around for a long time.

No one can fault the president for wishing to inject some mercy into justice. But you can't temper justice with mercy until justice starts to operate. The wiser judgment for Ford would have been to let the charges against Nixon take their course, as they have with others who were involved in the Watergate cover-up. There would have been time then, at some point, for the president to intervene and use his pardoning power. He would thus have sated the people's hunger for compassion, but he would also have appeased their passionate sense of injustice.

The pity of it is that the nation had come to recognize Ford as a decent man, and had welcomed the change in climate at the White House. Ford built up a moral reservoir of credibility with the people. I hope I am wrong, but I fear he has blown it with his blunder.

★

WRITING "HOT HISTORY"*

Imagine the most powerful man in the world, but a deeply flawed man. Imagine him, in a moment of overweening hubris, presiding over a secret, lawless scheme to ensure his reelection, convinced that only he can carry the burden of world power and prevail over America's inner enemies. Imagine this scheme surfacing in an accidental minor outcropping, then being covered up, and eventually being tracked down and exposed. Finally, imagine the unraveling of the man's power, of his regime, of the man himself, in the last agonized days.

It is the story of the unraveling that Bob Woodward and Carl Bernstein have told in *The Final Days*, in overwhelming, microscopic detail. Call it investigative journalism, call it hot history—call it whatever. The fact is that the two authors did it in the way most natural to them—as a story to be "covered." They started a few days after Nixon resigned, organized their file system, deployed themselves and their staff, and fanned out in every direction. Their method was that of truth-through-interviews, to get at people fairly close to the action and to weave a skein of first-, second-, and third-hand reports from the interviews.

Does their book change the broad outlines of the picture we already had of the Watergate unraveling? Basically, no. Does it give any new meanings and new dimensions of depth to the story? Again, no. But there are unexpected details—minor surprises that flash out of the otherwise somber narrative—that have been widely picked up by the American and world press. A few of the portraits of second-level figures get filled out—notably, President Nixon's chief of staff, Al Haig; his counsel, Fred Buzhardt; and his press secretary, Ron Ziegler—and

---

*This article originally appeared in *Saturday Review* (May 29, 1976).

one gets a more intimate view of Julie and David Eisenhower than before. As for Nixon himself, the colors are harsh, sometimes grotesque. It is the portrait of a man losing control over himself as he loses control of the struggle to keep from being impeached.

The *Newsweek* excerpts, and the news releases and press stories based on them, were so lurid in their overkill that the book itself, with stretches of sober, sometimes prosaic detail, seems a relief. Yet in conversations I had with each of the authors, I put to them some of my reservations: on perspective, on the tests of evidence, on detachment and bias, on the trust they ask the reader to share, on the differences between a journalistic foray and a historical siege.

They had thought about the problems, and they had answers. Of the two, Woodward was a bit more skeptical than Bernstein of the way the excerpts had been managed, yet both insisted that the press would have overplayed them anyway. (My own view: maybe the press was overeager, but the lady was seductively arrayed.)

On the evidence question, it would be foolish to treat a journalistic book as if it were a court of law, in which the rights of the accused have to be jealously guarded against hearsay, and the witnesses are raked over in cross-examination. I mentioned to them the injunction of the German historian Leopold von Ranke to tell the story "as it actually happened" (*wie es eigentlich gewesen ist*) and to be sure to have two witnesses to every event, not in collusion with each other and neither of them self-deceived. The authors cheerfully accepted it. I am ready to believe that in the vast majority of interviews they succeeded in checking and double-checking the information. But the self-interest of many of their sources—their public face, their desire to rid themselves of the Watergate taint and get a better role in the drama of history—seems to me an insurmountable obstacle, unless the reader knows who the sources are and can make his own assessment of them.

This is, of course, the nub problem. It is the more serious because the authors—given their major role in tracking down the cover-up in their *Washington Post* articles—had themselves been actors on the stage of history and had a stake of their own in the story of the final days. A heroic effort at detachment might mitigate some of their inevitable bias, but, offhand, this particular pair wouldn't have been my first choice to venture the heroism.

Consider the difference between the two enterprises. The first was the digging out of a plot and a cover-up, getting at the particulars that would suggest the larger outline. The second was the filling in of an outline generally—if vaguely—known, as faithfully (and colorfully) as possible. A bias and sense of shock about Nixon and Watergate would be helpful to energize the reporters in the first venture, whereas a similar emotional set would be a hindrance in writing history—even contemporary history.

But the larger problem is the anonymity of the sources. American readers are likely to be prove-it-to-me people. The basic decision the authors made was that there was to be no attribution, of a particular conversation or detail, to a particular source. Which means they are asking us for blind trust. Not only must they have "relations of trust" (as they put it) with their sources, but also they expect the reader to trust their assessment of the trustworthiness of the sources. It may have been the only way this particular kind of book could have been written, but the leap of faith it asks for is more of a jump than most of us can make.

Take one of the details I know something about. Of the Supreme Court case on the Nixon tapes, the authors say that Chief Justice Warren Burger came up with an "inadequate" opinion to satisfy the rest, and "finally Justice Potter Stewart undertook to co-author the opinion." As it happens, I tried out this assertion on the chief justice, who was astounded by it. He told me that the process of shaping the unanimous opinion was a long one, but that he had been in charge all along and had no "co-authors." Since it is unlikely that any of the justices would have been informants for the authors, it must have been one or two of the clerks—but which? Justice Stewart's? Anyone who knows the Supreme Court knows its internal splits and should be wary of them. I feel the same way about an earlier passage telling what the justices said to one another in their conference room, which is so secret a place that the last appointed justice has to serve as the only messenger boy. I'd love to see the file on that one.

The trouble is that we can't see any of the files. Woodward told me that they would be turned over to a library collection, to be available at some distant date. In the long run we'll know, but it will be after all the reviews and the gate receipts are in, and in the long run (as John Maynard Keynes used to say) we'll all be dead. Think of how we would feel if Richard Nixon, in his forthcoming memoirs, were to make the same claim to our leap of faith in trusting his anonymous sources.

I don't play down the creativeness of investigative journalism, old style or new style. The old style was the Richard Harding Davis stuff, or the muckraking *Shame of the Cities* stuff of Lincoln Steffens, or John Reed's stories about the Mexican War or his reporting on the Russian Revolution in *Ten Days That Shook the World*. This kind of journalism is still heady stuff, as witness the Redford-Hoffman film, from the Woodward-Bernstein *All the President's Men*. It gives a beautiful sense of what goes on in a city room and in an editorial conference, and glorifies the detective-reporter in a way to double the journalism-class enrollment next year and make folk heroes out of Woodward and Bernstein.

For a time the phrase *new journalism* afflicted us, but it is now, happily, passing. If it meant anything, it meant a sense of glorying in the reporter's subjectivism. We know that there can be no absolute detachment. As Lord Acton put it, the only true detachment is that of the dead, because they no longer care. But we can make an effort to recognize and appraise our own values, and therefore our bias, and still strive to live up to von Ranke and tell it "as it actually happened," not as our partisan attachments tell us it *should* have happened. Even as a crusader Steffens forced himself to tell the story of the cities straight. Anything else would destroy his credibility, which depended on his tough-minded grasp of the reality. This is still a requirement for journalism, old or new.

Part of the problem of a book like this is the climate it appears in. Nixon's turnings and churnings as he gets boxed in ever tighter, the portrait of him as, in effect, having gone bonkers, is one that fits in with the prevailing mood about him today. There was always the chance—after impeachment, after the trial that would follow—that he would have to go to jail. With the resignation and pardon, it didn't happen that way. But as we retraverse every hour of those closing days, we take part in an adjourned session of the trial that wasn't held. We follow the grim windings of the House Judiciary Committee in its deliberations and votes; we are present when Special Prosecutor Leon Jaworski considers the problem of plea bargaining with Nixon and meditates on how it might be to get a president to turn state's witness against his former aides.

Which of us, as he reads, isn't caught up in the flood of his own memories of the whole enactment? That excellent historian of the Near East, Bernard Lewis, uses a revealing title for his new book of lectures on history. He calls it *History—Remembered, Recovered, Invented* (Princeton University Press). If Woodward and Bernstein have indeed written history, then much of it is remembered and much recovered. The remembered elements serve as a frame for the recovered elements. But the remembered history wasn't just in the memory of the people interviewed but in our own memories as well. This is a case in which Carl Becker's phrase, from his famous lecture on history, applies: "Everyman his own historian." In a more or less rudimentary way, what is true of traditional societies is true of each of us—that we share a collective memory of our recent past as a people, of our folk heroes and folk villains, and that we filter any new information—the history dug up and recovered—through the history remembered. Whether there are also some elements of history invented in the Woodward-Bernstein account is a question we won't be able to answer until the time capsule to be buried in the library is someday opened.

Which again raises the question of the line between good journalism and good history. I suggest five criteria for deciding. First, have the tests of evidence been applied rigorously? Second, has the author tried to make allowance for his own bias and his own value cluster? Third, to what extent are the returns in? In the current book, with a few exceptions, the palace guard—primary and secondary—are targets, not witnesses. We won't know the truth about the maneuverings until we have the memoirs of Haldeman, Ehrlichman, Dean, Ziegler, Haig, St. Clair, and of Nixon himself and can compare them with *Final Days*. Until then, with the best of intentions, the authors are limited to the accusatory brand of investigative journalism. Nixon and his cohorts remain targets, not subjects.

The last two criteria are equally important. You have only a truncated history until you have had time enough to note the consequences of the events and decisions you are writing about. We see Franklin Roosevelt and Harry Truman more clearly now than in 1955 because we have seen the consequences of their decisions. Which means that the early accounts and estimates, however necessary, are often cruelly inadequate approximations of the historic truth. Finally, the historian must try to make some sense and pattern out of the raw material he has dug up, seeking to be fair and just, and tell it as it actually happened, but seeking also to extract the meaning and implications of the whole story.

We can, of course, get too stuffy about this. In the current case the authors have done what they can best do, which is not to find meanings but to gather events and memories, and set them down chronologically, in a kind of Book of the Days very similar to the Book of the Years of the earliest chroniclers. We can parallel Clemenceau's remark about not leaving war to the generals by saying that we ought not to

leave history to the professional historians, who are in danger of stifling it. The craft of history is always in need of rebarbarizing by the
energies of talented amateurs, lest it come under the dictatorship of
the mandarins. A good example of such an amateur was Gene Smith,
who used to work as a reporter on the *New York Post* and who wrote an
account of the final days of Woodrow Wilson (one of Nixon's heroes)—*When the Cheering Stopped.* It was good history as well as good
journalism, and it passed all five of my criteria with colors flying.

Unless we know the implications of what we know, we don't know
much. That is why every good journalist-historian must have in him at
least some ingredients of the psychologist, philosopher, and social analyst, and would do well to add to the accusatory drive a brooding
sense of irony and even compassion.

Not for Nixon's sake, but for our own. Here is the epigraph for
the last volume of war memoirs by a talented amateur historian, Winston Churchill: "How the Great Democracies Triumphed, and so
Were Able to Resume the Follies Which Had so Nearly Cost Them
Their Life." I suspect that a future historian will someday write a similarly ironic epigraph about Watergate and Nixon and his resignation,
and the follies that we will probably have resumed that nearly cost us
our life.

Richard Nixon himself, the central figure of the story as enacted,
is, of course, the subject of the book and the target of all the observa-
tions. Yet no Nixon—clear or complex, coherent or divided—emerges
from the myriad interviews. "Psychohistory is bullshit," Bernstein told
me. He has a right to his view, but it suggests an impatience with the
nuances of character and the interior maze of agonized contradictions
in Nixon's mind.

An investigative journalist can perhaps get along without these
subtleties in his relentless focusing on the "facts." But for a historian
there is no democracy of facts that are all born free and equal. Why
didn't Nixon take some of the other courses open to him—making a
bonfire of his tapes or sweating through an impeachment and even a
criminal trial without surrendering on the "confidentiality" issue?
Why didn't he, even earlier, risk everything on an open confession to
the people and thus redeem, if not absolve, himself? What brought
about his downfall? Was it his own indecisions and waverings, or was it
the breach of faith that his own party leaders finally felt, or was it the
rebellion of the much maligned "bureaucrats" who fed what they knew
to the congressional committees and even to investigative reporters?

These are hard questions, which require hard answers. Someday we'll get some of them, and then the whole story of the deterioration of Nixon and his band can be told, along with its implications. The American people will welcome it, because their historical consciousness requires the presence of a sense of the past in their minds, to give the nation continuity, and because they need to get their bearings in history if their civilization is to survive.

RONALD REAGAN

COMMANDER OF A COUNTERREVOLUTION

As Ronald Reagan, midcourse in his second term, turns into the last lap of his bid for history, it is already possible to draw some conclusions with reasonable confidence: His is the most surprising presidency since Truman's; he is the most effective president since Eisenhower, and he wields the greatest dramatic flair and realignment clout since Franklin Roosevelt. In contrast with the tenures of Johnson, Nixon, Ford, and Carter, when Americans wondered whether their country was governable, Reagan has showed convincingly that it is.

That, certainly, is the prime thing history will say about him. For the rest, we can still only look ahead and speculate. But first a hard look at the making of a psyche and a political mind, to trace how so unlikely a life could have prepared this president for his exercise of power.

His boyhood was objectively a rough one in a family with an alcoholic father who scrambled to make a living as a shoe salesman in Illinois small towns. Perhaps his feeling for a loved problem-father led to an early emotional distancing and a defensive denial that has persisted. Yet what Reagan retained was an almost Arcadian sense of a Huck Finn boyhood. Out of a family that remained warm and cohesive through all its struggles there came somehow a genial personality and a sense of inner security.

His college years at Eureka were those of an attractive, self-assured, popular youngster who was good at sports and dramatics, breezed through his exams, and was seen as a class leader. He managed to get a Depression job as a radio sports announcer in Des Moines, and that led to a start in Grade B movies and a Hollywood subculture that has swallowed young talents more promising than his.

This essay originally appeared as "The Surprising Presidency" in *Notre Dame Magazine* (Autumn 1985). The three columns that follow provide later assessments.

Reagan's acting career has been a shocker for president watchers who hold actors and the world of make-believe cheap. Yet politics is theater, and there has been an actor in every president concerned with a presentation of self, from Washington and Lincoln through both Roosevelts to Kennedy. In Hollywood, Reagan learned role-playing and the arts of the scenario, where he delivered lines with his own reading on a stage set by others. Ultimately he applied this scenario as actor on a world stage.

But the exploration of make-believe in Hollywood went along with the beginnings of a political mind that was shaped in the three great social upheavals he experienced—the New Deal in the 1930s, the Cold War years of the late 1940s and '50s, and the counterculture and war years of the 1960s.

The '30s made him a New Deal Democrat, devoted to Franklin Roosevelt and his works and philosophy. FDR as model sank so deeply into his imaginings that even his later conservative defection could not extirpate it. He has played the role of Franklin Delano Reagan with more gusto than any in his acting life.

The postwar '40s taught the young liberal, now head of the Screen Actors Guild, the nature of takeover tactics by Communists and how to counter their power plays. It was an education in the reality principle—the ultimate one in politics.

Reagan's acting career took a downward curve, perhaps because (as he felt) he had become too controversial to get the roles he wanted. Luckily his new job, touring General Electric plants in the 1950s as the featured speaker at employee gatherings, revived in him what Hollywood had all but blocked out—those things that were on the minds of middle-class workers. It was his return to his boyhood world and the values of Middle America. He formed a speaking style in his give-and-take communication with them which "the Great Communicator" would never lose.

Yet as he moved into his early fifties, he was still a minor figure in a minor world. Like Harry Truman, he had a long moratorium, which made him wonder whether his best talents would go unused. The turning point came in October 1964, when Barry Goldwater could not make it to a Los Angeles fund-raiser and Reagan batted for him. It was a campaign version of his basic G.E. speech, including a passage on Communism as "the most dangerous enemy that has ever faced mankind in his long climb from the swamp to the stars." It caught fire, made Reagan a statewide Republican figure overnight, brought him a campaign bid from a little group of rich Californian kingmakers, and led in 1966 to his election as governor.

Running as a "citizen politician," Reagan caught on to something that eluded his professional advisers—how important the issue of the campus protests and violence was to California's middle-class voters in the great social upheaval of the mid-1960s. The citizen politician was becoming a true political man, unifying the faction-torn Republicans and thrashing the incumbent governor in a megastate that the Democrats had all but taken over.

Governor Reagan kept his image as a breaker of liberal icons, yet managed to negotiate with the Democratic legislative majority in a series of trade-offs on social programs, education, and spending. What he learned during the eight stormy years of his governorship, he acquired because life—not education or politics—had prepared him to learn it.

He fared worse as a presidential contestant, trying too early in 1968 against Richard Nixon, making campaign and staff blunders against Jerry Ford in 1976. We all took his moving concession speech, the high point of the convention, as a graceful swan song.

But in 1980, at the age of sixty-nine, he made a third presidential try. He was overconfident in Iowa, pretending to be king and conqueror when the battle had only begun. But he took charge of the New Hampshire debate ("I paid for this microphone"), changed his staff command, got his act together, and was never headed off. In the election he had the luck to run against a failed president, and he turned America into "Reagan country," presiding at the rebirth of a party whose collapse in 1964 had first brought him into politics.

Ripeness was all—and tenacity too. Reagan seems so sunny a figure that we forget his dark years in the desert, parched for hope. The impressive post-Roosevelt presidents—Truman, Eisenhower, Reagan—all came to the White House after a long wait, in the fullness of years, untortured by an excessive power drive, unriddled even in adversity by identity crises, knowing who they were, richer than their critics guessed in the experience relevant to the presidency. "You're in the Big Leagues now," House Speaker "Tip" O'Neill told the new president. He had reason to rue his condescension.

Reagan pushed five themes in his first term—tax and spending cuts, freeing the economy for investment and entrepreneurship through deregulation, beefing up defenses, regaining authority and respect in world affairs, aiming to restore traditional values. They were largely a success because he had mastered two supposedly incompatible skills. One was to take and retain strong positions with which people could identify. The other was to struggle, cope, negotiate, bargain, compromise to get something accomplished. We call one "ideology," the other "pragmatism." Reagan has stressed the first but used it to enlarge his gains in the second.

Only the economy might have doomed him, and it was a close thing during 1982 and 1983. Someone cracked that George Bush's earlier epithet for Reaganomics—"voodoo economics"—was unfair to voodoo. But heartened by "supply-side" tax and budget cuts, and strangely married to a bastard form of Keynesian deficit financing, a new entrepreneurial economics emerged as a surprising amalgam and turned the economy around.

The presidency is an ongoing struggle against political entropy. How much claim on history will Reagan as political strategist have?

I see the two Reagan victories, in 1980 and 1984, as together forming a watershed event when the historical stream of the presidency changed course. Curiously, Reagan is the only president since Roosevelt who has had a "revolution" named for him that stuck. Only Roosevelt before him gave more direction to the long tides of national tendency. Roosevelt did it by grasping the nettle of the crises of his time—the Depression and the war—and plucking from it the flower of safety. He illustrated Hegel's dictum that "a great man actualizes his era."

Reagan was not a "great" man, but he too, in his own way, has grasped the nettle of his time and found followers. He actualizes his era by bringing to consciousness the accumulated discontents of a middle class which finds its dreams and values threatened. Add to this, more recently, the young across-the-class spectrum drawn to him by the prime event they associate with him—the entrepreneurial and information revolution and the sense of an "opportunity society" it has revived.

Some heavy political costs come with the territory of the Reagan revolution. He will not be absolved by history for a mammoth deficit, a threatened safety net resulting from budget cuts, a heavy trade imbalance, a loss of land and home by subsidy-dependent farmers, a bitterness over the "social issues" of abortion, church-state relations, and employment quotas.

By its very nature a second term has lame-duck elements, since the president no longer has any coattails to promise or withhold. Yet, picking the right issues, Reagan might lift the level of his tide high enough to sustain a party realignment, and focus on a campaign for his place in history.

This campaign of history he is likely to pursue to the end of his term. It means taking risks with his popularity, but in a second term there is much to place at risk. There are critics like Walter Dean Burnham of M.I.T. who call the Reagan presidency "divisive, not unifying," and add that "this will continue and . . . intensify." Since Reagan has so often accused the liberals of tenderness of mind, it is fair to point to his Social Darwinism and speak in turn of hardness of heart.

But unlike Jimmy Carter, compassion is not writ large in Ronald Reagan's lexicon of governing. Ninety percent of the blacks and 70 percent of the Jews voted against him in 1984. But his defenders respond that an expanding economy means more for the poor than statist antipoverty programs, and that a resolute foreign policy is the best preventive for a creeping anti-Semitism. History is written by presidents who are linked with the productive energies of their societies and with a favoring equilibrium of forces and prestige globally.

A more disturbing light on the working of Reagan's mind came with his hapless adventure among the Waffen SS graves in the German cemetery at Bitburg. It was a self-inflicted wound because it called into question Reagan's intuitive understanding of symbols, and of the burden of history that the Holocaust imposes and that no consideration of "reconciliation" with Germany could diminish. It showed his knowledge of the past as spotty and selective and that his feel is for surface images, not the deeper levels of the symbolic.

Yet Reagan has continued to prove himself a survivor. The assassination attempt of 1981 was an organic challenge to his will to life, but Reagan pulled through the surgery and trauma and returned to the political fray with the zest of a man who has been out on the thin edge of life as well as of history. Four years later, in surgery for cancer of the colon, he again outraced the Pale Rider on the Pale Horse.

With Reagan, as with Dwight Eisenhower, Americans were made aware of the tenuous character of the life journey, but they also admired the tenacity with which each man pursued it. In Ike's case it was a war hero turned politician, in Reagan's a politician turned folk hero, but in both, the brushes with death helped rather than hurt the hero image.

It was only when the question of mental competence was raised that the image was threatened. After the first Mondale debate, when an overbriefed, overcoached, and overtense Reagan performed poorly and his eager critics found code phrases to hint at senility, a resilient Reagan in the second debate retrieved himself with an impressive display of life force.

As the second term began, it was a jolt for a man so dependent on delegation to his White House staff to suffer an almost total changing of the guard, with the turnover of his California group. Yet his continuing sense of command belies the easy view that he is only a creature of the men who surround him. At a time when the American imperium is too complex and demanding for any one man to handle, what is required of a president is that he put his recognizable signature, as it were, on the flux of events he cannot control. Reagan has continued to do that.

For history, the signature—and the consequences—are what count. Presidents do what they can to nudge history and remind it what to emphasize. In his second term Reagan put the issue of tax reform at the top of his priorities list because it had overtones of populism. He counted on a widespread feeling about the unfairness of the tax structure and on a rankling sense of injustice. But the response was disappointing, although the option to build one up is still there, and he may yet wager with history that the broad direction was right.

There is a "Teflon" theory about Ronald Reagan prevalent among his liberal media critics—that the persona Reagan presents to the world is a largely fictive one, a patina contrived by his publicity aides. If true, they have managed by a miracle to allow no break in the interplay between surface and substance. The truth is that, like FDR and unlike many other presidents, Reagan as a natural and private man is at home with his persona, and the two personalities flow together and fuse.

But the private man is there, authentically. Even in his relation to his children there is an element of reserve. This is true of his friendships and loyalties as well. But the strongest tie of all is to Nancy Reagan—so strong that the question of her political influence with him is largely irrelevant. He does not need a Colonel Edward House, as Wilson did, or a Harry Hopkins, as FDR did, because Nancy is there and, as he put it after his cancer surgery, "she is my everything."

In the area of global policy Reagan had a set of attitudes and tactics but lacked a global philosophy and a grand strategy. Given his views on Communist power, he was determined, like Truman and Eisenhower, to contain its expansion. But while his critics had foretold trigger-happy confrontations with the Russians, Reagan largely resisted the temptation to be reactive. Even on occasions like the Soviet shooting down of a Korean airliner over Asia and the killing of an American military officer in East Germany, Reagan—despite his strong language—stuck to a policy of restraint in action.

Containment has a number of possible meanings. For Reagan, in overall terms, it has meant two things—American *readiness* and *resoluteness*. He spelled them out in his rising defense budgets, in carrying through the deployment of intermediate missiles in NATO countries despite antinuclear demonstrations, in launching a massive research program for a "High Frontier" defense technology in space. These were all meant to signal that America had broken with the liberal presidential culture and its policies of accommodation.

Reagan has had no clear presidential model in global policy, although at times his mix of covert and overt methods, as well as of rhetoric in language and restraint in action, is reminiscent of Dwight Eisenhower. The difference is that Reagan's support of the anti-Sandinista guerrillas in Nicaragua became too openly covert to be politically acceptable to either domestic or hemispheric opinion. Yet it challenged the Soviet monopoly of guerrilla movements, and it was part of a larger effort to keep them off balance, in a global "revolutionary" strategy new to democracies.

But in Central America, as elsewhere, he had to operate within a post-Vietnam climate characterized by fear of war entanglements and a lingering liberal empathy for "revolutions," even when inspired and organized by America's enemies. In Lebanon, with its Byzantine religious fealties, he met with military disaster when he exposed a "peace-keeping" Marine detachment to fanatic suicide attack, and with political frustration and powerlessness in the terrorist hostage-taking of airline passengers.

The small-town Illinois boy, trying to govern an imperial complex by common sense and intuitive insights, found that the world was more riven by cultural splits than he had thought, and less responsive to American readiness and resolve as he embodied them. Yet in an Age of Terror his decision to intercept the plane carrying terrorists from the cruise ship *Achille Lauro* and deliver them to court process was a gutsy one. Since its direction was toward a collective social contract, it might also prove historic.

While he was a novice at world politics, he knew how to set the stage for Soviet-American relations as world theater. Since the very nature of nuclear weapons meant that they could not be used in reality, the next best thing was to actualize them as part of the political play. As a result, Reagan managed to bring the leaders of the "evil empire" back to the Geneva arms talks. He was better at this than the three ailing Soviet party secretaries who died off during his first term. The accession to power of Mikhail Gorbachev meant that Reagan acquired a Soviet peer in political theater, and their summit meetings came inevitably to be regarded as tests of images and of wills.

Something of the same dramatic mood applied to the strange new world of the Strategic Defense Initiative ("Star Wars"). It was meant to shift the center of gravity in the arms competition from increasingly lethal offensive weapons to an offensive-defensive deterrence mix. It stirred Soviet fears, largely because the American superiority in laser and particle-beam technology gives the United States an advantage in the initial stages.

A number of strategic thinkers have well-based anxieties that it may destabilize traditional nuclear deterrence for a time. But its long-range effect could be a greater sense of defensive security for both camps. As an episode in man's long, still unimaginable journey away from self-destruction, Reagan's innovative willingness to make the weapons shift has obvious dangers, but it may give him a claim on history in an area where few thought he could make any appreciable difference.

Thus I leave him at midcourse, near the end of the first year of his second term. Historians, looking back at him, may see in his lineaments the features of the American values system, and of the advancing arts of enterprise and technology on which he counted heavily. His future in history is likely to be linked with their future, but most of all with the evidence that the Reagan revolution has brought a new political culture into being and redefined the terms of political debate and discourse.

★

DECEMBER 21, 1986

Along with everything else happening in the Iran affair we are having to revise our overall picture of Ronald Reagan as man and president. In a sense he is sitting for a second portrait for the history books.

The man whose place I covet right now is Edmund Morris, who is slated to be Reagan's biographer and who has a front-row seat at whatever isn't too hidden in the White House operations. Since Morris is working on his second volume on Theodore Roosevelt, the activist president who did some rough behind-the-scenes intrigue in building the Panama Canal, he can't be too surprised at the traits his next presidential portrait sitter is exhibiting.

What has been wrong with the Reagan portrait thus far? Many have too long had the wrong angle of vision on him, catching only the engaging, whimsical public face. We have viewed him centrally as actor, communicator, and wizardlike orchestrator of a permanent public relations campaign.

The few commentators who have had a more positive view of him (I count myself among them) have stressed the secure, confident Reagan, with his sense of command and his ambitious undertakings in reversing the style and substance of the presidencies of the 1960s and 1970s.

Each of these takes on Reagan has its merits. But what we have been watching in the past month suggests another Reagan, with another style underneath his open one, and another set of motivations.

All political portraiture, like all political thinking, is metaphor because the instrumentation behind our eyes is symbolic. *Time* correspondent Laurence Barrett was on a true track when he called his portrait of the early Reagan administration *Gambling with History*. His metaphor now turns out to have been right. There is considerable of the gambler in Reagan, impatient at obstacles and frustrations, willing to circumvent them covertly even at high risk to himself.

It is the extent of Reagan's covertness that has to be painted into the rest of the portrait. On that score he is like Dwight Eisenhower, the most covert of the presidents, who may have learned it from his use of intelligence in World War II. What its sources were in Reagan's life is one for his biographers still to discover.

What is clear is that Reagan felt frustrated about the incursions of Congress into global policy, and with no great trust in the traditional diplomacy of his own foreign–policy elite he turned to the second and third echelons of his secret point men—the little foxes, I call them—and let them pursue his purposes through their own methods.

My phrase refers to Admiral John Poindexter, Lieutenant-Colonel Oliver North, General Richard Secord, not to Reagan. He is not a man of small purposes. History will judge him by the success or failure of his large ones—supply-side economics, the big tax cut, and, yes, the big deficits as well, the big tax reform, the effort to reverse the expansion of the welfare state, the global network of anti-Communist guerrilla movements, the massive weapons buildup, the Strategic Defense Initiative.

Reagan's logical and cognitive faculties are nothing to boast about, and the "black box" of his memory is pretty black indeed. But as with "Teddy" Roosevelt, the imaginative faculty is strong in him—the capacity to latch on to the grand scale, especially in foreign policies. He doesn't think small. He showed it in the Star Wars idea and he showed it again, for better or worse, in the scale of his bargaining at the Reykjavik summit.

Because the trouble in his covert operations lies in his careless delegation to the little foxes, the Grand Inquisitors are now after them—and him.

★

AUGUST 23, 1987

Why do so many presidents get mangled in ill-fated policies they dream up and can't carry through? There was FDR with his wretched Yalta agreement, Harry Truman with his unfinished Korean War, Dwight Eisenhower with the U-2 spy flight by Francis Gary Powers, which the Russians shot down and which Ike lied about, John Kennedy with the "perfect failure" of the Bay of Pigs, Lyndon Johnson with the morass of the Vietnam War, Richard Nixon with the stupidity of Watergate, Gerald Ford with the Nixon pardon, Jimmy Carter with his helplessness over the Shah's overthrow, and the Iran hostage-taking and his failed desert rescue mission.

Then there is Ronald Reagan, who seemed to live a charmed life as president during his first term, only to run into trouble at the Bitburg cemetery and then the ghastly Iran-Contra mess.

Why this sorry record of misjudgments on the part of able chief executives, some of whom (FDR, Ike, JFK) have even come down as hero figures? Why do presidents who ought to know better get so destroyed by history and their own natures?

The briefest answer is that, given politics and policy-making in America, the presidential task requires supermen—which, of course, they are not. But there are other critical factors as well.

The Constitution and the structure of policy-making in America are divisive and fractious, and they make a cohesive foreign policy un-sustainable. The sharp constitutional split-up of powers between the president and Congress—which neither observes—is intensely frus-trating to a president who tries to pursue a policy that Congress and an adversarial intellectual establishment oppose. Ronald Reagan and his support of the Contras is a prime example.

Thus we get a succession of tempestuous administrations in a fever-chart alternation of loves and hates between the chief executive and the people. When the president reaches out and uses covert and devious means to prevail over his opposition, when he runs afoul of the law, we also have a bloodhound intensity of tracking down his malfea-sance.

Along with divided powers and fractious branches of government we have a stern Catonian "rule of law," which cuts the president down as a miscreant. This not only ends the policy in question; it also dam-ages the credibility and authority of the presidential office.

What makes it worse is that no foreign–policy experience is pre-served in the succession of presidencies. There is nothing in America that could function as a council of experienced men, such as the Sovi-ets have in their Politburo. Presidential-election victories are canni-bals: they eat up all predecessor decision-makers and their experience, and they insist on starting afresh. To create a counter-establishment for conservative presidents is especially hard. Eisenhower and Reagan each won two presidential terms, but they failed to create a media and foreign–policy elite that could act as a support system for their more controversial initiatives.

Finally there are the character wounds that presidents have picked up in a lifetime of ambition and struggle, and have also inflicted on themselves. If character is destiny, then the self-woundings of presi-dents on their path to summit power become a particularly destructive destiny.

There have been biographies of Richard Nixon, Lyndon Johnson, and Jimmy Carter by writers trained in the psychology of the life jour-ney. They have tried to read the character of their subjects into their presidential decisions, and their early life encounters into their charac-ter. Sometimes they overdo their emphasis, but in skillful hands it is worth doing.

The Iran-Contra episode marks a disaster for Ronald Reagan but a bonanza for his biographers. They are already crowding around the fallen hero, to rethink and rewrite his life in the image of his wounds.

★

JANUARY 8, 1989

Like other important presidents, Ronald Reagan leaves us with the feeling that his presidency has been a complex mixture of light and shadow, the desirable and undesirable—yet a mixture that is anything but negligible.

The prime paradox about Reagan can be put quite simply: How come that a president with little intellectual range and depth has managed to steer a nation through the storms and shoals of the 1980s and brought it to port in pretty good shape, to the plaudits of the people if not of the pundits?

Take the dark side first. To start with, Reagan must carry the blame for a deficit beyond conception, and for an Iran-Contra initiative too messy to be called a misadventure. He leaves with a nation still coping with the menace of a drugged America, unable to cut off the supply or diminish the demand. He has made little headway toward easing the burden of debt-ridden Third World nations. His administration is struggling with waves of refugees washing on American shores. It is deep in the mire of commitments to savings-and-loan outfits whose deposits were guaranteed but with few controls over their wild speculations. Leveraged buyouts accomplished with junk bonds are the ultimate symbol of the ethos of greed, which is the flip side of their roaring capitalism. And the very fact of national prosperity, along with renewed passion for a home, gives a special pathos to the homeless.

Yet there is a portrait in more vivid hues. Reagan will be remembered also as the president of a prospering and expanding economy, with little inflation and unemployment, of a business entrepreneurial system that has released the open-market energies around the world, of reform that has lowered the tax level and closed many loopholes. He will also be remembered as the president who rearmed America with a clout adequate to its commitments abroad, gave its people a sense of confidence about their world role, strengthened America's role as "first among equals" in the Western community, and—wonder of wonders—established a post-Cold-War relation to the Soviet Union.

But a balance sheet, however favorable, does not allow for the intangibles in a president's tenure. Reagan has too grudgingly been assessed as a genial Dr. Feelgood type who wooed and hoarded his great popularity, careful not to spend it on unpopular decisions.

This strikes me as abysmally wide of the mark. Because James Monroe, who presided over an earlier Era of Good Feelings, was a lightweight, it does not follow that Reagan's similarly happy era makes him one as well.

The true category for him is that of the shaping presidents who defined an era and had "revolution" rightly attached to them. In the nineteenth century it was true of Jefferson and Jackson, in the twentieth of Wilson and Franklin Roosevelt. All four were Democrats, leaving Reagan as the first Republican to stake out a claim to this defining role.

He did not have to be a giant intellect, like Jefferson or Wilson, or a complex, magnetic personality like Roosevelt. He is a lesser figure in himself, closer to Harry Truman as an uncommon "common man" out of the American grain. Yet he had a strength of his own that will allow the historian to speak of "the Reagan era" on which he put his stamp.

It is the hedgehog stamp, not the fox's, of a man who has only a few ideas but holds them tenaciously and turns them into reality. Many critics have accordingly made the blunder of seeing him as "Manichean," with a good-and-evil political theology. Yet the adjective fell victim to the summits and had to be scrapped when the Russians sued for an era of peace and Reagan responded. The point that many miss in the Reagan paradox of rigor and flexibility is that only a president who called Russia an "evil empire" could in time embrace Gorbachev and not be lynched by the right.

The Reagan presidency was not a thing of illusion and nostalgia. It was grounded in a few ancient realities he had made his own—the importance of self-reliance, the limits of governmental action, the reach of the entrepreneurial system, the extension of freedoms abroad to whomever claimed them and was willing to fight for them, the proposition that a nation alert at once to foreign dangers and also to changes of posture will not have to use the weapons it commands.

PART III

ELECTING
A PRESIDENT

FOREWORD

Max Lerner wrote about every presidential campaign from 1940 through the primary season of 1992. His early writing about presidential politics often has a sharply phrased partisan edge. Later work tends to be more reflective and explanatory, with historical parallels dominant concerns.

In a 1988 interview in *The Quill*, Lerner remarked that columns in the 1940s and 1950s were confrontational by choice and that he changed his approach. "Generally, my earlier ones were about the conclusion I had reached," he said. "Now I try to lay bare my process. Every column has to be an adventure in recovery and possibility. I like best the ones that send me back over the years—to people and places I had almost forgotten, to ideas I picked up somewhere and have made my own."

—R. S.

1940

ROOSEVELT vs. WILLKIE

FROM THE VERY BEGINNING Franklin Roosevelt has been a crisis president, and there is little reason to suppose that he will cease to be president at a time when the crisis is deepest. This is bitter hemlock for reactionaries of every stripe to drink. But let us be clear at the outset: the chances are overwhelming that the next president of the United States will be that man now in the White House.

He will be there for four more years, not because he wants to, but because the people want him there. I don't need the Gallup or *Fortune* figures to prove it, although they do help confirm something we would know without them. The people want him there, not because the New Deal has been a success, or because we fear to swap horses while crossing a stream. For the first, there is the persistent fact of some 11 million unemployed and the extremes of wealth and poverty as accented as ever. And for the second, in a democracy the time when you are crossing a stream is exactly the time when you are forced to swap horses—if the horse you are riding is not much good. Only the Hitler blitzkrieg availed to force Chamberlain out and Churchill in. And to steer close to a grim play on words, without the change of horses the large part of the British army which crossed the Channel back to safety in England would today be mingled with the soil of Flanders and France. The point is that, for the people's purposes today, Mr. Roosevelt is a good horse. And they know it.

That knowledge goes deeper than party politics, deeper than political and economic experience. It reaches down to the prerational stuff in us out of which symbols are fashioned. It is the surge of these impulses that has already as good as swept aside the third-term tradi-

---

This essay was published as "FDR—Next President" in *The Nation* (June 22, 1940), just before the Republican and Democratic conventions.

tion. I do not mean to be mystical: the events which have made the president the only possible Democratic choice are clear enough. They are the war in Europe, the onward thrust of Nazi power, the new awareness of the revolution in war technology and of the nakedness of our defenses, the persistence of the worldwide forces out of which the Nazi revolution arose—all converging with the presidential election. But this forms only the outer framework. Within it there have been our own inner tensions at work. With the crumbling of what had seemed the enduring bastions of the European order, our deepest political emotions have been released. I mean the blank fear of our failure to survive as a tolerably democratic society; and the urge toward group cohesion, which means in this era the urge toward national unity; and—so rare in a democracy—the desire to submit to a leadership great enough to match the great times; and, finally, the longing for a symbol at once of security and of forward movement, of moderation and yet of aggressiveness.

Mr. Roosevelt comes closer to being such a symbol than anyone within our experience. Yet if he falls short of it—and how should he not?—measure by how much less he falls short than the other candidates. Their names have been successively before us during the past few months. Yet, in comparison with Roosevelt's, how far away and archaic some of those names already seem. Who was John Nance Garner? Was Paul McNutt once taken seriously as presidential timber? What graveyard crew will undertake to exhume Arthur Vandenberg and Robert Taft? Was that Thomas Dewey and Burton K. Wheeler that the Nazi tanks rolled over as they swept on to Paris? What are Cordell Hull's chances in a world that demands in its leaders, if not youth, then at least color and forcefulness? The fact is that Hitler and Stalin and Churchill now dominate our imaginations so monstrously, and the harsh age in which they have become leaders has so stretched our political horizons, that men of ordinary candidate stature seem puny. Roosevelt alone among the candidates can claim our attention as a leader-symbol along with the Europeans.

Who will oppose him? It still requires, despite Dorothy Thompson, two to make an election. The Republicans, confronted by the clear probability of Roosevelt's nomination, have striven desperately to find the other man. But Roosevelt has had so big a lead that their hearts have simply not been in the effort. Even as I write, only a week before the opening of the Big Show at Philadelphia, there is a funereal air about the preparations. The only real candidate the Republicans

have is Wendell Willkie, and—despite his being a former Democrat
and a big public-utility man, both circumstances violating the outward
political decencies—I would stake a good deal that he will be the
choice. Willkie has brought novelty and freshness into Republican
politics; his outward limitations have been in themselves challenges; he
has known the value of mingling candor about his hopes with skepticism about his chances—an irresistible combination whether in a lover
or a candidate. If it is Willkie who is picked to oppose Roosevelt in the
election, it will not be a wholly uneven battle. For Willkie has middle-
class "independent" appeal. His strategy will be to go along with Roosevelt on the intervention issue, but play himself up as the younger and
stronger man for the war crisis. The theme will be a dual one: that the
problem now is to organize American industry for defense, and to do
it without embracing economic collectivism—and who could be more
nearly ideal for both purposes, we shall be asked, than a shrewd and
successful utility executive? If Willkie is nominated, only Roosevelt
can beat him. And there can be little doubt that he would.

What sort of president would Roosevelt make? This is not a
whimsical question, despite our having had two terms of him. For he
would be president in a world half lost to Nazism, in which whether or
not we go to war we shall have a war economy and a political organization of concentrated powers. How does the Roosevelt we know look
in the light of the new world we can only dimly discern?

The Roosevelt we know is a mirror of our own best energies, our
own possibly fatal confusions. Perhaps because of that fact no one has
yet taken the dimensions of the man in an enduring study. It is not that
our writers lack the art, but that in the face of so elusive a figure they
lack the confidence to use it. The political portraits, whether done in
bile or saccharine, are dismal things. Emil Ludwig's full-length study
was pretentious as well as inaccurate. But John Chamberlain, although
working, as usual, within too limited a medium, has done a canny job
in his last book in showing Roosevelt as a master tightrope walker. And
Harold Laski's book *The American Presidency*, while in form a study of
the presidential office, is in effect a commentary on the most fateful
American president.

I say "fateful" as applying both to the time itself and to the man's
apprehension of it. Roosevelt has always had a sense of history. The
well-worn story of his remark to newspapermen during the bank holiday of 1933—"I shall be either America's greatest President or its
last"—is typical of a perspective few presidents have had. One thing

Roosevelt has said clearly: he has no intention of being another
Buchanan. Which implies that all the basic conditions that characterize a country on the eve of a civil war are true of our period. But to
avoid being a Buchanan in the face of impending civil war one must be
something of a Lincoln. How much of Lincoln does Roosevelt have in
him? More, I am convinced, that any president since Lincoln or before. I know that in externals they are poles apart. In the one an easy
graciousness, in the other a clumsy grace; the one modern, alert, cos-
mopolitan, and the other a backwoodsman even for his own day; the
one aristocrat, the other plebeian. Yet the resemblances are real. Each
of them managed somehow to catch the accents and express the aspirations of the ordinary people of his day. But beyond these, and more
important, each was forced by the exterior tension of events to complete an interior crisis out of which his real greatness emerged. Lincoln
was a brooding man of thought whom the Civil War compelled to action. Roosevelt is a man of action whom the crisis of the Depression
years and the international collapse have compelled to thought. The
more memorable figure is undoubtedly Lincoln, the more effective
president probably Roosevelt.

Yet Roosevelt has not been effective on the crucial question of unemployment, which is America's dynamite dump. Nothing can be
clearer than his failure to translate his own deepening perceptions and
his generous sympathies into a working program. I need not spell out
that fact here. What needs, however, to be said is that while Roosevelt
will no doubt be linked in history with the pragmatic and piecemeal reforms of the New Deal, he is at once smaller and bigger than the New
Deal. Smaller because the New Deal is not one man's creation but the
product of mass aspirations. Bigger in the sense that his personal
stature has survived the relative failure of the New Deal and the scat-
tering of its battalions. It may not be rational, but it is true that many
would vote for Roosevelt who would reject most of his works. His
presidential tenure offers an uncanny perspective: here is a man who
lost or had to compromise on most of his goals, yet he has emerged
with prestige and popular appeal probably as great as ever.

But to the unemployed and the disinherited, to WPA workers,
and to youngsters just out of school and without a job, it is scant consolation to have symbol without substance. They still cling to the Roosevelt banner, partly because Europe has become a word of fear and
bewilderment, partly because a war economy might make jobs for
them, mainly because they are still convinced that Roosevelt will

somehow keep moving forward without revolution or dictatorship. In short, the Roosevelt following today more than ever is a following based on fear, faith, and expectation rather than works. Nor have these people ever really been taught either the elements of the Roosevelt achievement or the sources of the Roosevelt failure. They do not know the great forward stride made in the development of the administrative agency; few of them understand that the president managed somehow to resolve a great constitutional crisis; many are forgetting the solid achievements in the protection of the worker, the farmer, the investor, against the more obvious harshness of capitalism on the decline. And as for the springs of failure, no one has pointed out to the people the role played by the opinion industries in bolstering every reactionary movement, by big-business sabotage, by the demoralizing anti-labor and anti-alien agitation, by the lack of audacity in genuine economic planning, by the failure to build enduring political support in a party realignment, by the crumbling of administrative morale.

When the people support a political leader through fear and faith, ignorant both of the sources of his past failure and of the conditions of his future success, that leader is in a dangerous position. He has as a politician encouraged expectations that as a policy maker he will probably be unable to fulfill. I believe Roosevelt must know that. I think this insight, rather than the persistent rumors about physical exhaustion or some new ailment, goes far toward explaining the sense of tiredness the administration conveys, and the very real and not feigned unwillingness of the president to stand for a third term. Being a political leader is at best one of the loneliest things in the world; but being one under the conditions Roosevelt has recently had to face must be desolating. Having to cajole a hostile and often stupid Congress and handle a bitter and sometimes venal press, having to mend political fences while building administrative structures, having to keep in sight the forest of national welfare despite the trees of special interests, having to see more clearly than most the logic and stakes of the international scene, and finding oneself balked in translating that insight into foreign policy—all that does not make a president's lot a happy one.

I do not know whether Roosevelt himself is conscious that if his past role as president has been difficult, his future role as president would be even more so. Thus far he has relied mainly on two techniques. One has been the balancing of interests between various groups, always with an eye to getting out of the trading of gains and concessions as much as possible for the underprivileged. The second has been the alternation of periods of swift legislative and administrative advance with "breathing-spell" periods of consolidation. And usually there has been the understanding that even the best army is as weak as its officers, and therefore a concern for filling the key administrative posts with progressives. These standards seem now in process of abandonment. If gains have come out of the recent attempts to balance interests in Washington, they have not been for labor and the low-income groups. The past two years have been a long and continuous breathing spell, with almost no advance toward economic planning or social legislation. And the key posts, especially in the new war-industry structures, are coming increasingly to be filled by men who can by no stretch of the imagination be called New Dealers.

I think I can guess what rationale might be offered for these moves. The important thing, we might be told, is the supreme national effort in the international emergency; party lines and class lines must be transcended, and along with others the administration must give up its pet preoccupations and its social hobbies; the new powers the government is getting in the national-defense economy are inherently mistrusted by the corporate capitalists, and their consent must therefore be wooed; when we have met the immediate emergency and can come back to interior problems, we shall have an administrative plant that is a going concern and can then be turned to the uses of economic democracy. And the New Deal can then go on to its most daring phase—of attempting to run a peace machine with the same efficiency and the same sense of national welfare as a war machine.

I do not know that anyone in the administration actually thinks this. I do know that the next president, if he is a liberal, will have to face the issue raised above. Mr. Roosevelt has always been a master of the strategic retreat. Perhaps the present New Deal doldrums fall under that category. But surely he must know that the world America faces in the next decade bears few resemblances to the world of the 1920s or even of the '30s. He must know that whether we go to war or not we are already *at war* in the realest sense, because under any contingency we shall have to embark on a national-defense program that will channel from a third to a half of our national income into war preparations, reduce living standards and real wages, transform our economy into at least a semiplanned war economy, play ducks and drakes with our civil liberties, and sweep Latin America into the ambit of something approaching a good-neighbor imperialism. We have all been forced to grow up in the past months and can afford to call things by their right names. If, as seems increasingly clear, American survival depends upon such swift and heroic measures, I should rather have Mr. Roosevelt in the White House than anyone else who would stand a chance of being elected. (I assume Roosevelt has given up his hope of getting the political boys to accept Robert Jackson or William O. Douglas.) But I pray that it be a Roosevelt like the one who from 1934 to 1936 put through the basic program of New Deal social legislation, a Roosevelt who understands with Churchill that wars are never won by retreats and evacuations, no matter how brilliant. That applies to war on the social and economic fronts as well as the military. For there is as surely a world revolution today in economics and politics and social morale as there is in war technology.

1944

ROOSEVELT vs. DEWEY

To READ THE PROSE of Governor Thomas Dewey, as embodied in his speech at the Lincoln Day dinner, is to be back again in your high-school days, listening to one of the assembly addresses. The speaker is respectable and successful, the cadences are impressive, the allusions vaguely historical, the phrases sound as if they ought to mean something—but the meaning, if any, has nothing to do with your world.

I am probably the wrong man to judge, because I have never liked Lincoln Day speeches. I do not like to see Lincoln *used*. And I am as loath to see the governor of my state use him to smear the president of my country as I would be to see the crudest ward politician pawing the flag to get the perquisites of office.

Lincoln, says Dewey, "knew that he was not perfect, not all wise. He would have been the last to call himself indispensable. . . . Lincoln loved and respected the American people. There was nothing in his soul of the paternalistic contempt for their intelligence and their character which . . ."—and you can finish the sentence for yourself. It is sickening to me to see Lincoln's memory twisted by politicians to make a trap for fools, distorted so that every sentence is aimed not so much to characterize Lincoln as to blast Roosevelt.

But to move from the manner of the speech to its substance: the big thing that Dewey tried to say on Saturday night was on states' rights. He contrasted Lincoln as a symbol of the rights of states, with FDR as a symbol of "the autocratic rule of a swarm of bureaucrats rivaling in numbers and in tyranny those by which our enemies live."

This is, of course, the veriest eyewash. I have heard some agonized Republicans wish that Dewey would change his political advisers. Well, I wish even more that he would change his literary advisers and his historical research staff. If he did he would find that it is an im-

possible task to conscript Lincoln to the purposes of an attack on national power and a homily on local government. For Lincoln and the
Republicans came into power as the champions of national action as
against state sovereignty. The men who "fought and died" for the
Union cause during the Civil War did so not, as Dewey implies, to resist national encroachment but to keep a nation strong enough to survive. It was the Southerners who were fighting for John C. Calhoun's
conception of states' rights. Dewey seems to have his history a bit mixed.

He tries to save himself, as an afterthought, by saying that the
problem in the Civil War was secession by the states, and now it is abdication by the states. But surely he is not serious, but merely playful
and whimsical, if he means to imply that we must prepare for another
civil war, against the New Dealers who are destroying our Constitution. Again he has his history mixed. The man who, of all American
presidents, stretched the Constitution most was Lincoln. He went so
far as to suspend the writ of habeas corpus and the operation of civilian courts—which we have not dared do today even in Hawaii. One
may argue that he had to, being sorely pressed by civil war. But in any
event this does not make him a good stick with which to beat the New
Deal dog. And surely it is shocking, in the midst of a war for human
freedom, for one of our leaders to charge our own president with a
tyranny rivaling that of Hitler and Tojo.

Or, rather, it would be shocking if we were to take his words with
any seriousness. I have about come to the conclusion that a speech by
Dewey or John Bricker must be taken like a Chinese play: not as a description of real life, but as an oft-repeated ceremonial symbolism to
put the customers in a proper frame of mind. Dewey does not present
a shred of evidence for his thesis on states' rights—except the fantastic
assertions that Governors Lehman and Poletti left the New York State
government in chaos. He makes no effort to apply his viewpoint of
states' rights to any specific issue—like the soldiers' vote, or social insurance, or flood control, or national action against unemployment. To
talk specifically might alienate votes.

He is still, in short, the cautious young man on the political trapeze.
There is not a single point of difference between his views and statements and those of Harrison Spangler, the mahout of the old-line Republicans. Spangler is, of course, more maladroit—far too maladroit
for smart Republicans like Henry Luce, as witness the satirical write-
up of him in *Time*. But both men stand for the same things. Nor is
there a particle of difference between Dewey's views and those of Governor Bricker. On the whole Bricker has, in the past few days in Wash-

ington, been the more outspoken of the two. He has actually come out
for a tax system that will not bear too heavily on business. Dewey has
contented himself with such brilliantly daring commitments as states'
rights, local government, the consent of the governed, and a free constitutional system. Prodded for being too careful, he has thrown caution to the winds, and taken a strong stand on what were the burning
issues of the election of a century ago, in 1844.

The one new thing Dewey has done in his Lincoln Day speech
has been to talk about the peace. I suppose that, given his temperament, this took courage. He came out in favor of the Mackinac
Republican Declaration of last September. He claimed that the Republicans in the woods at Mackinac foresaw the Moscow Conference,
and converted Secretary of State Cordell Hull to internationalism, so
that he was practically their envoy. And he said that we must avoid "a
self-willed executive who wars at every turn with Congress"; otherwise, we will have "a repetition of the same catastrophe which happened in 1919."

I wonder whether the governor appreciates the full gall in his
words. Himself once an opponent of Lend-Lease, a leader of a party
which—except for Wendell Willkie and a few others—has mainly devoted itself to mocking Henry Wallace's internationalism and which
cooked up a stew of double-talk at Mackinac that delighted such isolationists as Vandenberg and Taft: he now wants to cash in on the
Moscow Conference, without in any way giving his own views on postwar international action.

And worse than that. He takes the tragic behavior of the Republicans in 1919 in sabotaging the peace treaty, and their disgraceful behavior in 1943 in sabotaging price control and an adequate tax bill and
food-cost subsidies and the soldiers' vote bill, and he elevates them
into an argument for electing a Republican as president. This is to
plead that the reward of the mutineer should be the leadership of the
army; the reward of noncooperation, the presidency. It is a political
philosophy that combines blackmail with anarchy: "If you don't let us
run things," it says in effect, "we'll still have Congress, and we'll wreck
the peace."

Such a mood does not jibe very well with the painfully assumed
humility to be found elsewhere in Dewey's speech. The governor
would have us believe that he believes in government "from the bottom up" whereas the New Dealers govern "from the top down." This
is belied by his own conduct at Albany, where he is top man with a
vengeance—where the Republican legislators know nothing until

Dewey has told them, think nothing until Dewey has phrased if for them, and do nothing until he has given them the green light.

The most revealing passage in the speech is the one in which Dewey seeks to discount the greatness required for presidential leadership in our time. He deplores the idea that we need "extraordinary men whose intellectual attainments transcend the range of normal minds." He says that our problems "will not lend themselves to single, brilliant solutions." I can understand that he is worried, because most people regard him as too small a man for the big job of the presidency. And so Dewey, in his modesty, is trying to overcome the handicap by cutting the presidential job down to his own size.

But this won't do. Obviously we do not want anybody who thinks of himself as a superman in Hitler's fashion. And least of all does that apply to President Roosevelt. No one in his senses wants us to build up the idea of an antidemocratic elite. But that does not mean that any politician will do for the presidency. Lincoln never ceased to be a common man, but he was also a man of transcendent ability, insight, vision. He was a great leader—the greatest argument we have had that a democracy can generate leadership. We shall do democracy no service if we leave leadership as an idea to be monopolized by the totalitarian states.

Here then one gets the anatomy of Governor Dewey. In a painful attempt to be both honest and amiable with Dewey, Walter Lippmann the other day called him "a young man who has certainly grown and is surely growing." "No one will hold it against him," he added, "if it took him a long time to understand the war." The most recent speech shows that he still does not understand either the war or the peace. I suppose we ought to encourage a young man who is struggling to get ahead, and to understand his world. But I do not see why we should make him president, and let him carry on his education in public, at the expense of future generations.

★

JUNE 29, 1944

In nominating Thomas Dewey and John Bricker, the Republican Party leaders have chosen two little men for the greatest posts the American people have within their grant. They have done so on a platform that is a weary collection of old lumber with not-so-ingenious trimming. And they have done so in a time more fateful than any in our history, and in a world whose dangers and stakes are so vast that the nation must perish in it whose leaders lack knowledge and boldness.

The fact that Dewey and Bricker are Republicans is less important than the fact that they are small men, living in a provincial political world. There are Republicans, like Wendell Willkie, who might as candidates have given the independent voter some pause. And there will be many Republicans this year who will cross party lines, or will be too disheartened to vote. The crucial fact is the precipitous contrast between the stature of the task and the stature of the Republican designees for it.

I wrote yesterday that when the American people have voted for President Roosevelt they have voted for a man, a program, a direction. The Republicans have just concluded a convention in which their job has been to offer us something different in all three respects. Let us examine how they have done that job, and what they have to offer.

First, the men. As we look back at the whole campaign for the nomination, we can see now what the logic of Dewey's choice has been. The very qualities that make him the Man Whom Nobody Loves make him also the man who has not deeply offended any political interests. Since the Republican Party leaders had nothing affirmative to say to the country, they chose a man whose tactic has been to play safe, and whose outstanding quality thus far has been silence. It is fitting and proper for a party that has shown itself the party of negativism, that its symbol should be a cipher.

This does not mean that Dewey has not taken positions in the past. He has. But they have been the positions of a man who simply did not know how to calculate the forces loose in the world, and who thought it safer therefore to keep his eyes not on the world, but on the conventional prejudices of potential voters.

At a time when the great need was for collective security, he warned against "entangling alliances." Two months before Dunkirk he declared himself for isolationism. During the blitz against England he endorsed the stridently anti-British *Chicago Tribune* publisher Colonel Robert McCormick's man, Charles Brooks, for the Senate in Illinois. At a time when the Finnish war had made Russia unpopular here, he called the 1933 recognition of Russia "most unfortunate," although he did not protest against our recognition of Hitler's government. And when he spoke of "a perversion of government abhorrent to the conscience of mankind," it was the Russian government he was describing, not the German. Two months ago he had changed his mind enough to

say that "there were faults on both sides" in Russian-American relations. And the Russian leaders whom he had called "assassins" and
"murderers," he now called "hard-headed, realistic leaders."

When the Lend-Lease bill was first introduced into Congress, he
called it "an attempt to abolish free government in the United States."
Later, when Wendell Willkie had come out strongly for Lend-Lease
after his return from England, Dewey came out mildly for it. From
that day (February 12, 1941) until Pearl Harbor, Dewey refused to be
drawn into any discussions of foreign policy, on the ground that he was
head of the United Service Organizations drive. This meant that he
was conveniently noncommittal during the hottest days of the Great
Debate between the isolationists and interventionists—a man who
thought that a public figure had a right to be neutral in the greatest
moral battle of our time; neutral as between the doctor and the disease,
neutral as between life-affirming action and life-denying inaction.

This is the man whom the Republicans have chosen to lead America in carrying a world war to victory and organizing a postwar world—
a man who has shown shrewdness but no boldness, cunning but no
wisdom, tactical ability in politics but no understanding of the deep
forces of his time and his world. And a man, we must add, who has had
no experience, and has shown little interest, in the large political decisions within which the technical world of military, diplomatic, and
economic experts takes on meaning.

As his running mate they have chosen, in Governor John V.
Bricker, a man who is saved from being a complete cipher only by the
fact that he has cultivated dangerous company. Bricker proved that he
could not be wholly ignored by the simple expedient of doing what
Dewey had neither the need nor the stomach for doing—allying himself quite unashamedly with the rabid isolationists in and out of the
Republican Party, and with the lunatic fringe of native fascists.

Bricker's nomination was obviously the result of two factors: men
like Governor Earl Warren could not be forced into taking it, and so it
was open; and second, the "nationalists" (a polite name for isolationists
in foreign policy and reactionaries in domestic) decided that since the
post was on the auction bloc, they might as well appropriate it. This
may make Dewey unhappy, but he is now wrapped up with Bricker in
a single package that manages to be at the same time uninspiring and
unsavory.

As for the Republican platform, it was an effort to find a common
denominator for all the factions within the party. But when one of the
factions to be included is isolationist and fascist, and another interna-

tionalist, the common denominator that results is merely irrelevant. The Republicans worked hard in their platform to weld together all the dissident elements in the nation and appealed to all the interest groups. But a chorus of dissidence does not add up to a program. Nor does the sum of conflicting interest groups form a direction toward which the nation can move. It is notable that scarcely an echo of the real world of today—the world of Cherbourg and Caen and Mogilev, of Teheran and Cairo—penetrated into the private world of the Republican Convention members.

The Republican platform reminds me of nothing so much as the words in the closing paragraph of James Joyce's *Finnegans Wake*: ". . . it's old and old it's sad and old it's sad and weary. . . ." The Republican direction is nowhere when it is not backward. And the Republican candidates are an invitation to organize apathy.

✭

OCTOBER 10, 1944

It is in the nature of the American character to preach civic purity and practice political roughneckism, to make virtuous protestations about well-behaved campaigns but to like them dirty. The present campaign, despite all the public resolves to be good on the part of the political managers, is developing into a dirty one. In this respect, it is like the campaigns that have preceded it—but with a difference. That difference is worth exploring.

Just for fun I have been digging into the history of American politics in the narrowest sense of that term—the struggle for votes, the business of getting and keeping or losing power, the history of party and election battles. I have dipped again into the books by Claude Bowers on the struggles of the Jefferson-Hamilton period and on the party battles of the Jackson period, and into W. E. Binkley's excellent historical work, *American Political Parties*.

When you read again the things that were published about the private lives and public characters of Jefferson and Hamilton, Jackson and Van Buren, Lincoln and Grant, Cleveland and Blaine, you get a taste of how salty and scurrilous the American political tradition has been. Presidents in office and the aspirants for the office were accused not only of treason and corruption, but also of sensuality and effeminacy, of adultery and bastardy and cuckoldry, of concealed paternity and tainted blood. Nor were the wives and mothers of the candidates left untouched. In fact, in comparison with the dirty charges you can dig up in the American campaign annals, columnist Westbrook Pegler seems to write like Fanny Fern, and John O'Donnell of the *New York Daily News* has the unmistakable lavender fragrance of *Godey's Lady's Book.*

This long historical view may cause us all today to preen ourselves on our political virtue. And, in fact, in a recent survey of the subject, Samuel Hopkins Adams writes that compared with the good old times, the present campaign "in which the standard charge is that Mr. Roosevelt is too old and Mr. Dewey too young," would make our ancestors "look down upon us as wishy-washy milksops."

But hold up a moment. Things are not quite that lovely—at least not in the campaign that is now being waged against President Roosevelt

I want to thrust aside, for the thing I am trying most seriously to say, the purely personal attacks. The present campaign is no better and no worse than previous ones in that respect. Adams is wrong in saying that the only charges hurled are those of ignorant youth and crabbed age. Maybe I don't get let in on the anti-Dewey talk. But I've read enough anti-Roosevelt talk to leave me with a queasy stomach.

In yesterday's *Daily News*, for example, John O'Donnell says that Al Smith's death and Wendell Willkie's will help Dewey because they carry the moral that Roosevelt is next. He says that the real issue is the president's paralysis, and that it has left such ravages on his face that he doesn't dare allow a full-face photograph to be published. Despite the vigor of the president's recent speeches, I hear repeated rumors of people who want to bet that President Roosevelt will not survive the election by six months. (P.S. The bets never materialize. It's not the money that is being offered, but the poison.)

But this is not what makes the campaign a stench to all decent nostrils. That's old stuff. The president has had it used against him each time he has run. He has survived it, and the country has survived it.

The real point is that the present campaign is concentrating far more on group division than on personal abuse. Its technique is not individual libel, but group libel. Time was when you accused the opposition candidate of having had an illegitimate child. Now you use a much subtler and more dangerous technique: you say he is the candidate only of the Jews, the foreign-born, the labor bosses, and the Communists.

Oh, you don't say so outright. That would require a kind of forthrightness of malice, and would not be respectable, and so you leave that to the lunatic-fringe publications, such as Gerald Smith's. What you do instead is to invent a phrase that will carry all the loaded implications I have mentioned, without carrying any responsibility along with it. The phrase is "Clear it with Sidney." Sidney Hillman is a Jew, and was born in Lithuania, and is the head of a trade union, and the papers have tried desperately and fantastically to make a Communist of him. Put these things together, and you can see how much sheer disruptive dynamite the phrase "Clear it with Sidney" carries.

Be sure that the Republicans are trying to make a good thing out of the phrase. The master minds among their big advertising agencies have fixed on it as the only thing that can spread the propaganda of fear and hate among American farmers and middle-class people. They put it on the radios in one-minute spots. They run limerick contests with it. They feed the latent bigotry of this time and this place with it.

Will it work? I don't know. But I do know that it is dirtier politics than any that has been practiced in our country since the Ku Klux Klan beat Al Smith because he was a Catholic. Only, the Klan scurrility was kept underground. The stuff about Hillman ("It's Your Country— Why Let Sidney Hillman Run It?") has become the major and unabashed strategy of the Republican National Committee itself.

Can it be that these men don't know that this is the crux of the fascist technique, used successfully by Hitler and Goebbels? Can it be that they don't know that after the campaign is over this sort of stuff leaves a residue that will never be wiped out—a residue of racist hatreds and anti-labor hysteria that is the matrix from which racism grows?

Sometimes I think they don't know and ought to be told. And sometimes I think that they do know, but just don't care.

★

NOVEMBER 8, 1944

The American people have spoken, and again it is FDR. We on *PM* have a deep sense of satisfaction at the results.

This is not the time for gloating over a political victory. It was one of the great and crucial struggles of American history. Yet the victory of the administration forces was (at least for us) never an end in itself, but always a means to an end. The end is the fulfillment of our victory in the war and the determined organization of a lasting peace.

To that task everyone of us who deserves the name of American must rededicate himself, regardless of party. For the task ahead of us is so broad and massive that, by comparison with it, party labels are irrelevant, and differences of political opinion are piddling.

A great America will, however, study every chapter it has written in its history so that it may turn to the next chapter with strength and clarity. What was the big meaning of the election through which we have just passed? What light does it shed on us as people? What guidance does it give us for the future?

Let me make it clear first that the results are a resounding personal victory for President Roosevelt, but that they are also more than that.

They are more than a victory for a *man*.

They are a victory for a *record*—the record that the whole American nation has made under a New Deal administration and its leadership. They are a mandate to extend that record.

They are a victory for a *direction*—the continuation of the progressive road that America has traveled for twelve years, in peace and in war. They are a mandate to keep building that road into the future. This means that we must apply to postwar social construction the same national energies and techniques that we have applied so successfully to the destructive job of war. And it means that America must retain the leadership in building a coalition of peoples for peace like the one we have built for war.

But even when you have said these things about the election results, something more important remains.

I can best get at it by recalling the nature of the campaign. In it were invested all the resources of high-pressure manipulation of the people's minds. Not only did the president have against him the large majority of the press, with the great power it wields. He had against him the Big Money, and the concentrated economic power of the nation, and the slick publicity techniques. The issues that were raised— Communism, aliens and alien doctrines, labor dictatorship—seemed to the intelligent observer many light-years distant from the real issues. Yet they had an explosive emotional dynamite packed away in them, and no one knew whether and to what extent it would wreak havoc in the ordinary American mind.

We all know that there is in every man far-reaching depths of the irrational. Whoever fears for democracy does so because he wonders how far the irrational can be exploited, and with what results.

He wonders, in short, whether the people can take it.

Well, if you were among those who wondered, you have had your answer.

The answer is: The people can take it.

The moral is: Never sell the people short.

Despite the slogan shrapnel and the propaganda blockbusters, they kept their counsel and kept their heads. They had their eyes fixed on the object—what man and what record they trusted, and in what direction they wanted to move. I know of no more triumphant vindication of the democratic idea than the American people have furnished in this election ordeal.

There were many single elements about the election that were exciting. There was the demonstration that labor can act politically, not only for its immediate selfish interests, but also in terms of the national interest and of world perspectives. There was the proof that to many people the issue of America's place in the postwar world transcended every other, and with that conviction they even crossed party lines.

But the most exciting things of all were the strength and the clarity that ordinary Americans showed.

They will need that strength and clarity for the future.

For one man, no matter how generous and farseeing, is not a whole nation. He has made mistakes in the past, and he will make more. He will have to be supported where he needs support, strengthened when he wavers, challenged when he deserves a challenge. The program for postwar America must be given solidity and substance. The direction for the future must be made sharper, less hazy.

All of that we can achieve as a people. But to do so, we must work and organize to give a great nation a great future, just as we have worked and organized to give it once more a great leader.

★

APRIL 15, 1945

THE DEAD PRESIDENT—AND THE LIVING PRESENT

Obituaries are stiff and generally hollow. The occasion is too deep for a few dry garlands of praise to be laid on the grave of our dead president. It is more important to assess the sources of his strength, and from it to take strength for what lies ahead of us.

More than anyone since Lincoln, he was the people's president. When people heard he had died, they looked at each other with unbelieving surprise. In Savannah, where I first heard the news, the Negro who told it to me asked, "Do you think it can be true?" The man with whom I was talking at the time—a community leader—said, "The world has died." The sailor on the train said, "I can't get used to the idea." The pretty young woman with the small son said, "Do you think now we can stop another war?"

Some of the verbal tears that are being shed for him have "crocodile" written on them. But most of the grief is real. Democracy is a funny thing: you can throw a man out of office when you want to, but when you find a man you really trust you hold on for dear life. We have learned that democracy does not dispense with the need a family feels for a father, the ship's crew for a captain. Roosevelt was both, and for a long time, because our crisis was of long duration. Now he is gone, and the people miss him.

The grief for him is great. Yet, as Mrs. Roosevelt said, we have more reason to be sorry for the nation and the world than for him. For Franklin Roosevelt had lost his private life. He had suffered the ultimate martyrdom of becoming a public leader. The killing pace of the presidency, which he had survived for three terms, finally caught up with him.

His problems and turbulences are now over. The "tired old man" has gone to his rest. The man who tried for so many years to move his legs does not have to try any longer. The man who had to bear so much of the world on his strong and wise shoulders has now slumped them forever. The good earth of his Hyde Park, that he loved so, will now hold him.

He should have lived at least a bit longer. Long enough to see Berlin taken, and the junction of the American and Russian armies in Germany, and Adolf Hitler in a prisoner's box turning his fishy eyes to an unbelieving world. Long enough to see the ratty hide of Japanese fascism drying in the setting sun. Long enough for the opening of the first conference of the United Nations as a going concern.

But these are perhaps narrow dreams, personal symbols. Let me ask, rather, in seeking further the sources of Roosevelt's strength, how the historians will assess him, writing with cool detachment and hindsight.

They will, I think, say he was the man who led us through the greatest crisis in our history since the Civil War. They will say that he was the greatest figure that twentieth-century democracy produced. They will call him the leader of the Great Coalition—the master planner of its war strategy, the architect of its peace structure, the symbol of the hopes that people all over the world have for a lasting world security.

How about his leadership? The historians will say that under ordinary conditions he might have proved an ordinary leader, which was also true of Lincoln; that the times evoked his greatness, but also that the greatness was there to be evoked. He grew with each occasion. He had the capacity for learning rapidly from events, and the gift for transmitting what he had learned to the people—gradually enough for even the lowliest person to absorb it. He was a master educator without ever becoming the priggish schoolmarm, and a consummate politician whose stature always extended beyond his politician's skills. He was the aristocrat who had placed himself at the head of the people's movement, the man of great affairs who never lost the common touch, the man of mastery who always remained a democrat and could never become a dictator.

But we are grown people in a grown-up world, who must put away our grief for our dead president, and face the living present and the looming future.

They will be difficult. But how much less difficult they seem now than if we had not had Roosevelt's leadership. The end in Europe may now be a matter of days, and in the Far East a matter of months. The strategy of military victory has been mapped. In every important military and diplomatic post there are people who developed under Roosevelt, and worked with him.

The pattern of peace has also been begun. Roosevelt had the vision not to repeat the mistakes of Wilson: he started building for peace long before the war was over, and its ardors and sufferings forgotten. He remembered to bring both of the great parties along with him as he explored the path to peace. His weakness here lay in concentrating too completely on the understanding among the leaders of the Big Three—in making the beginnings of the security structure too much a matter of personalities, too little of institutions. It is easy to see how this weakness flowed from his own sense of strength. He was the leader of the Big Three—the man closer to both Churchill and Stalin than either of them was to each other. With his death the greatest leadership tripod in history falls.

It is no derogation of President Truman to say that neither in experience nor in personality will he be able to take FDR's place in the

Big Three. But the completion of the world security structure need not be a problem in personal leadership. The pattern has been begun: the rest of it is clear enough to follow—if we have the will.

There is the nub of it: *if we have the will.* It will require great will to surmount the tasks ahead of us. We know now that there can be no world peace except through a firm understanding with our allies, the British people and the Russian people. The problem is to apply that knowledge in action. We know now that America can survive in the world economy only if we help the rest of the world to rebuild itself, to repair its ravaged energies, to develop production and markets. The problem is to apply that knowledge to action. We have learned in a war economy the techniques that we will be able to apply to a peacetime American economy, and set men and machines and capital to work building instruments of life rather than of death. The question is whether we have the will to apply those techniques in action.

Most of all, we have learned under Roosevelt how to go through economic crisis and war crisis without destroying our civil liberties, without breaking man's basic decency to man. We may well have to apply that knowledge also in action in the calculable future.

America will yet be able to produce great leadership to see us through the years ahead. But only if we are a great people. We shall have to place every iota of our common will, our unity, our determination behind President Truman and those who are working with him. If we fall to quarreling over personalities, and if we give to party what was meant for mankind we shall be lost.

It will do us good to think about Franklin Roosevelt as we set about our tasks. He had courage: it is we who must have courage now. He had tolerance: we shall need all the tolerance we can muster. He had vision: we must not walk in blindness.

1948

TRUMAN vs. DEWEY

So President Truman finally had to announce his candidacy for the Democratic nomination. His move is, at least in part, an effort to hold together the disintegrating Democratic support for him. Seeing his political strength crumbling, Truman has announced to the nation that if nominated, he will accept and run.

No doubt. But the question of whether he is to be nominated and elected is not for him to decide, but for the Democratic and liberal voters of the nation. I think it is going to be hard—terribly hard—to persuade them that he is the man whom they want to lead the liberal forces to victory.

What looked a month ago like an impossible pipe dream of liberal Democrats—the chances of scuttling Truman as 1948 candidate and nominating someone better—has now become a real possibility.

Partly it comes as a result of Henry Wallace's progressive movement. But only partly. For the strength of the Wallace effort is a sign, rather than a cause, of Truman's lack of a real hold on the imagination of people. The revolt of the Southern Tories, at the other end of the political scale from the Wallace left-wingers, is also a sign rather than a cause: a stronger president could make an unpalatable political move stick, while a weak one cannot make even the right move stick.

The real cause is President Truman himself. The component elements of the Democratic Party have always been uneasy partners, but in a time of world crisis like the present one it takes a figure of great stature to hold them together. Roosevelt could. Truman can't. Truman is his own worst enemy.

He has talked of the need for Democratic liberalism, and his Jackson Day speech was wholly on that theme. But to talk liberalism and act liberalism are wholly different things. The only strongly liberal move he has made recently was his civil rights program. It deserved—and still deserves—praise. But it came late, after the Wallace forces had beaten him to the punch. And it was not believed. Both the Negroes in the Northern states and the reactionaries in the South figured it as a wholly political move: it enraged the Tories without rallying the liberals.

Aside from that one gesture, Truman's recent record has been the sort to make him impossible as the liberal candidate of a liberal party. He has gone on with military intervention in Greece and Turkey, has yielded to those who pressed for more of the same kind of intervention in China, and his current moves on guaranteeing the military borders of Western Europe mean that the Marshall Plan is in danger of being transformed into a military alliance. His recent record on appointments—his scuttling of Chairman James Landis of the Civil Aeronautics Board, Chairman Mariner Eccles of the Board of Governors of the Federal Reserve System, and Surgeon General Thomas Parran—shows a tragic unconcern about rewarding courage and ability in the government service. Finally—and beyond all else—the administration sellout on the Palestine partition and the UN shows Truman as a man willing to be tough against everyone but the enemies of justice. Our generation has seen many sellouts, but one would have to go back to Munich to recall a sellout as cynical, as bedraggled, as contemptible as the State Department's weaseling out of its commitment to partition under the UN.

I wrote in this space on February 19: "Either the Democrats must change their cynical and bungling policies, or they must change their presidential candidate." These two are really linked, for Truman is what he is, and his policies will stay or go with him. He is a man of good will who is bewildered in a crisis world and doesn't measure up to the size of his job. He has allowed himself to become the instrument of the big generals and the big corporations, and he has made their military-minded and property-minded policies his policies.

What I have thus far written is wholly on the score of principle. It sums up why I do not believe that Truman should be nominated. But there is an additional reason on the score of practical politics. From this distance I do not see how he can win if he is nominated. The movement of the pro-Wallace liberals is increasingly away from Truman rather than back toward him. Even the anti-Wallace labor movement has little enthusiasm for Truman. The Southern Tories have broken with him. I despise the motives that animate these Southerners, and in a contest between Truman and them my own sympathy is wholly with Truman; yet the political fact of the break is there, and must be reckoned with. The victory of Leo Isacson, with support from Henry Wallace and the American Labor Party in a special Congressional election in the Bronx, shows the extent to which the minority groups, which count for a good deal in the crucial industrial states, have been alienated from Truman. The big-city Democratic bosses, who would like to cling to Truman if they could, are now faced by what is for them a hard fact of life: the probability that they could not win with him. And it is in the nature of a boss as a political animal that he won't consciously back a likely loser.

The Democratic politicians are worried. On Thursday and Friday there will be a strategy meeting of all the big Democratic machine bosses. For the time being, no doubt, they will continue to assert their loyalty to Truman, and Truman will continue to be a candidate to succeed himself. A man who has had that much power, even when it has been thrust on him, does not easily abdicate it. And the men who put him into power, and whose position depends partly on the system of patronage, do not easily abandon their titular party chief. But politics is an unsentimental affair, as is so much else in American life. In business, money talks; in politics, it is the final votes that talk. The hard fact is that barring a miracle Truman can no longer deliver the votes. Five times in American history the party politicians have scuttled a vice president-become-president when the time came for a new nomination. Five instances ought to be good enough, if what you are looking for is precedent. But the decisive fact is that Truman does not deserve the nomination, and in all probability could not be elected if he got it.

Are there other leaders to whom the Democratic Party could turn? There are: Justice William O. Douglas, General Eisenhower, former OPA Administrator Chester Bowles. Any one of them would give the nation good leadership. Any one of them would do a good deal to reunite the split Democratic forces. Any one of them would stand a good chance of winning, even with Wallace in the field, and would be sure to win if Wallace were to withdraw before November. A ticket made up of two of the three would give the Democrats a new outlook and future.

That is the crucial problem—the problem of building a base broad enough so that on it could be built a new structure of Democratic unity. Whether justly or not, Truman has today become a divisive and not a unifying force within the Democratic Party and among American liberals. His policy has become a divisive policy—exactly because it is reactionary in the foreign field and indecisive in the domestic.

What we need is a Democratic leader who will unify the liberals and give the nation the guidance it needs in a crisis age.

✮

JULY 18, 1948

Philadelphia—It was two in the morning, the hour when vitality is at its lowest. The sweating delegates, correspondents, cameramen, and assorted camp followers waited grimly for the presidential candidate to appear. After the drama of the civil rights fight, everyone figured the final presidential speech would be anticlimax. And the convention managers, evidently fearing only a halfhearted reception for their candidate, tried to forestall a flop by asking that there be no demonstration.

Both the audience and the managers were wrong. The last act went over big. He spoke too rapidly, too jerkily, too emotionally. But he was caught up in what he was saying. It was a harangue, I suppose, and it was what the polite people call "demagogic." But it carried conviction, because it was the truth, and had been waiting to be said for a long time. It had no taste. The candidate used un-Deweylike words like "lousy" and called the Republicans the "enemy." But the Republicans richly deserved both the adjective and the noun.

Somehow a rapport was built up between this stumbling, fumbling little man and an audience which neither loved nor admired him. They sensed that this was the most militant presidential acceptance speech in either major party since Bryan. They liked the fact that he came out of his corner fighting.

I had mixed emotions as I listened. I knew he had not grown a new skin or sprouted wings. He was still the Truman of the Truman Doctrine, of the Palestine switches. The natty clothes, the jaunty step, the eyes sparkling clearly through steel-rimmed glasses, the set of the jaw gave a squarish look to the insignificant face. The whole appearance bespoke not a great man but a stubborn mediocre man whose mediocrity was straining to fill out the large outlines of his great office.

At the moment the enemy were the Republicans, the real-estate lobby, the money changers in the temple. But I remembered when the enemy had been the Russians, the railway labor chiefs, the CIO, the Zionist pressure group, Henry Wallace, John L. Lewis, the anti-Truman opposition within the Democratic Party. The enemy changed, but always the burning intensity was unflaggingly personal.

It was a great speech for a great occasion, and as I listened I found myself applauding. I thought how different this speech was from Dewey's acceptance speech. Dewey was stilted and frozen inside, and his stilted words froze his audience. Truman's words, tumbling out, released the fighting energies of his audience. Yet I could not help remembering that the administration managers had that afternoon fought against the Americans for Democratic Action's civil rights amendment; that Missouri, the president's own state, had voted against it; that the group of conservatives who make administration policy, and use the president as a puppet, had been pushed for the moment into the background, but were still there; that the president's newfound militancy was a campaign militancy; that he justly blamed the Republicans for the domestic policy, but foreign policy was the area of his own presidential power, and in that area his policy was Republican policy.

I came away from the convention with few illusions about the candidate and his managers, much as I welcome their militancy. But I came away with a sense of respect for the vitality of the Democratic Party itself, and the way in which its great tradition of progressivism defies the stifling forces of an era of fear.

In these closing sessions of the convention, something very like a miracle had happened. The battered liberals, who had lost every preconvention fight, came back under ADA leadership to win the crucial battle for civil rights. The Southern reactionaries were beaten, and the fight for the soul of the South will now have to be fought out where it belongs—in the Southern communities themselves, rather than in the councils of the party. A convention that had until that day been an inert collection of empty men came to life under the leadership of a group of new young men whose faces will be seen and whose names will be heard in the next four years.

Truman will, in all probability, be beaten; but Democratic progressivism is not dead. Its aliveness is underlined by the fact that in this hour of its great crisis its candidate knows he must assume the mantle and militancy of FDR if he is to stand even a chance of winning.

As I watched the climax of the convention—the sloughing off of the old and tired, the secession of the rotten, the new vitality of the mediocre, the beginning of the new—I thought of Walt Whitman's line: "Out of the cradle endlessly rocking. . . ." He had written it about himself, he had meant it for America. The processes of birth and death and agony and rebirth are as real in politics as in organic life.

★

NOVEMBER 7, 1948

The warmth is coming back to American life. I have never seen so much confessional breast-beating and sackcloth-wearing on the part of usually cocky commentators as after this 1948 presidential election. I say this with a wry penitence; if there weren't so many sinners stamping down the sawdust trail to testify to their unworthiness and shout contrite hallelujahs, I would myself join them in confessing that I was not very bright in my election forecast.

By this time the reasons for the upset have been spelled out clearly enough—Dewey's outsmarting himself, Truman's courage and canniness, labor's labors in defeating Taft-Hartley men, the farmers' clinging to the price-support program, the Roosevelt tradition and the strength it still has.

Why is everyone so happy about the election, including many who voted for Henry Wallace or Norman Thomas or even Thomas Dewey? To answer by calling it the biggest political upset in America's history isn't enough. The emotional force with which the whole thing hit us was due not only to surprise at the result, but also to the explosion and release of pent-up resentment. Dewey went around the country delivering not campaign speeches but acceptance speeches. He treated Truman throughout the campaign as an insignificant item in a meaningless dream, as the little man who wasn't there. But the dream developed into nightmare and the nightmare into reality. Harry Truman turned out to be the little man who *was* there. And when we discovered it, we all cheered.

But our resentment is not entirely directed at Dewey, or even at the hapless Roper-Gallup-Crosley trio of pollsters. What links Dewey and this trio in our minds is that they are symbols of the same thing—the effort to supplant human life by the slide rule, to run the political animal as if he were part not of a biological universe but of a mechanical one.

Our emotion comes from a rebellion against the machine principle. Dewey had everything figured out, and we were simply parts of his blueprint of power. Roper and Gallup also had everything figured out, and for them we were parts of a calculating machine, which unfortunately counted only heads but couldn't tally the psychic intensity inside them. Hence our emotional explosion. But Dewey is now a dazed failure, and the pollsters have become scapegoats for every smart aleck to slaughter with his tired witticisms. The truth is that in attacking them we deflect our fury from ourselves for having been taken in by the machine principle.

Truman believed in himself and his methods of campaigning, but up to the last minute he was not sure he could infect enough of the people with that belief of his. The same thing applies to the people who voted for him and (mainly) against Dewey. They were silent people, because in most sections of the country the whole weight of the respectable was thrown in Dewey's direction. They kept their thoughts to themselves, kept them even from the poll takers. Each of them waited until he was in the polling booth. And each, in his own mind, thought of himself as part of the minority, voting against the nation's grain.

Each lit a feeble little match in the night's darkness, thinking he was alone. And when he looked around him, behold, there was a forest of matches, and in their spluttering of combined illumination the American people saw themselves and their strength and democracy's greatness.

★

JANUARY 20, 1949

On this day of President Truman's inauguration, one may ask, What is it that impels a man to move heaven and earth to get into the world's toughest job?

There is no question about how punishing a job the presidency is. It eats men. It left John Adams and his son, John Quincy Adams, embittered men. It made Jefferson and Jackson the targets of the most extreme abuse. It quite literally killed Lincoln and Garfield and McKinley and Franklin Roosevelt. It broke Woodrow Wilson's heart and, in a somewhat different way, Hoover's.

It is not so much an office as an obstacle race and a Gehenna combined. You have to deal with a Congress that remains only briefly in a honeymoon mood. You have to listen to every pressure group and seem to give in to none. You have to handle the press and trust you will be the bird on the front page every day, but mainly for the brilliance of your plumage and not to be roasted, boiled, fried, carved up, or flayed alive. You have to seem knowing about an administrative structure so vast that no dozen men could know its details. You have to run a foreign policy that girdles the globe, yet be aware of what opinion is sprouting up from the grass roots of every hamlet in your own country.

You have to keep yourself from being run by the generals and admirals who run the biggest military show on earth, and also to hold at arm's length the corporation bigwigs who run the biggest economic show on earth. You have to be statesmanlike in language, yet present an image of boldness and decisiveness. You have to be a nonpartisan national leader without ceasing to be a very partisan party leader. You have to attract talent, yet see to it that plenty of gravy gets to the patronage boys. You have to have your wrist broken shaking hands and your memory tortured remembering faces. You have to be remote and dignified, as the world symbol of the greatest democracy in history; and at the same time warm and earthy, so that no one will regard you as glacial and high-hat.

You have to remember to smile even when your temper is at the boiling point and your digestion is gutted—for a frown might send the stock market tumbling and the chancelleries of the world into hysteria. You have to forget you were ever a private man with a private life. You have to get used to seeing the members of your family roasted for things over which they have no control. You have to learn how to take it, but be restrained in dishing it out. You have to assume that your mistakes will be magnified and trumpeted from the market place, and your achievements either ignored or credited to some kingmaker in your inner circle. You have to wake up every morning and go to bed every night in the midst of a fresh crisis. You have to learn how to ride the whirlwind and command the storm, with only your own limited mortal capacities to aid you.

What makes men hunger for a chance at such a martyrdom? The immediate answer, of course, is the power and the glory. The American presidency is today the most powerful office in the democratic world, and in some ways more powerful even than Stalin's. For while the head of the American state does not have the arbitrary power that the Russian leader does, the consequences of his power are more far-reaching. A decision he makes will change the destinies of people in Paris or Tel Aviv, and on the steppes of Asia and on the banks of the Congo. Such power is a heady stimulant, and a man would be scarcely a man to be immune to it.

Another answer lies in the dreams the young men dream in our American culture. They are the dreams not of the contemplative life, or the philosopher's wisdom, or the saint's saintliness, but of always being midstream in the current of action and excitement. The style of American culture is the style of continuous dynamic movement, and the dream of the presidency is the ultimate dream in American life because it is a dervish dance of activity, the succession of your pictures in the papers and your name on every lip. This is at once the strength and the weakness of America.

Finally, there is no other culture in which the head of state has so direct a relation with the people. Martin Van Buren, writing in his autobiography about Andrew Jackson, pointed out that Jackson got his strength from contact with the people. "They were his blood relations—the only blood relations he had." In a symbolic sense this must be true of every president. It is the old fable of Antaeus and how he kissed the earth his mother and renewed his strength thereby.

1952

EISENHOWER vs. STEVENSON

JULY 22, 1952

THE SPEECH THAT ADLAI STEVENSON delivered at the convention yesterday may very likely make history not only for the Democratic Party but for the nation. The conviction that swept across the whole convention afterward was that it had to be this man, whatever his own personal doubts. To many of the delegates Stevenson had been only a name up to that time. They inclined toward him because they needed someone like him, but they must have had strong doubts about pursuing this phantom figure. What the speech did was to give the convention a taste of the quality of mind, the sharpness of phrase, the strong yet balanced judgment that are Stevenson's mark. After that there could be nothing that would stop the Stevenson draft movement—not even, I suspect, Stevenson himself.

It is a good guess now that Stevenson will win the nomination, either on the first or second ballot. The Democrats smell victory over the Eisenhower-Nixon ticket. Despite the whole large field of ready and willing candidates, none was clearly the man who could organize victory. Stevenson was. The ovation he got was a mark that the Democrats felt they had found the one solution to their problem and the nation's.

Who is this man on whom the Democrats have so early and—as it seems—so decisively fixed their choice? He seems to know his limits, and (in fact) the limits of government and politics. He knows how to get along with a legislature, how to organize a staff, how to reach the people. But essentially he is a lonely man, carrying on his struggles inside himself.

In a picture of him the other day the photographer, whether by design or accident, caught with his camera and put into the foreground the large lettering of the title of a book on Stevenson's desk. It was a recent novel by Vincent Sheehan called *Rage of the Soul*. I thought there was a remarkable symbolism for Stevenson in the phrase.

For there is a rage of the soul in a sensitive man confronted by the complex nature of the problems of our world, and the very limited way in which we can "solve" them, as we put it. Politicians, by their nature, shut their eyes to this fact, and the only rage they experience is when their candidacies fall through or they fail of election. Stevenson may have good private reasons for not seeking the presidency, and he may quite genuinely want to serve another term as governor of Illinois instead; or he may feel that the nomination is worth having only if you can get it without strings, so that you can conduct your own kind of campaign and be your own kind of president.

These may all be partial motives, yet one cannot help finding among them also the sense of torment when you are torn between the rigor of your public duties and the luxury of your private sense of the complexity of things.

It has been argued that Stevenson has no moral right to refuse the presidential nomination if it is offered to him. That is a sound moral position—if you want to take it. Certainly the duties of a citizen include not only the rights of suffrage but also the obligation of office—provided you are called to it.

Yet I feel that this approach from the moral duties of citizenship is too Boy Scoutish to satisfy someone like Stevenson. More persuasive would be the mood of a convention which simply refused to play any longer that cat-and-mouse game that the Democratic Party leaders had come to play earlier, and which assumed that once the nomination was achieved there could be no further argument about it. The ovation he got should have convinced Stevenson that this was the mood of the delegates, and that in the end they simply would not take No for his answer because they were telling him, not asking him.

This is new in politics, but so is a man like Stevenson. We are learning that the exact degree of Stevenson's liberalism or moderateness of view is less important than the skill and reflectiveness, the literateness, the freshness of spirit he would bring into the White House. He may lack a degree of steel and decision, but the course of a campaign will supply it in part, and four years of the world's toughest job will harden any personality.

☆

JULY 24, 1952

For five days I have been sitting in a hot room by a television screen, watching one of the authentic miracles of our time—the visual record of every detail of a national political convention. I covered the Republican Convention two weeks ago on the spot in Chicago. When I undertook to sit this one out in New York in order to get a basis for comparing the two methods, I had almost resigned myself to a dullish, second-hand experience. I was wrong.

For during these five days I have been one of 60 million Americans who have watched intently while a group of hard-working men and women prepared to submit to the suffrage of the people. We have been watching history in motion on the TV screen—60 million of us turned into working historians.

The political parties are awake to this fact, and there are signs that the convention rostrum and hall will increasingly become a stage on which a drama will be enacted primarily for the TV audience.

I hope fervently they will not in the future phony it up too much. The great charm of convention TV now is that it is a documentary. To be sure, there have been some efforts to stage it for the TV audience. Yet what is impressive is to be found less in the thundering passages of the speeches, often tolerated only with boredom by both the convention audience and the TV audience, than in the moving human passages between the party's personalities and the delegates.

On Tuesday there was a moment, during the ovation given to Eleanor Roosevelt, when a great collective emotion was caught and expressed before a vast national audience. Last night such a moment came again during the Barkley ovation after the speech, when a succession of people came up to shake Vice President Alben Barkley's hand and embrace him. TV audiences will, I am certain, learn to recognize the genuine and sift it out from the hokumed-up carnival stuff.

I found that there is one thing TV does not give you that you get when you are yourself on the convention floor—a chance to look around, get your own total impression, and make your own selection of significant detail. Instead you get the selection made by the TV photographers and engineers. It may be better than your own—but it is someone else's selection, not yours, and you feel more passive than when you can do your own picking.

And also your own interpreting. The performance of the individuals and teams who do the commentary on TV has still to catch up with the technicians who bring you the scenes. I have found a good deal of timidity among some of the commentaries, dull repetitiveness in many, a sense of confusion where it was unnecessary, and in some cases sheer ignorance.

But it is ungracious to carp at these marks of immaturity when you are confronted by the generous abundance of TV fare. Here is a picture of America in cross section, which each must learn to read for himself.

Here are little huddles of intense, whispering men, earnestly talking tactics; here are several Negroes rising to applaud Barkley as he tells the story of the Negro soldier from Birmingham whom he met in Korea; here is a women putting on lipstick with great technical care and adroitness; here are two women gossiping while they chew gum; here are a boy and girl, very late in the night, sitting among almost empty benches listening intently to the droning platform-reading; here is an old man in workingman's clothes, cupping his ear to hear better. Here beauty is caught for a fleeting moment, arrested and held within a television frame in scenes that sometimes remind you of those wonderful details from the big canvases of the Italian painters.

Best of all, here are political parties forced by public opinion to give the people access to their every deliberation, to open every channel and crevice to the access of the public gaze. Even the hot and smoke-filled committee rooms are invaded by the TV eye. Whatever happens in the coming election, no one will be able to complain that the victors sneaked in their victory while no one was looking. For we are all looking, 60 million strong, and tomorrow perhaps 100 million. And politics will never be the same again.

✷

SEPTEMBER 24, 1957

Aboard Eisenhower Special—The Republican campaign last night took over the techniques of television soap opera in Hollywood, combined them with the atmosphere of a political convention in Cleveland, and won at least a round in the struggle over the Nixon secret fund.[1]

It was the most extraordinary climax to the most dramatic political story in the history of presidential campaigns. What other campaign meeting, assembled to hear a presidential candidate, had ever before begun with a piped-in broadcast in which the candidate's running mate defended his political honesty by giving a national audience the story of his life and love? And in what other campaign meeting had the presidential candidate afterward thrown away his prepared script on a national issue like inflation and spent his time lauding the courage of his running mate, making clear his admiration for him, and then promising to bring in his judgment in the next act?

The dramatic skill of Nixon's television performance threatens to overshadow a more important drama that has been played out on Eisenhower's campaign train during the past six days, ever since the Nixon story broke. I mean the drama of General Eisenhower's struggle with his conscience.

It is General Eisenhower who—in spite of the fact that for the moment Dick Nixon stole the show—has been and remains the central figure in the whole drama. It was Eisenhower's campaign for virginally honest government that was thrown into confusion by the disclosures about Nixon. It was Eisenhower's own moral sense that seemed at first to have been outraged. It was on Eisenhower's campaign staff that the plans for the Nixon show were laid, although they were announced from California. It was to Eisenhower, as well as to the national audience, that Nixon addressed his most tremulous final plea for justification.

Let me describe the setting in Cleveland last night. The press watched the Nixon television show in a room on the second floor of the Cleveland auditorium. Eisenhower and his party watched in another room. When the curtain-raiser was over, the real show began. George Bender, Republican congressman from Ohio, who was the cheerleader of the Taft forces at the Chicago convention, introduced the notables, including Senators Robert Taft, John Bricker, William Knowland, and Karl Mundt.

Then the general appeared. I have heard him speak more than a

---

[1] The *New York Post* revealed the existence of a fund set up by wealthy Californians to help Richard Nixon. Controversy over the fund resulted in a television address that became known as "the Checkers speech."

score of times during this past week. He has rarely been effective, but last night he was. Dramatically he threw away his prepared inflation script—which was a good thing for the country as well as for him. He was a different Eisenhower—keyed up, responsive to the audience, and with an obviously deep emotional involvement in what had been happening.

With nostalgia General Eisenhower recalled the episode of General George Patton, and the famous slapping scene. "He committed an error. He made amends for his error." And it was clear that Eisenhower was putting Nixon into Patton's place. "I happen to be one of those people," he added, "who, when I get in a fight, would rather have a courageous and honest man by my side than a whole boxcar full of pussyfooters."

General Eisenhower seems to have shifted his ground. When he now speaks of Nixon committing "an error," he is speaking in technical terms—in terms of the morally indifferent question of whether a senator is technically wrong or right in letting his friends help him carry his expenses in fighting Communism. And when General Eisenhower now says—as he said last night—that his final criterion in judging Nixon will be "Do I myself believe that this man is the kind of man that Americans would like for their vice president?" he is opening himself to the test of the stream of telegrams and letters that is bound to come in after the effective Nixon performance.

It is hard to escape the conclusion that this is not a new script or an accidental one. It is part of the political game and there can be no valid objection to the Republican professionals using their best skill on it. But when General Eisenhower lets the high moral purpose with which he started be shifted and twisted until he ends up exactly where the most cynical and manipulative of the professionals do, it is hard to escape the feeling that one has watched the crumbling of that moral purpose.

On the level of political soap opera, there can be no question of the effectiveness of the Nixon performance. No hero as handsome as Nixon, as clean-cut in looks, as tremulous and pulsating in his delivery, has hit the political circuit for a long time. The pretty and adoring wife, the mortgages on the houses, the saga of a poor boy who became senator—these were surefire stuff. They mark a new era in campaigning.

But it isn't enough to say, as Nixon did, that the fund was not secretly given or handled. If it had all been aboveboard from the start, how explain the outcry Nixon raised when the disclosure was made?

How explain his insistence that it was an Alger Hiss plot? There could be no plot or smear in revealing what had all along been an open transaction.

It isn't enough to say that he got no funds for himself. Where there is a double compensation, there is bound to be a personal advantage for anyone in political life.

It isn't enough to say that only the rich can afford to stay clear of such subsidies. Other senators on the level of Nixon's own means have been able to get along without either corruption or subsidy. It means a real burden, but they are bearing it.

It isn't enough to say that he saved the government money by not sending out his speeches with the government frank, and by getting rich men to pay for them. By this same logic, why not let the same group of rich men pay the salaries of the senators as well as their postage and office expenses?

It isn't enough to say that he gave the rich men nothing in return for their subsidy. In the original interview Dana Smith had made it clear that Nixon was chosen for the subsidy exactly because the rich men knew that he voted right from their viewpoint. One of the fatal defects in the speech was Nixon's failure to talk about his voting record on housing, on price control, on tidelands oil.

Nor is it, finally, enough to say that he was using the money to fight the Communists. The fight against Communism is not something separate from Nixon's other duties as senator. It was part of his public image and his public function.

What Nixon owed the American people was a straightforward answer to the question of ethical wrongdoing. What he gave them instead was a slick and glossy job of television art. It will take time for the people to strip away the phony from the real. But I have faith they will do it.

★

OCTOBER 16, 1952

The Eisenhower story since the start of the campaign has been what the novelists call a "deterioration story"—the lack of inner fiber that would make a man strong enough to cope with the tragic pressures and conflicts of life.

No one—not even the most committed Republican—has been able to ignore the succession of compromises and surrenders from the first advent of Senator Everett Dirksen on the postconvention scene to Eisenhower's acceptance of McCarthy's veto of part of his speech. Since they cannot be ignored, they must be explained.

I start with the fact that Eisenhower was a real hero in the military phase of his career, and not a fake one. He is alert and resourceful and has a quick intelligence. He has a genial feeling for people, likes them, and likes to be liked. Within the grand strategy of the Allied coalition, and under the leadership of Franklin Roosevelt and George Marshall, he was able to carry through a massive and delicate military operation.

What then has happened to Eisenhower now? He no longer has clarity or conviction, he has made needless surrenders even in terms of political advantage, and he has allowed the magnificent capital of the popular belief in him to leak away and be wasted.

I think one answer is that Eisenhower is in the wrong medium when he runs for president as the glittering leader symbol of the Republicans. He is out of his element. His element was the conduct of war, and to it he was trained, and in it were all his conditionings. In the conduct of war you learn both to take orders and to give orders with the single objective of victory. What people feel about you is not important: It is only the results that count. But in the conduct of politics, there is a subtle give and take of appeal and response between the leader and the people.

As long as Eisenhower was a soldier, he had a belief in himself and in his capacity to assess the technical advice given to him by his subordinate officers. But in the medium of politics, for which he is untrained, surrounded by tangled problems of economics, legislation, and foreign policy of which he is profoundly ignorant, he turns to those who are more expert than himself—and he has no experience of his own in assessing their advice.

As a result he feels for the first time deeply insecure, and feeling insecure, he tends—as all technicians do—to reduce all the problems to technical problems. That is to say, his test of what to do about William Jenner or Robert Taft or Joseph McCarthy, about the issue of taxes or the Korean War is: What will get us the most votes? Thus, in this new medium, the former great leader turns into the great opportunist. And when he finds that each new compromise succeeds only in losing him more votes than he has gained by it, he grows more reckless with the next compromise in his effort to recoup his falling political fortunes.

One of Eisenhower's troubles is that, while he is unschooled in the arts of political leadership, he carries over from his war experience the image of himself as a strategist. Thus he is not wholly putty in the hands of the political hacks and the agency men. In part, at least, he takes pleasure in fighting the political campaign as he might fight in a military one. Calling it a "crusade" becomes merely one of the stock military devices.

This behavior of Eisenhower's has sent his supporters into a tail-spin of dizzy doubts, self-torturing, and almost comic rationalizations. It has led even the very intelligent Alsop column to the profound remark that, after all, "Eisenhower is Eisenhower"—meaning, I suppose, that what he has done does not define him in any sense. It has led others to talk of the "calculated risk" that Eisenhower took in first reconciling himself to Taft, Jenner, and McCarthy, before he turned to the wooing of the liberals.

Men's capacity for self-delusion is great, and it is unkind to break the spell. But in the interests of clear thinking I must continue to observe that the Eisenhower story is the tragic one such as the Greek dramatists dealt with in the "Fall of the Hero"—a man caught in a struggle in which the very qualities that once gave him distinction serve only to destroy his integrity.

Tender is the night of blurred emotion with which some still cling to their former idol. But the great decisions of a nation must be made in the harsh daylight.

★

OCTOBER 22, 1952

With all the pollsters swarming over the nation, I have been polling myself and I find—to no one's great surprise, not even mine—that I'm for Adlai Stevenson. Since every voter ought to give his reasons, here are some of mine:

... Because (as Hamilton Basso has remarked) Stevenson is for the English sentence.

... Because he doesn't have a dog named Checkers, or a wife with a Republican coat.

... Because his finances are uncomplicated enough even for me to understand.

. . . Because he doesn't act as if he were taking a course on how to make friends and project his personality.

. . . Because he doesn't say "Goodbye folks" as the train pulls out of the station.

. . . Because he doesn't treat me as if I were an item in an agency survey of customer response to a product.

. . . Because I don't want the advertising boys to tell me to "love that General."

. . . Because I want a man in the White House who has read a book, even if he hasn't written one.

. . . Because he has been a late starter, but is the kind of entry who will be there at the finish.

. . . Because he doesn't carry with him the smell of the McCarthy stable.

. . . Because he doesn't insult my intelligence.

. . . Because he is the prime target of the team of Nixon, Jenner, McCarthy, and Taft.

. . . Because he has a sense of history in the nation and of reverence for the individual.

. . . Because he has a friend called Harry Truman.

. . . Because he is a democrat and not a publican or a pharisee.

. . . Because he is no weather-vane changing with the wind as it moves from East to West and North to South.

. . . Because he treats Americans like adults, refusing to tell them that their problems can be solved by patent medicines and that the boys can be brought back from Korea in time for Halloween.

. . . Because he has exploded the myth of the twelve-year-old mind.

. . . Because he can tell a joke and a story, and has saved the campaign from the solemn banalities declaimed by mediocrities.

. . . Because he has shown that he knows how to say No.

. . . Because he can say things like "You've got to vote like a Democrat if you want to live like a Republican."

. . . Because he doesn't stoop to conquer the states' rights Dixiecrats.

. . . Because people have switched to him, not from him.

. . . Because my favorite Republican, Senator Wayne Morse, has come out for him.

. . . Because I don't mind the agency boys writing the ads of the nation, but I hate to see them taking over its government.

. . . Because he has made the right enemies in his own party—James Byrnes, Harry Byrd, and Allan Shivers.

. . . Because he knows how to keep his dignity amidst the embroilments of a messy campaign, and not only when to talk but also when not to.

. . . Because Stevenson is naive enough to think that a campaign is meant for a discussion of issues, and I like that kind of naïveté.

. . . Because he can hold together the Great Coalition of labor, liberal, and internationalist groups that Roosevelt built.

. . . Because he has not only talked civil rights for Negroes, but has put them into practice in the Illinois National Guard and civil service.

. . . Because he is a civilian who will have strength enough to stand up to the generals instead of a general who buckles when confronted by a strong civilian.

. . . Because he doesn't think that fighting Communism is a game to be played in the headlines, but a life-and-death struggle with the world as arena, which will be won only in the hearts of men.

. . . Because he can understand the sources of neutralism in Europe, and save our democratic alliances.

. . . Because he prefers to look in the future of India and of all Southeast Asia instead of lamenting the past in China.

. . . Because he will use intelligence and will and a long patience to prevent an atomic war.

. . . Because all the people I like don't like Ike.

1956

EISENHOWER VS. STEVENSON

FEBRUARY 4, 1956

THE INDISPENSABLE CANDIDATE

THE TRAGEDY OF PRESIDENT EISENHOWER'S sickness is deep and real, yet there is also something almost grotesque about the way in which the Republicans have pinned all their political hopes on this frail mortal vessel and hang immobilized upon his decision to run or not to run again. If he decides to run, two sentences from his January 19 press conference—the first full one since his attack—may well be used against him. "It would be idle to contend," he said, "that my health can be wholly restored." And again, "My future life must be carefully regulated to avoid excessive fatigue." The presidency, one should add, is scarcely an office whose holder can hope to "avoid excessive fatigue."

Political opinion in America is genuinely baffled about what the answer will be to the "big question." Each Eisenhower utterance makes the pendulum of guessing swing first one way, then another. There have been so many equally confident rumors and counter-rumors that not even the "inside dopesters" (who abound even more in politics than in the rest of American life) can seem credible—because they can't pretend to know what goes on in the head and heart of a convalescing man. The president might give his answer before the middle of February, or he might conceivably wait until March. If he waits it may well be at the expense of another heart attack—for Senator Knowland is eating his heart out with rage and frustration at being kept from launching his own candidacy. He has declined nomination

"The Indispensable Candidate," "Convention Eve," and "The Electronic Convention" appeared in *The New Statesman and Nation* on the dates given.

in New Hampshire, the first of the primaries, but he has not disowned a group that is campaigning there on his behalf and will run a slate of pro-Knowland candidates in the primary in March.

The work of the government, meanwhile, goes on under the steady hand of Sherman Adams, with the top decisions (as in the turn-of-the-year messages to Congress) being left to the president. "There is nothing in the messages," the *New York Times* observed, "to suggest that we are being governed by a coronary occlusion." Yet to a remarkable degree the normal processes of politics—and of government too—hang undecided in a limbo between the *will-he* and the *won't-he* of the decision. Until it is announced, neither the Democrats nor the Republicans can be sure of either their campaign strategy or their closely linked legislative strategy. Administrative decisions tend to mark time, and foreign policy cannot be shaped with any confidence that it will be maintained.

It is a situation unparalleled in American history—a sick president who can accept or reject the eagerly tendered nomination, or who can in effect pick his successor as candidate because no one will have much chance of winning without Ike's support. Eisenhower may not be the "indispensable man" in the White House itself (Stevenson would in some ways make a better president), but he is clearly the *indispensable candidate* for the Republicans. Without him they seem doomed to wander in the desert for another four years as they did during the twenty-year dry spell from 1932 to 1952. Since there are more Democratic than Republican voters, Eisenhower must use his prestige to get a major part of the uncommitted ("independent") vote and even a fair share of Democratic ones. He can be pretty sure of achieving this, since he is a widely respected and even beloved figure, whose image as a man of peace has reached to every class. That is why almost all the "wings " of the Republican Party are flapping feverishly for Eisenhower to run, except for the Neanderthal wing, which prefers Knowland. But even the Republican primitives, under Knowland, Jenner, and McCarthy, might swallow another Eisenhower candidacy with only a mild choke.

It is a great personal triumph for a man to have achieved, as the sick savior of his party's political fortunes. The party leaders came to him, in their hour of anguish and need, as if for extreme unction. Once they had been certain that four more years of power were in their grasp—only to have the prize all but vanish because of a mysterious "occlusion." For a time the whole nation assumed that the sick president was wholly out of the political picture, and there was a dispirited canvassing of other Republican possibilities, including the four Californians—Richard Nixon, Earl Warren, William Knowland, and Goodwin Knight. Then the mood changed. The president's doctors grew more optimistic, and Dr. Paul Dudley White became a political prophet and declared he would vote for Ike a second time. Magazine articles appeared, playing down both the seriousness of a heart attack and the rigors of the presidential office. National polls of heart specialists showed that two-thirds of them thought Ike could bear the burden of another term—though this mainly proves that American medicine votes Republican. The hucksters had again taken control of Republican strategy. They even entered Ike's name in the New Hampshire primaries, and he didn't withdraw it.

There was much talk of a "regency," also called the "Commodore Group" after the New York hotel where it often meets. This included a number of pre-1952 Eisenhower backers and advisers, who are still close to him: General Lucius Clay, who formerly worked with Ike in Germany, U.N. delegate Henry Cabot Lodge, Sherman Adams, Attorney-General Brownell, and Thomas E. Dewey. With the president's brother Milton Eisenhower, these are the men with whom Ike is most likely to take counsel on personal and political matters. The Alsops reported confidently the belief of this group that the president had decided to run, and it was rumored that Henry Luce had given his Washington staff of correspondents much the same report. If Nixon was to be ditched as a liability on the vice presidential ticket (because he was too lightweight a figure to take over the presidency in an emergency) the report was that Eisenhower's running mate would be Dewey, who had himself been twice a presidential candidate and was therefore of the right stature to run for vice president in such a context.

But these expectations might easily, in the next few weeks, prove frail and sagging reeds. The president talks with great sobriety about the difficulty of the office, about his need to avoid fatigue, about the danger of changing leadership in the midst of a presidential term. To be sure, he may speak thus as part of the camouflage of a man who wants to run again, or he may do it as a way of holding his party and Congress together as long as possible before he bows out. Either tactic is possible, and Eisenhower has shown himself far more of a political tactician than he would seem to be. As I write this the odds are again against the president's renomination, but they may change once more. The decision is still his, and anything can still happen.

Those who argue that Eisenhower would have been reluctant to try for a second term even if he had not become sick are, I think, quite wrong. I have all along felt that he wanted a second term, as indeed he had wanted the first one, and some time before the heart attack I went out on a limb to say so. The president had come to enjoy his office, along with the power of decision that went with it. He had a firm sense of party ties that grew stronger each year, and a feeling of pride at having kept his party together and given it a new popular strength. He also had a sense of mission about keeping world peace intact—and he still has.

The heart attack changed a good deal in Eisenhower's own thinking about the future. At first he must have despaired of ever trying for another four years. Yet as he grew stronger two trends of thinking may well have contended in his mind. One was the argument of some of his advisers that the whole burden of the office could be taken from his shoulders, except for the big decisions: certainly it had been true, even before the attack, that Eisenhower used the military approach to his job, with everything briefed and distilled by the staff below him until it reached him in the form of a one-page report, all the details being delegated to the chief of staff. Along with this argument there may have been the natural urge of a convalescing man to resume his work in order to show himself and the world that he had the vigor to overcome such obstacles. Roosevelt had something of the same feeling about his paralysis. Contending against this was the sober knowledge that another coronary attack might come at any time, and that it was scarcely responsible to incur such a risk for himself and the country. It has been, and still is, a lonely debate going on in Eisenhower's mind. He talks of it with dignity and detachment, and while he may be taking counsel about it—especially from his brother—no one except himself can think it through for him. The biggest single argument in favor of his running is that the Republicans will, in default of his candidacy, be sunk without a trace when the nation polls in November.

I have mentioned the four candidates from California, which is so important a state because it is the fastest-growing one in the nation, the second now in population, and has a tradition of politicians who had to get much of their strength across party lines. As far as Nixon is concerned, there was a chance to test the nation's confidence in him when the president was so ill that many expected he would be unable to fulfill his duties at all: at that time only a small Nixon claque clamored for giving that too cheeky and opportunist young man a chance to sit in the White House. As for Knowland, he heads the preventive-war group and would pull only those votes: the idea of Knowland in the White House would be far worse than that of a super-huckster—it would be that of a fanatic let loose among the stockpile of H-bombs. As for Knight, few take him as seriously as he does himself.

There remains Chief Justice Warren, formerly governor of California and several times an unsuccessful contender for the presidential nomination. There is little doubt, on his record and personality, that he would make a great and even liberal president. He has a direct and rough-hewn quality, is a good administrator, and enjoys politics. The fact that he is on the Supreme Court would not in itself compel him to refuse the nomination: Hughes took it in 1916, was almost elected against Wilson, and was later reappointed to the Court as chief justice. But there is another factor that makes it extremely unlikely that Warren could be induced to run. His great work on the Supreme Court was in getting a unanimous Court decision in the school-segregation cases. This decision has embittered the South, and has started something like a new Southern rebellion. The Republican problem about Warren would not be so much the loss of the electoral votes of the normally Democratic South: the Republicans could afford to lose the few Southern states that broke away into Eisenhower's camp, and could more than counterbalance them with a heavy Negro vote in the North, which regards Warren as a hero of our time. The real problem is that Warren's candidacy would be seized upon by White supremacists in the South as proof that the Supreme Court decision had been politically inspired from the beginning, and it might jeopardize any future attempt by the Court to deal with the problem of Negro civil rights.

Thus a refusal by Eisenhower to run may well leave the Republicans with Nixon as their only recourse—or perhaps a political unknown like Governor Christian Herter of Massachusetts. All the straw polls indicate that Nixon would be beaten not only by Stevenson but also by Estes Kefauver and Averell Harriman, if the vote were held now. No doubt a campaign would throw all the heavy Republican resources of publicity and TV in Nixon's direction, and he might be refurbished by their aid and also the support of Ike himself. Yet it is a doubtful and bleak prospect for the Republicans.

Aside from these considerations there seem to me to be far more serious ones that Eisenhower should take into account. The presidential office has become the fulcrum of American government, the only part of the government that gives real direction to policy, and the president—certainly since Wilson and the two Roosevelts—has developed strong and direct ties with the people. If Eisenhower were to run as a semi-invalid and get reelected (as well he might), a precedent would be set for an inactive presidency, which might damage the office itself. It is one thing to have an active, functioning presidential leader who bears the brunt of the political battles yet remains a symbol for the nation as a whole because he becomes identified with every national policy. It is quite another thing to have a president who is a sort of chairman of the board after the structure of the business corporation and is used either as a front man for disguising what the "boys in the backroom" are doing or else remains in the shadows while other men carry on the active work. The presidency is no place for any man to measure out his strength carefully in a semiretirement. I am confident that President Eisenhower will see the truth of this, and will decide accordingly.

There remains the question of the Eisenhower image and how it may still be used by the Republicans. It is the image of a great soldier who has become a man of peace, and who can therefore be trusted either for military or diplomatic decisions. But alas for the Republicans, the ineffable John Foster Dulles has done much to obscure this carefully contrived popular image of Eisenhower. The notorious current farce—the *Man on the Brink*, otherwise known as the Dulles Follies—may prove disastrous for the Republicans because it depicts American foreign policy as having been shaped by a reckless plunger who used the theory of "deterrence" to gamble with American and world destinies. But if Dulles was such a gambler, one cannot fail to conclude that either the president was one also, or else he did not know what Dulles was about. Either of these conclusions would be bound to hurt whatever candidate the Republicans will finally run. If it is Eisenhower, he will have to refurbish the image of the man of peace. If it is someone else, it will be all the harder for Eisenhower to rub off onto him his own prestige as a peacemaker.

★

JULY 21, 1956

CONVENTION EVE

Now that President Eisenhower has again declared himself ready to be a candidate, breaking the news with an elaborate casualness, Americans are on the eve of the most bizarre presidential campaign in their history. It will be one in which the Republicans will stress Eisenhower's ruggedness while attacking anyone who dares mention his health, and the Democrats will insist on every public occasion that the health of an invalid with an exiguous life expectancy is strictly his own private affair. It will be the first American campaign ever conducted in the manner of Rembrandt's *Anatomy Lesson,* with the new tribe of medico-political doctors acting as the unacknowledged legislators of opinion. It will be a campaign waged as a great civil war of X rays, testing whether the American voter is still one of the incalculables or whether he is the Electronic Man, responding to a feedback circuit.

While no one can foretell the result, the shape of the struggle to come is already fairly clear, allowing, of course, for some "acts of God" like those that have dominated the past year. President Eisenhower has proved that the greatest wonder of contemporary America is not the Grand Canyon or Niagara Falls but his own persisting popularity and physical resilience. He has now survived a massive heart attack and a major intestinal operation, and survived them not only physically but politically. Never in American history has this happened to a president and presidential candidate. It bears witness to several things: to the deep affection Americans of every class and both parties feel toward him; to the canny way his managers have handled the whole medical and nomination issue, especially Sherman Adams and James Hagerty; to the new role of "public relations" skills in American politics, and the almost unanimous support that the big communications empires have given the Republican managers; to Eisenhower's own greatly underrated instinct as a politician.

The performance is the more impressive because he has so little factual base. Two weeks before his heart attack the president told a group of his party associates, "Human beings are frail—and they are mortal," and he warned them against pinning their flag too tightly to one mast, and being "dependent on one man." Such words from him or any other Republican today would be heresy, yet he was right then. He is not the indispensable president—as witness the abilities Adlai Stevenson would bring to the office. Nor is he the indispensable Republican candidate, as witness Earl Warren, who would win the election handsomely and would cut into independent and Democratic votes more deeply than Eisenhower himself. But Eisenhower is indispensable to the Republican leaders. His popular appeal has been pretested. Moreover, they know where he stands, while Warren would be an unknown quantity. Eisenhower has been flexible enough to take over much of the Democratic welfare-state program, yet in basic economic matters has proved himself deeply conservative.

He has also proved himself a passive president and party leader, never pushing presidential power hard against congressional, nor federal power against the state's, nor his own party leadership against the "dinosaur wing" of the Republicans. Bored with the day-to-day decisions that spell out policy he has relegated them to a staff headed by Sherman Adams, so that on issues like the response to the internal Russian "new era," or the question of foreign economic aid, the Eisenhower administration has spoken with a Babel of conflicting voices. He has shunned controversial topics. He has failed to press hard for the legislation to which he has committed himself. Yet in a total evaluation it would have to be said that in some of the clinches (Geneva, the McCarthy Senate censure, the veto of the natural-gas bill and the first farm bill) he has somehow managed to assert his power and has shown much of the guile of the fox, if little of the regal wrath of the lion. Most of all he has known how to maintain before the people the image of a nonpolitical, kindly daddy figure, far above the battle of politicians—and thereby shown himself one of the shrewdest politicians in the history of the presidency. Even in his illnesses the daddy figure has applied—for daddies do get heart attacks and have to undergo operations with strange technical names, and good children wait for them to get better, following the whole medical odyssey of an ileum with absorbed interest and never losing their faith.

The Democrats believe there is a junta that has maneuvered Eisenhower into running, but surely this is only half of the scissors. The other half is that Ike, too, wants Ike to run. Robert Donovan, who was given extraordinary access to administration material to write *The Inside Story*, says that Eisenhower spent "five weeks of torment" at Gettysburg when he was recovering from his heart attack. He is not a Cincinnatus to retire contentedly to his wife and plough, but a man who needs to be nourished on the power and glory of his office. The ileitis attack, as evidenced by the prevailing medical literature, is a more serious matter than Ike and his circle have dared admit. Its danger to his candidacy must have frightened Eisenhower a good deal more than its danger to his life. As a good soldier and a good politician he has come to care less about length of years than about tenure and power. Hence the studied casualness with which he let it be known that he is still running.

Despite the evidence of the pollsters that the election will be a runaway, it is not a wholly valueless garland that the Democrats will bestow at their August convention, although it may prove a prickly one

to wear. Anything can happen before November to make the straw
polls archaic. There is already some evidence that the health issue is
more seriously present in the minds of the voters than before the president's ileitis attack.

The clearest development in recent months has been the transformation of Adlai Stevenson from an "egghead" candidate into a
human and earthy political figure. Like the Lincoln he admires,
Stevenson thrives on adversity. After his defeat in the Minnesota primaries by Kefauver (largely, it would now appear, through a skillfully
planned infiltration of Republican votes), he settled down to the "weight
lifting" local contests and went through a barnstorming and hand-
shaking ordeal from which he seemed to get a wry sort of enjoyment.
His "comeback," culminating in the California primary in early June,
was so complete that it not only eliminated Senator Kefauver effectively from the convention race but seriously dented the hopes of the
other hopefuls.

While it is reckless to predict the course of an American presidential convention, I am willing to go out on a few limbs. "I am now
the man to beat," says Stevenson, and while his first challenge will
come from Averell Harriman (to whom Estes Kefauver will throw his
own strength), the real showdown is likely to be with Senator Stuart
Symington. The "moderates" who will control the Southern delegations are strongly opposed to Harriman and would certainly prefer
Stevenson, but many of them—and also many of the Northern and
Midwestern conservatives—would scuttle Stevenson if Symington
made a show of strength. But Symington, who has made headlines
only with his sustained efforts for the maintenance of big armaments,
especially in the air, is not a likely opponent of an Eisenhower whose
main appeal is that of a peacemaker. While tenacious of principle,
Stevenson has been careful to take no positions that would play into
Eisenhower's strengths, or would divide the Democrats.

As for Harry Truman's role at the convention, he will clearly be
one of the decisive voices there, along with Sam Rayburn, Lyndon
Johnson, and the city political bosses. But Truman, as a good party
man, is concerned only with getting a candidate who can win, pledged
to a clear platform and a militant campaign. While not a Stevenson en-
thusiast, he will back him strongly if he is the convention choice, as he
is likely to be.

For second place on the ticket the names most frequently heard
are those of Senator Kennedy of Massachusetts and Mayor Wagner of

New York—both younger men and both Catholics. Both are good men, but it is a sign of the continuing shadows cast by the 1952 red-baiting speeches of McCarthy and Nixon alike that it should be thought desirable to flank Stevenson with a running mate who can keep the Catholic vote.

The real anguish of the Democrats, however, is over the issue of civil rights for Negroes in the South. The Emmett Till lynching in Mississippi and the Autherine Lucy case, keeping her out of the University of Alabama, stirred South and North alike, and marked a major effort of the Southern diehards to sabotage the Supreme Court decision on school desegregation. There are two phases of the Southern rebellion that will have an impact on the elections—the vote of the Southern states and the vote of the Northern Negroes. Of the two the second easily holds more danger for the Democrats, although the first has received more public attention.

For a time there was talk of Southern secession from the Democratic Convention, but the trouncing defeat that "moderate" Lyndon Johnson gave to "Dixiecrat" Governor Allan Shivers of Texas in the state Democratic convention surprised even the moderates and settled for good the issue of secession—unless the nominee were to be Harriman, who has become (quite wrongly) a symbol of wrath for the Southerners. The historical fact is that since the Wilson election in 1912, no Democratic president has needed the "solid South" for his victory, although it has helped to have it. Because of the great election odds against him, Stevenson is more likely to need it. But the contemporary fact is that the Southern Democrats have nowhere else to go except the Democratic Party, on which they depend for their seniority in Congress and their wholly disproportionate share of committee chairmanships. While Eisenhower continues to be popular in the South, and has carefully avoided doing or saying anything that would alienate southerners in the current civil rights controversy, the South associates the Supreme Court decision with the name of Earl Warren, a Republican.

The Negroes in the big cities of New York, Pennsylvania, Ohio, Michigan, Illinois, Missouri, and California have achieved something close to a balance-of-power position in the presidential voting. Since the days of Roosevelt and the New Deal they have voted strongly Democratic, but in 1952 Eisenhower made inroads into this monopoly. The name of Senator James Eastland of Mississippi, fanatic champion of white supremacy, who became head of the Senate Judiciary

Committee in a Democratic-controlled Congress, has become a powerful argument against continued Negro allegiance to the Democrats. The leaders of the powerful Negro organization the NAACP have been flirting with the idea of turning to the Republicans, and it is expected that one of Nixon's duties in carrying the brunt of the campaign speaking will be to make a powerful play for the Negro vote. To counter this, Stevenson will have the active campaign support of Mrs. Roosevelt, who remains a great symbol for American Negroes. In the primaries in Washington, D.C., and California, Stevenson did best in the heavily Negro districts, despite the gaffe he made in an earlier statement on "gradualism" in the civil rights struggle.

What is really bleak for the Democrats is their lack of money and therefore of TV time. Scarcely out of debt on the 1952 campaign the Democrats now face an even more expensive one, in which the corporate money and the bandwagon money will all be at the service of the Republicans. The Republican National Committee has announced that it plans a $7 million presidential campaign, but every study of past expenditures confirms the hunch that the announced figures are only a fraction of the money actually spent. It has been estimated that the Republicans spent between $50 and $100 million last time, and the figures this time (including the congressional races as well) are likely to be higher. The Democrats can come nowhere near matching it. As a result they despair of being able to get to the people their version of the issues. The situation is made worse by the crassness with which a one-party press (which is more than an epithet in America) has played down the Democratic viewpoint.

Two unpartisan leaders of the "opinion industries" have made an effort to bring back a competition of ideas into American elections, but their efforts have not been embraced. Philip Graham, publisher of the *Washington Post*, tried to organize a public TV appeal for campaign funds for both parties, but it was sabotaged by Leonard Hall, the Republican National Chairman, who backed out of an earlier agreement to go along. Frank Stanton, CBS president, proposed that the TV chains grant equal time on a public-service basis to both major parties, but there has been no visible enthusiasm among Republicans.

The Republicans will have in this campaign not only the Man and the Money but the effective slogans as well. Their two watchwords will be Peace and Prosperity, and they plan to combine the two in the slogan that under the Eisenhower administration "everything is booming but the guns." A few things might happen, of course, to upset this slo-

gan. The farmers' income has not kept up with the rest of the economy, but the Republican strategists have tried to deal with that temporarily by setting up "soil bank" subsidy payments. To deal with the
inflation danger the Federal Reserve Bank has tightened interest rates,
and tight money is never welcomed by the "ins" in an election year.
The clumsy handling of the Middle East crisis by Eisenhower and
Dulles has alienated the "Jewish vote," but it is probably too slight to
count for much. The Big Giveaway is more than ever an issue, but
Eisenhower's natural-gas veto will count against it.

The only foreseeable pattern on which the Democrats might win
rests on the assumption that the real campaign issue will be none of
those I have mentioned above, but the question of presidential health
and the presidential succession. Whether he likes it or not, the president will be the focus of anxious and watchful eyes all through the
campaign. If he gets a cold it will be a setback, if he has to cancel a
speech it will be a disaster; but if defiantly he drives himself too hard,
he risks a real breakdown.

"A vote for Eisenhower is a vote for Nixon" is the slogan on which
the more earthy Democratic strategists are pinning their hopes.

★

SEPTEMBER 1, 1956

THE ELECTRONIC CONVENTION

San Francisco—What J. B. Priestley calls the New Society—and what
Graham Wallas saw a half century ago, peering with his owl-like wisdom into the darkness ahead—had its formal unveiling in full-fledged
splendor at the San Francisco Republican Convention. The idea of a
convention as a democratic arena—"a darkling plain swept by confused alarums of struggle and flight"—still had some force at Chicago,
but none at San Francisco. It was wholly an electronic convention.

The decisions had been reached beforehand, not even in the traditional last-minute "smoke-filled room," but in the Eisenhower high
command. There were no rival candidates, either to Eisenhower or to
Nixon. It was a one-button convention, with no competing buttons for
anyone outside the orthodox "team." It was a sewed-up convention,
with no scope for delegate freedom and no recourse from the deci-

sions. And since the delegates had nothing to do except to say "Arkansas passes" or "Texas passes," when asked for other nominations, it became perforce a carnival convention—a mink-bedecked, diamond-studded, champagne-flowing Mardi Gras, discreetly Babylonian, with not enough genuinely high spirits to make it even lustily vulgar.

This convention established at least two "firsts." It was the first in American history to nominate both its candidates without a dissenting voice, doing better even than a Soviet collective farm or a Nasser election in Egypt. It was also the first to have been "produced," like a Hollywood movie or a TV "spectacular," with George Murphy in charge of the general production and Robert Montgomery in charge of the TV delivery and histrionics of the two candidates. Even the seconding speeches for Eisenhower were staged with the same mechanical precision: the managers picked the seconders—a Texas Protestant mother, a Catholic ex-football coach, a young Southerner, a Negro woman professor, a Midwest farmer, a Catholic member of a steelworkers' union, and a Boston Jewish woman—as if they were using an International Business Machine. Even Providence was drawn into the production when Nixon left dramatically for the bedside of his dying father on the day he was to be nominated, and returned the next day to accept the nomination and tell his TV audience that his father had rallied because of the "tonic" effect of the choice of his son.

In the effort to give a lifeless convention some color there were elaborately staged "demonstrations" for "Ike and Dick" that were overprepared and synthetic. At one point, when a maniac member of the production staff thought of releasing a barrage of toy balloons from the ceiling just before the president rose to make his acceptance speech, and the TV screen showed some unbelievable shots of the President of the United States pelting and being pelted by balloons, a Japanese correspondent watching it smiled his most courtly smile and commented, "Very childish, don't you think so?" Perhaps it was this element of childishness that saved the convention from being even more of a portent than it was. It is hard to believe that the TV audience was wholly taken in by the blandishments and failed to see some of the idiocies of a convention that was half a Shriners' conclave and half a political-party monolith.

The monolithic part contained the element of menace. The personality cult of Eisenhower has been building up ever since the 1952 campaign and has reached unparalleled heights since his illnesses. Yet in itself it would be tolerable—especially since the cult object is ingratiating and not over solemn about it. But that cannot be said of the drive to put over the Nixon nomination, which had elements of behind-the-scenes manipulation along with an open hysteria.

There are many who now doubt whether the Nixon nomination could ever have been stopped. I think it could have been if the president had acted firmly six months ago, when he was recovering from his heart attack and knew how important the second man would be if he were himself reelected. The president has expressed, with a formal correctness, his sense of Nixon's "dedicated" and "efficient" and "able" work, but I don't know anyone close to the high command who has been willing to say that the president wholly trusts Nixon to carry on his work. But Nixon has been the darling of the Hoover-Taft-McCarthy wing of the party, mainly because of the Alger Hiss case but also because his record in Congress was on the reactionary side. He also carried many of the campaign burdens in the 1952 and 1954 campaigns, and built up a party following among the professionals. When Eisenhower, who lacked the courage in 1952 to drop Nixon under fire, again hesitated to decide one way or another about him in the early months of 1956, Thomas Dewey saw the wave of the future and went over to Nixon. The alliance of the Taft and Dewey professionals was too powerful to beat. The only thing that could undercut it was the fact that Nixon is heartily disliked not only by most Democrats and many independents but even by a segment of Republicans.

This is what Harold Stassen tried to use in his belated campaign to dump Nixon, using sample poll figures that have every mark of being authentic and that show Nixon as a weak running mate. But Stassen started late and clumsily. At the convention itself the feeling against him as a party "traitor" was skillfully maneuvered into a pro-Nixon sentiment. Stassen himself was surrounded by a near-lynching hatred, and one of his supporters—the head of the Missouri delegation—was actually roughed up. Stassen never had much of a chance with the delegates, but when the psychic intensity of the Nixon forces frightened off any chance of Eisenhower intervention, Stassen folded and seconded Nixon's nomination in pathetic surrender. His final failure of nerve was exceeded only by the cowardice of the anti-Nixon people who had not dared to speak when Stassen started his drive.

There are some Republicans who are heartened by the "liberalism" of the two acceptance speeches, and argue that Eisenhower is trying to rebuild his party and take it away from the isolationists and the primitives. They forget that the right wing of the party is quiescent now only because Eisenhower is the only resource the party has, and only through him can they stay in power. The right-wingers showed their continuing strength by refusing to follow Eisenhower on crucial parts of his congressional program. On the crucial test—the Nixon nomination—they showed that they could outmaneuver the liberal wing if Eisenhower kept his hands off.

Once he is elected they will no longer need him. If it should happen that he cannot serve out his term, they will have a successor in the White House for whom they have high hopes, even if they, too, do not wholly trust him. If Eisenhower does serve out his term they will come out in the open in 1960, renewing the deep internal struggle for the soul of the Republican Party. The reason why San Francisco was a phantom convention was that the automation, the hoopla, and the monolithic surface concealed the existence of this struggle.

✮

NOVEMBER 7, 1956

When you measure the massiveness of Eisenhower's victory you glimpse the full outlines of the American urge to cling to normalcy in a time of world disorder, and to worship at the shrine of an immaculate daddy figure in a time when little children are afraid.

It isn't just the morning-after mood that brings to my mind a sentence from a letter of Tom Wolfe's, the last letter he wrote—"I've made a long journey and been to a strange country, and I've seen the dark man very close." It has been a long campaign for all of us. In a real sense the campaign began with General Eisenhower's first illness, when he had to decide whether he would run and the country started to decide whether it wanted him. We have seen many strange things in the course of this long journey. And we have glimpsed, much too closely, the particular "dark man" I have in mind—the figure of an American electorate that shuts its mind to logic and reason and the evidence of events and makes a cult of one man's personality because it has been shrewdly fashioned and shrewdly sold.

The victory belongs not to Eisenhower but to the traits in the American people that have made him the dominant figure on the political horizon. The victory belongs to what is popular and fashionable, to what is familiar and comfortable because it is mediocre, to the "adjusting man" who adjusts to what everyone is doing. It is the triumph of conformity.

It is too easy for us to talk of the Republican "slogans" as the key to the landslide. If slogans alone could win, then Madison Avenue would become the permanent ruling group of the nation. The real point is that this time the slogans "took" because of the elements in the contemporary situation and contemporary character that prepared people's minds for them.

Despite the anguished mood of those for whom the election results are dismal, the republic will, of course, survive even four more years under the Republicans. American industry will continue to boom, not because of the wisdom of those who own and run the country but because of the magnificent technological plants and skills we have. Money will continue to flow. Violence will continue to erupt all around the rim of disintegrating empires, and daddy will continue to issue reassuring bulletins.

It should be clear from this that the Republican victory leaves me unconvinced and unreconstructed. I accept the verdict of the jury in the sense in which we all accept wrongheaded verdicts that seem to go against all the evidence and are the product of a mental fixation the jury had even before the trial began.

But the fact that Eisenhower's popularity has been vindicated doesn't make a peerless leader out of a confused man struggling with hackneyed thoughts. Readers of *War and Peace* will remember Tolstoy's description of General Kutuzov, who felt that a general can do little more than watch the battle and smile reassuringly while he pretends to know what is happening and why.

General Eisenhower is our General Kutuzov. He continues to be a powerful symbol because he meets the needs of those who want to believe in something, and who fix on a man because they are too shallow and scared to think for themselves. Nietzsche wrote that "it is only the great thought that gives greatness to an action." There is no greatness of thought in Eisenhower, just as there is no real passion of belief in those who voted for him. Their victory seems a curiously joyless affair, as if they had a bad conscience and retained a lingering doubt about the verdict they rendered.

Some very good men went down under this Eisenhower wave, and some evil men have been floated on the wave into positions of power in Congress. The election has proved a triumph not only of conformity but also of coattails.

It is as if those little levers, all in a row, were lined up like good little soldiers. Once you pulled the first it took a giant intellectual effort not to pull down all the rest. "We do not ride on the railroad," said Thoreau. "It rides on us." One might say that the people didn't run the election; the election ran the people, by the same principle of mechanism that made them respond to the slogans and the smile and the arms held high as a sign that all will forever be well.

But just as Eisenhower's victory doesn't make him a great man, so Stevenson's defeat doesn't make him into a small one. Whatever his mistakes of strategy (and it is always the loser who turns out to have made all the mistakes), he fought hard, he stuck to his ideas, he went down with integrity as well as with grace. He would have made a president of the first rank. Even in defeat he may have contributed more to the processes of democracy by the nature of his campaign than Eisenhower contributed even in victory. For while Stevenson's proved a lost cause, Eisenhower has proved the lost leader. It is a tragic waste of great human material to send a man like Stevenson into political obscurity.

But it is idle to shed tears over political might-have-beens. The causes for which Stevenson and Kefauver fought still remain to be fought for in the years ahead. Two years from now and four years from now the factor of the personality cult will no longer be present in the elections. The Democratic Party is still a strong party, and it contains fresher energies and younger and more committed men and women than it has contained for some time.

Meanwhile there is the reality of an ailing president who, with all his faults, is a man of goodwill; and behind him the reality of an heir apparent whom all the synthetic perfumes of his recent campaigning have not washed clean.

1960

KENNEDY vs. NIXON

JULY 14, 1960

LOS ANGELES—THEY HAILED the conqueror, and a new hero came into a political culture where hero-types die hard and bring heartbreak when they die, and in which a new political man is struggling to be born.

Before we push the past wholly into the obscurity of musty files and memoirs it is worth saying that no good fight for a deeply felt cause is ever wholly wasted or lost. Lyndon Johnson fought a lusty fight, yet the notable one was that of the Stevenson cohorts.

Their wished miracle was never achieved, the dream and hope on which they operated never materialized. There is a wistful sadness among the Stevenson faithful who brought to the nomination proceedings the only note of passionate caring that was sounded all day.

While the outward struggle was between Johnson and Kennedy, there was a more subtle one between the Stevenson and Kennedy forces. The North-South fight was marked by genuine differences of social outlook, which will form a continuing problem during the campaign. The Stevenson-Kennedy fight was not over basic issues, since both men represent the liberal wing of the Democratic Party. It was a matter of choice between two different kinds of leadership, two moods and temperaments whose differences are not easy to define yet are important to understand.

One way of putting the difference is to see it as one between a reflective man for whom action comes at the end of a complex analysis, and an action man for whom reflection is a prelude to action. Perhaps the best epitaph on the Stevenson hero-type was the general post-mortem comment in his camp: "We started too late"—something that could never be said of the Kennedy hero-type. There is a heady sense of triumph among the men who planned, organized, and executed the Kennedy victory with a precision rarely achieved in the loose and sloppy entity called the Democratic Party.

Adlai Stevenson was the kind of political figure who, like a great novelist or artist, creates a world that bears his unmistakable stamp. If I didn't understand this earlier I understood it when I watched the demonstration at the convention.

The people who took part in it—Negro and white, young and old, poor, middling, and rich—couldn't have explained their almost fanatical intensity by any position Stevenson has taken on any particular issue. All you could say was that he had about him an awareness of greatness. They were caught up in his world of intangibles, as a reader is caught up in the world a novelist weaves out of his own and the reader's sensitiveness and dreams.

I was going to say that Kennedy will in time create his similar world, but that would miss the whole point. Kennedy as a new political figure is interested in the means by which a given end will be achieved. We are entering an era in which political leadership, like almost everything else in our culture, is handed over to the technicians. Give them the ends, and they will find the means. That is the kind of man this new political man is. That is Jack Kennedy.

He is easily one of the most brilliant political technicians who has come on the American scene since Franklin Roosevelt. We can count on his skill, his timing, his perceptiveness, his adroitness of maneuver. Above all, we can count on his intense will to complete whatever job he takes on, and to win.

What this means is that John Kennedy will be as good as—and no better than—the frame of ends and values within which he works. He is not the sort of man who can himself create this frame. But he has the right instincts, as Harry Truman had; and he has the perceptiveness to select from the thinking of those around him those ends that are most in tune with the nature and needs of our times.

This has already been illustrated by the forthrightness and generosity of the Democratic platform, which was fashioned so largely under his influence, and presumably with his complete assent.

But the crucial tests of the ends and values to which Kennedy will commit himself are still to come. One is the selection of a vice presidential running mate. This is more than a technical matter to be settled by the often mistaken lore of political professionals. If Kennedy fails to choose a genuine liberal to run with him, much of the impact of the Democratic platform will be lost.

More important is the kind of campaign he wages, and whether he does it with a bold imaginativeness or with a niggardly failure of commitments.

The Democrats have a new man. He has a chance to rise to greatness or to remain merely a good technician.

★

Los Angeles—In his first two acts after getting the presidential nomination, candidate Kennedy managed to make a blunder and start a commotion.

His little speech after his nomination, by omitting any mention of Adlai Stevenson, showed an unnecessary lack of generosity and raised a serious question as to whether Stevenson will get that long-dangled job as secretary of state.

And his choice of Lyndon Johnson as his vice presidential running mate has plunged the convention into a furious debate as to what this move shows about Kennedy's thinking on his larger campaign strategy, and his quality as a political leader.

My own view is that Kennedy acted out of a political instinct which, if properly understood, sheds a good deal of light on his political quality. He refused to let the vice presidency go to a free convention choice.

He made the choice himself out of motives and reasoning that must have seemed good to him. This was his first act of leadership since his nomination. It must be set down as an act of major political cynicism, by a man who is confident that he will get away with it.

Put most baldly, Kennedy was faced with two choices in making his decision. One was to pick a running mate who would symbolize his concern about the liberal farm vote and civil rights vote, on both of which his support is pretty shaky. The other was to pick one who would symbolize his concern about the disaffected Southern states and the economic conservatives within the party.

He made his choice clearly and dramatically. What it amounts to is a political gamble that he can count on the liberal voters because, given the Nixon alternative, they have nowhere else to go, but that he must woo the South and the conservatives.

On grounds of sheer political cynicism the Kennedy decision may be wrong or right, but the important fact is that it was made on these grounds by a man whose every move is being watched for indications of what kind of man he is.

I don't know whether it was the result of pressure from Johnson and the Southerners, or whether Johnson had to be persuaded. You can buy both versions here at Los Angles, but the question is not crucial. Whether he had to be pushed or did the pushing, Kennedy must take responsibility for the decision.

Nor is it even a question of Lyndon Johnson's own basic qualities. I happen to think that he is a man of great ability and maturity, and that on civil rights he is a Southern moderate with a considerable fund of realism. He will preside well over the Senate, and will be available to use his persuasiveness among his former colleagues.

But this first act of Kennedy's was a crucial symbolic act. If he capitulated to pressure his courage must be questioned. If he took the initiative then his basic drive toward liberalism must be questioned.

One of the favorite defenses offered here by some of the Democratic intellectuals who believe in Kennedy's liberalism is that he is following a pattern set by Franklin Roosevelt when he ran with Garner in 1932 and when he later scuttled Henry Wallace as vice president in 1944. This is part of the larger perspective that sees Kennedy as the Roosevelt of 1960.

He may be, but not on any evidence I am yet able to see. The civil rights picture in 1932 was not what it is in 1960, nor was Garner in any sense a symbolic Roosevelt choice.

As for the 1944 decision, it came after Roosevelt had established the pattern of his presidential leadership over the course of twelve years. Kennedy is not yet president, and the nature of his leadership and political direction is exactly what is in question.

During the early days of the convention the argument for Kennedy as a militant liberal was based on the fight he put up against the Johnson candidacy and the forces behind it, and also upon the civil rights plank. If Kennedy's defenders used this reasoning they cannot regard the choice of Johnson as anything but a refutation of their logic and a repudiation of their hopes.

There is serious question as to whether Kennedy's move was a smart one, even if it is seen in terms of political cynicism. I don't believe that the Democrats can take the support of the liberal farm states, the trade-union groups, and the big-city Negro votes for granted. Nixon will prove a formidable antagonist and will know how to exploit every point at which Kennedy is vulnerable with these groups. The Democrats will have to give some evidence that their platform declarations are more than words.

Kennedy and his advisers may discover one of the truths of American political history—that for the Democrats the courageous decision on liberal principles almost always turns out to be the politically smart decision as well, and the one that plays angles without principles leaves only a dusty answer behind, without victory. I hope they won't make this discovery too late.

★

SEPTEMBER 27, 1960

History has often turned on the hinge of a single event, and the current, fateful presidential campaign may in the end prove to have turned on the first Nixon-Kennedy debate and its successors.

Up to then the campaign had gone sluggish. Each of the candidates was running, as the phrase has it, like a dry creek. Each was working away at his campaign in a kind of isolation, local segment by local segment. The prevailing mood was of apathy, doubt, indifference, lack of commitment.

What was needed to make the campaign come alive was a direct confrontation of the candidates. This the first debate provided. It was no Lincoln-Douglas affair, but it had drama, dignity, and tension. The UN debates helped, since the audience that had watched them must have wondered why the living drama of the world crisis could not rub off on the contest that was to decide who would lead America in that crisis. For the first time also, an audience of the leaders of the world's nations was able, like the American audience, to size up the two candidates as they confronted each other and the world, faced the same problems, answered the same questions.

I should guess that this debate furnished Kennedy with his first real breakthrough. The vast audience had a chance to compare two programs for the nation, two visions of its future, two men as personalities. It was an exacting thing to watch, demanding much of the viewer-listener, since he had constantly not only to absorb what he saw and heard but also to make reassessments of both men at each point. An hour is not a long stretch for this purpose, but it is long enough for

a judgment to emerge. On all three scores—program, vision, man—
the judgment seemed to me strongly to favor Kennedy, at Nixon's expense.

Curiously the whole debate turned on the nature of the welfare
state that has come to stay in America. If the debate had been between
Kennedy and Barry Goldwater the issue would have been sharp. Between Kennedy and Nixon it was blurred by Nixon's I-agree-with-
your-ends-but-not-means attitude. But Kennedy had the advantage
because on every phase of the welfare state they discussed—minimum
wage, health insurance, farm aid, federal aid to education—Kennedy
was affirming while Nixon was qualifying, Kennedy was on the offensive while Nixon was on the defensive.

If anyone doubted Kennedy's liberal position before, there is no
longer any basis for doubt. But along with the program itself, what
counted was the passion behind it. Here is a man who in a brief spell of
time, under the stress of events, has found maturity because he has
found conviction. His answers were not learned by rote, to be repeated
parrotlike; they came readily and swiftly because they were part of
what he felt.

But the sharpest difference lay in the two men themselves. Both
were being sedulously careful, of course, to present themselves at their
best. Kennedy tried not to look boyish, Nixon tried to dispel the old
picture of the hatchet man and to present an unfailing sweet reason-
ableness. But there are limits to what you can do in doctoring your image. The truth manages to come through.

Nixon emerged as an anxious man, overeager, overexplaining, re-
peating himself, assuring everyone of his opponent's sincerity and his
own. At one point his tension was so great that he offered by inadver-
tence to "get rid of the farmers" before he stumbled into the clear to
get rid only of their surpluses. If a team of psychologists were watching and comparing notes, their reports on Nixon as a personality
would be worth reading. The product of an age of anxiety, he showed
the characteristic marks of his era.

Kennedy, by contrast, was alert, crisp, quietly confident. His
economy speech revealed a spare and muscular mind. An intellectual,
he sought neither to hide nor parade that quality. He spoke and
thought swiftly, and his words—while rarely memorable—were the
right words in the right place. He could demolish an argument in two
sentences. He knew his stuff, as Nixon did too, but he marshaled it
more effectively.

Curiously the whole issue of "experience" had the sawdust stuffing knocked out of it. Kennedy has had the same length of national experience as Nixon, who sounded boyish in his effort to puff up the consequences of his trips abroad. As for the vaunted ability to stand up to Khrushchev, Nixon was so busy being sweetly reasonable that the image of the tough talker grew tarnished. If anyone emerged as strong enough to express America in the world crisis, it was the Massachusetts senator, who cares so deeply that he is angry at what the amateurs have done.

★

OCTOBER 28, 1960

Cleveland—I have spent two days deep in Republican territory at Omaha, Lincoln, and Norfolk, Nebraska, speaking to teachers on non-party themes, and now I am in Cleveland, where the smell of victory is Democratic. But whether among Republicans or Democrats there is no question that Kennedy's brand of campaigning has left an impact. Several weeks ago I wrote a column on the mind, personality, and character of Richard Nixon. This is meant as a companion piece on John Kennedy.

It is too early to measure all his shortcomings and his full stature, but all of America has now had a chance to study him and a pretty clear estimate is emerging. If elected he would be a young president as presidents go, but he is young chiefly in the sense that he still has dreams and that nothing seems impossible to him, about either his own future or America's.

He was born to wealth, and doors closed to young Americans of lesser means have been open to him. I doubt however whether this should or will count against him, despite Nixon's current not-so-oblique jibes at his private resources. The America of Franklin Roosevelt, Averell Harrimann, and Nelson Rockefeller is beyond resenting this accident of birth. What most people ask is that the money be used meaningfully and that the man for whom they vote should strain his energies beyond money values. Even more they ask with whom the man identifies himself. As someone has remarked, in this campaign Kennedy is the poor man's rich man and Nixon the rich man's poor man.

He has a mind of his own, divergent from his father's, uncaptive to the hierarchy of his church, persistent in refusing to follow its declared policies on anything that would diminish the traditional American separation of church and state. When the hierarchy has asked for public aid to parochial schools, Lodge and (to a lesser extent) Nixon have bent to its pressures, while Kennedy has construed the constitutional precedents strictly against such a breach of the wall of separation, and has had the strength to resist the pressures.

Even more important, he *has* a mind. It will be a refreshing thing once again, after so bleak an interval, to have a man with intellectual tastes and capacities in the White House. The curious notion, so widespread in the 1952 and 1956 campaigns, that it would be dangerous to have brains in the presidency, has been burned away in the fiery furnace of recent American reverses. John Adams and Thomas Jefferson, Madison, Lincoln, both Roosevelts, Wilson—these men had minds, whatever the political furniture with which they embellished them. Kennedy, in his own way, is not too far behind them in his concern with ideas and with the life of the mind.

His own mind is spare, economical, hard-driving, as so much else about him is. It lacks the verbal magic of Adlai Stevenson, yet it has energy and always it hits at the jugular of a problem. It has command of what material it needs. It is a mind moreover that can command others, pick their brains, use their knowledge and skills, infect them with the will to win.

Just as Kennedy's education has been secular, so his conditionings have been mainly in the liberal direction. He has had to learn many things from hard experience, but he has been open to its lessons. He is not afraid of the burdens of big government and knows that there can be no fulfilled individualism for the lowly and the lonely except in the frame of state action against what oppresses them.

He is part of the tough-minded liberal American tradition of self-criticism. Aloof as his life has been from the life of the mass of people he does not have the contempt and condescension for them that his adversary has shown. He has talked to them on the assumption that they are mature enough to know the truth about their country, and intelligent enough not to be treated as children.

Nixon has been talking about the "hydra-headed" Democratic leadership. He should be more interested in another Greek myth—that of the Medusa head, which men were fearful of facing lest it turn them to stone. To be willing to face the Medusa head of today's world a man must know himself—know who he is, what he wants, where he is going, how he proposes to get there. This is what we mean by identity, and Kennedy has identity.

He has grown perceptibly in the course of his hard campaign for the nomination, and even more in these recent weeks of the fierce fight for the election. He has the stuff of growth in him, and if we dare project into the next four years the path and pace of his growth in the past year he would—if elected—make one of the strongest and most effective presidents America will have had.

In this growth he has found somehow that relation between leader and people—beyond cold logic, beyond what is visible of him to them—which every president has had since Franklin Roosevelt. I am speaking of some circuit of relation set in motion between him and the crowds who come to see and hear him and even touch him, of the spark of human connection with them that Richard Nixon has never been able to achieve for all his straining, just as Hoover and Landon and Dewey never achieved it.

He will, if elected, once more attract to Washington and the government's service the kind of talented, brainy, committed young Americans who flocked there from the universities in the days of the New Deal and who have since been replaced by wooden men. America will have a hard struggle to win the future even with them. Without them it has little chance.

★

NOVEMBER 8, 1960

Boston—Jack Kennedy came back here to the Boston of his boyhood and university days and was given an idol's reception by a crowd that went gaga at the prospect of having one of their own in the White House. He didn't say much because he didn't have to. The crowd knew where he stood and could have finished every sentence they interrupted with their animal roar of acclaim. He has said his say for the past year and it has been a good say, with clean edges and with manly assertiveness. His last broadcast ended a brilliant campaign, which deserves to be rounded out by a resounding victory.

Thus we write an end to the whole business. Nothing quite like this, either as spectacle or experience, can be found on the same scale of magnitude and intensity anywhere in the world or in world history.

Call it what you will—nonsensical, fanatical, hysterical, comical, synthetic, boisterous, rancorous, incredible. Call it carnival or medieval
ordeal by fire. Say in world-weary fashion that it lasts too long, costs
too much, solves too little, and exhausts everyone, victors and van-
quished alike. Say you have had it and are relieved that it won't return
for another four years.

But when it comes to achieving a succession of power in a society,
don't pretend you know of any other way that is so dramatic, authentic,
exasperating, incalculable, impressive, and expressive as an American
presidential campaign. And even in your last cynical and sophisticated
moments, don't pretend that you would have it much different if you
had a long, clean parchment in front of you and freedom to write a new
constitution.

Jack Kennedy ended his final mile unflaggingly, with the same
combination of buoyancy and earnestness that made him master of the
campaign. Whatever its outcome, he received what Bostonians have
come to call the "last hurrah" with grace and hurried on to Hyannis-
port. I shall be returning to New York today to cast my vote. But before I do I want to raise my own too-feeble last hurrah for a remarkable
man who will—if the votes fall right—make a remarkable president.

It is usual, in a final preelection column, to say some sacred nonsense about how everything is now over and may the best man et
cetera. I won't pretend to such an Olympian above-the-battle calm.
The campaign, or, rather, the subterranean campaign, against
Kennedy was not a clean thing. The roots of bigotry went deep and its
shadow was sinister. If Kennedy is beaten overwhelmingly this factor
will not have been the decisive one. If he is beaten by a narrow margin,
meaning by a bigotry margin, it will be an ugly scar on the American
conscience.

But I find it hard to believe he will be beaten. We have, in our
time, witnessed few movements of popular feeling as strong and assertive as the upsurge of feeling for John Kennedy since the first TV
debate. It matches the feeling for Roosevelt and is more intense than
the genial, glowing feeling for Eisenhower. The Nixon people have
drummed up their crowds too and they have been vociferous. But what
a distance between the thunder of sunrise in Kennedy's receptions and
the heartbreak of declining day in Nixon's.

It has been said that Kennedy marks the coming of a new generation on the stage of American political history. This ignores the fact
that Nixon belongs, at least chronologically, to the same generation as
Kennedy. Their ages are separated by only four years, yet there is a

weariness in Nixon's thinking even when he is most violent in his language, while there is a sense of newness in Kennedy's, even in his platitudes.

If Kennedy wins it will be despite the electoral tandem of Nixon and Eisenhower, which should have proved one of the strongest of our time, since Eisenhower's age and prestige were added to Nixon's youth and energy.

If Kennedy wins it will be despite the Republican edge on TV time, the last splurge (now estimated at $600,000) on the four-hour telethon, and the support of newspapers for Nixon by a circulation ratio of some four and a half to one.

If Kennedy wins it will be despite the encrusted primitive anti-Catholic feeling among many fundamentalists and even among some who style themselves liberals. It will also be despite the alliance of Nixon with the more backward elements of the South.

This is to say, that if Kennedy wins, America will have experienced a coming-of-age, in overcoming much of the darkness and fear within it. Most of us can never recognize a great historic crisis unless it gleams safely at us from the past. Americans are in such a crisis now, and if they make the right choice they will be once again a nation on the edge of greatness.

★

NOVEMBER 9, 1960

It has been a hard race and a close dragged-out finish. But some things are clear about it.

One big fact about the Kennedy victory is that neither religion nor economic power, neither fear of inflation nor the magic of President Eisenhower's name could stop it. An even bigger fact is that enough Americans hungered for greatness in their presidential leadership—enough, at any rate, to overcome the handicaps with which Kennedy started.

Americans can be proud about having fought out, on a major battlefront, one of the great battles of their history—the battle against the bitterness of religious bigotry within the heart. The political landscape will never be the same again. The fight was tough but the stakes were high. Never again will an able and promising candidate be ruled out completely because of his faith, even for the highest office in the nation.

I might add that what has happened about a Catholic candidate will happen, in time, about a Jewish candidate, and in the fullness of time, about a Negro candidate.

It is also good to note that Richard Nixon's vaunted political cleverness did not avail, nor did the fact that so much of the massed economic power of the nation was behind him. The world thinks it knows America as a plutocracy. It is good for the world to discover that there are things in the gift of the American people that cannot be bought, and that the people cannot be maneuvered into believing what is against the evidence of their experience.

They were told that America had prosperity and economic health, yet they knew that there were pockets of suffering in the economy, and they had warning signals of a hard road ahead. They were told that for individuals to spend was virtue, but for the people as a whole to spend in the public sector was some kind of crime, yet they sensed that these fears were archaic. They were told that America's world position was highly satisfactory, yet they knew differently. They were told that the position of the Russians in the satellite areas could be undercut by sending high American emissaries on peace trips, and again they knew differently.

It was Kennedy's task to keep before the people constantly the crucial aspects of the reality principle. He was able to do it, where Stevenson before him had failed. This was partly because, as a Catholic, he was less vulnerable to the charges of appeasement. But mainly it was because his knowledge and his self-command inspired confidence, and his attractiveness as a person opened the minds of many to what he said. Intellectually, some may resent this role of personality in a campaign, but the nation is lucky that for once a good mind and a good social program converged with a popular-leader symbol.

The dialogue of leadership—between the people and the man they trust—has begun anew. It will have to go on for the next four years—or even the next eight—under conditions of massive difficulty. The struggle between the world democratic bloc and the world Communist bloc will be a grim ordeal. To keep it going on the plane of politics, economics, and ideas, without slipping into nuclear and germ conflict, will require iron nerves and great understanding. To take some positive steps toward the reduction and control of the suicidal weapons, and toward a stronger UN authority that may some day have a monopoly of these weapons, will require courage and vision.

I don't say that these were the decisive issues on which the people made their choice. It is improbable that they ever formulate the problem in this fashion. But, in simpler but crucial terms, they did feel that only if America becomes stronger will it be able to become more flexible in its foreign policy. And they evidently did respond to the image of vigor, courage, and freshness in Kennedy's leadership.

They will not, I think, be disappointed. The years we are now entering bid well to be a new era of policy, leadership, national energy, and direction in American life, comparable to the great era of Roosevelt's New Deal. Kennedy, as I have several times emphasized in the past months, has the stuff of growth and greatness in him. The presidential mantle will soon be fitted on him for size. There is ample room in it for a big man. I think Kennedy will fill it out.

As for Richard Nixon, he has seen the cup of power—which several times he had come so close to quaffing—dashed finally from his lips. He fought hard and frantically for it, and there is some pathos in his story that even his opponents will recognize. Yet I cannot help feeling that his leadership would have been inadequate for the years ahead, which will require a mind that can grasp the intangible forces loose in our world and can marshal the full resources of brains and purpose in the democratic world for an unparalleled struggle.

A new era is opening, a new wind is rising, a new spirit is abroad in the American land. I have seen that spirit on the faces of young people not only in the campaign but also on university campuses and even in the high schools. They have once again the sense that things are possible for America and for the cause of freedom, and in that cause they want to be used and they want to be wanted. America's destiny is in their hands as well as in the hands of the new president. We shall need their brains and energy and commitment. Let us start.

★

NOVEMBER 26, 1963

THE WORLD'S GRIEF

Paris—Nothing quite like this response has happened in living memory, not even the worldwide grief at the death of Franklin Roosevelt, and of Pope John, nor the excitement in Europe when Woodrow Wilson came to the Peace Conference. I have watched the long lines of people, simple people, waiting to sign the register at the American Embassy, and what I see in their faces gives me hope. It is something reaching across the national barriers to what ties us together in a common plight and a common destiny.

Those who watched the massive spontaneous funeral procession of successive nights in Berlin, winding its way through street after street, illuminated by candles in the windows, must have felt the same hope. There were even candles in the windows of East Berlin. I don't doubt that the sense of stunned grief and dismay at John Kennedy's death has made the greatest break thus far in the Iron Curtain.

One can understand the American shock. But how about the rest of the world—the captains and kings gathered in Washington at the obsequies, in the greatest array of power and talent in our time, and the electric shock that ran through common people everywhere? Certainly there was the element of unsurpassed political theater, along with the human tragedy. In point of sheer drama I count the shooting at Dallas, the death in the hospital, the capture of the suspect and his death in turn, as the most dramatic happenings in modern world history. Even the two great parallel events—the death of Lincoln and the death of Gandhi—do not surpass it in drama.

Lincoln and Ghandi were greater men than John Kennedy. But he headed the world's greatest power mass and the whole free-world camp. To see so much power and promise ended so precipitously—that caught the world's imagination. But there was something more elusive as well. There was the fear of what might happen if as firm a hand and nerve could not be found again at the nuclear controls, and if the curious interplay of mind and will which Khrushchev had with Kennedy could not be achieved with another.

This common fear lay behind the mass response, and it is in this fear that I find a prelude to hope.

There is a quite general amazement in Europe, especially in France, at the failure of security in forcing protection upon Kennedy. Given the history of the attempts against de Gaulle, the French are a security-conscious people. When de Gaulle made a recent provincial tour and spoke in Lyons, every rooftop was controlled, every house overlooking a vulnerable point on the line of march was canvassed. It is not only the political plotters who must be kept in mind. Every modern society (and not only America) must reckon with the mentally unstable who have an impulse to kill the man at the summit, not out of political commitment but out of a puzzling confusion in the mind.

That was, one would have thought, the case with Lee Harvey Oswald, who seems to have been one of the American lumpen proletariat, fluctuating between the radical left and the radical right, a rootless fellow who felt the world was against him. But the killing of Oswald by Jack Ruby and the coyness of the Dallas police heads about the evidence against Oswald have sowed a new doubt in many minds. The hints in the Paris papers are that Oswald may not have acted alone, that someone wanted to silence him, that the police of Dallas are involved, and that the cover-up impulse may come from the ultra-right and not the left. All sorts of wild rumors thrive in this atmosphere. That is why it was wise for the Justice Department to step into the Oswald case and announce that it is still open. Only a complete public report will dissipate the fog of doubt.

The Russians are of course doing their best to depict the Oswald-Ruby affair as another case of the Reichstag fire, an American version of fascist provocation. This may be a response out of habit, but more likely it comes from the anxiety of the Russian leaders at the worldwide response to the Kennedy killing: it is meant even more for home consumption than for foreign propaganda. I feel that Khrushchev, who is an all-outer at whatever he does, might well have made the trip to Washington, as de Gaulle did, were it not for his fear that the Chinese would use it mercilessly against him.

As for de Gaulle himself, he doubtless made the trip because he was genuinely moved at the death of his young ally and antagonist. But the wide and spontaneous French emotion at the death may also have stuck in his mind. De Gaulle has antennae that reach out to what his people are feeling, far below the level for reasoning itself. Perhaps he feels that he went too fast and too far for his people, in breaking up the American grand design for Europe, and in opposing to it the old idea of a *"Europe des patries."* As one Frenchman put it to me: The least de Gaulle could do was to render to Kennedy in death what he could not grant him in life.

★

THE NEW CHIEF

Paris—The role of the hero in history is not one to be exacted of every leader. We are as unreasonable in asking Lyndon Johnson to be another Kennedy as we were once in asking Harry Truman to be another Roosevelt. One recalls, in fact, that even John Kennedy suffered for a time in the estimate of the intellectuals because his political style was not Roosevelt's. Yet even before his death he had become a considerable hero. And Harry Truman showed that he could earn the designation of president, by his own will and personality, even after it had been bestowed on him by fate.

There is every reason why this should prove true of Lyndon Johnson as well. No vice president has a chance to show his true potential, simply because his lack of power strips him also of authority. Nor is any man of spirit likely to shine in the shadow of another man. Johnson's greatness came when he was Senate leader and could fashion his own strategy to achieve the administration's ends. The question now is whether he can show equal greatness in fashioning the ends themselves, along with the strategy for achieving them.

If a president needed a "philosophy" of action, in any explicit sense, Johnson would be hard put to it. His philosophy has been to get elected, stay elected, put his associates in his debt, collect on the debts, make friends, influence crucial votes, accept compromises, and drive hard to win what and when he can. It is a traditional American politician's philosophy, and it applies especially to men who are not intellectuals and are not at ease with them. But it is not, as was true of Roosevelt and Kennedy, a philosophy of direction.

If we remember that the formative phase of his career came in the New Deal days, when he was a fledgling congressman, that he served effectively under Truman and Kennedy, that he got the first civil rights bill of this century passed, that he has been willing to embrace the doctrine of deficit spending in order to stimulate the economy, it is pointless to underscore his "conservatism." He is a conservative in the sense that he comes from the great oil-chemical belt in Texas and will not break with the men who hold power there, and in the sense also of believing in the art of compromise. But he is not a conservative like Eisenhower, who has a deep set against the welfare society, and certainly not a conservative in the curious meanings that have recently accrued to the term in America.

The big difference between Johnson and Kennedy lies not so much in political philosophy as in their focus of interest and their personalities. Like de Gaulle, Kennedy cared primarily about military and foreign policy, and the rest—except for civil rights in crisis—came close to boring him. Johnson's focus, except for the issue of space exploration, has been domestic. His tactical brilliance as a parliamentarian should enable him to get measures through Congress, even through a Congress that stymied Kennedy almost completely. But he will now have to feel more at ease with the whole scope and sweep of world politics, in a world in which he will have to pit himself against Khrushchev and de Gaulle.

Will he manage it? He has one trait that will help: his feel for power. Within his own domain he has known how to get at the root of power. The trouble is that his domain has been parliamentary. None of the great leaders of the modern world have been at heart parliamentarians, not even Churchill. They have known how to pick men, and how to harness them in unlikely teams, but, most of all, they have had a sense of history and of timing, and iron nerves in a crisis, and have been attuned to the needs and mood of their people. That is the crucible in which Lyndon Johnson will be tested.

I should not underrate him, even by these standards. Some of the European papers have written him up as some kind of political ham with a talent for buffoonery. But this man is no buffoon. He may lack Kennedy's intellectual and literary tastes, and certainly the men he gathers around him eventually will be different from the Kennedy circle. But he has a political style of his own. American to the core (as Harry Truman was), a Texan, a politician, an optimist, he has the sweep and exuberance of the continent in him.

Above all, there is the fact that the presidency makes the man, almost as much as the man makes the presidency. Johnson may make the mistake of starting to campaign for the next term before he has made his impress on this one. But if he avoids that trap, we may once again see the presidency raising its incumbent to his fullest stature, as it did with his former chiefs—Roosevelt, Truman, and Kennedy.

1964

JOHNSON vs. GOLDWATER

SAN FRANCISCO—WHEN Barry Goldwater finished his acceptance speech I half expected some visible sign from on high to signalize that the deity to whom he had made such continuous appeals had found them acceptable. There was more than a moral fervor in the measured portentous sentences; there was a religious overlay such as no presidential nomination acceptance speech in recent American history has matched. Not only, one felt, had the Republican nominee promised to liberate the American people from bondage, chastise the Communist heathen abroad, add further to the stocks of the already overflowing nuclear stockpiles, and do away with violence in the streets. He also promised to bring back to Washington a Republican president and a Republican Congress, and to restore to the throne of the universe a Republican God.

Yet one felt it was a false and hollow Armageddon he invoked, where the forces of the Republican faithful would stand and do battle for a right-wing, lily-white, arms-rattling version of righteousness. There was nothing in the speech about the economy, doubtless because it is prospering; nor about how to resolve the strains of the Atlantic Alliance or the bloodshed of the Vietnam War, doubtless because he doesn't know.

There was no recognition of the most promising development of our decade—the split between the two world Communist camps—nor how to exploit it for the free-world camp. There was not a word about how the wished-for "flowering of an Atlantic civilization" could be brought about in a Europe whose only striking recent sign of unity has been the almost unanimous recoil from the Goldwater presidential image. Worst of all, there were ringing phrases about the free man and the whole man while ignoring the immediate claim of millions of Negro Americans to be free and whole men.

Goldwater gave his convinced supporters the gospel they wanted and recognized. Yet he made not the slightest conciliatory move in it to heal the internal split in the party, not to keep the liberal and moderate Republicans, the human-rights Republicans, and the internationalist Republicans either from sitting this one out or from defecting outright to Lyndon Johnson and the Democrats.

Not only were his bland generalities about freedom, property, and the whole man devoid of any content for these discontented segments of the party, but there was even a direct slap in the faces for the dissenters by the only sentence that brought the faithful to their feet: "I would remind you that extremism in the defense of liberty is no vice." It was a sentence that was meant to give aid and comfort to the John Birch Society and its satellites and subsidiaries, but was also meant to stop short of any underwriting of the sit-downs in defense of the liberty of Negroes.

There is only one way of reading the whole tactic implicit in the speech. Goldwater and the men around him are tender of the feelings of the know-nothing fringe groups that have attached themselves to the Republicans, but are willing to humiliate the more moderate Scranton-Rockefeller-Lodge-Romney-Eisenhower-Nixon-Hatfield groups. They will admit them to the new Republican fellowship only if they will abase themselves publicly, not only letting themselves be stripped of power but also accepting the scorpion and the rod. The walkout of Senator Kenneth Keating and almost half the New York delegation at the first possible moment, when the speech ended, was crucial not only for political survival but also for self-respect. I suspect there will be an epidemic of political apathy among the liberals and moderates in the whole Republican Party. The Goldwater command has left them no alternative.

There is no element of surprise in this harsh takeover of the party by its reactionary wing. There were plenty of signs that it was coming. The choice of William Miller, the farthest right of all the potential candidates, as vice presidential nominee was a clear sign of things to come. The booing of Governor Nelson Rockefeller during his convention speech, the ugly treatment of Governor Mark Hatfield for his attack on the John Birch Society, the short shrift given to the mild proposed platform amendments—these too were signs. Most important of all has been the hysterical identification of New York and other Eastern cities with a sinister conspiracy of intellectuals, foreigners, Communists, Negroes, international finance, immorality, godlessness, and street murderousness.

Every party and faction has the right to call itself what it wishes. But unless words are to be twisted out of all their past meanings, the team, the doctrine, the leadership, the overtones and undertones of the new Republican dispensation are not those of "conservatism" but of reaction. After the purge of men and ideas has been completed, the only men who remain wholeheartedly in tune with the Goldwater command will be the reactionaries.

★

JULY 26, 1964

(An open letter to Sen. Barry Goldwater, on his defense of extremism)
Dear Barry Goldwater:

When Governor Nelson Rockefeller expressed his sense of shock at your now classic sentence about extremism, you seemed a bit shaken, tried a few verbal feints, then passed the burden to Rockefeller by asking him to "put down in writing his definition of extremism." Very sensibly the governor, being a good politician, refused to do your work for you. But since I am only a writer and teacher, I am happy to try my hand at it. Maybe it will help in the discussion that is now sweeping not only the country, but Europe and Asia as well.

First, let us get rid of some fake gambits that you and your lieutenants have tried, and that don't do you credit. One I call the patriotic-war gambit. "Is it extreme action," you asked Rockefeller, "for our boys to give their lives in Vietnam?" A soldier who fights at his country's command, after a decision made by the president and Congress under the law of the land, is no extremist in any sense that makes sense: he is simply a good soldier. How different this is from those who, without any command from the nation and without any respect for the constitutional rights or the civil liberties of others, rail against them, defame them, threaten them, seek to silence them. It is a shabby thing, Senator, to wrap the flag of the soldier around such men. It debases the soldier and debases the flag.

Next let us get rid of the Patrick Henry gambit, which tries to equate the extremists of today with the leaders of the American Revolution and the Founding Fathers of the nation. During the San Francisco debate on the "extremism" amendment to the platform Senator Peter Dominick of Colorado tried to mock the amendment by reading to the convention what purported to be an anti-Patrick Henry editorial from the *New York Times* of 1765. Even in terms of convention ethics this was a low blow, since the *Times* didn't exist in 1765. When called on this, Dominick said he would do further research and let the people know. We are still waiting for the results.

Your vice presidential running mate, William Miller, seems to take the same line in explaining your meaning. So does Charles Percy, running for governor of Illinois, who is unhappy about your sentence. The American Revolution is over, and a defense of Patrick Henry at this date scarcely deserved all the heavy emphasis you gave the sentence in your speech. And do you really mean that the John Birchers, the Klansmen, the fascist and Communist crackpots, the members of the White Citizens Councils are modern versions of Patrick Henry, Sam Adams, and Thomas Jefferson?

Having disposed of the fake gambits let us get down to cases. Abstract definitions and excerpts from dictionaries are of no use here. Your speech came in a definite context. For several years you have been getting support from far-out right-wing organizations and individuals. Many are in California, many in Texas, but they are to be found throughout the nation. Nixon repudiated them when he ran for governor in California, and they hated him. They hate Senator Thomas Kuchel, Governor Nelson Rockefeller, Governor Mark Hatfield, all of whom have spoken out against them. Are these the people you defend as patriots?

Within this concrete context the best definition of an extremist is a simple and direct one: he is an all-out fanatic, whether of the right or the left, obsessive, irrational, hate-filled. He has the right to his doctrine and (within the law) to his actions. He does not have the right to have you stand up for him and defend him.

Your sentence, Senator, was either a deliberate shocker or an almost incredible howler. I suppose you are stuck with it until your lieutenants, who are now trying to explain it all over the lot, will explain it away. You are asking for a "summit conference" of all the Republican moderate and liberal leaders, perhaps to explain that you didn't mean what they all know you meant.

I have spoken of the context in which the definition has to be made. Let me fill out the context a bit more. The nation has had two recent experiences with the actions of extremists. One happened on November 22, 1963. An obsessed, irrational, hate-filled fanatic sent the killing bullet into John F. Kennedy's brain. You will recall that when the news first came no one knew whether it was a fanatic of the right or the left who had sent that bullet. It turned out to be an extremist of the left: it could have been an extremist of the right. In his own confused tormented mind he thought he was acting "in the defense of liberty" (to use your own phrase).

In Mississippi recently some men felt so passionately about their version of Southern freedom and states' rights and white supremacy that they killed three boys. In Harlem and Brooklyn there has been bedlam on the streets, and some passionate believers in black supremacy have tried to exploit the honest bitterness of thousands of Negroes. White or black, these extremists do not deserve your defense, Senator. Yet how easy for them to come in under the umbrella you have (unwittingly, I hope) held out for them.

★

OCTOBER 26, 1964

"What kind of country do you want?" Barry Goldwater was asking, and the crowds at the whistle-stops in his aficionado territory—Orange and San Diego counties in Southern California—shouted back, "Goldwater country." It's not a bad question, even if it got the conditioned answer.

A Goldwater America would set back America's alliances a generation, America's world prestige a half century, and America's internal unity a century. Rightly or wrongly it would serve notice on the world that any people wanting a welfare society had better settle for a Communist one because the world's greatest democracy is uninterested in showing how a juster and more creative life can be built for the many without scuttling the freedoms of any. It would build up rather than relieve the sectional tensions and—by moving away from consensus politics—add class and ideological tensions to those we already have.

The choice is not between a Goldwater and a Johnson America but between an exclusive and an inclusive concept of American society, a rigid and a fluid one, an archaic and a modern one. Goldwater's campaign has been not only against the presidential office itself (despite his feeling for military power he shrinks from the capacious powers of the presidency) but also against the twentieth century. He promises to roll back the universe and give us yesterday. His picture of world Communism dates from the Stalin era, his economics goes back to the pre-New Deal days of Hoover, his international politics to the turn-of-the-century days of McKinley, his concept of race relations to the post-Civil War days of Booker T. Washington, his cult of small-town America to Jefferson's day, his social theory to Adam Smith and the eighteenth century, his worship of military force and of war as a showdown to Machiavelli and the beginning of the nation-state system.

His mind is a patchwork quilt of faded and outworn ideas from past centuries and dead societies. In a sense he will never understand, he is an echo, not a voice. Yet the sloganeering to which he lends himself has a quality of slickness in the manipulation of the mass mind that belongs very much to the Big Media technicians of our own time and place. If Goldwater loses, it will be for other reasons, not because of any failure to make use of the devices and resources of the modern mass politics he professes to despise.

Lyndon Johnson too is a borrower: his political attitudes were shaped under Texas populism, his social welfare thinking under FDR and the New Deal, his ideas on world political strategy under Harry Truman and John Kennedy, his legislative tactics under Sam Rayburn. Yet the result has the imprint of his own lively personality. He is not the echo of no longer viable societies; he is his own unmistakably persuasive voice, a man who achieves a consensus not so much by compromise as by finding the unifying elements that override the divisive.

There are many liberals and moderates in both major parties who say they will vote *against* Goldwater, not *for* Johnson. It is true that, despite the enthusiasm of the campaign crowds, Johnson has not caught hold of the thinking, creative groups in America as Kennedy did. It has not yet sunk in on them that John Kennedy is dead, and that his political style died with him. It is time we begin to judge Lyndon Johnson not by the measure of the style and personality of a man he was never close to, but by how well he fulfills his own.

Seen thus, Johnson is, if anything, more like Harry Truman than Kennedy: a man who is nothing if not political; a man adept at every nuance of power and persuasion, who has already deeply enriched the art of politics and will enrich it further; a very uncommon common man, rooted in the popular soil where (as Truman did) he still clings to the cronies who accompanied his rise. Whether you like or dislike these things about Johnson, you had better recognize them for what they are.

Of one thing I am certain. If he is elected he will leave the presidential office stronger and more resourceful than it has ever been in its history. In this sense he will prove a historic figure. Already he has shown, in only one year of office, a striking capacity for meeting crises with coolness and making the right decisions. In fact it would be hard to point to any recent president whose first year was as crowded with achievement and as free of major blunders. Give him a chance to continue and he will give as good an account of himself, on the stormy voyage of the modern state, as any captain America has had for a long time.

That is why I am for Johnson as against Goldwater. I should add a postscript about the men in the wings. In a nation where passions are bitter and mental stability precarious, we must reckon with a warped mind somewhere in a crowd, or with the crushing burdens of the presidential office. At the thought of a Hubert Humphrey in the White House I get a feeling of security. At the thought of a William Miller there I get a shiver of the absurd, as from the stage world of Ionesco and Genet.

★

NOVEMBER 4, 1964

It was a tidal-wave victory, not only for Lyndon Johnson and Hubert Humphrey but also for American good sense. The dramatic element in the election results was the massive repudiation of the two Republican candidates and of the Republican Party wing they represented.

I can't remember an election that was more completely dominated by the word "No." The "No" was hurled at a man, at his ideas, at his world vision, at the direction in which he wanted the country to go. "What kind of country do you want?" Barry Goldwater kept asking his audiences toward the end of his campaign. The American people have now given the answer. They don't want it to be a country of the radical right, which largely got Goldwater the nomination and has formed the principal cadre of his support. They don't want it to be a country in which the government would be ineffectual and inactive on domestic policies and would cut itself off from its friends and allies in world policy.

The size of the tidal wave, in both the popular and the electoral majority, is of first importance. Not only does it reassure Americans about their own perspective and sanity: even more, it is a message sent across the oceans to foreign peoples and their leaders, friend and foe alike. It tells them—in Europe and Latin America, in Asia and Africa— not to overestimate the reactionary potential in America and not to underestimate the strength of democracy in America. The larger the margin of victory over the radical right by the broad liberal-moderate spectrum of American conviction, the clearer the message.

The most meaningful part of the total rebuke was in the way in which it set the "white backlash" in perspective. There is little question that the backlash attitudes have in the past six months become a reality to be reckoned with. But the crucial fact about the election was that these attitudes did not get translated into Goldwater votes except in the Southern states; Goldwater's views on the economy and social security, on war and peace, thrust the resentments on the racial struggle into the background. That means more than a rebuke to Goldwater. It means that Americans kept their sanity, put first things first.

If Goldwater had won, many of us would have had to revise our whole conception of the American national character and of the quality of our civilization. The results have proved a triumph not just for two candidates and a party, but also for the America we know and love. This America is generous despite its petty prejudices, forward-looking despite its pockets of reaction, levelheaded despite its little whirlpools of hysteria.

It would be a mistake therefore to see the election results only in negative terms, as a rebuke. They are also an affirmation of belief by Americans in their own broadly humanist tradition and in what their civilization can fashion out of the future. In good measure, that affirmation has used Lyndon Johnson and Hubert Humphrey as its symbols.

Johnson has now achieved presidential election on his own. With a margin of victory such as no president has had before, he has a mandate that is also heavier—and more frightening—than has ever been handed to a president. I am convinced he will make a formidably effective president and—in terms of his decision—he has a chance to be a great one. And I suspect that his greatest efforts and development will come in a field he has not stressed before—foreign policy.

There are many who fear that the tidal wave will not only sweep Goldwater and his radical right off the main stage but also the Republican Party itself. I don't think so. It depends on what the Republican leaders, now that they are in a position to rid themselves of the incubus of extremism, do about it. If the Republicans have learned the lesson of the 1964 elections and if they return to the policy of consensus, they have the resilience to become again an effective opposition. If they again allow themselves to be captured by a hyperthyroidal minority of primitives, they well deserve what happens to them.

1968

NIXON vs. HUMPHREY

APRIL 3, 1968

THE BEST RESPONSE I HAVE HEARD on President Johnson's decision not to "seek or accept" the Democratic nomination came not from any of the stunned presidential candidates or any other politicos. It came from a news vendor in New York. "It's good for peace," he said. I concur.

It is good for peace on two scores. It will rid the president of suspicions that would otherwise have clung to his every move toward negotiations—suspicions that he was doing it only for political advantage. Thus it will allow him to act with greater fluidity for peace, and with a more united country behind him.

Second, it will rid Ho Chi Minh of any belief that the president will not dare to continue the war through the election campaign for fear of being rejected either by the convention or by the people. If Ho Chi Minh can get this lingering obsession out of his mind, he may be persuaded to come to the negotiating table and make a bargaining deal for peace.

On both scores—a cleared atmosphere at home and a stripping away of illusions in Hanoi—the move is good for the nation and the world.

What does the president's exit from the current political struggle do to the campaign? It will help Robert Kennedy by removing the heavy armor with which the pro-Johnson delegations had been invested, and will open them to a new Kennedy blitz. Since Eugene McCarthy has not been the president's principal enemy, his political fortunes will continue to depend on the results of the primaries.

The impact on Nixon may be a harsh one, since the removal of his most vulnerable opponent will stir up a wide demand again for a real

Republican alternative to Nixon. The Republican delegates who have felt confident that Nixon could win over an unpopular Johnson will think twice about what he will do against either Kennedy or Mc-Carthy.

This could mean the revival of the Rockefeller draft idea, or even the emergence of John Lindsay as the only other Republican who could give Kennedy a real race of it in both New York and California, and divide the Negro, liberal, big-city, peace, and youth vote with him on pretty equal terms. If, however, the Republicans feel that the candidate running against Kennedy or McCarthy must be hawkish—which is a possible conclusion—Nixon's hold on the nomination will be strengthened.

The man whose political fortunes are the biggest question mark, and who has been hit hardest, is Hubert Humphrey. If any present or future bid of his for the Democratic nomination is to pick up real strength he will have to run within the nimbus of Johnson's new image as a peace-seeker, differentiating himself from Kennedy and McCarthy by a greater tough-mindedness about Asian Communism. It would be a hard road.

But can Johnson himself be wholly and finally ruled out? Is it really, as he has put it, an "irrevocable" decision? Within his present intent, my answer would be clearly yes. I don't go with those who regard every word or act of Johnson's with tenfold suspicion, and who cynically view his refusal to run as merely another slick maneuver. I believe he means it.

Not only has he had almost five grueling years in the White House. He is also a proud man who doesn't want to subject himself to the humiliation of possibly failing to get renominated or reelected. Most of all he is a man whose ruling passion now is to focus on the war and the peace. Only thus will he be able to get that vindication from his people and from history on which his self-image most depends.

But if vindication does come, can political acclaim be far behind? Overnight the national sentiment about Johnson has already been radically transformed. No longer does he have to fear being mobbed by a hostile crowd. He can count on heartfelt applause wherever he appears. Even Bobby Kennedy must grant him "magnanimity." The whole climate within which he moves has been changed. With a single act he has removed the credibility gap. It is wholly possible that, when August comes to Miami, with it will come some real peace negotiations. What the delegates will do then is today incalculable. But in a surprise-studded year they might even turn to the former whipping boy and devil figure, Lyndon Johnson.

Certainly his withdrawal has cleared many poisons from the atmosphere. It will help the peace, and even the conduct of the war, and the way the world feels about America.

★

JUNE 21, 1968

We were talking about heroes the other evening, and someone wondered whether any of the candidates would fit the term. Hubert Humphrey says his say, sometimes at length, always with verve, but his strength lies in responsible judgment, not in the heroic mold. When Robert Kennedy was killed the last remaining American of potential hero material died, although no one can be sure that Kennedy would have been able to fulfill the potential. Rockefeller is more in the Humphrey style, with a certain bluster and high spirits that belie the hero image because there is always a tinge of loneliness in it. As for Richard Nixon, whatever else he may be he is a nonhero.

And Gene McCarthy? To be an antihero is something else again. The McCarthy who has just scored a considerable victory in the New York primaries confirms what I wrote the other day—that in this campaign nothing can be taken for granted, and there is no closure until the end. He refuses to be written off. But his strength is of a maverick, not of a hero—the exact opposite of Kennedy's political style. His persisting strength, especially among those who share the peculiar new amalgam of enthusiasm and a jaded "coolness," ushers in the vogue of the antihero. It is a style worth examining.

The hero dreams of greatness and offers it to his followers, as a form at once of blessing and communion. The antihero flees from the very idea of greatness as he flees from power, either for himself or his nation. Power for him is an ordeal to be survived, a cross to be borne, a cup to be drained but without joy or illusion about what it contains.

The antihero as presidential candidate is a political style that would have been unthinkable except in an era of deflated ideals, which contains also the antinovel, the antipainting, and the antistudent. It fits in with the mood of a people who find that growth is choking the cities, affluence is drowning the economy, commitment is overflowing into violence, imperial power is paralyzing the imperium, and an impossible overextended war is stretching the whole civilization to its bursting point.

How comforting it is, in such an era, to have the antihero ask Emerson's old question, "Why so hot, little man?" Only this time it is closer to being "Why so hot, big and powerful empire, why so hot?"

I should very much like to see a confrontation of the candidates in a series of encounters that would show their style and personality as well as their stance on issues. With Rockefeller pitted against Nixon neither would look heroic, but Rockefeller's direct style should come off better than Nixon's canny one. With McCarthy pitted against Humphrey you would get the cool antileader against the ebullient leader who asks for a chance to show what he can do when he is on his own, and not as someone's deputy.

One trait of the antihero is that instead of building up to climaxes he throws his lines away. This would have been unthinkable on a public platform, before a huge crowd, where your presence has to fill the stage and your voice the auditorium. But on a TV screen, especially on the miniscreens that have invaded the landscape, it is possible to throw your lines away and get your effect. The dry wit and the understated appeal have a chance for the first time.

I have been talking of antiheroes and heroes, not of great men. A great man—one thinks of Goethe as the type-figure—is a creative one who fills the space around him with his authority. In this sense there are not many great men left in our world, simply because anyone's authority—official or personal—seems somehow an offense to us. We are incapable of that suspension of disbelief without which there can be no climate for greatness. The only great man today that most of us would be likely to agree on is Picasso. Even de Gaulle, who seemed to have authority before it began to get shabby around the edges, has come into question. But while no longer great, de Gaulle still plays the hero and will continue to. For to be a hero is a matter of role-playing and role acceptance.

It is also a polarizing role, alas, as witness de Gaulle's unhappy effect on France in polarizing the nation into two hostile camps. I fear that this was true also of Robert Kennedy's hero role. None of the men left in the presidential race is a polarizer. They look to conciliation as their historic role. We shall have to judge their chances of achieving it by asking which of them combines best the necessary gift for action and sensitiveness to thought.

✭

Miami Beach—When the Republicans passed up Nelson Rockefeller and chose Richard Nixon they were consistent in at least one respect. They stuck to the peculiar suicide drive that has marked their choices since 1932, except when they had a hero candidate in General Eisenhower. But Richard Nixon is no hero.

For a moment, when I was watching Tom Dewey give his quadrennial report on the malfeasances of the Democrats, I had a sudden stab of recognition. This was Richard Nixon in 1988—graying, a little jowlier, with more sunken eyes and more beetling eyebrows, talking to a convention twenty years from now as the elder statesman of the party. And being hailed, applauded—and ignored.

What kind of man is the Nixon who is in the national spotlight again today? We don't know how good a Republican candidate he will make, still less how good a president he would be. It is terribly hard to extricate the reality of the man from the angle of contrived public images. But we do know that in the past four years, which have spelled his thrust for the nomination, he has worked hard, seriously, intelligently, and has made only a few blunders, and those not fatal.

But surely that could have been said also of Tom Dewey in 1948. He had been nominated in 1944 and had lost against a champ, FDR, just as Nixon ran against John Kennedy and lost in 1960. Then Dewey came back to run again in 1948, beating Bob Taft (the Ronald Reagan of that day) and Harold Stassen (the Rockefeller of that day), and was then in turn defeated by Roosevelt's vice president, Harry Truman. The question is whether Nixon will do better in 1968 against Johnson's vice president, Hubert Humphrey.

As with all historical parallels I have played up the similarities and played down the differences between Dewey and Nixon. The differences are considerable. Nixon did better against Kennedy than Dewey against Roosevelt. He has had actual national experience in the vice presidency. He has had an eight-year interval where Dewey had only a four-year interval between nominations.

The last may be most important. Nixon underscored it in a press conference here, when he spoke of "this period of contemplation and this period of withdrawal from the political scene." The terms are

Toynbee's in his idea of "withdrawal and return," repeatedly applied to de Gaulle's absence from power.

But Nixon is no de Gaulle. He takes himself more seriously as a historical figure than the voters are likely to take him. Despite his new habit of speaking of himself in the third person (as he did in the remarkable taped record of his private talk to the Southern delegations), he is not at all de Gaulle but only a sinuous congressman from California who used the break he got in the Hiss case to maneuver his way up the political staircase.

Yet the period of withdrawal was immensely useful for Nixon. It gave people a chance almost to forget his old hatchet image (how long do images last in the public memory?) and gave Nixon a chance to fashion a new and more "statesmanlike" one. Yet the old image has served him well with the delegates from the South and Southwest and Middle West, who still refuse to see in this rich Wall Street lawyer a member of the Eastern Establishment that they hate so implacably. Thus Nixon has made the best of both worlds.

He must get the credit for having done it with extraordinary skill. He knew his party as perhaps no one else today does—its wings and factions, its moods, its prejudices, its loyalties, its hates and hungers. He estimated better than most the weaknesses of Nelson Rockefeller's support, and how to circumvent Ronald Reagan's. He never took George Romney as seriously as some did. He saw a vacuum of leadership in the party's center, and he moved into it with all deliberate speed. And he did all this without having a state delegation of his own, from either New York or California, to use as a base.

This makes him a good political broker, a good party worker, a good convention operator. But does it make him a credible presidential figure? Does it mean he can deal with the dissident young, poor, and blacks in America for whom he has never shown any understanding? Does it mean he can deal with America's tragic splits and with its grave historic burdens?

To convince me and others that he can, he will have to show qualities beyond those he has shown—qualities hitherto undreamed of in Richard Nixon.

✮

AUGUST 21, 1968

There are two questions that every presidential convention has to answer. One is: What kind of president do the delegates want? The other is: What kind of party do they want?

Neither gets really answered, because neither is squarely confronted. The first is usually rephrased into "which of the available men, with whom we can live, will win for us?" The other usually follows from the first: "We want the kind of party that will be big enough for the rejected but that will rally around the chosen."

This fits what happened to the Republicans at Miami Beach, but not what is happening to the Democrats at Chicago. They say little about what makes a good president, but are waging a sharp inner struggle to decide what the identity of the party will be. All the candidates except Georgia Governor Lester Maddox agree that the delegations must represent the new black voters as well as the whites although they disagree on what state delegations should be changed. The real trouble lies elsewhere—with the effort of one segment of the party to use a deep difference on the Vietnam issue as a reason for rejecting not only the front-running candidate but also the party itself, and for starting a new fourth—or will it be fifth?—party.

Meanwhile, what counts most for the nation remains woefully undiscussed: What kind of president does America need in a time of global turmoil, racial conflict, and widespread unrest? I see a president's qualities under five headings, although obviously the divisions are artificial, since all must be part of the same living, functioning man.

1) Qualities of knowledge, intellect, and insight in a job that demands more of these than any other in the world. Good staff work can repair some of the defects of knowledge, but intellect and insight cannot be delegated. This is where experience in government and in life counts. Being an egghead helps, but it isn't essential. A man must have been through the battles, touched all the big problems, sweated blood in striving for their solution.

2) Qualities of personality and character. Is the man credible as a person? Can you trust him? This is where the quality of courage comes in, provided it doesn't go with a martyr complex. This is where integrity comes in, again provided a man doesn't believe he is the only

one who has it. This is also where you have to balance consistency with the capacity for change. Here is the graveyard of many politicians, who succumb to being Machiavellis or who change their skins of opinion and personality with every changing wind, or who—in the opposite direction—become so pure that they become isolated, as Woodrow Wilson did in his time of troubles.

3) Qualities of maturity and judgment. The problem here is not to be governed by impulse or ideology, nor to wreak your inner personal conflicts on your decisions, but to act (or refrain from action) with a cool and calm intelligence. Age has little to do with it, but what you have made of your experiences and your mistakes has much to do with it.

4) The quality of command. This includes many things—energy that communicates itself to others, and the quality of will, and the capacity to make decisions and live with them until they have to be changed, and clarity amidst the confusion of others, and direction amidst the cross-purposes of others. This is where an activist conception of the presidency comes in.

5) The quality of relation to others. A president has always had to act as educator and carry on genuine dialogue with the people. But today he must know as never before how to relate to those who feel out of things—to the disinherited Negroes and poor, to the young who feel estranged from a world they never made, to those in the cities, white and black alike, who feel endangered by the increase in violence. The candidate who most clearly had this quality of relating, Robert Kennedy, is dead. Those who remain have shown it only spottily, not strongly.

I leave for the last a quality related to all the others—the president as a symbol. He must be able to attract and organize the best brains in the service of the nation, and give the world the sense when he speaks and acts that he does so not for one class or race or generation but for the whole society.

Is this perfectionism? I don't mean it to be, but only a touchstone to see which of the available men comes even within hailing distance of it.

☆

AUGUST 28, 1968

Chicago—Amidst the welter of reports about the confusion and disarray at Chicago, let me enter a dissenting opinion.

At Miami Beach three weeks ago none of us were able to see any America we could recognize as a reality. There was none of the sweat and struggle that is the mark of America in an era of revolutionary change. There was only a cotton-wool vacuum, with hoopla and boredom, with speeches of sweetness, light, and concord.

Here in Chicago you see America plain, with no holds barred, no warts missing from the portrait, with everything there including credential fights and platform debates, with the Georgians Lester Maddox and Julian Bond, with the old mood represented by the old South and the new mood by three candidates from the Middle West and by the intellectually alert delegations from California and New York, with lively responsible spokesmen for the new black voters of the South, with Chicago Mayor Richard Daley and California Speaker Jesse Unruh as potential kingmakers, with hippies and Yippies and the New Left, with soldiers and Secret Service and a maddening security tightness, with newsmen and photographers being clubbed by overreacting police squads, with a crippled transport system and phone services, but with unflinching resolve to show and face what America is really like.

This is the America I have seen and come to recognize as I have crisscrossed the nation in the last few years. It is better to have it shown in full glare here in Chicago, with its unlovely as well as its exciting aspects, rather than have it hidden from view behind contrived public-relations veils.

From the swirling events, following each other with bewildering speed here, five men stand out and with them three major issues. Three of the five men are, of course, the three willing and professed candidates. Jesse Unruh and the California delegation put the party and nation in their debt by staging a debate among the three men—the best political debate of presidential candidates that I have thus far seen.

All three came off creditably, with McCarthy's understated anti-hero style again evident, and McGovern's remarkable antennae for communicating with his audience, and Humphrey's cool nerve and grasp of reality along with his rhetoric. But to one uncommitted, if not unengaged, reporter, McCarthy added least to what he had known about him. McGovern added most, but it was Humphrey who came through best as the broadest-based credible and responsible presidential timber.

The other two of the five men I have mentioned are of course Lyndon Johnson and Edward Kennedy. If there was ever any hope in Johnson's breast that a hopelessly deadlocked convention would seek him out again, it grew slimmer as Humphrey's forces rode out the inevitable storms at the start of a convention.

The undercurrent of drama streamed around Senator Edward Kennedy, and the question of whether he was waiting for a draft or had set his decision against it with finality. Of the Kennedy friends with whom I talked, the steadiest opinion I found was that, even if he could have the nomination now, he was not ready for it, either psychologically or in his political growth.

I was reminded somewhat of the 1948 experience of the Republicans, when Eisenhower as a war hero might have had the nomination in a draft but turned it down to run in 1952. There are no presidential candidates today who are war heroes, but Edward Kennedy is a symbol at once of the assassination wars and of the truncated Kennedy promise. The draft movement strikes me as premature. Ripeness is all, both for Kennedy and for the nation.

As for the issues, that of how to end the war and get a viable peace is being battled over. But there are two others, about which the convention has been less explicit. One is the issue of whether the "new politics" group among the Democrats will leave the party and form a new one, as the far-out SDS-*Ramparts* magazine radicals want McCarthy to do, or whether they will regard the Democratic Party as offering them a broad enough tent within which to continue their striving. McCarthy's refusal thus far to say he will support Humphrey if he is nominated is the tub he has thrown to his own little extreme-left whale, to appease it.

The final issue is how to balance legal order with social justice. Despite my somewhat rueful experience with a detachment of Chicago police whom I chanced to encounter (about which I shall write in due course, after the convention business is settled), I am aware that the Democrats cannot give Nixon and Agnew a monopoly on the voters who are crying for law and order. How the Democrats resolve their stand on this issue may go far to decide the election itself.

☆

AUGUST 30, 1968

Chicago—Surely there was a better way to handle the young protest-ers and demonstrators than the way the Chicago police used. No one can doubt that the tough leaders of the National Mobilization Com-mittee wanted a confrontation on nomination night, nor that the po-lice violence served the purposes of these men admirably. Looking back with hindsight it was a mistake to keep them from marching to the Amphitheater, where they have been stopped without making a shambles of a street-corner in the heart of the city.

It was a mistake to put the burden of clearing the street on an overburdened police force that has been tense for weeks and psycho-logically unprepared for what it had to do. It would have been better to use soldiers and the National Guard as the prime force for keeping civic order and insuring a peaceful demonstration, and reserve the po-lice for smaller disturbances.

If the police had to be used as the prime force, they could have limited themselves to making arrests instead of clubbing their targets with an indiscriminate fervor.

The obvious result of the methods used has been to increase the polarizing of the opposing groups within the Democratic Party, to sharpen the already sharp gap between the generations, and to hand over to the untender mercies of the far left groups an array of young people who have been radicalized by the whole experience. Mayor Da-ley and his Police Commissioner couldn't have done this more effec-tively if they had meant to.

The leaders of the far left groups have been handed two beauti-fully effective slogans with which to win over the young people. One is the "raw deal" which they insist the convention gave the peace forces, the other is the cry of "police brutality." Both of them add up to a case against the system. That is why Dave Dellinger, one of the heads of the National Mobilization Committee, claimed that his group had won a tragic victory—but it is a victory. For with these slogans the far left can make the same kind of appeal to America's youth that the far left made in Paris during the riotous nights at the university barricades in May. What I have been witnessing in Chicago is very much the scenario I saw when I was in Paris.

Most of the youngsters in the demonstrations were not revolutionaries, but decent idealistic kids with a passion for peace in their hearts. But a number of those who planned and organized the demonstrations, and used the youngsters for their purposes, are tough professional revolutionaries who welcome the chaos because it is their only way of radicalizing the young, the poor, the estranged.

It doesn't take many such tough and hardened men to control the larger movement: anywhere from 2 to 5 percent will do it. Without the police excesses they would have been ineffectual. With those excesses they have largely succeeded. Both sides—the revolutionaries and the police—planned for massive violence, and both predicted it, and because they did, it came. It is a case again of the self-fulfilling prophecy.

I had an experience earlier in the week which has made me a problem of social order and the police. Several of us from the media—including Hugh Hefner, Jules Feiffer and myself—walked down Wells Street in Old Town around 1 a.m. to see what was happening. We got tangled in a group of spectators and stragglers from an earlier "hippie" demonstration, were chased down a side street by a police car, were threatened by a small phalanx of guns held by cops who jumped out of the car, and barely managed to get away without serious trouble except for an injury to Hefner by a police club.

Compared to what happened to at least thirty newsmen and photographers during the week, this was a very minor event. We suffered no bloody heads as they did. But we did learn, with an immediacy we had not experienced before, something about the rage of the police in such a situation, and the helplessness of ordinary Americans who are luckless enough to encounter them when they are "cleaning up" some area. As I reviewed the TV clips of the bloody melee at the Hilton Hotel with its display of force beyond what was necessary, I got a shock of recognition that went back to our own experience in Old Town.

In the case of the National Mobilization Committee encounter there was something added—a rage on both sides, a polarizing rage which embitters both the young militants and the police. I say again that on both sides this isn't the way to do it. We had better find another way, more temperate, more humanist, or we shall find the dream of social peace turned into a nightmare of civil conflict that can only play into the hands of the extremes on the left and the right.

☆

SEPTEMBER 3, 1968

Hubert Humphrey's victory in the convention hall was overshadowed by the primitive violence on Chicago's streets. He had to deliver his remarkable acceptance speech to a disrupted convention of a fragmented party in a nation stunned by what its people had seen on their TV screens. It is an almost impossible assignment that Humphrey now takes on, with the odds heavily against him and in Nixon's favor.

Perhaps the only thought that can console him in his agonized situation is the reflection that he will now have a chance to show his true mettle as a political man and as a human being, and that he will be watched with some sympathy by a people who have always had a weakness for the underdog.

Humphrey chose to speak about three commanding themes—peace, social order, and national unity. But the greatest of these, summing up the others as well, is unity. Caught between the need to keep President Johnson's support and the need to bring the McCarthyites back in the party, between the Southern governors and the big-city liberals, between the Daley forces and the conscience of the party, Humphrey had to hold a delicate balance between them and yet give a driving vigor to his vision of a "New Day."

The fact that he managed as well as he did, and got away with it, was testimony to his tactical political skills as well as to his oratory. Let it be said that he came through his first big test.

But there are others ahead for which the art of taking positions skillfully will not be enough. Humphrey will have to make the positions he takes persuasive, by adding to them that extra personal dimension that marks a man capable of leading and governing. He has to win over a good share of the intellectual community whom Johnson estranged and whom the Chicago events have further embittered. Eugene McCarthy's defection is in itself important, but even more it is a symbol of the embitterment of a whole segment of the party. If Humphrey could bring McCarthy back into the Democratic fold, it would help him with the young people. In turn, if he could make himself credible to the young, he could have a leverage for bringing McCarthy back.

Humphrey's plight is that he has to persuade this group of something they are determined not to believe—that he is not Tweedledee to Nixon's Tweedledum, and that he is not puppet to Johnson's manipulation of Vietnam policy. Of the two, it is the latter that is crucial.

Humphrey is at a disadvantage here, because as vice president he will be associated in the nation's mind with the president's policy whether he agrees with it or not. Every move in that policy between now and November will raise questions about where Humphrey stands on it. If he fails to disengage himself from the president, he will have little or no chance to win back the disenchanted. If he does disengage himself he must brave the anger of a sensitive and powerful man who may today be more concerned with his own place in history than with the political future of his vice president.

If I were in Humphrey's place I think I should risk the break with the president when my conscience could no longer carry me along with his policies. The defeated minority plank on Vietnam, had it been adopted at the convention, would have given Humphrey a place to stand from which he might have made such a break. Without it he will have a harder time to fashion a persuasive position for the break. But the break, if and when it comes, will be by that fact all the more dramatic, and therefore the more credible to the nation as a whole. It would open a gap between Humphrey and Nixon on foreign policy, as well as the existing gap on domestic.

It is hard to guess whether McCarthy will return to the party if Humphrey does not make so risky a break. His present argument is that he must focus on electing another ten liberal senators. The fact is that McCarthy, after Chicago, may become a symbol of the embattled young militants, and thereby become a prime target for the groups that stress "law-and-order" in the cities.

If that happens, his support in states like Illinois and Ohio might prove to be a doubtful blessing. The pressure to bring McCarthy back into the party thus may come from the state and congressional candidates for whom the party split will prove ruinous.

I leave for another piece the even more vexed problem of how Humphrey can make himself credible, not on the McCarthy left, but on the Daley right, on the law-and-order issue, how on this score he can head off defections to either the Nixon-Agnew camp or the Wallace camp.

I don't put the task beyond him, but it will take some doing. His excellent running mate, Senator Edmund Muskie, may play a role here because he comes from the ethnic suburban groups whose fears have been most aroused. Many Americans will watch them with sympathy, but many also with an I-want-to-be-shown detachment.

★

SEPTEMBER 4, 1968

No one can doubt that there is a swing to the right in American politics, but this is compatible with another swing—one toward a radicalism of basic attitudes, on both the right and the left. This is becoming an era of competing far-out positions: that of the youth on the Chicago streets and that of the police answering them by cracking their skulls; that of the Black Power far-outers, who have just met in Philadelphia and discussed an all-black private urban militia, and that of the George Wallace forces in his American Independent Party; that of a Black Panther fourth party, and a planned fifth party (the New Party) made up of dissidents from the Democrats, and doubtless a sixth party still to come.

Such a fragmentizing of positions goes with a polarizing of emotions and with a "No Compromise" mood on both sides of every great issue. A number of people, who probably have never thought of themselves as far-outers, have said to me: "I'm sick of compromising. Let's have action." I am sure that many other people, in that 70-plus percent reported to be supporting the Daley position, have said much the same thing: "We're sick of coddling the young and the rioters and the hippies. Let's have action."

We have already seen the result on the Chicago streets. We shall probably see more of it.

This is no time for hysteria. I saw the police in action in Chicago, and I feel strongly that they overreacted, out of frustration and rage. But to those who have said that this is Nazi Germany, I have to say, no, it isn't Nazi Germany, but it may usher in a kind of Weimar period, which could pave the way for something worse. Especially if any groups, black or white, left or right, start talking about organizing private defense forces. For it was these private paramilitary organizations that marked the Weimar period before Hitler, along with a terrible frustration and a polarizing of rage.

And to those who tell me that they are tired of the American two-party system, and are fed up with its compromises, and they prefer

George Wallace or Eldridge Cleaver because at least you know where he stands ideologically, I have to say again, watch out. Ideological politics are exactly what America must stay clear of.

Yes, the convention system needs changing, and yes, the major parties need realignment and are already in process of realigning. But the idea of regrouping in two sharply defined ideological camps, each pitted against the other with hatred and rage, each seeing the other as the enemy, each feeling that anything goes in the final struggle against the other—that way lies political madness and national catastrophe.

If you doubt this, then look at the record on the European continent, from the Atlantic to the Volga, where for centuries they had the ideological politics of race and class and religion. The result over the centuries has been class warfare, racial hatred, religious genocide. What an example to imitate!

I may be called ideologically soft, but I am glad America has had a two-party nonideological system, with enough differences between the parties to evoke traditional struggles, enough similarities to create a large group of Independents, and with each party broad enough to contain Ronald Reagan and John Lindsay, Strom Thurmond and Nelson Rockefeller; then the Democratic Party ought to be broad enough to contain even a Richard Daley or a Eugene McCarthy.

Each may want to throw out the other, and at this moment Daley's actions and Humphrey's response seem to have soured McCarthy against his party's ticket, perhaps for good. But any American leader embracing an ideological politics, in which all party members have been purged clean of ideological heresy, is not doing the nation any good.

My own thinking runs not in terms of ideology but of a basic frame of human decency and a confronting of competing ideas within that frame. That, I take it, is what the Czechs and Romanians are struggling for, as against the ideological purity the Russians demand. My protest against what happened in Chicago was that it broke the frame of man's humanity to man. For, in the end, it is man who is the root—not ideologies, not parties, not slogans, not races or religions, but man himself, and the human nexus that ties him to his fellow man.

★

OCTOBER 2, 1968

The most important single thing about Richard Nixon is Richard Nixon, and the most important single thing about Hubert Humphrey is Hubert Humphrey. That may sound like tautology, but it is also the nub of the presidential campaign. The choice lies not so much between the positions the candidates take as between their personalities and credibility as leaders. It turns not on where they stand but what they are. This applies to an extent to George Wallace too, but less so, because his positions are in themselves so extreme.

All the doubts about Nixon converge on the central doubt, not about his skill or will but about his credibility, just as the doubts about Humphrey converge on his quality of command. Nixon has performed wonders with his own public image, transforming it almost beyond recognition in the space of six years (his low point was the California gubernatorial election in 1962). But the changeover job has been too successful. Its very completeness raises questions about the sleight-of-hand techniques by which it was accomplished.

These doubts have been fed by his vagueness on the substantive issues where a sharp stand might hurt his image. This has been especially true of the war and foreign policy.

The war is not the crucial issue of the campaign, as compared with domestic violence, but it raises the central problem of Nixon's credibility. Both Nixon and Humphrey historically have been hawks on Vietnam, Humphrey in his vice presidential capacity in a war administration, Nixon even longer, ever since he proposed American military intervention to swing the balance to the French side when Vietnam was still Indochina. Both have tried to move away from this position. But Humphrey, still caught with Johnson on his back, is doing it by spelling out specific phases of the war and peace, however incompletely, while Nixon has maintained silence, except for his wishful and vague promise to seek an "honorable" peace.

But what is an "honorable" peace? How does Nixon propose to achieve it? Alas, the answer has been silence. At first no one pushed Nixon on this, and later he used the start of the Paris talks as a moratorium for his silence. But how long does the moratorium last? If we are to wait while the Paris talks last, then we shall wait until Nixon is president before we know his views on the war.

I don't recall any comparable silence on the part of a major candidate in a major democracy since Harold Wilson refused to talk about foreign or military policy at the Labour Party conference in 1963, before the election that brought him to power. Wilson got away with it, and everyone thought it terribly clever of him, as they do now of Nixon. But Wilson brought England to disaster because he out-clevered himself, and the question about Nixon in my mind is whether he too will not out-clever himself, and whether the qualities needed for an election will be adequate to the problems of the nation and the world.

One must raise the same question about domestic issues. How does Nixon propose to deal with the bitterness of the Negro in the ghetto, and with the white-black split? His earlier answer—"black capitalism"—has evoked very little response from black Americans and there is nothing in it that is not contained in the "total coalition" approach already being tried, which Humphrey accepts as part of his plan for the ghettos.

Actually, as Wallace has grown to be Nixon's real headache, rather than Humphrey, Nixon has shifted from his interest in ghetto economics to a law-and-order approach meant to snare the voter who is seceding to Wallace. This is at once Nixon's hope and his bind. If it proves true that Wallace is taking two votes from Nixon for every vote he takes from Humphrey, then Nixon must move in Wallace's direction, as he has been doing in his attacks on the college students and on the Supreme Court decisions guarding the constitutional rights of accused men. But the more Nixon does it, to head off Wallace, the more he loses his chosen image of the cool moderate, and the closer he comes to the image of the "old" Nixon.

His credibility problem operates in both directions—toward the moderates and toward the Wallaceites. As he woos the second, he endangers the first.

1972

NIXON vs. McGOVERN

W E ARE SMACK IN THE MIDDLE of one of the exciting experiments of our time—an effort to establish a direct democracy in a system of political parties which at best was a secondary democracy and at worst a set of local kingships.

A vivid example was the recent vote of Arizona Democrats, at a grassroots level, in choosing the 500 delegates to a state convention, which in turn will send delegates to the Miami convention. The remarkable fact was the unparalleled turnout of what may be called the "new consciousness" voters—women, young people, Chicanos, blacks, students, and activists for various causes. Whatever happens in the national convention and the presidential election itself, these groups had their day—and the day was golden.

The implications need thinking about. One is about "participatory democracy," a phrase that had an intense earlier vogue and is now fading out. All democracy, if the term has any meaning, is participatory; the question is how direct it is, and how effective it is.

The danger in a vast society like America's is that in making party choices, habit and convenience become the masters, and little party oligarchies get control and hold it, and the democracy becomes very indirect, and the voters at the base of the pyramid get frozen out, exerting little if any direct suasion on the few professionals at the top.

This is not a good system. It leads to deals in smoke-filled rooms at the top, and cynicism in back rooms everywhere. It leads to a sharp separation between the pros and the inert mass of voters.

Worst of all, it leads to a sense of exclusion and powerlessness among those who need most to feel included and feel some sense of power. Dry rot develops exactly where new green shoots of energy should be coming up.

The result can be a growing hopeless feeling that if there is to be change, it cannot come "inside the system," only outside, and that gains and growth within the continuity of history are impossible. Witness, as evidence, the riots and blood outside the Chicago convention in 1968.

Writers on party power talk a good deal about the "iron law of oligarchy," but what is happening in America today suggests that the iron law is not so iron, and can be broken.

But there is a second implication worth noting. A political party is an organization for a purpose, and the purpose is to win elections—not party elections, but the larger elections, from national down to local.

The Democrats today are the party that is going through the revolution of direct democracy, while the Republicans—with their presidential candidate clear and all but chosen—are sticking to their old machinery. It is not they who had a bloody riot in 1968, nor is it they who lost the election because of it.

Their chances of winning the "new consciousness" voters this year are minimal, and therefore they have less urgency about wooing that vote and getting it out. They will run on President Nixon's record and on whatever persuasive power his name has, and leave the democracy to the Democrats.

The question is whether the new internal democracy of the Democrats will help or hinder them in winning the election. The Arizona Democrats not only have stirred up the grassroots voter inside the party: they have also given him the heady power of plural and distributive voting.

In a district choosing ten delegates to the state convention, each voter had ten votes and could distribute them among the delegates in any way. Obviously this gives some advantage—as all primary elections do—to the high-visibility candidates, who offer either personal or ideological drama to the voter.

Hence, while Muskie came first, as expected from his standing with the state's Democratic officeholders and professionals, Lindsay and McGovern came second and third with impressive votes.

The question is whether either Lindsay or McGovern would, if nominated at Miami, have a winning appeal to the nation's voters as a whole, not only to the liberal Democrats but also to the middle voters of both parties, and especially to the "ticket-splitters," especially in the suburbs.

There is weighty evidence accumulating that it is these middle voters and ticket-splitters who have recently been the decisive element in state and national elections. That is why the pros, who want to function within the new reforms, still lean toward Muskie.

They may well be asking the tantalizing question now, "What will it profit a party if it gain direct democracy and lose the elections?"

★

SEPTEMBER 20, 1972

Washington—Two big mysteries currently engage Washington in guessing and gossip—what happened at Watergate and did Air Force General John Lavelle's superiors know about his unauthorized bombing of North Vietnam?—and both mysteries still mystify. The McGovern hope is that some anger about them will spread, and erode the Nixon margin of advantage. My own soundings across the country suggest that while Watergate may conceivably become a code word, it hasn't yet. I doubt if Lavelle ever will. It leaves only a massive apathy.

Every campaign becomes, at some point, a battle of coded words and ideas. This one is no exception, but the coded battle—in which the issues are somehow scooped out and only the verbal husk remains— has come earlier than in past campaigns.

In this battle, the Republicans are on the offensive. For a time it looked as if the Democratic codes might have it all their way. With the war and the young and women and unemployment on their side, they seemed the wave of the future, and who could stop them?

Well, the wave got turned back, or maybe it never got started. Most of the coded ideas—youth, the "new politics," tired old pros, taxes, populism, credibility—have dropped out of the effective McGovern vocabulary. If anyone brings them up these days, it is the Republicans, for negative effect.

What is the residual McGovern vocabulary today? The war is still his big issue, and the code words are "precious young lives," and "dying far from home for a corrupt dictatorship." Another is "special interests." For a time the ITT affair, with the charge of trading a political contribution for a favorable Justice Department anti-trust suit settlement, made some noise, but it ended not with a bang but a whimper. Then came the charge that the Agriculture department had given the big corporations an inside track on wheat sales to Russia. There is evidence to back up the charge, by the department's own admission. How heartbreaking it must be to the McGovern campaign managers to see that even here the "special interests" issue hasn't struck fire with the voters.

The code vocabulary of the Republicans is much longer, richer, more available. Take President Nixon's quick visit to an Italian-American festival in Prince George's County, Maryland. All he had to do was use the words "work" and "family" and everyone got the message. He was talking of the work ethic as against "getting something for nothing." He was talking of family loyalties as against the uprooted and alienated "kids." "Quotas" became a coded signal at the Republican convention. It is working overtime for Nixon among the "ethnics," and has become one of the major symbols in areas of Jewish voters.

There are other obvious—and overused—elements of the Nixon code vocabulary: "abortion," "amnesty," "drug culture." All that the speaker has to do is mention them, and the audience gets the idea. This is true also of "welfare" and "giveaway," not to speak of "busing." For a time "Eagleton," was a code word. And of course "Nixon" and "McGovern" have become code words, each used negatively by the other side. But "McGovern" these days has far greater intensity of impact.

The Watergate issue exudes a pretty messy smell thus far. Commentators have been wracking their brains to explain why it hasn't excited the voters and given the campaign a special charge. But the answer is stunningly clear. The committed anti-McGovern voters, with their minds made up, respond to a code so rich and emotion-laden that they won't let Watergate shake them. As for the marginal voters, they are so skeptical of politicians, anyway, that nothing about politics will surprise or move them.

The Nixon power advantage is also clear. Trying to get something out of the emotional drug issue, McGovern charges that Nixon has allowed the war to cripple the campaign against heroin imports. And, suddenly, there is the president appearing on TV at a conference on heroin, big as life, talking tough about stopping up the supply routes of the vicious drug dealers and cracking down on countries that don't help.

Or take the McGovern charge about the wheat deal and the special interests. It may get some farm votes. But what strikes most people about the deals with Russia and China is the image of the American economy not only supporting its own people but selling mountains of wheat to its rivals, and exporting machinery and technology to them, too. "A pitiful giant?" Nothing pitiful there. A giant strong enough to supply his enemies as well as himself, and make them half-friends, and perhaps get a measure of peace.

As a cabbie said today, when we passed the White House, "He's a tough cookie in there." Which may be the final word in the code vocabulary.

★

OCTOBER 27, 1972

Indiana, Pa.—While Henry Kissinger is hard at work trying to nail down the ceasefire, other Nixon lieutenants are working hard to defend their party's activities in the Department of Dirty Tricks.

From the investigative reports piling up, the "Watergate caper" now seems more than solitary and more than a caper. It went deep and ramified far in the party structure. In its early phase it was directed less against George McGovern than against his rivals in the primaries, especially Ed Muskie, trying to blast him out of the race as the dangerous anti-Nixon candidate.

Its later phases are more obscure. But it seems to have gone further in dirty tricks than most episodes in the long history of political sabotage. It had recruiting agents, a network of "contacts," a willingness to concoct forged letters, and a knowledge—amateur or professional—of the technology of bugging. It also had plenty of money to spend.

In brief, it had everything—manpower, money, organization, high spirits, low cunning, a flaring imagination, and a devil-may-care insolence. Everything but ordinary everyday decency.

It was a child of its time, drawing upon two subcultures within the prevailing cultural climate.

One is the espionage subculture. Anyone who is a hopeless, hung-up suspense-story buff, as I am, knows of a recent feature of that genre, sometimes called the Department of Dirty Tricks, or the Agency of Disinformation, or whatever the Russian or French or Chinese equivalents may be.

Under whatever name the purpose is always the same. It is to create confusion and divisiveness among the enemy, get its leaders fighting with each other, and spread chaos in its ranks. A former CIA man arrested at Watergate, Bernard Barker, called it with some pride, the "paramilitary mind," which is a way of saying that if you are involved in a battle you can't be squeamish about means.

The second source seems to be the hippie-activist counterculture. I have been reading Dotson Rader's long lament (in *Evergreen Magazine*) over the publishing fate of Abbie Hoffman's book, *Steal This Book*, which evidently scared off a number of publishers as a monster collection of rip-offs, complete with how-to illustrations.

But learning day after day about Barker, Donald Segretti, Dwight Chapin, and assorted others involved in campaign misdeeds, what better term describes these stories than a giant Republican rip-off? Abbie Hoffman and Jerry Rubin wanted mostly to boggle the bourgeoisie and show a fine contempt for property, propriety, and the system. But the high stakes of the Republican rip-offers were the presidency itself.

Here you have the archenemies of a system in the radical counterculture and its arch-defenders in the conservative power structure uniting (whether in reality or fantasy) in a similar rip-off ethic. It suggests how far that ethic has penetrated the climate.

Finally there's the question of why the voters have shown so little high dudgeon against low tricks. I write this from a university town in the deep-mining coal country of Pennsylvania, where the students come from families of miners, farmers, small-town tradesmen.

It has been Roosevelt, Truman, Humphrey country, could have been Muskie country, could still be George Wallace country. It is not McGovern country.

McGovern came out this way a few days ago and brought Ed Muskie to campaign for him, and Muskie asked his fellow Slav workingmen to vote for McGovern. But will they?

The men and women who work here and live in battered small houses and in trailer clusters, set in valleys of mist and mud, have to cope with a hard life. The familiar populist theme is still true here. People are discontented. They carry a floating anger.

But Wallace's angers come closer than McGovern's to their own. They take to tough men. Even Tony Boyle, head of the Mine Workers, whose role in the murder of union rival Joseph Yablonski has never been cleared away, gets a good hearing here for his contest with Arnold Miller in the mine presidency election.

We talk much about populist angers, but forget that what angers George McGovern doesn't necessarily anger many of the men here.

Curiously they even turn their bottled-up workingmen's angers against McGovern. I suspect his talk is too moralistic for them.

If they were sore at Nixon for other reasons, the rip-off ethic might make them sorer. But since they see Nixon as a tough customer in a tough world, this added evidence of toughness doesn't bother them as much as some of us think it should.

★

NOVEMBER 1, 1972

A commentator owes his readers a candid, reasonably detached, continuing scrutiny of the campaign. I hope I have not done that too badly. At the end he owes them—what is far less important—his own summing up. Anyone who won't confess to some sweat about reaching such a judgment this time is lucky. Neither candidate is much of a hero, neither wholly a Devil. I have little enthusiasm for either.

I might let it go at that, but since I have never sat out a presidential election I won't start now. I set down here some angles of vision that suggest why my own trial-balance tips toward George McGovern.

On the Agnew buildup. The strongest aspect of Nixon's past eighteen months in office has been his new diplomacy, shaped with Henry Kissinger's help. But how long will it endure in the face of its internal foes? The Republican right wing abhors it, as Spiro Agnew does. They are already building Agnew up for 1976.

If he makes it, he will undo much of what has been done for a new Great Powers diplomacy and for a meeting of minds on reducing nuclear power. To hold his right wing in line this year Nixon was ready to pay the dangerous price of a probable Agnew succession. But why should I be asked to pay that price?

On moral insensitivity. The shadow of Watergate and the Republican political rip-offs has hung over the campaign. There are too many signs that people around Nixon—not all of them irresponsible underlings—were either overzealous or overclever, and some criminal. The president condemns the Watergate crime, and nothing has yet been proved in the courts. But despite this protective cocoon of legalisms, Nixon has shown a moral insensitivity to the whole surrounding fabric of rip-off and sabotage.

On domestic policy. Latterly Nixon seems to have neglected or forgotten even some of his more liberal domestic programs, including a continued drive for de facto desegregation, the Philadelphia Plan in labor hiring, a strong system of educational subsidies, and an energetic housing program. In the next four years, we may expect the resumption of forward movement from McGovern, but not from Nixon. For the working people, George Meany has consistently said that Nixon's economic controls hit wages harder than profits.

An administration must be tough-minded, yes. But I am troubled to see compassion for the lowly—if it ever existed—turned off so abruptly. There is a difference between toughness of mind and hardness of heart, whether on ending the war or civilizing the civilization.

On the party structure. I am not a party loyalist, but I don't want to see the Democratic Party shattered. Whatever the presidential outcome, the continuance of a Democratic majority in both Houses will be healthy, especially on a future reform in the balance of war powers between executive and Congress.

On managing social change. There were runaway changes in the America of the 1960s, and they needed to be contained and channeled. The present mood has turned dangerously toward stagnation in important areas where channeled change is still needed. There are popular intolerances that the president and his party have used politically, instead of calming them. With his fixation on foreign policy and his boredom with the domestic scene, I suspect that Richard Nixon will have neither the interest nor the will to pursue this calming policy.

On Nixon's margin. I have few illusions about what the election results will be. But if Nixon is to win, it would be better if he won with a narrower margin. It would make domestic policy more liberal in the next four years, place clear limits around the second term, and make Agnew's future less secure. It would also give Nixon less scope to play emperor of the American imperium.

I could wish this were a more impassioned election position, and there will be readers who would wish it were more partisan, one way or the other. But no one who has traveled the country as I have can ignore the fact that something in George McGovern has turned off many who might have supported him, and that there is something in Richard Nixon that even those who respect him cannot accept. It would be willfully blind to fail to see this, and dishonest to fail to say it.

I have strong faith in what the presidential office does to its incumbents. Richard Nixon has grown in it, especially in his vision of Great Power relations. He may still have growth in him. But George

McGovern starts with greater social generosity, and with a deeper streak of moral commitment to the life chances of ordinary people. He has less to live down than Nixon had at the start of his first term. He too would grow in the incumbency of the office. He has already shown evidences of such growth during the grueling ordeal of the recent weeks.

I add only that there are things I feel more deeply about than a choice between the candidates: that the current moves toward a cease-fire should not be dragged out too long and should become a reality, that American change and growth should have fresh scope, and that the basic fabric of American society should not be broken by social tensions and too bitter political division.

★

NOVEMBER 8, 1972

So Richard Nixon came through, and achieved the triumph he sought so doggedly, so skillfully. It was a personal and not a party triumph, since many Democrats who crossed party lines to vote for him crossed back to vote for Democratic congressmen and governors. It was thus also a personal defeat for George McGovern, who fought gamely against overwhelming odds but who was clearly the exactly wrong candidate for the Democratic Party to have chosen at this time.

There will be many postmortem canvassings of the reasons for the massiveness of the McGovern defeat and the Nixon victory. It was not because of the personality of the two men, since both were relatively colorless, and most votes were probably negative votes, cast against rather than for a candidate.

If I single out one meaning of the election results, it is not because I reject the other meanings but because this one is central, radiating out and cutting across all the others. Besides, it was too little discussed all through the campaign, perhaps because—like Poe's Purloined Letters—it was so obvious that it was overlooked.

I am speaking of the real "sleeper" issue of the campaign, unde-bated but present in the minds of most voters—the management of social change. Note that this has been the first presidential election since the great wave of dislocating and disruptive social changes of the 1960s. In 1960 Kennedy's victory came on the rising tide of change, when most Americans were hopeful about it. In 1964 Johnson's victory came when people still thought he could manage the domestic changes and before the war tide engulfed him. In 1968, at the height of the change, the narrowness of Nixon's margin of victory suggests how torn the voters were between a liberal and a conservative approach to change.

In 1972 they were no longer torn. The tide has been moving toward the deceleration of the social changes. Very early McGovern lost his credibility for both parties on what we call the "social issues," which are really the change issues. When they rejected him it was not because of any particular stand of his, or trait of his, but because they didn't believe that he was the person to preside over the future deceleration of change.

There was much talk about McGovern's wobbling and waffling, whether on taxes, welfare, busing, housing, or whatever. All of it came down to a central shift. His assumption at the start of the campaign was that Americans want rapid social change. He geared his primary campaigns to that assumption, and was misled by their results. For the nation as a whole it was simply not true. Richard Nixon was quick to see this, swift to take advantage of it.

When McGovern shifted, trying to say in effect that he too could be trusted to manage the deceleration of change prudently, it was too late. Besides, for the unbelievers the fervor of many of his followers canceled out his denials. In the popular mind—blue-collar, white-collar, ethnics, middle-class—the image had been formed, and it hardened. McGovern hammered harder and harder at corruption, at the war and even the peace, at Nixon personally, but it was as if he was on one track and the voters on another, and never the twain met. Rarely has a good man, with high ideals, fighting gallantly, alienated so many. His campaign was drenched in the pathos of alienation.

Nixon campaigned little, because he didn't have to, and because he thus gave few hostages to his future policies. There were no real pressures to make him commit himself, except on the cease-fire. It wasn't that the voters loved him, but that he was a known and not an unknown quantity. Between a candidate they knew and could therefore calculate, and one they didn't really know and hadn't given their trust to, they chose the first overwhelmingly.

Nixon's basic stance toward the next four years can be put quite simply: on domestic changes, he intends to place limits around them, and preside over their deceleration. On global policy, he intends to move ahead, along with his adviser Henry Kissinger, on further initiatives toward Russia, China, and the SALT talks. One might point out the fault line in this, between backtracking at home and dynamism abroad. But most voters either rode along with the contradiction, accepting it grudgingly, or else they saw Nixon as essentially a stabilizer in both areas, seeking deceleration at home and seeking global stabilization between the Great Powers abroad.

As for the Democratic Party, it retains its majority in both Houses of Congress, and can set limits on whatever hubris Nixon's landslide victory may evoke in him. It can also, as the Republicans did after the disaster of 1964, rethink its blunders, and learn from history.

1976

CARTER vs. FORD

Aᴌʟ ᴘᴏʟɪᴛɪᴄs ɪs ᴛʜᴇᴀᴛᴇʀ. But aside from the vice presidential choice and the acceptance speech, the theatrical highlight of this Democratic convention has been the still-unfolding character of the presidential nominee—the question of what manner of man Jimmy Carter is.

I can recall only a handful of nominees about whom this question was put so insistently. They were Franklin Roosevelt, Wendell Willkie, Dwight Eisenhower, Adlai Stevenson, John F. Kennedy. Each of them, like Carter today, came into the candidate limelight too fast to have revealed much about themselves. Each took the city of the politicians by surprise, if not by storm.

There are some signs that the manner of man Carter is, and the way he is likely to develop, may place him with these five. Not that he resembles Roosevelt, with his patrician dash and his joy in life, or Willkie, with his half-political, half-literary sense of adventure, or Eisenhower, with his genial soldierly fatherliness, or Stevenson, with his self-deprecatory intellectual bite, or Kennedy, with his combination of Faustian appetites and Apollonian grace.

Yet however different Carter is from them, he can be mentioned alongside them without a sense of absurdity. Clearly there is substance to him, and there is puzzlement about him. In my own view he comes closest to Willkie. In both cases you have the businessman-turned-politician, the outsider among professionals, grinning and cocky, conservative in instinct but with a passion for the underdog—in Willkie's case for civil liberties, in Carter's for civil rights.

We can take the what-manner-of-man question apart and break it into four other questions about presidential nominees. What are his political instincts? What will his policies be like? How will he make decisions, and how will he behave in crises? What is his inner essence as a man?

In his political instincts Carter may be closest to Roosevelt, with perhaps an even more ravenous power hunger than the squire of Hyde Park had. But there seems to be the same combination of strength and guile. Roosevelt as president was constantly attacked for the element of guile. If Carter gets to the presidency I suspect it will be true of him, too.

Machiavelli said that a ruler may rule either by inspiring love or instilling fear. But while Carter seems to prefer love, he has a capacity for command, which combines both.

It is too early to tell about his policies, even given the platform and the acceptance speech. They are likely to hover around the center—some a little to the left, some a little to the right. I have the sense about him, as I had about Stevenson when he was nominated, that neither his liberalism nor his conservatism is the traditional brand. If he gets to be president it will be interesting to see whether he can put together a new amalgam.

On one thing we are clear now. His decisions—right or wrong—will be his own, not someone else's decisions. His passion for reorganizing the governmental processes springs not only from a desire to streamline them but also from a desire to make his choices as president felt. This is all to the good. As for his behavior in the fiery furnace of crisis, we don't know yet. But the swiftness and skill with which he retrieved his "ethnic purity" blunder show a degree of coolness about him.

There remains the question of his inner essence as a man. He lacks the bravura style that we found in the five nominees I mentioned. As a Southern liberal in the White House he will feel (he has told us) a greater sense of inner security than Lyndon Johnson had. Unlike any president since Woodrow Wilson, his inner essence seems best expressed in religious terms.

Going back to the Machiavelli sentence above, Carter wants primarily neither to be loved nor feared, but to be followed. His conviction of being twice-born and having communed directly with God must mean that he sees the people as a flock to be tended and himself as shepherd. Like the Great Shepherd in the Psalm, his deepest drive may be to lead his people into the paths of righteousness. It will be a somewhat novel experience for Americans, if it happens. Politically it is not one that will give the Republicans much of a target to shoot at.

★

AUGUST 23, 1976

Kansas City—In his final day of triumph and decision Gerald Ford abandoned the Sun Belt strategy for a Heartland strategy. By his choice of Senator Robert Dole rather than Senator Howard Baker or John Connally, and by the fighting tone of his acceptance speech, he made it clear that his aim is to heal the war wounds within his party, and rival Jimmy Carter in an upbeat, evangelical appeal to the "old-time religion" values of the Heartland voters in every region.

By any other logic than that of the Heartland appeal the choice of Dole has to be seen as an unfortunate one. He is a bright but undistinguished farm-belt senator, chiefly known as a party wheelhorse. He is not associated with any major legislation, has little intellectual imagination, and no national constituency. He is a conservative who will not help Ford to broaden his base with either Democrats or independently.

But Dole had three things going for him. Of the list of six candidates whom Ford and Ronald Reagan discussed at their midnight meeting—Howard Baker, William D. Ruckelshaus, Robert Dole, William Simon, Elliot Richardson, and John Connally—Dole was the one whom Reagan liked best, or perhaps disliked least. Second, he has the aggressive qualities that Ford wants and needs in a campaign against a wily infighter like Carter. Finally, he is a man President Ford feels at home with, who won't threaten to outshine him, and who offers fewer problems for him—political or personal—than any of the more dramatic choices.

It was a low-risk decision by President Ford, rather than a bold one. Just as Carter turned to a strongly liberal Walter Mondale to make sure that the liberal dissidents wouldn't sit on their hands during the campaign, so Ford turned to a conservative party worker to make sure that the conservative dissidents and the party militants won't sit on their hands. But it is the presidential candidates themselves who will set the tone and strategy of their campaigns.

The surprise of the convention's closing session was the new image Gerald Ford projected in his acceptance speech. It is quite deliberately a Harry Truman image—that of the underdog fighter who has survived the first bruising round, who refuses to lose heart when the odds are steep against him, but takes the offensive with an indomitable optimism. That Ford spoke in the very shadow of Truman's old home, in Independence, made his effort at adopting a Truman image more poignant, while highlighting both the parallels and differences between the two men and their political philosophies.

More than anything else it is the Ford-Carter debates that will count. In any other situation an incumbent president would be foolish to debate with a challenger who is a newcomer. But President Ford has nothing to risk except his cellar standing in the polls and everything to gain. The real risks will be Carter's, who is the incumbent of the high ratings and who has thus far benefited from the haziness of his personality and views. Ford won't be as articulate as Carter or as fast in thinking on his feet, but he has little to lose. The stakes for him are the chance to project his cherished Truman image in a sustained way. What Carter in turn wants is a chance to consolidate his lead—to show his command of the issues, spell out his positions, and counter Ford's matter-of-fact mind by his own more agile and subtle one.

By rejecting both Howard Baker and William Ruckelshaus—the two contenders who could have helped him with the party's Watergate problem and his own problem of the Nixon pardon—Ford in effect declared his refusal to go on the defensive in his campaign. Instead he went on the offensive, not only against the Democratic congressional majority but also in vaunting his own record on peace, the economy, and the healing of divisions within the society.

This means that Ford's real target will be the image he will try to pin on the Democrats of the past—that of a freely spending and over-legislating party linked with a growing bureaucracy and with too rapid social change. The decisive and final symbol of this, deeply embedded in the memories of Heartland America, was the turbulent decade of the 1960s.

Ford's problem is that this was Nixon's rhetoric in 1972 as well, that Watergate has intervened, that he is running against Jimmy Carter and not George McGovern. By his "outsider" role Carter has managed to dissociate himself from the Democrats of the 1950s and '60s, and by his evangelist overtones he is less vulnerable to the usual Republican attacks on the sinfulness of the Democrats.

It will be a debate between the images of latter-day saintliness, both addressed to Heartland America.

★

There has been no true psychological profile of Gerald Ford, not even the instant histories that are beginning to appear on Jimmy Carter. It isn't for lack of time: the two years since Ford became president were time enough. Mostly it is because no one took him that seriously.

He seemed clearly a caretaker president, holding down the job until someone weighty enough, great enough, or mischievous enough to merit real study came along. There didn't seem to be enough tangle in Ford's personality and character to need untangling.

True, a couple of biographies of him were published, but he has seemed a man without a history as well as a man without a future. Even when he decided to become a candidate to succeed himself we all treated him as the candidate who wasn't there.

We were wrong. No matter how the election comes out, what happened during his contest with Ronald Reagan and in the closing days of Kansas City now forces us to do some rethinking on Ford as a person.

In an earlier piece on Carter I spoke of R. D. Laing's phrase the "divided self" and how Carter had overcome his division during his life history. What little we know about Ford suggests that the surface unity his personality showed did have a crack in it.

I speak, of course, of Ford's two fathers. He was born Leslie King. His parents were divorced soon after, his mother remarried, and his new father—Gerald R. Ford—adopted him legally and renamed him Gerald R. Ford, Jr.

As his biographer and former press secretary, Gerald terHorst, tells the story, the young Gerald, then seventeen, was working at a lunchroom in Grand Rapids when he saw a stranger standing at the counter. "Leslie," the stranger said, "I'm your father. Let's go out to lunch." Ford had only recently been told of his two fathers and his adoption. King was on his way to Detroit to pick up a new Lincoln, and had stopped at Grand Rapids to talk with his son. After that lunch he disappeared again.

One can read too much into the incident. Young Gerald had grown up in a secure family with his new father, was a football hero of his high school, was about to go on an athletic scholarship to the University of Michigan. Yet the abandonment by his father, and the episode of the sudden arrival and departure, couldn't help but leave a scar of doubt. There followed Yale Law School, where he did tolerably well (he was in the top third of his class), but was mostly silent during the class discussions, and was known chiefly as a "jock," was an expert dancer and took pretty girls to the dances.

After his navy years, Ford came back to Grand Rapids, got into politics, ran successfully for Congress, and has never left politics since. Very often the people who go into politics as a vocation are those who win—and perhaps need—the approval of others in order to validate their own sense of identity.

Ford was an extrovert, with that kind of protean skill and need. He did well in the political vocation, but he always followed a leader— an Eisenhower, a Nixon—instead of aiming at the top post himself. Even when Nixon was forced to resign, and Ford became president, he found it hard to assume the leader's role. He shrank from it, lest he seem a usurper—to others and himself.

Using the Carter analogy one may guess that Ford was "born again" when he ran for the presidency for the first time, encountered the unexpectedly stiff challenge from Ronald Reagan, found himself ridiculed by the media as an incumbent president who would be refused the nomination by his party, fought hard to a cliff-hanger finish—and overcame.

The acceptance speech was Ford's watershed. Ford was like a Lazarus come back from the pit of night. The young man who had been rocked by his father's betrayal, and had sought security at first in sports and then in the safe haven of second-rank politics, finally found the perilous joy of a fighting strength on the lonely height, where only trust in self can save you.

This will be the Ford who will face Carter in the debates—less verbal and articulate than Carter, less agile with ideas. Yet he won't be wholly a pushover, because it isn't the pre-Reagan Ford who will be there, but the post-Reagan Ford—prouder of his record, more confident of his abilities and qualities than he has ever been. When the two born-again contenders engage in mortal combat it will be worth watching.

★

OCTOBER 13, 1976

If you don't have a taste for the delightful ironies of role reversals and upside-down strategy shifts, this is not the campaign for you. I can't recall a presidential election with more lightning changes in the turns of battle than this one. Nor do I recall one where the gods of mischief were busier in deranging the minds of the combatants, and the goddess of fortune wilder in playing dice with their destinies.

For a time it looked as if Jimmy Carter had thrown the campaign away by his unwary interview with *Playboy*, where he spoke of "lust" in his heart, and his needlessly cruel characterization of Lyndon Johnson. Then, just as President Ford was moving into a dead heat with Carter, he in turn threw the campaign away by his even more unwary gaffe about Poland and Eastern Europe in the debate. The fact of single marginal episodes causing such havoc in the fortunes of battle cannot have escaped an observer who has any sense of the ironies of history.

There have been such episodes in past campaigns, like the "Rum, Romanism and Rebellion" howler, of 1884 that doomed James G. Blaine against Grover Cleveland, but they were the exception. The key to the new roll of chance in presidential elections lies in the decisiveness of the media. They serve as a multiplier factor.

Within minutes of the ending of the second debate, the TV screen was filled with assessments of damage Ford had done to himself. If anyone was unsure of the debate's outcome, his doubts were soon dispelled by the newscasters and commentators; much as had happened with Carter and *Playboy*.

Things were quieter before contraptions like the electronic tube, and before so much rode on the outcome of each election. When it took weeks for a dispatch to travel through the thirteen original states, no candidate could be either elected or defeated by the mischance of a single remark. What counted, in the case of men like Adams, Jefferson, and Madison, was the cumulative impression of a total career in politics.

But the media are with us, and things are as they are, and the candidates and their staffs have to seize the moment of fortune or misfortune and know what to do with it.

One can see how Ford made his howler: He was tense and unsure of himself under Carter's barrage of attack. He didn't want to yield anything to Carter that would seem to augment Russia's power in the world as compared with the free world. In his eagerness, Ford got muddled and failed to distinguish between the fact of Soviet power over its satellites and the fact of popular discontent within the frame of this power. It was a fateful blunder, and may mean the difference between a close election and defeat.

What makes it worse—and the result more ironic—is that the voters it affects are the blue-collar ethnics who had been deeply troubled about Carter and were moving toward Ford. The irony is also that historically, on the issue of the captive nations of Eastern Europe, the Democrats have been on the complacent side, the Republicans on the unyielding side. The idea of "building bridges" to nations like Yugoslavia, Romania, and Poland has been a favorite one among Democratic presidential advisers, even more than with Secretary of State Kissinger.

Carter is, of course, playing the issue to the hilt, with his talk of Ford having been "brainwashed" in Poland, and his "hard" line on the Communist and Arab states, almost interchangeable with Reagan's. He can't be faulted for pushing hard when things are going his way.

Yet Carter faces two major dangers of overreaching. One is that he will seem too opportunist as a quick-change artist in his topsy-turvy role reversal. The other is that he will seem too ruthless.

His style in the debate was the first sign of the new strategy of harsh attack on Ford. Since it worked he has intensified the strategy, hitting him on campaign financing, on the Arab blacklist, and wherever else he can get at him. One is reminded of a fighter pursuing his groggy opponent for the killing punch.

Usually Americans like the killer instinct in their candidates. But it is hard to recall recent presidential campaigns in which so intense an attack was unleashed. Even "Give 'em hell" Harry Truman directed his fire at a whole Congress, not his opponent.

What makes it more dangerous for Carter is that the image he had carefully built up was that of a devout believer in the Christian creed of humility and compassion. Smiting the enemy with fire, scourges, and pestilence seems more Old Testament than New. The Holy War is historically more Moslem than Christian.

✭

Even before the election, Americans have been holding an inquest, not on the results but on the expected wretched turnout of voters. Given the freeze on enthusiasm, and the probability that as many voters will probably stay away from the polls as will go, the question is: Why the apathy?

The simplest and most obvious response is the events-are-bad explanation. Everyone knows the litany of recent disasters that have made many lose confidence in political institutions and leaders. The theory is that the discouraging times have turned off the voter, making him feel that it doesn't make any difference who gets elected, because events are beyond the control of presidents as well as of voters.

This explanation leaves me cold. The highest voting percentages came between the Civil War and the 1890s. Those were not good days—the days of Reconstruction, sectional hatreds, corruption, depressions. In fact one might even argue that bad events make hot politics, and that today's apathy may be more related to the absence of a war or a sharp depression, either of which might spark a voter turnout. The politics of rage and outrage is more likely to excite voters than the politics of dreary discontents.

For a more fruitful approach I start with the need for political distance between an evocative leader and the people. Hitler is the classic instance, Gandhi and Nehru are others. Their followers saw them at vast mass rallies, sometimes traveling for days to catch a glimpse of them, but it didn't happen often. The rest of the time the leader was a name, a haloed figure, a memory. The best recent instance was de Gaulle, who loved to theorize about authority and appeal in a leader and who was convinced that distance was part of it.

But the media have abolished the distance between people and leader in America. In the earlier republics the people heard about their presidents and candidates, but rarely saw them. How many Americans ever saw Jefferson or Adams or Madison? In the 1850s the rural folk drove their wagons into the Illinois towns to hear Lincoln and Douglas, but it was an event to be recalled for decades. There was a fervor among his listeners when William Jennings Bryan campaigned, as witness Vachel Lindsay's nostalgic celebration of that boyhood event in his "Bryan, Bryan, Bryan."

Today we serve up the candidates every morning along with the breakfast-food ads, and every evening with the auto and beer ads, and it's hard to tell their spiel from the others. We get to know their pitch and cadences, their grin, their bald spots and hairlines, their stumblings as they recite the words agreed upon an hour or two earlier in their huddle with campaign managers, press secretaries, pollsters, TV advisers, state and regional experts, ethnic specialists, and speechwriters. By becoming familiar they also become commonplace without ceasing to be synthetic. We scold them, rail at them, turn the cold eye of indifference to them, dismiss them as we might dismiss a disappointing quarterback in a pro football game.

Another item that breeds contempt: We see them constantly as suppliants for our votes, weaving and dodging around issues, evading the hard questions, picking their way between the pitfalls that beset them. They become broken-field runners. The qualities that make them survive are less those of courage and strength than of adroitness in escaping the dangers of candor.

This is not due solely to the media. Even more, it is due to the pressure-group democracy that we have become—badgering the candidates, surrounding them with the psychic intensities of the aggressive and aggrieved, as with barbed-wire entanglement.

Thus at a time when the need is for symbols larger than life, the candidates are cut down to all-too-mortal scale and become antiheroes. There is a deep drive in all of us for someone or something to be loyal to—a party, a movement, a cause, a person. There is a hunger for trust. The voter feels frustrated in finding anyone who can evoke either his loyalty or his trust. And since he can't achieve it, he resents both the parties and both the candidates who have made it hard for him.

He may vote for one or the other, with a thin margin of belief to back his vote. He may vote for a minor-party candidate, to give the party leaders something to think about. Or he may get turned off—or never turned on—and not vote at all.

It is his way of saying, "Amidst the phoniness, I serve notice that I'm no phony. Where the differences are of little account, count me out." Except that we had better count him in—very much count him in—as someone to ponder over, someone to be disturbed about.

★

OCTOBER 29, 1976

Columnists assume, in their narcissism, that their readers are hanging on their decision about how to vote. I doubt that there is an overwhelming interest. But when I read an endorsement, whether for Jimmy Carter or Gerald Ford, I like to know the context of the endorser's present stand in his past stands.

In my own presidential odyssey my earliest vote was for Franklin Roosevelt in 1932. Many of my friends on the left scorned me because they thought he was a lackey of capitalism. But compared with Herbert Hoover, and given the need for an energetic attack on the Great Depression in its panic phase, Roosevelt was an easy choice for me.

I stuck with him in later elections, too—1940 was the only hard choice, because he was breaking the two-term tradition and Wendell Willkie was a good man. But American entry into the war seemed inevitable, and I preferred FDR as war leader.

In 1948 Truman's cronies troubled me, and Dewey seemed impossible. So I came out for Norman Thomas, but inside the voting booth I found myself voting for Truman after all. In the next two elections I voted for Adlai Stevenson. He would have been a more interesting president than Eisenhower, although Ike is getting moderately good grades from the historians.

In 1960 I voted for Kennedy over Nixon, in 1964 for Johnson over Goldwater, in 1968 for Humphrey over Nixon. I had never a flutter about any of those decisions. The 1972 decision, for McGovern over Nixon, was harder. I had no illusions about either man. But since Nixon was clearly going to win, I voted for McGovern to make Nixon's mandate as thin as possible.

This year I prefer Carter and Mondale to Ford and Dole, and to McCarthy and whoever he runs with. As a person and a mind I like McCarthy. But aside from the danger of his undercutting Carter, I doubt that this is the time for a crotchety president with no party, even if he is also the only candidate with irreverence, wit, and a sense of the absurd.

I have at times been more critical of Carter than his committed supporters have been. Ford is in some ways safer because we know him better, and Carter more of a gamble because we don't. But in a time of the shaking of nations and of the world economy, and a time also for rethinking the foundations of our national life, it isn't enough to hug the familiar road, especially when the jobless figures show it isn't a good-enough road.

We took a gamble on Roosevelt in 1932 and it worked, and on Kennedy in 1960 and it might have worked if he had lived. Many of us were willing to take a gamble on Stevenson. If we were never prepared to venture, then incumbents would always win and challengers always lose.

America today needs someone at the helm who will energize the collective intelligence and will of the whole people. Ford has not done this during his tenure because it isn't built in him to do it, either in his mind and imagination or in his conception of the presidency.

He has proved himself a man better able to say no to Congress than yes to the urgencies of the time. With some exceptions, like Henry Kissinger at State, Edward Levi at Justice, and William Coleman at Transportation, the group around him in Washington has similarly lacked dynamism.

An administration is more than a president. It is the people around him, the man who will succeed him if necessary, the people he appoints, the ambiance of energy or lack of it surrounding the whole. The most lurid fact separating Ford and Carter is the men they picked for vice president.

I can comfortably envisage Walter Mondale as president. My mind boggles at Robert Dole in the same role. I will feel better with Carter's Supreme Court appointments in the next four years than with Ford's, just as I will feel better about economic policy, energy policy, and the proliferation of arms sales.

Roosevelt had a Depression and then a world war to cope with; Truman coped with a postwar crisis; Truman and Eisenhower together with a cold war; Kennedy with a missile confrontation; Johnson with an internal acceleration of change along with a war; Nixon with his own inner nature as well as with phasing out a war and a cold war.

The presidency is a risky task, and whoever gets it will be a gamble. But it is better to pick someone who is likely to command the storms.

✶

NOVEMBER 3, 1976

It was a good victory for Jimmy Carter, even if it came after a flaky, shaky campaign and a hectic array of undecided states almost to the end.

It showed some important things about the America now entering its third century. One is that the South has been brought back into the presidential history of America, from which it was long excluded.

Woodrow Wilson was born a Southerner, but came to the presidency from New Jersey. Lyndon Johnson was a Texan who first became president not by election but by succession at Kennedy's death.

Carter's victory will give Southerners a new sense of political confidence, and will soften some of their chip-on-the-shoulder resentments about the national parties.

Carter's victory also brings a healing of the wounds between whites and blacks, especially between Southern whites and Northern blacks.

The overwhelming turnout of black voters for Carter, in big black population centers of the North like Detroit, Chicago, Philadelphia, and here in New York, is evidence that the big-city blacks no longer carry the memory of their Southern roots with bitterness.

Equally important is what the closeness of the election results showed about the future of the Republican Party. If America is to continue with its two-party system the parties must have some kind of numerical balance, if not in registration, then in their voting potential. Both parties must have a sense of hope and possibility; neither can afford to feel despair.

It is to Gerald Ford's credit that he gave his party back its almost-lost hope. He fought his way back from an impossible distance behind Carter, after the conventions, to a position all but abreast of him at the end.

It took courage, stamina, and an indomitable will, and in its closing weeks his campaign was tighter and better managed than Carter's, and he himself won back some of the authority he had eroded in the past.

He will leave his presidential post with a warm knowledge that almost half the voters wanted him to continue for a term of his own. He has not been one of America's great presidents. But my own guess is that the historians a decade from now will assess him more generously and justly than most observers did in the primaries and the campaign.

They will say that he came to the presidency at a time of deep wounds and divisions, when the legitimacy of the office had come into question. He did much to heal the wounds, close the divisions, and restore a measure of the legitimacy.

As for President-elect Carter, he had a close call. He almost became a Humpty-Dumpty, and narrowly avoided a great fall. But he did avoid it. He finally won the prize for which he had worked intensely for two years.

He showed errors of judgment and at times seemed his own worst enemy. But he also showed a capacity to sustain the tensions that will stand him in good stead in the presidency. He benefited from his showing in the debates.

But mostly he won by hammering away at the economic issue. The bread-and-butter question is still the prime question for American voters. At the crunch, the unionists, the young, the blacks, the low-income groups carried the victory for Carter on the issue of jobs and joblessness. It wasn't that they trusted him more than Ford, but that they preferred to gamble on his doing better than Ford with the economy.

Carter will enter the presidency as a man chastened by his misjudgments in the campaign. It is a good wheel of fire for him to have been caught on. It will burn out some of the immaturities in him and temper him for the trials ahead.

He will be judged in great measure by the kind of men with whom he surrounds himself in his top appointments. Up to now some of the "Georgia Mafia" have proved too callow and cocky to inspire much confidence about his capacity to choose people. He must overcome this initial impression.

One of the attractive things about Carter has been the sense of energy and freshness with which he entered the political arena. Roosevelt and Kennedy had that kind of energy. But there must also be a philosophy behind it—of government and society, and of the global economy and the world community.

It won't be enough for Carter as president to project his personal qualities into the center of the picture as he did in the campaign. He will no longer be a small-town Southern farmer and businessman selling his piety and virtue to the voter. He will be in the political big time, where tough-mindedness and mature judgment count.

We all pledge him our help, but he will need to stretch himself to grow to the dimensions of the presidential office.

1980

REAGAN vs. CARTER

JOHN CONNALLY IS OUT of the Republican contest, and it has been a $10 million flop. Gerald Ford is in—very much in. Ronald Reagan is still the hot candidate, with his South Carolina win. What's wrong with this picture?

There is a growing feeling, as we watch the primaries story unfold, that the role of TV in influencing the results is central, and that it isn't healthy for the American political system.

A strong argument can be made for this view. No matter how much fairness and detachment the news managers on TV channels try to muster, TV can be at once exhilarating and cruel to the candidates. It is image-making and image-destroying. It is sudden birth and sudden death. TV has become at once midwife and mortician: It presides with equal fervor over the birth of a political star and over its plummeting and destruction.

The argument is that we cannot afford to surrender this make-or-break power to a media elite whom we have never elected but who have become the real power group in the nation.

The alternative? Is it to go back to the old days when primaries were only a preliminary test run for the candidates, in only a few states, and when it was the convention itself that fought out the bloody battles, on the convention floor, and got all the media attention? The fact is that we cannot go back to an exclusive convention politics, even if we wanted to. Too much has happened. The developing primaries system has an irreversible momentum. Besides, the convention system wasn't all that good.

What gave it both its strength and its weakness was the role of the power brokers—state party chairmen, big-city bosses, national committeemen, key senators and congressmen, trade-union leaders. Before the full growth of the primaries system a convention was rarely ready for a first-ballot victory for any candidate: often the balloting went on for days and became a marathon of endurance between two or three candidates, while the power brokers maneuvered behind the scenes. Sometimes a convention was deadlocked and then a "dark horse" candidate emerged as victor as a result of power deals in a "smoke-filled room."

The strength of this system was that the power brokers could sometimes reach agreement on a "consensus" candidate who was a compromise and also electable. The weakness was that a compromise candidate, chosen to break a deadlock, might be a cipher like James Cox or a deadbeat like Warren Harding. Worst of all, the system gave a manipulative make-or-break power to men and women whose interests and judgment were not necessarily those of the voters.

The primaries system is media-focused and ruthless, yes. But it has great merits of its own. It tests the political intelligence of the candidates as well as their durability. It discovers how much realism they have, along with strong voices, good nerves, and good digestions. It separates the political men from the political boys.

But that isn't all. Its great merit is that, despite its seeming feverish pace, it is actually more reflective than the convention system alone, in both senses of the adjective. It reflects the mood of the people—a volatile mood sometimes, but still *their* mood, and not that of the power brokers at a particular moment when the convention meets.

It also gives the people a chance to reflect, from week to week and month to month, on the intelligence, character, psyche, courage, decisiveness, values, and trustworthiness of a dwindling array of candidates who have survived after others have fallen.

This is a consensus politics all its own. It may destroy a Howard Baker, which was sad, but it also comes up with a John Anderson. It may end with a George McGovern, yes, but it won't end with a Warren G. Harding. The convention will still have a role to play, and for the Republicans this year it will probably again mean a floor fight between Reagan and Ford. But the two men will have been tested to the limit before they get there.

★

MARCH 21, 1980

I have a theory about the remarkable strength that Ronald Reagan has shown in the primaries and will show in the election itself. We have, I think, come to the end of the affair that has been going on between the American people and the liberal dream since Franklin Roosevelt was elected in 1932. The voters see Reagan as signalizing a sharp turn away from the liberalism that ruled the country for most of the half century, under both Democrats and Republicans.

Ronald Reagan presents himself as the continuing and final hope for a breakthrough that will end this liberal affair. The reason that most liberal commentators are today surprised at his showing is that they have been living in an illusory liberal dream.

Mostly liberal commentators know Washington, New York, and Boston. They don't know the rest of America. As a media elite they are part of the New Class, which is the power elite of today. If a liberal showed a consistent record over a long period they would hail him. When someone like Ronald Reagan remains a consistent conservative they attack him as a reactionary and—in their own minds—see him as outside the mainstream of American opinion.

He was outside when he fought the Communist leadership of the Screen Actors Guild under the New Deal. He was still outside, although less so, when he made a bid against Richard Nixon in 1968—a Nixon who shared the liberal adversary with Reagan but who had no basic doctrinal position himself except to be elected. Reagan was less a conservative outsider when he fought Gerald Ford in 1976 and all but made it.

But by 1980 the current toward conservatism that has been running strongly since 1968, not only within the Republican Party but among Democrats and independents as well, has caught up with Reagan. He has not been its avant-garde leader: Howard Jarvis has been that. But Reagan has been its continuing symbol. The moderate conservatives would have preferred Gerald Ford again in 1980, as they did in 1976. But they will settle for Reagan, because he is now part of the mainstream for them.

This column was reprinted as a guest editorial, "The End of the Liberal Affair," in *National Review* (April 18, 1980), signifying its importance as a statement about Reagan's meaning, especially to a writer primarily known for a liberal perspective.

It is hard for the doctrinal liberals of both parties to accept this—
or even understand it. But Jimmy Carter understands it. He has all
along expected Ronald Reagan to be his opponent, not George Bush
and certainly not John Anderson.

The fact is that Jimmy Carter will have to run as more of a conservative than a liberal against Reagan. He was himself elected as an
anti-Washington outsider, which for most of his religious fundamentalist constituency meant that he was against the Eastern liberal establishment. Those who have studied the childhood influences that have
shaped Carter know that he has always tried to contain and reconcile
within himself the conflicting claims of the liberal rebellion of his
mother and the traditional Southern conservatism of his father. The
resulting image is sometimes that of a national leader, more often that
of a man deeply split inwardly.

Carter will find it hard to win against Reagan. The blow from the
Iranian parliamentary elections means that the hostages may still be in
Teheran by November. The Carter blunder over Israel won't blow
away, and the ambivalent, tortured performance by Secretary of State
Cyrus Vance before the Senate committee underlines Carter's long-
range policy of aiming at an accord with the PLO. Nor will the inflation picture be better in November: It is likely to be worse.

Reagan will benefit from all three issues. He will play the national
honor theme on Iran and the hostages. He has all along been far more
supportive than Carter on Israel as the anti-Communist bulwark of the
Middle East, and he will continue to be. On inflation he will stress a
tax-cutting program, which will have wide popular appeal. Unthinkable as it may seem, Reagan will carry New York as well as California
against Carter.

Along with his massive strength in the Sun Belt, from Florida to
Texas to Arizona, Reagan will put together an extraordinary coalition of
support. Jimmy Carter may turn out to be a one-term president after all.

★

JULY 16, 1980

The ticket is complete, the platform accepted, the battle joined. The
question about Ronald Reagan remains: If he is elected, what will be
his working philosophy as president? Not his speeches, not his programs—important as those are—but the animating ideas behind them.

The first idea is *restoration*. Reagan is convinced that America has blundered in moving away from a road once traveled and has gone up a blind alley, that we have abandoned true goals and Gods in pursuit of false goals and alien Gods. He is committed to restoring the free market, business initiative, productivity, the work ethic, the national pride, the traditional values system, the cohesive family, adequate defense, and America's position among the powers of the earth.

For Reagan this kind of restoration thinking isn't only rhetoric. It is what drives him, and gives him the relatedness he has to the middle class whose frustrations and anger he is expressing.

A corollary idea is that of the *rejection of retreat and passivity*. Reagan may never have read Arnold Toynbee on challenge-and-response—the responses that a strong civilization must give to strong challenges from without and within. But he has somehow become imbued with that idea. He and the group around him feel there has been a failure of nerve among America's political elite and intellectual elite—a failure to use strength when confronted by strength. He sees that failure all down the line, from weak-willed parents and a permissive morality, down to the failure of a defense buildup in answer to Russia's unparalleled military expansion.

Note that his policy is not always a backward-looking "restoration." It moves into the technological future, as do a number of the economic and fiscal initiatives that Reagan's advisers propose. But the movement into the future is meant as an effort to restore the values of the past.

The third major Reagan idea comes out of an emphasis on the healthy organism being allowed to *take care of itself* instead of saddling it with interventions and controls. This thinking comes out of Adam Smith's basic idea that if you leave the economy alone, individual self-interests will add up to the national interest and the common good.

But again—probably without reading him—Reagan has picked up somewhere Edmund Burke's idea of continuity in history and tradition, and the great damage that can be done to the health of the family, community, and society by too much meddling on the part of the state.

This philosophy can have a broad appeal to many groups—the old conservatives, the Gerald Ford free market economists, the Jude Wanniski and Jack Kemp right-wing Keynesians who want to use tax policy as a lever to move the world with, the Evangelical church groups, the Catholic right-to-life groups, the neo-conservatives, the "Committee on the Present Danger" defense groups.

These are disparate, discordant elements, and Reagan will find it hard to hold them together. But they furnish the core of a possible new coalition not only for Reagan but also for the future Republican Party.

Reagan's problem, intellectually, is that he wants the state to stay out of the economy, but he also wants it to set limits in the areas of privacy—on abortions, on pornography, on drugs. Even more, he wants the state to adopt an interventionist foreign policy wherever America is threatened abroad, and incur heavy governmental expenditures for the defense industries.

These are troubling contradictions. But despite them, what holds Reagan's thinking together is his vision of a tough-minded responsive America, acting decisively abroad through its governmental and defense power, willing to allow free and spontaneous growth at home in the economy and society.

Every politician has a philosophy of some sort behind his actions and programs. Reagan's, with all its contradictions, may be one whose hour has struck.

☆

SEPTEMBER 19, 1980

Whatever the impact of the debate between Ronald Reagan and independent candidate John Anderson, there is another debate going on, and it isn't being staged by the League of Women Voters. It is an assessment debate in the minds of the voters, about all three candidates. How to assess them—their abilities, personalities, character, leadership qualities?

The question of how they behave in the formal debate is only part of the input. More important is how they behave in the campaign as a whole, and what light that sheds on the kind of president each of them will make in the first four years of 1980.

I have Jimmy Carter in mind especially, because he is the incumbent president. "Issues begin to be paramount and personal characteristics of the candidates become less important," he said, starting a press conference with a self-serving passage about what a good president he has been, which belonged in Norman Mailer's *Advertisements for Myself*.

This hyperbole, if not hypocrisy, of Carter is part of his character. The fact is that, of all the presidents in American history, he is the one who has most persistently personalized the presidency. He has placed himself, his life, his religious experiences, his personality, his character, in the forefront of everything he has said and done. If ever there was an "I president" it has been Jimmy Carter.

This is the conclusion of every sustained study that has been done of him. It is the conclusion of *Jimmy Carter: In Search of the Great White House*, an extraordinary biography by Betty Glad, a political-science professor at the University of Illinois, which has been curiously neglected by reviewers. No biography of any president since Roosevelt has been so scrupulously researched and narrated with such cold detachment.

The Jimmy Carter who emerges from it is the one the voters are watching now. His ambition is mountainous, his sense of himself grandiose and ever-present. In pursuit of his goal there is little he won't do, however devious.

He has said that Ronald Reagan is not a racist, and that he never called him one. Not outright. But after attacking Reagan's use of "states' rights," he said that there is no room in America for "racism." What other meaning could there be for such a statement if it did not attribute racism to Reagan?

To hear him say, in the face of this, that his own campaign is "moderate" was a corruption of language so deep that it called into question everything else he said at the press conference, including the prepositions and conjunctions.

As it happens, I am no novice at watching presidents, candidates, and campaigners. I have seen the cleverest of the presidents as campaigners, Franklin Roosevelt, and the scrappiest, Harry Truman. I have seen bumbling ones, like Dwight Eisenhower, who was nevertheless a man with a granite integrity. I have seen witty presidents, like John Kennedy, and rambunctious ones, like Lyndon Johnson. I have seen presidents who played hard ball as campaigners, like Richard Nixon.

Jimmy Carter has a very special place on this list, as more than anyone else a president who has earned our total distrust in anything he says as a campaigner.

It isn't only that he uses his incumbency for partisan purposes. Every president has done it. A president is not only commander in chief, communicator in chief, educator in chief, decision-maker in chief. He is also politician in chief. He has to be a fox as well as a lion, if he is to wield and retain power.

The trouble with Jimmy Carter is that the only role he is truly effective at is politician in chief. It dwarfs all the other in-chief roles. If he gets reelected, after the kind of campaign he is waging, it will be because the voters have failed badly in their own inner assessment debate.

★

NOVEMBER 5, 1980

No greater upheaval in American politics has occurred for a half century, since Franklin Roosevelt's victory over Herbert Hoover in 1932. The reach and depth of the Reagan sweep belie the current wisdom that it came only as a protest vote against Jimmy Carter and inflation.

Ronald Reagan's triumph was too convulsive to be confined within so narrow an analysis. It expressed a wide range of discontents, not only with the economy but also with foreign and defense policies, with taxes, welfare, and social policies, and with the entire climate of ideas. It expressed, along with the discontents, some deep, pent-up social angers.

This wasn't a tremor. It was an earthquake. It was long preparing. It represents a long-range retreat from the liberalism of the New Deal welfare state. Early in the campaign I wrote of the support for Reagan as a sign of the ending of the long affair between Americans and traditional liberalism. Reagan is a symbol of the closure of the liberal dream.

Flowing from this inevitably has been the breakup of the coalition that elected liberal Democratic candidates for fifty years. It was originally put together by FDR, and renewed by Truman, Kennedy, Johnson, and Carter. Its breakup means not only the defeat of Carter but—even worse for the Democrats—the defeat of the whole galaxy of able liberal Democratic senators, including Birch Bayh, John Culver, George McGovern, and Frank Church. This was the cream of the liberal political elite, and the cream curdled.

Parties don't change in the American political system, but coalitions do. The blacks held with Carter and so did the upper-middle "New Class" professionals. But the Catholics, Jews, ethnics, blue-collar and white-collar workers didn't. The union leaders couldn't control their own members. Even the much heralded clout of the feminists didn't work: Reagan made headway with women voters, too.

Something like a class revolution has been taking place. Since the violent 1960s the middle-middle and lower-middle class has been seething with social resentments over the runaway changes in the culture. They, too, were part of the American dream—they had worked and scrimped, fashioned a trade or small business, built a house, raised a family. They felt threatened by the forces that seemed intent on taking this away from them.

This time the populist revolt was led by the conservatives. Economic distress is only part of the story. Also part of it are the reawakened religious impulse and the concern about the work ethic and about the endangered values system.

Don't omit a strong pride of national identity, badly bruised by the Vietnam defeat and Watergate and the humiliating Year of the Hostages. It isn't a macho jingoism, looking for a war to get into. Where Carter came closest to victory was in his attack on Reagan as a potential war-maker. Reagan had to answer it to win.

The Carter-Reagan debate had to be the turning point of the campaign. Reagan undid the Carter tactic by showing himself to be prudent and rational. But he couldn't have done it if he were not bolstered by the pride of American identity on the part of his listeners. He gave them hope of repairing that injured pride. Carter didn't—which was why his last-minute hostage ploy faltered and failed.

Some closing words about Reagan himself, as image and man. Liberals have refused to take him seriously—until the end, when they panicked.

Reagan comes close to being the first presidential folk hero since Dwight Eisenhower. Ike achieved it because he was a soldier and war hero, while Reagan was dubbed as only an "actor." But for the people who have parried their hurt national pride, their economic scars, and their social angers, he will develop an almost mythical quality.

He will need it, because the road ahead—for himself and the nation—is bound to be a hard one.

1984

REAGAN vs. MONDALE

W HO HAS THE RIGHT METAPHOR for it? Is what is happening to the two leading Democratic candidates a horse race, a dog fight—or what? But does it matter what we call it? It does. The metaphors we use express—and also shape—our picture of the reality behind them. And when we use the wrong metaphor it means we have the wrong reality by the tail.

This week's *Time* magazine cover picture of Walter Mondale and Gary Hart in a neck-and-neck horse race is a traditional one. Yet what is happening between them is not a race, whether between horses or humans, but something quite different.

The obvious difference is that a race is decided among the contestants, by their speed, strength, endurance, or whatever, while an election is decided by the voters.

But it goes beyond that. The voters are not just the calm, rational appraising judges who are part of our myth of democracy. They are themselves at the heart of the action, identifying with the candidates, cheering them on, until the line gets blurred between their roles as judges and as actors.

As for the candidates they use every resource and contrivance to woo and win the voters. They try to get inside their minds, tastes, and attitudes, and adapt themselves Proteus-like to all shades of their thinking.

Thus the winning or losing of an election depends less on the merits of the candidates than on the relations—mostly psychological—between candidates and voters. That is where the true battleground is. Its results get reflected in the "horse race" between the candidates.

But the results are the end product of a dynamic process, and the dynamic today is quite simply TV. It transmits the images of the candidates to the voters. It also transmits the images of the voters to themselves, as they see themselves reflected in the image of other voters.

Finally there is the "front-loading" factor—the bunching of the early primaries close together so that the impact of an early winner (especially a surprise winner) is multiplied with a dizzying speed.

The notion that the early primaries' voters are more "independent" than in other states is a dubious piece of rhetoric. The "independence" of each consists in following the lead of the voters in the preceding caucus or primary. After Iowa they clustered around the image of other voters who had clustered around Gary Hart, much as groupies follow other groupies who race to get at the new star.

What is being called "momentum" is actually an acceleration effect, close to hysteria, which is part of the psychology of mass feeling and action.

Once a new favorite is spotted unexpectedly the voters abandon the earlier favorites to be in on the sudden turn toward the winning side. The old and cold inevitability becomes a new hot inevitability.

It may be obscured by the glittering star appeal of TV, but presidential-election politics has always been war and is still war. It is nasty, unforgiving, heartbreaking, ruthless, cunning. It adds the dark element to the exercise of choice in a democracy.

But if we are asking for a metaphor the difference today is that it has become a war of images, fought out to the bitter end on a battlefield that is really a room of mirrors.

★

MARCH 14, 1984

In the wildest primaries campaign in U.S. history I suspect we are putting the wrong questions. We keep asking who won on Super Tuesday when the fact is that both Gary Hart and Walter Mondale "won"—Hart by showing he has a national and multilevel appeal, as in Florida; Mondale by displaying a new vitality and holding key states like Alabama and Georgia.

But the prime question is still unanswered—and even unasked. What shall we say about the prospects of a civilization whose voters show themselves as volatile and gullible as the Democratic voters have done since New Hampshire?

Nothing like it has happened in past preconvention campaigns. Gary Hart is the phantom candidate of our time, and the sickly thing is that the voters have been swarming over each other to embrace a phantom who has become suddenly a star. The school adolescents these days imitate Michael Jackson by wearing his thick belt, one white glove, and unlaced shoes. But voters are not adolescents—or *are* they?

Every new candidate to some extent invents himself. But Gary Hart invented himself with a vengeance—name, age, Naval Reserve status, Kennedy pedigree and mannerisms. His own past seems porous—whenever you poke into it, it gives. What Freud said—that we are becoming "prosthetic men"—may be even truer of politics, where we seem to be embracing the inauthentic man who has replaced bits and pieces of his past with synthetic material. In Hart's case, we did it in a mad rush, like the children who followed the Pied Piper.

Hart must get credit for sensing the popular mood while others didn't, for breaking the logjam of not very appealing Democratic candidates, and for extending the electoral options. As for the media, they accelerated everything into a high volatility. But neither Hart nor the media could have done *that* unless the volatility were already there, in the people themselves.

What has happened has been the convergence of a contrived but appealing candidate, a dangerous media power, and a voter volatility factor.

There may be a corrective at work. The fact that Mondale has been able to hang on, if only by the skin of his teeth, suggests that the media elite is catching on, if too slowly, to what is happening, and that some of the voters may be concerned about the character factor in a man who offers to govern the most powerful nation in the world.

The wild acceleration has been slowed down a bit. But for how long? I am skeptical of the commentators who say the Democratic contest will go to the convention. It depends upon how real the slowdown of the campaign is, and how credible Mondale will be as the only alternative for Hart—which is a big question mark.

"There has been a latent desire in this country for 10 or 20 years," Hart told Roger Simon of the *Chicago Sun Times*, for "a break with the past—the . . . destructive past." He mentions John Kennedy again as his model for such a break.

But, alas, with all his grace and the hopes he raised for the future, Kennedy with his "New Frontier"—and Lyndon Johnson after him with his "Great Society"—unleashed the destructiveness Hart bemoans—the "assassinations. . . Watergate. . . tremendous struggle."

What this shows about the health of the political culture and what it bodes for the civilization are not good.

It is more dangerous today to unleash an unthinking "dynamism" of the future than to follow the continuities of the past. There is a genie locked into the psyche of the American people which is best left undisturbed. The wild volatility of the current campaign is a sign of it. The leader who opens the jar and releases the genie is a leader America will rue.

★

JULY 20, 1984

"I want to be president of the United States," said Walter Mondale in his last acceptance sentence. As if we had any doubts about it! But can he govern America? He held the convention together by his sheer delegate strength and by making concessions right and left. But governing a medley of group wills and egoisms like America itself is a quantum leap removed.

No one was able to do it after Eisenhower. Kennedy tried and was killed, Johnson tried and it broke his career and heart, Nixon tried and had to resign, Ford tried and never got elected, Carter—Mondale's president—tried and laid a giant egg.

With all the ingenious ways the Democratic chieftains found to hang the Reagan effigy high on the TV screen, the fact persists that thus far Reagan alone—since Dwight Eisenhower—has shown that America is governable.

That is what Mondale will have to run against. He will have to show he can produce a better economy and a better foreign and defense policy than Reagan, and convince the doubters that he has the strength to say No as well as his everlasting Yes.

Mario Cuomo and Geraldine Ferraro used their immigrant family roots to advantage in their speeches. Walter Mondale included some paragraphs on his own life story, especially about "my dad" and "my mom" and "the values they taught me."

These lowly origins of the current version of the log-cabin myths are important for presidents, except in the case of Franklin Roosevelt and John Kennedy, who were not Republicans. Nor was Ronald Reagan exactly born to the purple.

Once you open your life history thus you invite scrutiny of it. In

Mondale's case the childhood poverty and insecurity may account for some of his excessive caution and perhaps also for the yielding to pressures that have become his political trademark.

Some politicians have climbed the ladder by imagination and risk-taking. Not Mondale. He has relied on pushes up the ladder, always first by appointment, not election, by men he cultivated who were Number One. Until now he has been the admirer, not the admired, the follower, not the initiator.

The succession of men who helped him move up is well attested: Governors Floyd Olson, Orville Freeman, and Karl Rolvaag of Minnesota, Senator Hubert Humphrey, President Jimmy Carter. When Mondale finally took the plunge for the presidency after the 1980 Carter-Mondale defeat it was the first big risk-taking he had finally decided upon.

There is nothing wrong in being prudent, and in having others pull you up by your bootstraps. But it isn't the benchmark of an initiator, nor does it justify Mondale's claims on the power to lead and the ability to govern.

In the 1984 primaries Mondale was tested by the challenge of a more daring (and erratic) Gary Hart and barely came through the test. This time it was the army of trade-union and teacher volunteers that saved him, and the guidance of savvy AFL-CIO President Lane Kirkland, and the tactic of continuing concessions to every important pressure group, both before and during the convention.

In keeping the convention from falling apart Mondale was helped by the ogre symbol of Reagan, which made Jesse Jackson and the other feudal leaders postpone their power appetites.

If Mondale should win an unlikely victory they would again clamor for their power rewards, and the whole array would become a jungle of warring possessors and pursuers. America would again become ungovernable, and there is nothing in Mondale's life history to suggest that he has the strength to govern the ungovernable.

★

SEPTEMBER 5, 1984

It is an eerie campaign, strangely skewed in the latest polls, with an asymmetry of twenty-three points in Reagan's favor and a swamping electoral college majority of thirty-nine states for Reagan, three for

Mondale and the rest uncertain. It is a national judgment out of line with any objective view, which would hold that Reagan and Bush are not nearly the models of leadership brilliance or Mondale and Ferraro nearly the dogs the polls would suggest.

What seems to have happened is a polarization of credibility. The voters seem turned off and tuned out on Mondale and Ferraro and seem to be listening to Reagan and Bush.

Consider as symbol the Labor Day parade in New York City. The unions mustered an army of marchers for Mondale and Ferraro, but the sidewalks were deserted. It was a ghastly and ghostly TV scene, demoralizing for the principals.

How explain it? Some immediate answers come to mind: The improved economy, the low popular esteem of labor, Mondale's difficulties in holding his coalition leaders together, the blunder of trying to name disgraced former Carter official Bert Lance to the post of Democratic National Chairman, the collapse of the high expectations raised by Ferraro, the failure of the Democrats to woo the white along with the black Southern vote, the gingerly approach to the high-tech revolution because of the strength of the union component in the Mondale coalition.

But somehow overshadowing these is the image of Ronald Reagan, which thus far dominates the campaign. And one of the zanier aspects is the extent to which Reagan has appropriated Franklin Delano Roosevelt to his purposes.

One would think it would be Mondale, as the Democratic heir, who would claim FDR. But there are dangers for him in identifying overmuch with Roosevelt's welfare-state legacy, so Mondale has mostly emulated FDR's coalition but failed to generate the sheer personal magic to dominate it, as FDR did.

What Reagan has done is one of the neatest tricks in the history of national elections. No one has repudiated FDR's programs more sharply and sought harder to roll them back. But no one, at the same time, has succeeded so surprisingly in appropriating FDR's style and image.

Reagan could be sued for impersonating a national monument. He has FDR's grin and laugh, his jauntiness, his inner security and total self-confidence. He has his backward tilt of the head as he delivers his one-liners, and everything but his cigarette holder. He has his campaigning stress on a politics of hope and of the future, and his unquestioning optimism about America, which rallied the young voters. He has in full measure a capacity to use the media technology of his day to grab the attention of his listeners, presently called his "Great Communicator" role.

The other day a reporter, scarcely a Reagan partisan, noted how he revels in the fray and called him a "happy warrior"—the very term FDR used about Al Smith because he thought it described himself.

Joan Mondale, conscripted into the trenches in Connecticut, volunteered that Reagan has "salesmanship" and her husband "leadership." But part of leadership, as FDR showed, is the capacity to make a political personality credible. Reagan doesn't match Roosevelt's skill in translating the prevailing political culture into new programs. But his public persona is too powerful to be written off as salesmanship.

He is helped by what helped FDR—the spreading sense that we are living at a time of the passing of an old order—in Reagan's case *Roosevelt's* old order. Reagan doesn't dominate that passing to the extent that FDR did, but he does preside over it—and the voters seem to sense it.

I have to conclude that either a dazzling act of impersonation is taking place or something of historic import is happening. Perhaps both.

✫

OCTOBER 19, 1984

I had a call from a CBS News producer. How concerned was I about the new TV dominance in presidential campaigns?

My answer was that I am concerned, yes, but I don't lose sleep over it. The new information technology is a fact and we must take it in stride and learn how to channel it to the public good.

With print, the eye was the prime sense organ, processing the words through the brain. With radio it was the ear. With TV it is the eye and ear together, with the visual images easier to follow than the verbal.

But it is still the brain that is in charge, processing image and word, conveying them to the mind to make some sense of them for the individual self.

All of this is elementary in the current research on the brain and the senses. But we need to recall it amidst the pervasive gloom about the impact of the media.

TV offers us a superb technology of audiovisual images that can bring us closer to the total person—provided we can learn how to grasp what we see and hear.

That is a big proviso. Overnight millions of people have become debate aficionados. But what is it that gives them a charge? It is two candidates involved in the presentation of self. They try to present their most attractive self, the persona. But we should also be watching and listening for something else—the mind, spirit, experience, life history, values, character.

Are we doing it? Not much. In the first debate we watched an aging king faltering in his kingship, and a clever challenger showing his spirited debating skills. And we waited until TV told us who had won and multiplied our own judgment, thereby creating public opinion.

Yet we are not choosing a debater but a decision-maker. The debate tells us more than we knew before about how the candidate's mind works and the positions he takes. It doesn't tell us about how he has operated or would operate in the crunch of decision.

This is TV's weakness. The tyranny of the visual image dominates it. If we knew enough about presidential history and about the candidate's life we could read the meaning of the images in that context. But we don't. And so the viewer's total mind doesn't have the information it needs, and we don't see the total person.

What can give us that context? The print media, especially books. But the millions don't read them. Here too TV has already begun to fill the gap, as witness the remarkable *MacNeil/Lehrer NewsHour* on PBS, which makes the commercial news shows seem thin, and presents events in depth. It can serve as a yardstick of what TV is capable of.

We are still in the childhood of media development, and in our own childhood as a culture of viewers who must decode what they watch. The media are not idiot-proof or adolescence-proof. But neither do they have to encourage both.

We have to learn that the devil is not in the technology, although its owners and practitioners have a lot to be responsible for. The fault is in our social imagination, which could demand nonpartisan documentaries on great presidential decisions and in-depth interviews with the candidates about their life journey. Every technology can be used diversely, and a culture gets the kind of use it demands and deserves.

★

It was a stunning personal victory for Ronald Reagan and a glowing Republican Party victory, but much more. It was a historic election because it changed the climate of the political culture and shifted the center of political gravity.

That is what realignment elections do, which is more important than the question of whether the victorious party picked up fifteen or twenty-five congressional seats. Presidents govern or fail to govern because of climates.

There is, of course, the "bounce-back" theory—that if (or when) Reagan has to commit a tax raise to get a lock on the deficit, the Democrats will bounce back.

But it would be shallow for them to convince themselves, in an understandable fit of economic determinism, that the Reagan victory came only with the favoring economic wind and will go with it.

The recovery had much to do with the victory, but while it was necessary, economics alone is not adequate to explain the sweep of forty-nine out of fifty states. Something else was there, and the something else was what we call the "new patriotism," which is in reality a new sense of national confidence and national identity. The something else is also a new valuing of old values, especially by the young and very young.

If this is true, then two things follow. One is a shift of the center of political gravity to conservatism. Since party labels are a matter of ingrained habit, it may remain true that Democrats will continue to outnumber Republicans, although by a smaller margin. While Democratic liberals will remain Democrats, they will be seen as less liberal ones. Republican conservatives will be seen as even more conservative. As a result of this election, the entire political continuum has shifted a few degrees to the right. And its shift is most marked in the changing youth culture.

That, rather than a party "realignment," is the dynamic of presidential "revolutions." It was true of Jefferson, Jackson, Lincoln, FDR. All four shifted the center of gravity to a new sense of collective identity, and all four got the smell of success when the young generation embraced their cause.

Reagan's difference from them is that while those giants also transformed the intellectual elite and the media culture, Reagan is unlikely to. His triumph is a personal, not a cultural one.

His 1964 TV speech, amidst the ruin of Barry Goldwater's hopes, got the attention of the California kingmakers. In the twenty years since then, this actor and TV host, this seemingly ordinary citizen-politician, has turned into an extraordinary force in changing the way Americans have defined themselves. He has combined the opportunity politics of career hope and entrepreneurial confidence with the politics of national assertiveness, and both of them with the values politics of family and religion. It is a heady brew.

His ideology and worldview have remained steady. They have not shifted with the times: The times have caught up with them. In that sense, Reagan has weightiness, as all political values leaders have had. He is a "great communicator" not because of any unusual passion or oratory, but because what he says comes home to the Americans seeking to define themselves.

The one citadel he hasn't breached is that of the liberal and media intellectual elites, who have commanded the political culture since FDR. In the four years to come, that is where the political blood will be spilled, and that will be the fire next time.

1988

BUSH vs. DUKAKIS

THIS IS NO WAY TO CHOOSE a president. Watching the desolate Democrats and the fratricidal Republicans at the start of their 1988 election year, many Americans are coming to understand that a crisis of the entire nomination system is closing in on them.

Among the Democrats, to borrow from Yeats, the best of the public figures lack any conviction of candidacy, while the available ones are full of a passionate intensity. Among the Republicans a mean and nasty war has broken out between Bob Dole and George Bush. If anything like it is sustained for the next six months, the convention victor will be too bloodied to take on his Democratic antagonist.

The Bush-Dole carnage is clearly aimed at the "front-loading" effect, giving acceleration and permanence to a bandwagon "momentum" that is all process and no substance.

The debates become a squaring off for this momentum, presenting a medley of men who have programmed themselves with clinching one-liners, a setup that trivializes and personalizes everything.

"Bad money drives out good money," says Gresham's Law. Similarly, the needling questions between the candidates drive out the memory or possibility of any sane and serious exchange. It is as if we were being asked to vote for who will do best on one of the TV political panel shows rather than who can best heal the wounds and watch over the greatness of America.

There is probably no way the media revolution could have been kept from exerting a major impact on the presidential selection process. But it didn't have to limit itself so largely to the endless repetition of revealing snippets that furnish the hot history of personal bad blood between the candidates.

All campaigns are power battles, but they can be something else as well. The ground a candidate stands on, how he has come to it in his life journey, when he thinks the country was derailed, where he wants it to go, how he means to get it there, what he sees as its sickness and its perils but also as its strengths and health—these questions should be at the core of the battle, as they were in FDR's day, and in Harry Truman's and Dwight Eisenhower's, even as late as Jack Kennedy's and Richard Nixon's.

For such an enterprise TV could furnish a magnificent technology, to reveal a man's thought and vision in the lineaments of his face, and in the grammar and syntax of his body language as well as his words.

What we get instead is a buzz saw of inquisitorial demands for total correctness on single-issue dogmas, total harmony with the views of the party activists, total virtue. The kind of prosecutorial questions that are thrust at the candidates—and that Dole and Bush are thrusting at each other—splinters and diminishes the entire process.

We have it wrong. Politics can be an honorable art, yet we are trivializing it. We should be magnifying the possibilities of light and depth in it that the new technologies offer.

I listened to Bob Dole and George Bush operating on the hypothesis of skullduggery—each accusing the other of holding something back from the light that he dare not reveal. It is a far cry from the Lincoln-Douglas debates, held long ago in Iowa's sister state, Illinois, at a time of peril for the nation! Then, each debater struggled with that danger, throwing all his intellectual and moral resources into his effort. What we get instead as the key to the present "debates" is the accusation of "cover-up," a term that immediately conjures up Iran-Contra, and, beyond it, Watergate.

It makes me wonder a bit. Is 1988 doomed to be a replay of the 1976 virtue campaign that gave the nation Jimmy Carter?

★

AUGUST 14, 1988

How do you go about judging the candidates? The media tell us more than we want to know about their lives, careers, families, loves, hates, exploits, abilities, foibles, political positions. Yet about the things that count in forming a judgment on who will best run the nation and manage the Western alliance we know desperately little.

What to do? Count this piece as a wry confessional about my own past choices.

I voted four times for FDR—and we got the New Deal but we also ended with Yalta and the abandonment of the Jews to the Holocaust. I railed against Harry Truman until his rip-roaring 1948 convention speech converted me—and he justified my vote. I voted for Adlai Stevenson and against Ike twice, only to have Ike, in time, join Harry to form the best brace of presidents of the century.

I voted for Jack Kennedy and then for Lyndon Johnson—and we got years of riots, assassinations, and another war. I voted against Richard Nixon in 1968 and, reluctantly, in a last-minute decision, for him (against George McGovern) in 1972. Looking back I may have been wrong both years, but perhaps Watergate and McGovern cancel each other out. I voted for Gerald Ford in 1976 and—considering what happened with Jimmy Carter—I might have been right. I voted for Ronald Reagan both times and I suspect the Reagan years will stand up pretty well in history.

All this is hindsight, and I will have to account for it to my maker. But 1988 is now, the choices are uninviting, the prospects numbing, and I go back for guidance to the bitter and hard-won experiences of presidential history.

I am independent of both major parties, and tolerably armed against most of the blather that passes today for campaign rhetoric—which will wither and stale tomorrow.

I am convinced that a voter forming a judgment, if he is not a terminal party faithful, will have to do two things. He will have to test the candidates from now to November, taking the measure of each against the great tides of our time. He will then have to fit the result into his own basic intuitions about how a civilization should be governed.

Take the first—the testing of the candidates. A president doesn't write position papers on tax collection or day care. His campaign speeches, with gestures, persona, and all, stop on Election Day. A president has to deal with bothersome crises, big and small, often of his own making. He has to recognize and respond to great happenings, perhaps even try to bring them about.

Right now there are thunderous events converging on a world scale. I am speaking of the Iran-Iraq cease-fire, and the Angola–Cuba–South Africa peace agreement. Add to it the congressional measure for helping the Contras without giving them arms. Add further the conversion of the European Common Market, slated for 1992, into an operative economic and political entity on issues going beyond trade. Add finally, the emergence of a new cluster of prospering Pacific Rim economies in Asia, which an American president may one day help shape into a Pacific Common Market of industrial powers.

We need to pressure each of the candidates, whatever else he is doing, to tell us how his experience fits into such events, what he makes of them, how he would wrestle with them, whose advice and help he would call on.

It isn't enough to hold conventions, draw up platforms, stage debates, which become formal, prepared performances as slick and contrived as the candidates can make them.

There is a chance to turn the events of the next months into a continuous national workshop or seminar—whatever you want to call it—in which the candidates and their backup teams will be the principal performers. I want to see George Bush and Michael Dukakis and their skeletal shadow cabinets, if they have them, tussle with problems exactly like those they will face in office.

All of us will want to compare them on the judgment they show, their resourcefulness, their grasp of the perspectives of history, their knowledge of the actors on the stage, their account of the options and their choice among them, their boldness and prudence, their toughness of mind, their generosity of spirit, their feel for the difference between the immediate and the long-range.

For myself, the biggest question is that of the center. If it is true that when "things fall apart, the center cannot hold," then we need a president who can make the center hold.

⋆

SEPTEMBER 29, 1988

George Bernard Shaw called boxing the "Allegory of Capitalism." In our time the prizefight, in the form of the presidential debates, has become the allegory of electoral democracy.

The first Bush-Dukakis debate reached an apogee—or nadir—of the tendency to see the campaign as a fight. The two candidates danced, jabbed, feinted, slugged it out—one in white trunks, the other in red. The media mavens served both as referee and judges.

The theory is that, unlike actual boxing fights, there were no fight judges. In fact, scarcely were the proceedings over before the cry "Who won?" echoed from every direction on millions of screens. There was talk of "no knockouts," talk of who won "on points," differences about how the "points" were to be counted. In the absence of actual judges the media, moving into the vacuum, assumed their role.

They did it in part by taking early polls, in part by soliciting discussion by experts, in part by asserting their own judgments. NBC, in the earliest watcher poll, gave Dukakis a nine-point edge. *Newsweek* and *USA Today* saw it as pretty much a dead heat.

I don't quarrel with either result. My own view of this exercise is that Dukakis was more aggressive, Bush more defensive, that Dukakis showed his tried debating skills and Bush his experience, that each came through with his characteristic personality and intellectual style—and that we learned little new about either of them. I also suggest that the stress on the debates, and on the postfight declarations of victory and defeat, form a helluva of a way to run an election.

Presidential elections are not prizefights in a ring, on fight nights, with declared "winners" and "losers." They are occasions for the formation of voter empathy and identification with one or the other candidate. The convention and acceptance speeches serve their function in this long process. Appearances by the candidates—fitfully and inadequately covered by the media—serve a function. So do debates, if the viewers and voters are allowed to form their own judgment.

Suddenly the debates, by their theatrical setting and their prizefight allegory, are being allowed to hog the show. In a sense it is inevitable, if the campaign is seen primarily as a media event. The same media, which over the months have offered only snippets of the candidates as they threw grenades at each other, now offer a sustained ninety minutes, opening gong to closing gong. Obviously it is a chance no viewer can miss, a media event whose hour has come.

The trouble lies not with the debates but with the "win-lose" metaphor they invoke. It lies with the postdebate instant polling and the handing down of decisions, based on the debating skills of the contenders rather than on the positions they have been taking over time.

There are two big questions raised here. One is the question of who passes win-lose judgment. It is the people—the voters—who are supposed to make the ultimate decision, at their own pace, in their own way. They stand in danger of being suckered into the delusion that the media have a right to make it for them—by instant polling and snap judgments, minutes after the closing gong.

There is a skewing of time here that distorts the long, sustained process of judgment. That process should cover the entire period from the conventions to Election Day. There is no point to hurrying it.

I am not one of those who complain at the fact that many voters have not yet made up their minds. It is healthy to suspend judgment and to keep the campaign handlers and managers guessing. Nor do I rail, as some do, at the temperamental quality of the periodic polls. They are the moving mirror by which we see ourselves as part of the larger democracy.

What I am questioning is the usurpation of the people's long-range judgment by the media's instant declaration of winners and losers. If the networks want to assume the responsibility of calling the election, let them. For them to do it by the surrogates they use is irresponsible.

My final question is about the use of the debate as the decisive agency of electoral judgment. The American people are not picking a debating star to send to the debate Olympics. They are picking a president, on the basis of his positions, judgment, experience, vision. The debates can contribute to that, but only if the voters insist on putting them in perspective, and on reclaiming their judging role, which is being usurped.

★

OCTOBER 27, 1988

We have it wrong. A long presidential campaign isn't a horse race. It is more like a protracted double courtship. Two suitors vie for the prize of the lady, by foul even more than by fair means, and she has a chance for some long and hard thoughts before finally giving herself to one of them.

Toward the end of what seemed an endless—and issueless, soulless, and nasty—campaign I have to offer a mildly dissenting opinion. Any close reading of campaign history, during the half century from 1936 on, documents the fact that no campaign has been free of rancor, whether in its utterances or in its whispers.

The best campaigners, from FDR to John Kennedy and Lyndon

Johnson to Ronald Reagan, achieve a delicate polar balance. They attack and attack, but they also celebrate and celebrate the country and its symbols. The George Bush camp of seasoned national politicians learned from this; the still-unseasoned Michael Dukakis camp didn't.

Every recent study of the role of optimism in politics supports the view that the lady's winning suitors are the ones who stress love and hope while vowing eternal commitment to the defense of both against their pessimist detractors.

This may at times violate the reality principle, as with the stubborn national deficit. Yet it is based on the proposition that the lady's not for burning but for winning. It goes with what we all recognize as the deep optimist strain in the American national character.

It also goes with the great current selfhood revolution in America, especially in "behavioral medicine" and the mind-body connection, which stresses that it is the life-affirming patient who will beat the odds. The political moral for our time is never to bet against the campaign paradigm of prosperity, peace, and national pride.

I venture also a reflection on form and substance in political ideology. The Bush forces have used symbols and imagery with wicked effectiveness against selected Dukakis positions on "the L word"—liberalism. The conventional wisdom is that it is all semantics, cunning wordplay on the political emotions.

If that were all, it wouldn't fly. There is substance in it that will outlast the current fracas. The campaign may be boring and nasty to the high-minded, but if you are history-oriented, you will see it as a *defining* campaign.

Things are happening to both liberalism and conservatism that never happened until now. The very fact that neither candidate has any real charisma diminishes the personality factor and sharpens the question of whether the energies of the liberal era are nearing exhaustion.

If they are, in fact, this is not the "end of ideology" but only the beginning of a reorientation of liberalism and conservatism, and a regrouping of their champions as they vie for long-range popular support. Something like a redefinition happened to liberalism under FDR, to conservatism under Dwight Eisenhower, to liberalism again under John Kennedy, to conservatism again under Ronald Reagan. A Bush victory, if it happens, would underscore the further need for redefinition.

A substantial Bush victory would also put a crimp into the fashionable theory of thirty-year political cycles, which premised a sequence of liberal realignment victories in the 1930s, the 1960s, and therefore the 1990s.

Right now the auguries are far from supporting it. If anything, they support the hypothesis that while all decades are equal in length, some are more equal than others. It looks as if the 1980s will confuse and confute the cyclical predictors, and will have a long reach into the 1990s.

Rather than stressing victory and defeat I stress the need for redefinition of the credos of both camps—the winner's as well as the loser's.

There is more in the earth and heaven of many issues—of crime and punishment, of group interests and national interests, of individual rights and of limits to them, of isolationism and intervention in critical world areas, of judicial activism and judicial restraint—than is dreamt of in liberal philosophy.

There is also more in the earth and heaven of other issues—of right to life and family choice, of a chilling austerity about the alienated and an empathy that seeks social action, of naked greed and a concerned entrepreneurship, of a Himalayan indebtedness that defies an expanding economy—than is dreamt of in conservative philosophy.

If the 1990s prove to be a time for redefining our philosophies, then it will be good for the soul of America—even if it isn't cyclical.

✭

NOVEMBER 13, 1988

The Bush minisweep was a strong victory for a man, a philosophy, and a direction. Yet it was accompanied by slight Democratic gains in the House and Senate and in state elections. In losing the presidency once more—the fifth out of the last six elections—the Democrats have continued to make a habit of it. They are even turning it, as House Member Patricia Schroeder ruefully puts it, into a fine art. But they have also mastered the art of tenacity in hanging on to their legislative majorities.

It raises the question, more strongly than ever, of whether we are moving into a protracted phase of coalition government. If Republican presidents try to function with Democratic Congresses, each will have in effect a veto on the proposals of the other. This would apply to the third branch as well, the federal judiciary. Its new appointments will be in the hands of a Republican president but subject (as the stormy Robert Bork hearings attested) to veto by the Judiciary Committee of a Democratic Senate.

It is all very well to have a government of checks and balances, but not if it becomes a government by deadlock.

The Israelis had to resort to coalition government for a time because neither major party could muster the votes to govern with. That isn't true of an America where one party has won the last three presidential elections by landslides or near landslides. But George Bush will find, as Ronald Reagan did, that a president cannot govern by himself. He needs a Congress that cares about country more than about party.

Bush started well, with an impressive display of judgment and a heal-the-wounds goodwill at his first postelection press conference. His early Cabinet appointment of James A. Baker at State was meant to reach the entire Western community, of which America is "first among equals." Baker is a symbol of the moderate conservatism that characterized his role as Reagan's chief of staff, opening him to criticism from the hard right. He shares that angle of vision with the president-elect.

Don't overlook the personal factor in Bush as a man. James David Barber is right in saying that the danger in the campaign was not its "negativism" but the "myopia," which failed to draw conclusions from the life history of each candidate. Indeed the TV fare which interviewers and commentators offered gave us little to draw from.

The Bush we saw from his acceptance speech at the convention through the postelection press conference is not a "new" Bush but the Bush of his whole life, fortified by his campaigning and his victory. After his Senate defeat by Lloyd Bentsen, and his 1980 defeat by Ronald Reagan, he emerged from the shadows of his "wimp" image and of his vice presidential obscurity under Reagan. He moved into the hot light that beats upon a throne in a democracy—emerged as his own man, with an inner security deep enough to weather the turmoil ahead, and strong enough to allow him flexibility.

Does he have a "mandate"? In its literal sense—of "entrusting"— he does. More than enough voters of every section, religion, race, and class, of both genders, have entrusted the arts of government to him to make it a mandate.

They know his philosophy as that of a moderate conservatism. They know his election spells continuity with the Reagan tradition, but that he will choose his own Cabinet. They know—best of all—that he has been privy to the decisions of both Reagan terms, that the territory of decision-making has become his universe, and that he will not need on-the-job training.

He starts with two handicaps. One is his vice president, of his own choosing, who was given a too hard time in the campaign, but has not by any means convinced the nation of his presidential potential. Bush will have to live that down by other appointments, and Dan Quayle will have to live it down by showing growth.

The other is the monster deficit that Bush inherits, along with happier hand-me-downs, from the two Reagan administrations. The first step there is to make a bipartisan commission, with its studies and reports, the central means of resolving it.

Strong parties are the lifeblood of a democracy. Ours need strengthening, not weakening. Yet they can be strong without being totally blinkered. "I have been one acquainted with the night," wrote Robert Frost. Bush has been acquainted enough with the night to move—even with his resounding victory—more than halfway toward the Democratic Congress. The Democrats have been even more acquainted with the night by now. But will they move toward the president-elect?

It will be the only way to prevent government by deadlock.

1992

CLINTON vs. BUSH

NOVEMBER 10, 1991

SUDDENLY THE IMPOSSIBLE has become possible. What Democrats have panted for, and Republicans have dreaded, has finally been vouchsafed. I mean some sign, from heaven (or wherever), that the Democratic presidential sickness is not terminal, that God is not a permanent Republican, and that George Bush may prove eminently beatable in 1992.

The sign comes from the elections, especially Harris Wofford's impressive senatorial win for the Democrats in Pennsylvania. It also comes presumably from the downturn of economic indicators that made the Democratic victory possible. Never mind that this puts the Democrats into the dubious position of an unseemly rejoicing over bad economic news. The more important question for the nation, given the control of both Houses by the Democrats, is why they have not armed their liberal vision earlier with a program that would rescue the American economy. Alas, there is little evidence that Democratic economics is visibly any better than Republican economics.

The only thing clear is that Americans seem to have fallen into what was, in Jimmy Carter's time, called a mood of "malaise." This is due to the faltering economy, which makes a recovery from the past downturn uncertain. Yet one cannot help noting that the extent of the current gloom is not justified by anything the economic indicators show. The gloom seems to be feeding on itself, in the manner of a self-fulfilling prophesy. What we need now is a president, from whatever party, who is psychologist enough to tell us—as Franklin Roosevelt did in 1933—that "The only thing we have to fear is fear itself."

One of the natural outgrowths of the economic gloom has been the feeling that in pursuing his foreign-affairs policies, President Bush has neglected his home base in domestic affairs. The "Look Homeward, Angel" message the people are sending him is unmistakable enough to have prodded him into canceling his Asian trip.

The lesson of Wofford's victory in Pennsylvania is that the administration has failed to measure the depth of discontent among the voters and their anxieties about losing their jobs along with their health benefits. For them, there is a more immediate concern at the present moment in history than what Bush and his secretary of state were able to accomplish in bringing the Arabs and Israelis face-to-face at Madrid.

This is a bitter brew for Bush. Only a short time ago, in the flush of the Desert Storm victory, his standing in the polls soared and he seemed all but unbeatable in 1992. It is a sign of how transient even great events are in the febrile mood changes of a democracy, and how rapidly the media-driven political culture consumes and disposes of them.

All of this comes, with an added irony, at a time when America, its economy and its democracy, have become models for the newly liberated nations to follow. What it should teach them—and us—is that there is never a time when you can take the public mood for granted in a democracy.

Bush and his White House staff committed the political sin of growing too smug about their support at home. They forgot that the best foreign policy needs a domestic base of relative contentment. It is equally true that the best domestic policy cannot flower in a climate of isolationism from the convulsions of the world around us.

If the Republicans need to reflect on the lessons of Pennsylvania, the Democrats should study the results in New Jersey, which is equally a bellwether state. The vote is turning against Governor Jim Florio's tax increase for a strikingly liberal program. New Jersey voted the Democratic legislators out, and gave the Republicans whopping majorities in both Houses. The political analysts, who celebrate a politics of resentment, must recognize that it can cut both ways.

★

Is Governor Bill Clinton's problem part of the Gary Hart syndrome—a question of how the political culture of the time deals with a candidate's adultery? Evidently Clinton, who thinks in "strategic" terms, must have thought that Hart's strategy was wrong, and that he self-destructed by pushing his luck and getting caught in flagrante delicto by a media watch.

So Clinton hinted at his past to reporters, hoping that the dead past would bury its dead. It didn't. It came to life all too vibrantly, with telltale quotes from a taped phone conversation that was a carefully laid trap. The quotes found their way to a national gossip tabloid. The moral for politicians is: Put not your faith in a past lover who feels wounded, strapped for cash, and starved for recognition in an overnight celebrity market.

The political fallout from the Clinton case will yield some evidence of how far—if at all—we have moved to some sort of sanity about sex in politics. Tactically Clinton handled his crisis better than Hart by seizing the chance, with his wife, Hillary, to present their case in a special segment of *60 Minutes*. They took a family-values ground— that whatever had happened earlier, they were a family now, with love and respect for each other.

Thus far, while the jury is still out, Clinton remains a battling contender. His audiences are, if anything, larger and more attentive, their questions are not hostile, his answers are detailed and programmatic, his fund-raising is not bleeding, his campaign is still a going concern.

Not that this disposes of the Bill Clinton syndrome. His case is a product of America's cultural crisis of the later 1960s, when he came of age. Like his generation he carried over a streak of its hedonism into his private life. A streak also of its risk-taking folly, since he knew that the life of a public man has only a highly porous zone of privacy.

What he may not have reckoned with was that America has taken over the pleasure principle without discarding its residual Puritan principle. It was the return of the repressed Puritan in the political culture that blew Gary Hart out of the water, and gave Bill Clinton the scare of his political life.

The crisis of America's political culture however goes deeper and is more embracing. We are in an election year when the incumbent Republican president has experienced a precipitous fall in his credibility, and will be facing a right-wing challenge in New Hampshire from Pat Buchanan and what Garry Wills has described as a group of "crazies" supporting him. This is the first time since the years of Father Charles Coughlin and Charles Lindbergh, in the middle and late 1930s, that the combined issue of anti-Semitism and isolationism has become something to reckon with in the political discourse.

The case of the Democrats, like the Republicans, continues to be one of the impoverishment of a political philosophy and of the available presidential talent. The liberal welfare state is dead beyond revival, which is why Bill Clinton—as one who seemed to recognize it—will be missed if he proves expendable. But so is the Republican "government is the enemy" philosophy. None of the candidates of either party has the combination of mind, persona, character, gravitas, and calling that a first-rate president must have if he and the nation are lucky. None even come near it.

The doldrums from which the American economy is suffering, as the leaders of both parties ought to know, are more than economic. We are only starting to learn that the Japanese are outstripping us in critical areas of technology, production, and export because they put their entire culture behind their economic strategy. Even if America had an economic strategy—which it doesn't—it is so divided culturally that it couldn't put all its talent and resources behind it.

That is America's larger cultural crisis. The question is when we and our leaders will wake up to it.

✭

MARCH 15, 1992

I'll go out on a limb. The primaries are as good as over. It will be George Bush against Bill Clinton all the scrappy, furious way.

But I refuse to go out on a second limb to predict the result. The reason is that elections are about metaphors as much as about the men who embody them. It is too early to say how the current Bush-Clinton metaphors will play.

One thing has become clear, however—that in the case of Paul

Tsongas, the assumption that as a cancer survivor he was a metaphor of an America suffering from a cancer of its own has proved unavailing.

I must confess to some personal experience here. I got a non-Hodgkin's lymphoma a couple of years before Tsongas. My doctors used state-of-the-art chemotherapy for it, and I added some will-and-affirmation therapies of my own crafting. I felt I was wrestling with the angel of death and life, a heady feeling for many cancer survivors. Thus I understand what Tsongas has been saying in his responses about his cancer experience.

But beware of carrying this mode of reasoning too fast and too far. Tsongas may well have become a clearer and better man because of his cancer, but it will not make him a better American president than he would otherwise be.

We must be equally wary of the questionable metaphor of an America on the verge of a racial civil war. One of our important thinkers, Andrew Hacker, is getting kudos for his book *Two Nations*, with its implications that we are headed for civil strife. This is mostly nonsense, even with its whole array of statistics. There is no Dred Scott decision, no Confederacy, no states' rights issue, no "irrepressible conflict" and, last, no Abraham Lincoln to guide us.

The fact is that no civilization in history—and I say *none*—has striven as mightily as the American to integrate the two races in communities of common efforts and shared values.

We must not allow ourselves to fall for these self-incitements that come out of a deeply embedded white sense of guilt and failure over the curse of the historic slavery institution and its outcomes. If we push our guilt far enough, we may indeed get what Hacker seeks to avert.

The truth is that we are suffering from the institutional failures of our own time. Our malady is the competitive decline of the economy, and the fragmenting of the polity and of the culture. Is there a metaphor that will encompass all these? There is. It is the metaphor of the organism. It is as actual and urgent for every form of society as for the individual life.

There is a new breed of black intellectuals who understands the prime need for building black/white communities in every area of effort. I wish there were more widespread understanding, in the universities as a whole, of the reality of communities as living organisms. It is our task as a people to keep creating new communities and keep the existing ones from being ripped apart.

Which leads me to a passing but inevitable word about what I must call "Buchananism." It is still too early to guess what impact Patrick Buchanan's campaign will have in the long run. We have a going organism now, still very vulnerable, of concerted white/black efforts at understanding. As Buchanan careers across the nation and its TV screens, it would be his inexpungable sin (yes, I mean sin) to rip that organism apart even further.

Buchanan doubtless thinks he can make peace with Bush at the convention, glory in his show of strength and go on to "win" in 1996 as Ronald Reagan won in 1980.

But win what? Not a nation but a bleeding entity whose efforts at community building will have been set back for decades.

Buchanan's leading metaphor is narrowly one of ambition and power. Who controls the "left" and the "right"? Who will fashion the party of "realignment"?

These would be interesting questions in another and less destabilized time. But it is the cruelest of ignorances to believe that we can inflict the kind of wound a militant Buchanan campaign will carry for the social organism, and not be paying its price, longer and higher than we count on, to our shame and rue.

PRESIDENT HUNTING IN AN ELECTRONIC WONDERLAND

T HE TWO NATIONAL PRESIDENTIAL conventions I recall most vividly both happened in 1948. One was the Progressive Party convention, a rebel offshoot of the Democrats, which nominated an intelligent farmer called Henry Wallace who had been close to Franklin Roosevelt and was fired by Harry Truman. For several sessions I had the benefit of the comments of H. L. Mencken, who sat by my side and bounced his epigrams off me. He found the show a sheer rollicking delight, a final proof of the degradation of the democratic dogma. I learned from him how to see and enjoy American politics as spectacle.

My other sharp recollection came as Harry Truman, well after midnight, rose to accept the Democratic nomination. With New York's fighting prosecutor who'd become governor, Tom Dewey, as his coming opponent, Truman's cause seemed bedraggled, almost hopeless. Yet in five minutes he had most of the press veterans standing on the tables, cheering him. I learned from him that politics can be more than spectacle and that the democratic idea can somehow triumph.

Do I miss the old conventions? You bet I do. Would I want them back? Yes, but there's no chance of it. Every media technology has created a presidential selection process in its own image. In an electronic era you cannot wish back the process that came with print media.

This essay was written in the spring of 1988. By the time it was finished, publications were looking forward to the fall campaign rather than backward to the nominating process, and it was never published. Max Lerner's last sustained examination of the electoral process, the analysis and cautionary advice remain pertinent today.

My two 1948 memories suggest how I feel about the 1988 campaign as the nominating season ends. I find the canned pieties of the candidates, as they mouth their thirty-second commercials, depressingly funny. Yet I cling to the possibility that somehow the new media too will come up with a Harry Truman—by whatever name, in whatever shape—capable of a gritty epiphany that will tell us that here is a man who can govern the nation.

The new era of media politics is here to stay. It began in 1968, when Eugene McCarthy ran second to Lyndon Johnson in a New Hampshire surprise, forcing the president to take himself out of the race. It has dominated the primaries and convention coverage since, and will continue its dominant role into the next millennium. The year 2000 will see an especially crackling primary campaign, asplash with millenarian promises. By that time the communications technology will have taken a couple of leaps forward and propelled us into an era of postmodern America that will make the 1980s seem archaic.

The technology is dazzling. It enables us to be everywhere instantly, watching and hearing everyone, part of every action. It tells us more than we want to know in some ways, but not nearly enough in others. It does not tell us the meaning or implication of what we are watching, but it does furnish contexts that supply meanings, sometimes the wrong ones, sometimes terribly unfair ones. Thus it can make heroes overnight, or villains, or destroy both.

Here is a quote worth pondering: "You can get awfully famous in this country in seven days. I mean, it's phenomenal. It doesn't take much." Who said it? Gary Hart. When? In 1984, in a documentary made in New Hampshire, months before the Iowa and New Hampshire results that were to prove Hart a true prophet. "Awfully famous" indeed. So much for Gary Hart, this prescient adventurer who predicted his own fate, this rising, shooting, falling, fallen star who owed his brief political life and sad political death to the dominant media.

To understand the dynamic of the season of presidential primaries there are three words worth some study: *perception, momentum, volatility*. They encompass the entire process by which the media have taken over the selection of American presidents. Suddenly a candidate is being watched by millions, day after day. They know little about him. What counts for them? I go back to Machiavelli, who told his Prince that what you *seem to be* is more important than what you *are*. It is one of the laws of power, as it is of love. Responding to the rule, an entire galaxy of media consultants, pollsters, issue specialists, speechwriters falls into place around the candidate as its central star.

The problem is to find or create the right profile of perceptions, sometimes to replace an old one. Jesse Jackson had trouble with his profile in 1984 and evolved a new one, with Bill Cosby taking the place of Louis Farrakhan as context. It works. Robert Dole replaced his 1976 profile as Republican hatchet man with a 1988 version of himself as the can-do legislator who is "one of us." It works. Pat Robertson replaced the miracle-working Evangelical preacher with the antipolitician whom the people "can trust." It also works. Sometimes it may even represent genuine change. It is mask-changing, but if you grow comfortable within a mask it can become the face.

The aim of course is always to be perceived as the winner, even when you are not. This is where *expectations* come in. The Greeks, in their sports, would tolerate nothing less than a winner. For Americans, in the wonderland of electronic perception, what counts is doing "better than expected." Better to have modest expectations that bring a surprise with them when you make second place, as witness Gene McCarthy in New Hampshire in 1968, Gary Hart in Iowa in 1984, Pat Robertson in Iowa in 1988.

A surprise performance gives you *momentum*, carrying your victory (however modest) from one primary to the next. The principle is that success (and failure) feeds on itself, almost cancerously. That's why it's best to have your victories early, when they will count, and your defeats late, when they will fade into the shadows. The principle is called "feedback," but "feed forward" may be more descriptive of the swiftness with which it operates. Gary Hart in 1984 used the metaphor of a "firestorm" or a "prairie fire." Both are apt—but note also that both are destructive.

Which leaves *volatility*. The volatile is the flighty, the unstable. The irony is that we seek stability in a candidate—someone steady, unfailing, trustworthy—while the process of finding him is as volatile as a runaway stock market. By an evolutionary process of natural selection our candidates are bound to become ever more cunning—to weather the volatile elements and survive. It does not follow that this makes them good presidents.

Is there a true metaphor to express this entire process? The traditional one is a horse race. The trouble with it is that it omits the role of the TV viewer who doesn't just watch the race but identifies enough with the horse to vote for him and help him win. The spectator becomes the rider and horse as well, all together. No such total fusion of roles has ever been achieved before in elections. It may account in part for the fascination the process exerts on us.

I add two other words that count in winning the nomination. One of course is *money*. Without it there can be no organization, no demographics, no advertising, no logistics, no infrastructure for making the whole complex venture work. The second is the *message*, a term the candidates come to use ad nauseam. For me the message and the messenger go together. I judge each by the other. Paraphrasing Marshall McLuhan, the messenger *is* the message. A successful candidate will have to achieve a credibility with the instrument itself—the TV tube—showing himself at home with it, as Ronald Reagan did.

Beyond that he must tap some force field of rages, prides, beliefs, which do not fit into the issue demographics that go with the conventional wisdom. In Iowa, in 1988, Richard Gephardt tapped into the economic fears and angers about Japanese competition. Even more strongly Pat Robertson tapped into the rages about morality, values, and the "social issues."

The primary system has to provide "surprises" every week. It does so by involving TV audiences in its unfolding spectacle. The viewers are not idle spectators. At some point a gut issue releases their anger, fear, pride. As America became increasingly an interest-group society, the old convention system, with its print messages, no longer reached them, and the TV-primaries system took its place. By establishing a "global village" TV offers to bring the old New England "town meeting" into every home, schoolroom, college campus, pizza parlor.

The chief trouble with the primaries' highly public sampling of American opinion, as in Iowa and New Hampshire, is that it starts too early, is too piecemeal, and overrepresents marginal constituencies, while it omits the great states that possess the bulk of the delegates. This fault line led logically to "Super Tuesday," which this year brings together a cluster or twenty states, mostly in or on the edge of the South, with a few others thrown in.

The principles I have suggested—*perception, momentum, volatility*—apply in the dynamics of the primaries, and the combination of *money, message*, and *messenger* apply as the support system. The important thing is to keep the dynamic from running away with the substance, propelling America into a wild chase through its electronic wonderland. For my view of American political health, whatever slows down the too early and too rapid accelerations is good for the parties and the nation.

I do not go along with any of the proposed nostrums to improve the primary process. For instance, I consider a national primary such a nostrum. The idea of the entire nation voting in primaries on a single day—a sort of Super-Super-Tuesday—sounds like the essence of democracy, but it is an invitation to disaster.

By their essential nature the volatile primaries are crapshoot gambles for the nation. They serve the people best when they are staggered, week after week, to even out the force of any one of them. They may even serve a purpose as an early warning system of long repressed discontent among the people, in some force field like the "social issues," which could sweep a dubious leader into overnight power.

I recall the dark days of the early 1930s, when Franklin Roosevelt regarded Father Charles Coughlin of Michigan, and Senator Huey Long of Louisiana, as just such leaders. I later lived through the time, in the Eisenhower 1950s, when—if there had been a national primary—Senator Joe McCarthy of Wisconsin might have swept to national victory with a gust of passion about the internal Communist danger. Walk warily. There are monsters in these trackless forests.

This applies as well on a broader scale to the long-bruited proposal for the direct election for president. Again it seems attractive as a way of achieving unalloyed democracy, without the inequality of the large and small states in the electoral college. But the founding thinkers of the Constitution, including both James Madison and Alexander Hamilton, foresaw that something would have to cushion the dangers of a naked plebiscite. They used the role of the states in the electoral college, voting as units, to enable them to retain their identity and still give the people the power of selection. There are many institutions in modern American life, including TV, that threaten to obliterate the identity and diversity of the states. It is wise to keep them from achieving a total triumph.

There is the story about George Washington, the wisest and wholest man that America has produced (Lincoln was the deepest). It has Washington pouring his hot tea from cup to saucer, to cool it, as a symbol of mediated democracy. In a postmodern America, with its still incalculable changes, we must retain an invigorating role for the people. But we do not want our history too hot, lest it scald us.

CODA:
THE LAST COLUMN

APRIL 25, 1992

A MEMORY OF PRESIDENTS

Who was the greatest president of the century? Clearly Franklin D. Roosevelt. Who was the worst? As it turned out, poor Herbert Hoover, both by ill luck and by wrong decisions.

I am carried on the tide of presidential memories. For whatever it is worth, as the longest enduring worker at this craft of president-watching, I am just short of a half century at it. This meant inevitably getting to know some of the presidents closely, from FDR on.

Considering the zany way we have come to choose our presidents we have done better than pretty well in their stature. There was a time, notably in the 1970s, when presidential psychohistory was all the rage. James David Barber built a reputation on his book *Presidential Character*, whose hero turned out to be Jimmy Carter and whose arch villain was, of course, Richard Nixon. The idea was to dig back into the president's past in order to predict how he would act in the crises of the future.

The progenitor of all of this was, of course, Sigmund Freud himself, who even took a crack at writing a psychobiography of Woodrow Wilson, with disastrous mechanical results. There is no way of predicting the behavior of the highly complex organisms who somehow assume command of the nation.

Every commentator has his own quirks about presidents he has studied. George Will proclaims Calvin Coolidge as his hero of Tory rectitude—and he could do worse. The virtues that were wrapped up in that dour Puritan package are in pretty short measure today.

For Paul Johnson's *Modern Times*, the talismanic name is Dwight

Eisenhower. Johnson sees Ike as the supreme American statesman of the century. Like FDR, Ike combined elements of the lion and the fox. But Ike's foxlike qualities were slier and more concealed, while FDR's lionlike qualities were more claimant.

My own hero, more modest than either, is Harry Truman. Deceptively an "ordinary" man, he was a stunningly extraordinary example of one. He combined the classic heroes whom he had studied in his high school library with the hard sense—sharpened to the point of genius—of the men who knew when and how to take command.

Over the years I have made lists (which of us has not?) of the "qualities" that constitute presidential greatness. But it is an idle dream. Leadership qualities are not abstract essences to be selectively tested. They are the intricate, multifold ways in which someone vested with power acts on it when called to action.

Always the tested action, always under stress, always in hitherto unheard-of and undreamed-of situations. Take Truman on the Berlin airlift as an example of willed, resourceful action. Or take Truman on the bomb over Hiroshima. Or take Truman fighting all his most trusted advisers to secure recognition for Israel's statehood.

Out of my confrontations with Truman, as it were, has come a rule-of-thumb imperative. Don't judge a president by his actions alone. Judge him by the consequences of his actions, within their context. For the one thing we can be certain about is that actions have consequences, and are to be judged by them.

Which means that Harry Truman was no rhetorician. I used to hunger for some signs of the flashing, unforgettable phrase, as in Woodrow Wilson or in John Kennedy or in FDR. But its absence was what saved him from being locked into actions that would in every case prove disastrous.

The glowing thing about Truman is that time after time, his actions have been affirmed by their consequences. This is history's ultimate vindication. It is why, with Truman as my model, I don't need to go into a phony Carlylean hero worship with high-flown posturings.

We could use a Harry Truman right now, instead of the synthetic men and the stilted figures on horseback who think American can be bought.

But Trumans happen only once, and are never minted again.